THE
MAGIC
OF JUJU

An Appreciation of the
Black Arts Movement

Kalamu ya Salaam

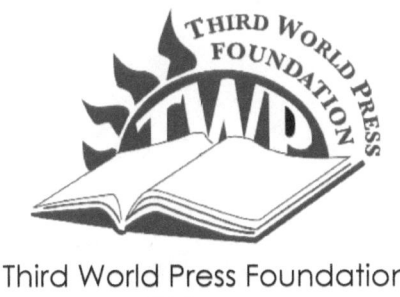

Third World Press Foundation
Chicago

This book is dedicated to the work and legacy of:
Hoyt W. Fuller (1923-1981) and **Stephen E. Henderson** (1925-1997)
and to the ongoing work and example of:
Dingane Joe Goncalves and **Jerry W. Ward**

First Edition
Printed in the United States of America

Library of Congress Control Number: 2016947462

ISBN 13: 978-0-88378-196-8

19 18 17 16   4 3 2 1

Citations:
This study is heavily documented and makes use of many quotations taken from either original publications or from collections, anthologies or reprints that were popular during the BAM era (1965 –1976). In a few cases, I have quoted at length because the quote is relevant because the source is not generally available, or because I wanted to provide factual support for both the context and the specific point I am making. All photographs are identified either by supplying source or photographer. I was not always able to track down the name of the photographer.

Cover Design by Keir Thirus and Solomohn Ennis-Klyczek
Layout by Relana Johnson and Solomohn Ennis-Klyczek

This book is dedicated to the work and legacy of:
Hoyt W. Fuller (1923-1981) and **Stephen E. Henderson** (1925-1997)
and to the ongoing work and example of:
Dingane Joe Goncalves and **Jerry W. Ward**

First Edition
Printed in the United States of America

Library of Congress Control Number: 2016947462

ISBN 13: 978-0-88378-196-8

19 18 17 16   4 3 2 1

Citations:
This study is heavily documented and makes use of many quotations taken from either original publications or from collections, anthologies or reprints that were popular during the BAM era (1965 –1976). In a few cases, I have quoted at length because the quote is relevant because the source is not generally available, or because I wanted to provide factual support for both the context and the specific point I am making. All photographs are identified either by supplying source or photographer. I was not always able to track down the name of the photographer.

Cover Design by Keir Thirus and Solomohn Ennis-Klyczek
Layout by Relana Johnson and Solomohn Ennis-Klyczek

CONTENTS

Preface...vii

Introduction...ix

Chapter 1
Defining the Black Arts Movement.....................1

Chapter 2
BAM's Historical Background............................13

Chapter 3
The National Birth of BAM...............................29

Chapter 4
Theory and Practice..49

Chapter 5
BAM Publications..65

Chapter 6
BAM Recordings..96

Chapter 7
Black Theatre..109

Chapter 8
BAM and Black Music....................................123

Chapter 9
Black Film and Television...............................137

Chapter 10
Dance...145

Chapter 11
Visual Arts..156

Chapter 12
BAM's Critics...161

Chapter 13
A Critical Assessment....................................182

Study Guide
Developed by Jiton Davidson..........................195

Photographs, Documents and Historical Archives
Compiled by Eugene B. Redmond.....................231

The Waves of Black Aesthetics:
The Deep River of the Black Arts Movement
A Dialogue between Kalamu Ya Salaam
and Margo Natalie Crawford...........................275

Index..308

PREFACE

The literary and drama/poetry performance wing of the Black Arts Movement (BAM) was the realization of nommo, the power of the word. BAM was a conjuration of "word" as a social force, "naming" as simultaneously a sacred creation and a political act. BAM was a forceful assertion: We are Black and intend to exist in our own way!

This study presents a broad overview of the birth, development, and dispersal of the Black Arts Movement with an emphasis on its literary wing. It details the social and artistic context which gave birth to BAM and discusses both its ideological and practical developments. Throughout this study I provide extensive citations from seminal BAM writers, theorists, and critics as they were originally published in important BAM journals and anthologies. I also examine the shortcomings and decline of BAM and present examples of both positive and negative aspects of its practice. Finally, I investigate the ongoing legacy and importance of BAM.

This study is primarily historical, rather than literary or theoretical. Although I do not present an in-depth critique of the literary work, I do offer a summary discussion of the political and aesthetic theories of BAM. I also offer a contextual history which specifically presents BAM's major shapers and influences.

Questions, comments, and suggestions from a series of "readers" have made a critical difference. I particularly want to recognize a handful of people who not only took the time to read and comment on the manuscript, but also offered information, resources, and insightful dialogue that greatly contributed to the manuscript's development. First, Dingane Joe Goncalves was constant in providing research materials and contacts with relevant people. Goncalves served as a sounding board for ideas as they developed, offering conceptual as well as detailed comments. Second in importance to the development of this project was the now-deceased Dr. Carolyn Fowler (aka Carolyn Gerald), the most knowledgeable critic of the Black Arts era. Dr. Fowler is responsible for prodding me to deal with the overall conceptual model that I used and for questioning me regarding specifics of research and citations. Also important in their raising of questions and citing of resources I had overlooked were Ernie Allen, Robert Chrisman, Tom Dent, Maulana Karenga, Haki Madhubuti, Carol Parks, Marc Primus, Ed Spriggs, Askia Muhammad Toure, and Dr. Jerry Ward. Of course, I am ultimately responsible for the information and viewpoints contained in this book. However, my effort would have been far more meager and less meaningful without the input from these knowledgeable individuals, as well as input from others.

My goal for this book is to give readers an accurate introduction to the history and significance of the Black Arts Movement. Although I point out the critical issues surrounding BAM theory and practice, this study neither replaces nor precludes the need for more substantial investigations, scholarly critiques, and historical analyses of BAM. This is only a beginning, an important effort in the ongoing struggle for cultural liberation.

Kalamu ya Salaam
New Orleans, LA – 1997
Provincetown, MA – September 1999

INTRODUCTION

Genesis. This study started out as an article, "The Black Arts Movement," for the *Oxford Companion to African American Literature*. In October of 1995, I was recommended by Dr. Jerry Ward to write the article he had been requested to write but was unable to because of an overload of work. The editors needed a fast turnaround and I thought, "No problem. I can do that." I knew I had much of the material on hand and had contacts with relevant people. When I began the article in 1995, I quickly realized there was no book-length study of the Black Arts Movement.[1] At first, I found it hard to believe, but then I understood. Why should I expect hunters, trackers, gun-bearers, and porters to write the history of the lion, especially if they had to cover a period when the lion was dominant? The realization that the lion's story had not been told was the beginning of this book. A little over one year later, I finally finished the first draft of the final manuscript. The manuscript took another year to complete. I consider the completed manuscript—now a finished book—just a beginning, an opening roar.

Basic Thesis. My thesis is simple: The Black Arts Movement is an artistic manifestation of the collective Black Power–oriented political activity that happened in the sixties and seventies. As an artistic movement, BAM is unique in American literary history because it is so closely aligned to a political movement. As I point out, seminal leaders of BAM were also important and nationally influential political activists.

My perspective is that of both a participant and critic. Since 1968, when I joined the Free Southern Theatre in New Orleans, I have been active as a socially engaged Black writer and BAM proponent. As is documented by my frequent writings in *Negro Digest/Black World*, my articles in *Black Books Bulletin*, *Black Scholar*, and by my editorship and articles (1970–1983) in *Black Collegian Magazine*, I was active as a chronicler and critic of BAM.

My primary task is to define and contextualize BAM. My secondary task is to identify the critical organizations, publications, and individuals, along with dates and places of activity. My tertiary task is to address misconceptions, myths, and unsubstantiated critiques that are often propagated in place of factual information about BAM.

Local/National/Local (L/N/L) Model. BAM was truly national in scope and not simply a regional phenomenon. BAM actually began in far-flung and uncoordinated activities across the country (grassroots/local). Key geographical focal points were as follows:

1. The West Coast Bay Area, which produced the seminal journals *Soulbook*, *Black Dialogue* and *Journal of Black Poetry*;
2. Chicago/Detroit, which produced *Negro Digest/Black World*, *Third World Press*, and *Black Books Bulletin*, as well as OBAC (Organization of Black American Culture) in Chicago and Broadside Press in Detroit;
3. New York/New Ark (Newark, NJ), which produced BART/S (Black Arts Repertory Theatre/School), New Lafayette and the National Black Theatre in New York, and Spirit House Movers and Jihad Press in Newark;
4. New Orleans, home base for The Free Southern Theatre, which traveled throughout the deep south and influenced the development of BAM activities from Florida to Texas.

These areas were key because the activities and manifestoes that came from organizations located in these areas set the tone and provided ideological leadership for BAM activities. First, there is uncoordinated and far-flung grassroots activity. Second, there is the development of a specific focus, as well as a naming, which provides diverse grassroots activities, with a sense of belonging to a larger national movement. Third,

there are the often innovative and diverse grassroots activities which represent specific examples of what is now a national movement. I used this L/N/L (local/national/local) model to grasp the chronology and define BAM activities.

In making my analysis, I use the following conceptual framework:

1. Contextualize BAM within the larger social/political environment of its period.
2. Emphasize both collective work and individual expression—consistent with BAM expressions—rather than focus solely on individual achievement.
3. Identify by name, date, and place the major areas of BAM work.
4. Focus on publications that advocated and documented the Black Arts Movement.

A Theory of History. Every history is based on a conceptual framework and a specific perspective. This study is no different.

How does one measure history? What criterion does one use to mark the beginning and the end of a historical period? Do you concentrate on organizations or individuals? How much contextualization is necessary to understand the historical importance of a specific movement? I finished the first and second draft of this study without consciously answering any of the above questions.

I failed to consciously formulate a historical conception that encompassed the entire momentum of BAM because I subconsciously relied on the assumptions of dominant culture. Among those assumptions is dating developments by the rise of a "great man." I had defined BAM's beginning with LeRoi Jones's (Amiri Baraka) coining of the phrase "Black Arts" and the founding of the Black Arts Repertory Theatre/School (BART/S). Although this viewpoint accurately pinpoints the naming of BAM, this viewpoint is inaccurate and misleading in terms of the development of BAM.

Who makes a movement? How do you measure the life of a movement? Certainly we cannot overlook nor minimize the impact of great leaders, but, on the other hand, neither should we minimize or overlook the existence of grassroots activity. Especially when we speak of resistance and alternative, it is important to understand that a true resistance is not simply a protest. BAM was not trying to be like Euro-centric cultural movements painted Black. BAM had a completely different worldview. BAM did not seek inclusion. BAM's goal was revolution.

Most written histories pay little attention to the activities of the masses. The focus is on the titular heads, the great men and women of the movement. In attempting to get a grip on how BAM started and developed, I kept bumping into this problem of viewpoint. Initially, I ignored the problem and attempted to write the history chronologically. This lead to a focus on the New York scene and spotlighting the Umbra workshop. But as I got deeper into the study and shared my findings with key veterans, a contradiction constantly emerged: Chicago and Detroit had significant activity prior to New York. The first independent journals were published on the West Coast; indeed, *Soulbook* preceded the founding of BART/S. I had a problem. The solution obviously did not lie in ignoring facts that didn't fit the thesis but rather in reformulating the thesis to fit the facts.

BAM's Decentralized Nature. While I had a number of assumptions when I started, the final shape of this study has been dictated by the confluence of my research with a focus on the self-defining nature of the Black Arts Movement. Each bit of research leads to more areas of investigation. For example, early on I formulated a hypothesis that BAM was not a New York based movement as is often supposed. I envisioned a bi-coastal development. But the truth is far more complex. The West Coast Bay Area is certainly a major focal point in BAM's development. But equally important, although much less formally recognized, is the activity in the Chicago/Detroit area, particularly Chicago. Indeed, as we will see, one might even argue that BAM-oriented organizations first surfaced in Chicago, even though they did not formally call themselves "Black Arts" institutions.

Moreover, another area of focus is the militant wing of the Civil Rights Movement, mainly but not exclusively SNCC (Student Non-Violent Coordinating Committee) led or inspired cultural activities. Two important cultural products of the Southern Civil Rights thrust were The Free Southern Theatre and The SNCC Freedom Singers, out of which came Bernice Johnson Reagon, who founded Sweet Honey In The Rock. In a later section, we look at this development specifically, but I mention this to illustrate that in the north, south, east, and west, BAM had regional focal points, which lead to local developments and thereby accounted for an unprecedented diffusion of BAM activities nationwide. Indeed, in many ways, from the very beginning there was a national/local dialectic of activity.

BAM is traditionally believed to have begun somewhere around 1965. However, there are multiple examples of BAM activity prior to this date. Though it is usually thought of as an outgrowth of BAM, Chicago, founded The DuSable Museum by Margaret and Charles Burroughs in 1961 is chronologically a BAM precursor. The Afro American Folkloric Troupe in 1962 in the Bay Area, the founding of *Soulbook* in 1964 also in the Bay Area, and the 1964 founding of the Free Southern Theatre in Jackson, Mississippi, also predate what is conventionally believed to be BAM's inception. More importantly, these activities highlight BAM's decentralized nature, evidencing simultaneous BAM activity in various parts of the nation. But the dialectic of BAM's decentralized nature is not complete if we look solely at pre-1965 regional and local formations.

While conscious of themselves as local entities, BAM leaders were attempting to establish a national movement. However, as more and more activity developed and as New York came on line, a critical mass was achieved, and BAM was born as a coalescing of these various formations into a cohesive movement aimed at the national development and articulation of arts and culture from a Black Power perspective. Even more than the founding of BART/S, the advent of the "revolutionary journals" (*Soulbook*, *Black Dialogue*, and *Journal of Black Poetry*) marked the beginning of an effort to explicitly generate a national movement.

This is the same course that the civil disobedience phase of the Civil Rights Movement took earlier in the sixties. The sixties opened with a major grassroots/local event. On February 1, 1960, four students from North Carolina A&T University initiated the first "sit-in." As Tom Dent notes in his book *Southern Journey*, the real significance of the sit-in went far beyond a bold, new tactic for civil rights struggle:

> These unique protests against segregation, dubbed the "sit-ins" by the media, marked the beginning of a new, activist phase in southern civil rights advocacy. It is important to note that the sit-ins were not initiated by racial leaders, but by college students who were virtually unknown. (5)

Here was grassroots/local activity, initiated by non-leaders, which was explicitly resistant to the status quo. There was no attempt to be "legal" or "non-confrontational." Moreover, this first sit-in sparked a virtual firestorm of sit-ins and similar activity (including the even more famous "freedom rides") across the South. The people were on the move and the leadership was forced to scurry to keep up.

After February 1960, the thrust of the Civil Rights Movement switched from legal activity (boycotts, picketing, and suits in court) to "illegal" activity such as sit-ins and freedom rides. In the early sixties, sit-ins and freedom rides were explicitly against the law. In this case, "the law" consisted of literal legislation in effect at the time in the various communities in question; "the law" was also long standing traditions at both the state and national level. In a similar way, BAM consciously resisted literary laws then in effect.

After the passage of the 1964 civil rights legislation and the 1965 voting rights legislation, the goal was no longer the desegregation of public accommodations and access to government; but rather, the focus shifted to the more radical demand of Black self-determination and empowerment, i.e. Black Power. In a similar way, BAM radically sought to establish an alternative literature that validated Black folk traditions and challenged White literary traditions as the ultimate judge of literary value for Black literature. In ways both obvious and subtle, positive and negative, BAM can be considered Black Power in the literary and performance arts sphere.

Performance Orientation/"Publication" Focus. There is one final conceptual wrinkle that needs to be ironed out before we delve into the formal investigation of BAM. The majority of BAM activities were performance oriented; yet I have chosen to focus mainly on publications. Why?

One reason for my emphasis on publications is of the research orientation of this study. Not surprisingly, the majority of the documentation that is available is material published in journals and anthologies. Relatively speaking, there is very little recording and audio/visual documentation of BAM performances in general circulation. Even then-popular television programs such as Ellis Hazlip's *Soul* and *Black Journal*, produced by Bill Greaves, are not generally available. Moreover, when these programs were popular, although viewed nationally, they were not the primary sources for disseminating BAM information. This fact brings me to the second reason I focus on publications.

BAM publications were the main ways in which BAM information was circulated. *Negro Digest/Black World* was the most widely circulated and referred to BAM-oriented publication, but the West Coast trio of *Soulbook*, *Black Dialogue*, and especially *Journal of Black Poetry* were also critically important. Two other publications were extremely effective: the anthology *Black Fire* and the special 1968 Black Theatre issue of *Drama Review*. Especially for the burgeoning numbers of community and campus-based Black theatres of the BAM era, those two publications contained play scripts which were performed in hundreds of communities.

Grassroots theatre companies used a mixture of the plays contained in BAM publications, locally created productions (which invariably included dramatized poetry readings), and major productions by playwrights such as James Baldwin, Lorraine Hansberry, LeRoi Jones/Amiri Baraka, Ron Milner, Sonia Sanchez, Ted Ward, and above all, the prolific Ed Bullins, whose slice-of-life, "ghetto-based" dramas were very popular. Because each community had their own poets, the influence of BAM publications, although considerable for shaping the overall direction of BAM poetry, was less of an impact in poetry than in formal theatre.

In the chapter on theatre, I focus on the performance objectives of the Afro American Folkloric Troupe as an example of BAM theatre in the first grassroots period. The national impact of that group was far less than merited by the work of the Troupe precisely because the Troupe was not broadly publicized in the media of its time.

An additional reason for my focusing on publication rather than performance is that performance has the inherent limitation of not transferring well in print. Printed language cannot communicate rhythms, timbre, tone, inflection in language, body language, nor dance and visual elements, all of which were greatly used in BAM performances. Resultantly, not having been in the audience, you do not have an adequate reference for you to appreciate what is only suggested by text.

Text alone does not convey the power of BAM poetry and plays—which means, on the one hand, that we have very little documented evidence to use to study BAM performances and, on the other hand, that the printed evidence we do have is admittedly limited and limiting. Nonetheless, what quickly became apparent around the country is that, in drama, it was better to have the script and to "interpret" the script in your own way than not to have the script at all.

This is why and how I approach this study. Throughout this study, the conceptual triad of L/N/L will dictate that I pay attention to what was going on in key areas prior to 1965. As much as possible, I list the names of founding members and the dates of founding. Finally, I emphasize elements documented by primary sources (mainly books and journals).

I believe this methodology increases the value of this book both as a guide for further study and as a reliable reference for a general overview. Certainly the "selection" of facts and figures and the interpretation of what has been selected is my choice, but by being upfront about the criteria for selection and by specifying my sources, I aim to make a clear case for the relative accuracy of this study. Additionally, much of the interpretation I offer has been comparatively tested against the views of numerous BAM participants and veterans. While some may argue with my opinions and take issue with the specifics of my methodology, the general historical information is accurate. Moreover, through on-going discussion and interviews with BAM veterans, I have been able to draw out information that previously has either not been published or not been contextualized as an element of BAM. This study is meant to be a beginning, not only in terms of being one of the few book length studies, but also in terms of establishing an analytical framework for the ongoing study of the Black Arts Movement.

Recent book-length studies of the Black Arts Movement include: Margaret Ann Reid's Black Protest Poetry: Polemicsfrom the Harlem Renaissance and The Sixties (2001); James Edward Smethurst's The Black Arts Movement: Literary Nationalism in the 1960s and 1970s (2005); Cheryl Clarke's "After Mecca": Women Poets and the Black Arts Movement (2005); Lisa Gail Collins and Margo Crawford's New Thoughts on the Black Arts Movement (2006), Regina Jennings' Malcolm X and the Poetics of Haki Madhubuti (2006).

CHAPTER 1
DEFINING THE BLACK ARTS MOVEMENT

Objectives. The Black Arts Movement's (BAM) objectives were three-fold:

1. to establish Black leadership of Black cultural expression directed to a Black audience,
2. to propagate the concept of the Black Aesthetic, and
3. to produce socially engaged art that promoted the Black Freedom/Liberation struggle.

This definition distinguishes BAM from a simple racialist position that any art produced by Blacks is "Black Art."

Black Arts Movement and Black Consciousness. A Black Power (sometimes called Black consciousness) perspective called for Black leadership and mass involvement; a Black Aesthetic; and socially engaged art which openly advocated Black freedom/ Black liberation struggle. These three points composed a triad that influenced BAM's development both locally and nationally. Between 1965 and 1976, the high point of BAM, all across America via involvement in neighborhood youth-oriented organizations, art collectives, and community-based arts agencies, Black artists were on the move, attempting to create artwork that spoke directly to Black people out of the triad of Black Power concerns. Moreover, this movement was dialectical in that it was not a simplistic following of one premise to its logical conclusion, but rather an ongoing, dynamic, and constantly developing interplay of theory directing practice and, in turn, shaping the development of new theories, and also

1

of individually developed dreams and ideals attempted and/or actualized by grassroots groups across the nation who, in the process of making the ideal into reality, created new dreams and ideals.

After the growth of local organizations, the second step in the local/national/local (L/N/L) dialectic was BAM becoming nationally self-conscious. LeRoi Jones' coining of the name for the movement is indicative of the fruition of this second step. In his 1984 autobiography, Jones, by then known as Amiri Baraka, recalls,

> One evening when a large group of us were together in my study talking earnestly about black revolution and what should be done, I got the idea that we should form an organization. On Guard had been long gone, because of its obvious contradictions. We needed a group of black revolutionaries who were artists to raise up the level of struggle from the arts sector. There was Dave Knight, White, Marion, C.D., Leroy McLucas, the Hackensack brothers (Sammy and Tong), Jimmy Lesser, Larry, Max, plus Corny and Clarence and Askia Toure. We would form a secret organization. Tong asked me what would it be called, it came into my head in a flash, the Black Arts.

Note that some of the names used are pseudonyms, specifically Sammy and Tong Hackensack, who are really Charles and William Patterson. Also note that "Max" refers to Max Stanford, the founder of the Revolutionary Action Movement (RAM). Stanford was a political activist and not an artist. Thus, at its inception, BAM was a marriage of art and politics.

The third step in BAM's dialectic of development was the adoption of the nomenclature and the general principles by Black and Black-oriented organizations nationwide.

A word about "Black-oriented" organizations is necessary to illustrate the varying levels of development. The Free Southern Theatre (FST) initially was an integrated organization that performed adaptations of "classics" as well as original work. One can easily imagine the bemused, if not confused, reaction of sharecroppers in the Mississippi Delta to the 1964 production of Samuel Beckett's *Waiting for Godot*. By 1969 FST was all Black and those same Mississippi Delta viewers were literally and profoundly "moved" by a pre-New York performance of LeRoi Jones' *Slaveship*. The audience was aroused to militant action.

In Mississippi, there were actual civil disturbances following the production. Moving its audience to action was an intended goal of this play and of BAM.

The FST *Slaveship* example has an interesting footnote. Gilbert Moses, one of the founders of FST, was the director of the group's version of the play *Slaveship*, which toured the Deep South. On the basis of his innovative work on that version (which used a portable set that could be carried in a van and set up in a variety of venues), Moses was tapped to direct a Broadway version, which played to critical and popular success. Although the nation as a whole became aware of *Slaveship* as a result of its Broadway success, it was the FST production, an outcome of BAM, that actually launched *Slaveship* as a national phenomenon. Those who look for a linear, progressive development and do not take into consideration dialectical developments make a major mistake. On one hand, FST was a chronological precursor of BAM. But, through the dialectical L/N/L process, FST also became a major proponent example of BAM's movement.

Karamu House, founded in 1949 by Rowena and Russell Jelliffes in Cleveland, Ohio, is another example of local arts movement, which both preceded BAM and then became a BAM-influenced institution struggling around the triad of BAM concerns: Black leadership/Black audience, Black Aesthetics, and social relevance to the Black struggle.

By 1970, most local, Black-oriented, arts organizations began referring to themselves as "Black Arts" organizations. There was Black Arts/Midwest, Black Arts West, BLKARTSOUTH, and so forth. That was how BAM developed. Moreover, these organizations generally followed the guidelines laid down in the BAM publications. For example, on July 24, 1975, Joe Briscoe, an aspirant BAM member in Sedalia, Missouri, wrote a letter addressing to Dingane Joe Goncalves:

> We are in the process of setting up a black cultural center to serve the brothers & sisters in this area. Theatre & poetry will be the foundation of our learning media so *The Journal of Black Poetry* is one of the necessary communication links we must have. Please send information about subscription price & a sample copy if possible, and any information and/or contacts

that can help our growth. We are small with much to learn. Our principle goal is to develop Pan-Africanistic thought. All help is needed & will be appreciated. (Goncalves "Letters")

Goncalves has a clutch of such letters literally from around the world that are similar to the one cited above and that demonstrate how closely people identified with BAM. This is how BAM developed, coalescing from grassroots/local activity, formalized on a national level, reasserted by the grassroots.

Internal Contradictions. When we review the staffs and editorials of BAM journals, we find that there is clearly no single leadership, no single line. In fact, if anything, there is an ongoing struggle around leadership and ideology. Sometimes this struggle for ideological leadership takes on a personal tone of ad hominem attacks. Sometimes former allies become bitter enemies and vice versa. By 1970, LeRoi Jones/Amiri Baraka became a leading, although not uncontested, figure. However, Jones/Baraka's popularity notwithstanding, there was no single centralized BAM leadership.

The lack of centralized leadership was both a strength and a weakness. The strength was *that* BAM organizations could reflect the particulars of their local situation and that the local grassroots artists could determine their own specific direction in implementing general BAM guidelines. However, the lack of a central leadership was also a major liability, especially when BAM formations were beset by financial strictures and ideological infighting.

For example, when John Johnson shut down *Black World* in 1976, there was no national leadership in place to negotiate with Johnson on *Black World's* behalf nor was there an organization in place to facilitate the development of a new independent literary magazine, which could follow up on the now defunct publication. An effort was made by Hoyt Fuller and others in 1976 to found *First World*, but the new journal was not able to sustain itself. The follow-up journal folded after only a handful of issues after Fuller, who had been serving as the journal's editor, suffered a heart attack and died in 1981.

Time and again, especially after the loss of key individuals or the closing down of key BAM institutions, BAM adherents were unable to mount an effective national response. The decentralized focus and the lack of centralized structure and/or leadership was a major debilitating internal contention of BAM.

External contradictions. There was a second dialectic at work, which was both externally and intentionally disruptive. Traditional American foundations defunded BAM institutions and established alternative "acceptable" institutions, targeting the BAM audience. Baraka points to the Negro Ensemble as an obvious example of this trend. He writes:

> Later, after the word "black" had cooled out some and the idea of even "black art" had sunk roots deep enough in the black masses, where it could not simply be denied out of existence, the powers-that-be brought in some Negro art, some skin theater, eliminating the most progressive and revolutionary expressions for a fundable colored theater that merely traded on "the black experience," rather than carrying on the black struggle for democracy and self-determination. Then the Fords and Rockefellers "fount" them some colored folks they could trust and dropped some dough on them for colored theater. Douglas Turner Ward's Negro Ensemble is perhaps the most famous case in point. During a period when the average young blood would go to your head for calling him or her a knee-grow, the Fords and Rockefellers could raise themselves up a whole-ass knee-grow ensemble. But that's part of the formula: Deny reality as long as you have to and then, when backed up against the wall, substitute an ersatz model filled with the standard white racist lies which include some dressed as Negro art. Instead of black art, bring in Negro art, house nigger art, and celebrate slavery, right on! (Baraka, *Autobiography* 214)

Yet, this is not the most insidious example of this dialectic. The most insidious is the development of "Blaxploitation" movies to push aside and replace the independent Black cinema movement, which was an active part of BAM. I will discuss this development in a later chapter.

Notably, the "alternative" and "establishment initiated" Black(?!) artistic thrusts are all distinguished by either a lessening or an eradication of the BAM ideological triad. Especially with the blaxploitation films, the directors as well as the producers of establishment "Blackness" were often Whites. The development of a Black Aesthetic was mooted in favor of a return to "craft" and "standards" (code words for the readopting of traditional Euro-centric aesthetical concerns) or in favor of an emphasis on entertainment. Needless to say, social engagement was downplayed or entirely eliminated. Time and time again this central antagonistic polemic is introduced by the establishment as a means of regaining control of Black artistic activity. Without an understanding of both the central internal and external contradictions of the sixties and seventies, BAM's achievements as well as BAM's losses can not be accurately assessed.

Other contradictions.   Examples of other dialectics at work include the internal effort to control Black publishing and to resist co-option by the external establishment or by establishment oriented and/or establishment sponsored forces who were ostensibly "Black." Internally, this is illustrated by the development of Black publications and presses, Black bookstores, and by an attempt to develop a Black book distribution system. Externally, this dialectic is illustrated by two boycott efforts: (1) The Ed Spriggs led boycott of Clarence Major's *New Black Poetry Anthology*; and (2) The boycott of *Essence* magazine early in its development. Both of these boycotts should be understood in context.

BAM was not a "skin game." Just being biologically Black was not sufficient. Instead, the triad of concerns gave the movement its definition and focus. Thus, in 1968 Ed Spriggs wrote "On The Boycott' black writers/white publishers: an alliance that boycotts black publishers" first published in *Journal of Black Poetry* and later reprinted in *Black Art Black Culture*, a collection of articles from *Journal of Black Poetry*. Spriggs raised a number of very important issues, which still retain their relevance. I quote him at length:

> What I want understood is this boycott thing, and it is necessary to deal with this...this did not come about due to a personal clash with Clarence Major. I mean it is not about C. Major the man, the poet, but the ideological stance that is him, a lot of other Black writers and until recently, myself. and another thing that needs clarification is that it aint about International Publishers per se, yeah, we dig where they at. along with a lot of other publishers in that same direction and Praeger, say, in the opposite...

I took a stand, boycott. it's time for that. it grew out of a telephone conversation with c major. while we talked the necessity to take the stand crystallized. repeat: black writers are being exploited even when they're talking abt black power thru the white press. i mean some cat's total economics and prestige depend upon the white publishers—not that they want it that way. we can break that up if we want to. our publishers will never be able to break out of this system if the boost doesn't come from the black writers. swamp our publishers with the level of material that we turn over to the white publishers and domestic and international distributorships will be a reality *before* the present system crumbles. there are many levels of power. let's move on up a little higher. We already have black publishers (no matter how minor some are) who consistently work with us. are we ready for that? c. major wasn't. even tho he had been published in dudley r's Broadside press anthology (*For Malcolm X*) and in the *Journal of Black Poetry. Journal of Black Poetry* is printed and published by black people entirely. Jamerson printing company does the job for the *Journal*. Julian Richardson, owner of Success Printing company does the job for *Black Dialogue*. Richardson and Associates are publishing a reprint of the *Philosophy and Opinions of Marcus Garvey* in paper and hard covers. san francisco could become the black publishing capital of afro-america if we had our souls where our mouths are. a lot more could be said abt the way we could support black publishers and what kind of changes we wld have to go thru to initiate that support. but we need to think, talk and act on this right away quick. we can take up the challenge now. we need to. unless some of us are already too revolutionary to entertain this kind of thing. it's still possible for us to get our cookies and help the black publishers get theirs too.

Repeat. it's abt discontinuing the freeze we have dealt out to black publishers by ignoring their existence. me? i'm nuttin on every thing directed to the mother country's houses that shat shld and cld be published black. so i wont get a poem here or a piece there. my life could never depend on it anyway. of course there are a couple of things due to come out that i let go of before i saw the necessity for this stance. no matter. we've got to stop the contradiction at the point that we become aware of them. black publishers are laying in the cut waiting for the righteous black writers. black writers can bail them out.

There are institutions to be built. we're young and strong enough to build but we've gotta have the vision. we have the power. if you don't believe it just ask dial, harpers, wm morrow, grove, merit, marzani and munsell or even international publishers. couldn't julian richardson, dudley randall and lafayette jamerson get into some very heavy drama if they could get just a little play from our co-opted black writers? you know they could. holes in yr front because you choose not to. fatten up. writers. black. seeking new dimensions of power. talk to me baby. we been laying back too long. (Spriggs, "On The 'Boycott'" 11, 13–14)

Today, there is not one major literary anthology widely used in Black Studies, Black literature, or related courses that is both edited by Blacks and published by a Black press. The absence of Black control of the presentation of Black literature is indicative of how completely the establishment view dominates the discourse about and the actual production of Black literature. Worse than the reality of this alien and often antagonistic domination is the reality that most Black scholars and writers see no major contradiction in the fact that the overwhelming majority of Black literature is produced by non-Black publishing concerns.

In a similar vein, orienting the arts on capitalist views, entertainment is generally acceptable in the nineties. But during the BAM era Blackness was more than a skin game. Thus, Askia Muhammad Toure's call for a boycott of *Essence* in protest of "firings" and of interim editor Gordon Parks' hiring of whites as art director and graphic illustrators. Undoubtedly, this protest helped push *Essence* towards a pro-Black position much faster than the magazine may have moved on its own. Toure writes in "Report on the *'Essence'* Magazine Affair," that

> Recently, in New York, Sister Hattie Gossett, an outstanding Black editor, was fired by the management of a new magazine for "inefficiency." (Sister Hattie had worked "efficiently" for a year and a half at *Redbook*, a national women's magazine. She quit her job at *Redbook* to join *Essence* in order to work for Black people.) Hattie Gossett is well known for her uncompromising Black views. We suggest that this is the real reason for her firing. About two weeks later, the editor, Miss Ruth Ross, a Black professional sister quit *Essence* magazine over an alleged "breach of contract." So *Essence* magazine is now without the services of the two Black women editors who were to help launch it.
> When word of Sister Hattie's dismissal passed along the grapevine, Black writers began to withdraw their work from the magazine. ... Blackhearts!! we urge you to BOYCOTT ESSENCE MAGAZINE THROUGHOUT THE COUNTRY, AS ANOTHER "GAME" BEING RUN ON BLACK PEOPLE BY SLICK NIGGAS HUSTLING "BLACKNESS" FOR PROFIT; AIDED BY AN UNCLE TOM EDITOR WHO HATES AND DESPISES BLACK CREATIVE ARTISTS. (Toure 33)

From the example of these two boycotts, we can clearly discern that BAM was more than a simple reversal of the racist notion that if you're white you're right and if you're black you're wrong. BAM understood that unity around biological Blackness was not sufficient to advance BAM's specific ideological goals.

Two other major dialectics at work concerned the question of integration, specifically interracial marriages and "the woman's question." BAM proponents were opposed to interracial marriages and were slow to respond to "feminism," which was viewed as a "middle-class, White woman's thing." The non-resolution of these contradictions led to splits between BAM and high profile integrationist-oriented Blacks as well as splits between BAM and Black women who prioritized politicality on gender issues. Alienated from BAM, many of these forces either forged new fronts of activity or joined existing establishment activities.

On this note, there is an interesting development. A number of high profile, male BAM spokespeople previously had been involved in interracial relationships. When they became BAM advocates, they took an extremely hard line against interracial relationships. I postulate that they were inclined toward the hard line because as men they generally did not have the day-to-day responsibility of rearing the children produced from the interracial unions. LeRoi Jones is, perhaps, archetypal in this regard. In his autobiography, there is very little mention of participating in rearing his children from his marriage with Hattie Jones.

On the other hand, Black women who had been parties in interracial relationships and who had responsibility for rearing the children of those unions did not take such a hard line. Alice Walker is an example of this. Undoubtedly, the Black male "holier-than-thou" hard line alienated a significant number of important participants and potential participants.

The splitting of marriages and organizations based on race was a particularly painful development for a number of people who were veterans of the Civil Rights Movement. Some of these veterans had made tremendous personal and political commitments to actualize integrated relationships. The advent of BAM strained many of those relationships to the breaking point. This strain accounts for some of the anti-BAM animosity often manifested in accusations of BAM's being "racist" or "crow-jim" (a play on the racist Jim Crow laws of the post-Emancipation era). While I do not intend to blow this contradiction out of proportion, at the same time I do not intend to overlook the racial split and the hard feelings that resulted. Some of those feelings are still being worked out by people who were "negatively" affected.

The "race" contradiction was not just a personal issue, but played into the politics of many BAM affiliated groups. This contradiction was most violently played out in the conflicts between SNCC and the Black Panther Party. SNCC set their hard line towards excluding Whites from the organization. However, the Panther Party held the belief that SNCC's exclusionary practices resulted from their past history of having Whites as leading members of their organization. As for the Panthers themselves, they took the position that they could work with anyone, having no hang-ups with Whites because they had never been controlled by Whites nor had Whites been leading members, whereas the Panthers believed that SNCC was obsessed with excluding Whites because Whites had once played dominant roles in SNCC. This, as well as the Panther antagonistic position on "cultural nationalists," involved a great deal of exaggeration and some outright falsification such as labeling Maulana Karenga as a paid FBI agent. In relation to BAM, the Panther's stance on Black/White coalition produced yet another point of alienation. After initially working together, BAM and the Panthers split forces in the late sixties. Emory Douglas, who was the Panther Minister of Culture and, to a lesser extent Eldridge Cleaver were both involved in early West Coast BAM activity. Emory did the cover for Sonia Sanchez's book of poetry, *Homecoming*, and also contributed artwork to *Journal of Black Poetry*. However, once the split intensified, Emory was directed by the Black Panther Party not to participate in any BAM activities. In hindsight, we can easily see that this was a self-destructive schism, but at the time the split played itself out as a major ideological battle.

Thus, the dialectic of assertion/alienation (i.e., the militant assertion of a political position alienates those who do not share that position) is established. When the position in question has both personal and social implications in terms of mates, friends, and associates, invariably what starts out as an ideological debate quickly degenerates into backbiting, infighting and self-destructive activities. Given its radical departure from the then existing norms, we should not be surprised that BAM was in constant internal turmoil as well as periodically mired in "bickering and backbiting."

CHAPTER 2
THE BLACK ARTS MOVEMENT'S
HISTORICAL BACKGROUND

Black Arts Movement Timeline. Our conceptual local/national/local (L/N/L) approach is now defined. The major contradictions have been considered. BAM itself is defined. With this much in place, we can now address the question of periodicity, i.e. when did BAM start, when did BAM end, why and how were the beginning and end dates chosen?

When discussing social movements, establishing start and stop dates is often an arbitrary exercise. BAM is particularly difficult to pin down to a specific start and stop date because of the nature of its beginning in far-flung, grassroots activities, which often appeared unrelated to each other. Nevertheless, if we claim that BAM was an important movement then we need to be able to locate this movement in history. In keeping with the L/N/L conceptual model, I mark BAM as beginning with a precipitating national event which stimulated local movement.

From this perspective, BAM begins in 1965, when the assassination of Malcolm X in February of that year propelled a number of forces into action, compelling them to make definitive moves and declarations. In March of that year, only one short month after Malcolm's death, LeRoi Jones joined forces with other Black activists/artists to found the Black Arts Repertory Theatre/School (BART/S). Also, the staff of *Black Dialogue* decided to dedicate their 1965 debut issue to Malcolm. Additionally, with the passage of the 1965 Voting Rights Act, the Civil Rights Movement was effectively ended, and the stage was set for "Black Power," which, by 1966, had already reached levels of national recognition.

I designate 1976 as a point where BAM began to transition away from its national spotlight. By then, Broadside Press had gone into hiatus and *Journal of Black Poetry* had ceased publication. In April of 1976, *Black World* was shut down by its publisher, John Johnson. In a later chapter, I will discuss the ramifications of these and other factors in the decline of BAM activity. Although I use 1976 as a formal end point for the purposes of this study, I do not mark 1976 as the death of BAM.

Well after 1976, the triad of BAM principles remained vital to a number of artists and institutions. However, after 1976, BAM was a much less dynamic force and often was in a reactive rather than proactive posture. In any case, I have chosen to focus on 1965 (national birth) to 1976 (institutional disruption) as the decade of BAM's apogee.

Political Context. Both inherently and overtly political in content, BAM was the first American literary movement with a national reach to advance "social engagement" as a sine qua non of its mission. The "revolutionary" literature of the Depression era, such as the communist-led John Reed clubs (which promoted the work of Richard Wright and other Black writers of that period) did not have the national reach that BAM had. The focal points for the production of most Marxist-oriented work was Chicago and the northeast corridor (particularly the New York area). BAM on the other hand was produced in the far west and in the Deep South, as well as in the northern urban areas.

I cannot overstress the national reach of BAM. The Black Arts Movement was neither a one-city nor one-region phenomenon. Individuals and organizations nationwide were actively involved and accounted for both its vitality and its diversity.

BAM broke from the immediate past of protest and petition (Civil Rights) literature and dashed forward toward an alternative that initially seemed unthinkable and unobtainable: Black Power. As a political reference, the phrase "Black Power" was not new. The slogan had earlier been articulated by Richard Wright, specifically in his 1954 book, *Black Power: A Record of Reactions in a Land of Pathos*, which described the mid-fifties emergence of Ghana as the first independent African nation. The more familiar, sixties use of the term originated in the Civil Rights Movement in 1966 with the Student Nonviolent Coordinating Committee (SNCC) which was often described as the most militant of the major Civil Rights organizations.

During the famous 1966 James Meredith march,[1] SNCC leader Stokely Carmichael and field worker Willie Ricks used the chant of "Black Power" as a counter to the speeches of Martin Luther King and other Southern Christian Leadership Conference (SCLC) leaders. While King was calling for equal rights, Carmichael and other SNCC workers would set up a call ("what do we want") and lead their audiences in answering ("Black Power"). At that time Black Power was often translated to mean Black political and economic control of predominately Black towns, cities, and counties in the Deep South, especially in Alabama and Mississippi. Credible sources contend that although Carmichael is often credited with popularizing the phrase "Black Power," in fact, Willie Ricks was the first person in SNCC to use the phrase and that Ricks passed it on to a receptive Carmichael who made it popular.

So what did Carmichael mean? In a July 28, 1966 speech, Carmichael comments:

> There is a psychological war going on in this country and it's whether or not black people are going to be able to use the terms they want about their movement without white peoples blessing. We have to tell them we are going to use the term 'Black Power' and we are going to define it because Black Power speaks to us. We can't let them project Black Power because they can only project it from white power and we know what white power has done to us. We have to organize ourselves to speak from a position of strength and stop begging people to look kindly upon us. We are going to build a movement in this country based on the color of our skins that is going to free us from our oppressors and we have to do that ourselves.

Carmichael continues:

> Everybody in this country is for "Freedom Now" but not everybody is for Black Power because we have got to get rid of some of the people who have white power. We have got to get us some Black Power. We don't control anything but what white people say we can control. We have to be able to smash any political machine in the country that's oppressing us and bring it to its knees. We have to be aware that if we keep growing and multiplying the way we do in ten years all

the major cities are going to be ours. We have to know that in Newark, New Jersey, where we are 60% of the population, we went along with their stories about integrating and we got absorbed. All we have to show for it is three councilmen who are speaking for them and not for us. We have to organize ourselves to speak for each other. That's Black Power. We have to move to control the economics and politics of our community. (Carmichael 474–476)

BAM cannot be understood apart from its beginnings in the Black Power movement. In the article "The Black Cultural Revolution," A. Muhammad Ahmed (formerly known as Max Sanford, a founder and leader of the Revolutionary Action Movement, or RAM) gives a detailed historical interpretation of Black Power's beginnings. Ahmed maintains that, "the mass protest-year of our struggle started on February 1, 1960, when four black students staged a sit-in at Greensboro, North Carolina. Within weeks, black students throughout the south were demonstrating against public aspects of segregation" (Ahmed 3). The sit-in is usually seen as part and parcel of the Civil Rights Movement, but as Ahmed details in his article, there was a vigorous ideological struggle going on within the broad Civil Rights Movement. The two camps may be simplistically identified as the assimilationist Civil Rights camp and the separatist Black Power camp. Although the assimilationist position as articulated by Martin Luther King/SCLC is perhaps the most well-known and most celebrated outcry of the Civil Rights Movement, the movement itself was far from monolithic.

Ahmed goes on to mention the involvement of the Congress of Racial Equality (CORE) in the 1961 Freedom Rides. Ahmed then pinpoints the 1962 founding of RAM as a leading ideological force in the development and spread of the Black Power ideology, an ideology that became the driving force of BAM. He writes:

Some of these students began intensive study of Black history; some of their ideological leaders were Marcus Garvey, Robert Williams, Harold Cruse, the Honorable Elijah Muhammad, Malcolm X and Dr. Dubois... As these black student revolutionaries began to formulate ideas for their party, some decided to leave school and go into northern black communities and organize like SNCC did in southern communities. After some debate a name was chosen for their black student party; it was called the RAM party, later to become known as the Revolutionary Action Movement. RAM won the student elections at Central State, its whole slate gaining control of student government. That was in May of 1962. (4)

Ahmed continues:

As a result of the mass activism in the north and south, a conference was held in August, 1963, called the "Black Vanguard" conference. The students discussed the forthcoming March on Washington and how it would be compromised, and began formulating ideas of involving brothers from the street in the forefront of the movement. They decided to continue nationalist activism in the north, slowly building a nationalist consciousness.

In the fall of 1963 the Grassroots Conference was called in Detroit, calling together grassroots leaders of the then Civil Rights Movement. The Grassroots conference took a black nationalist stand, supporting the Freedom Now Party, an all-black party organized during the March on Washington. (7)

In 1964 a group of black students at Fisk University formed a black nationalist student movement called ASM, the Afro-American Student Movement. ASM called the 1st National Afro-American Student Conference on Black Nationalism on May 1st to 3rd.... The convening of the 1st National Afro-American Student Conference on Black Nationalism was the ideological catalyst that eventually shifted the Civil Rights Movement into the Black Power movement. During the summer months, RAM organizers with the agreement of John Lewis, the then Chairman of SNCC, went into Mississippi to work with SNCC. RAM organizers soon came into conflict with white SNCC workers, who opposed an all-black force and the practice of self-defense; soon, RAM began a movement to force whites out of SNCC. (8)

A key participant in RAM's infiltration of SNCC was poet, journalist, and activist Roland Snellings (later known as Askia Muhammad Toure), who was also one of the main authors of SNCC's Black Power position paper. This history is important because unless we understand the root of Black Power's origins, we cannot appreciate its Black Aesthetic fruit.

In the first grassroots period, the key ideological figures of BAM were writer Larry Neal (who was also a member of RAM) and activist/scholar Maulana Karenga, who, in the early sixties, was head of the Los Angeles chapter of Attorney Donald Warden's Afro-American Association. Of course, the spiritual father of Black Power was Malcolm X, who inspired both Neal and Karenga.

Neal became the major cultural savant/writer. He published widely in publications as diverse as the New York-based, activist-oriented *Liberator* magazine and the Chicago-based, status quo-oriented *Ebony* magazine. From academic journals to the major anthology of the period, *Black Fire*, which he co-edited with LeRoi Jones, Neal's influential writings would be widely quoted by BAM participants.

Karenga, through the direct and indirect influence of his Kawaida philosophical formulation, became one of the central philosophers of Black Power. Karenga's direct influence was felt mainly through one 1968 essay, "Black Art: Mute Matter Given Force and Function," published in *Negro Digest*. However, indirectly, through the spread of Kawaida, and especially the formulation of the "Nguzo Saba" (seven principles) and the "Kwanzaa" holiday, Karenga had a major influence. Additionally, when LeRoi Jones became an advocate of Kawaida, Karenga's indirect influence became preeminent in BAM because of Jones' popularity and propaganda prowess in producing articles and pamphlets such as "A Black Value System" (in the debut November 1969 issue of *Black Scholar*) and *Kawaida Studies: The New Nationalism* (Third World Press: 1972), both of which were widely distributed and cited within Black nationalist circles.

Of course there were others who were significant forces in helping to shape BAM ideology. Significant among them are Ed Spriggs and Askia Muhammad Toure. In addition to being a founding editor of *Black Dialogue*, poet Ed Spriggs was also a visual artist who taught printmaking at BART/S in the spring and summer of 1965. Moreover, Ed Spriggs was among the first wave of BAM independent Black filmmakers. In 1965 he was part of a small film collective, which produced a half-hour documentary on the Ephesian Church of God in Christ in Berkeley, California. The film included the early work of Edwin Hawkins, who was the church choir director at the time. From 1969 to approximately 1972, Ed Spriggs, along with Larry Neal, Jim Hinton, Rufus Hinton (no relation), and Doug Harris formed a film collective which actively documented BAM and Black Power-oriented activities and events in and around New York City, as well as along the east coast down to Washington D.C.

Examples of some of their work included *Moving On Up* (a documentary for the A. Phillip Randolph Institute's Joint Apprenticeship Program in New York). In Newark they documented the Ken Gibson mayoral campaign, which was a showpiece of Baraka's initial forays into electoral politics, and they also documented the Black Power conferences which featured speakers such as Maulana Karenga and Richard Hatcher. In Washington D.C. they documented the SCLC's "Poor People's Campaign." From 1969 to 1975 Spriggs was head of the Studio Museum in Harlem, which was the site of the famous Africobra exhibit. Also of note, Hoyt Fuller's family selected Ed Spriggs to be the literary executor of Fuller's estate from 1981 to 1984. Along with the significant help of Richard Long of Atlanta University, Spriggs secured a permanent repository for Fuller's collection in the Atlanta University Center's Robert W. Woodruff Library.

Little known outside of intimate BAM circles, Askia Muhammad Toure was another significant catalyst who constantly sought to reach out to diverse peoples and involve them in BAM related activities. Toure was a member of the New York-based literary group Umbra, a key member of RAM, a writer for *Liberator* magazine, a founding member of BART/S, an organizer with SNCC, and a writer for *Black Dialogue*, *Soulbook*, and *Journal of Black Poetry*. When writing about the formation of BART/S, Amiri Baraka proclaimed both Toure's and Neal's importance to the school's foundation. He wrote that "Both Larry and Askia were among the chief catalysts for that blazing and progressive, though short-lived, institution...Larry Neal and Askia Toure were my models in the middle 60s for Black Art" (Baraka, "The Wailer" x, xii).

Of course there were numerous others, including organizers and theorists such as Imari Obadele, head of the Republic of New Afrika, a nationalist formation whose avowed goal was the securing of reparations and the establishment of an independent Black nation in the Deep South. Particularly important because of his international contacts and reputation was Robert Williams, the former Monroe, North Carolina NAACP leader who was forced out of the country after advocating and organizing armed resistance to KKK attacks in the late fifties. In exile, Robert Williams continued to be a beacon of resistance first while in Cuba and later in China. Williams operated Radio Free Dixie, a radio broadcast from Cuba into the United States, and also printed and distributed a newsletter, *The Crusader*.

On the religious front, the leader who had the greatest Black Power impact on Christianity was Jeramogi Albert Cleage, who founded Black Christian Nationalism and organized the Black-oriented Christian church, The Shrine of the Black Madonna. The task these and other leaders undertook was cogently articulated by Malcolm X:

> We must recapture our heritage and our identity if we are ever to liberate ourselves from the bonds of white supremacy. We must launch a cultural revolution to unbrainwash an entire people.
>
> Our cultural revolution must be the means of bringing us closer to our African brothers and sisters. It must begin in the community and be based on community participation. Afro-Americans will be free to create only when they can depend on the Afro-American community for support and Afro-American artists must realize that they depend on the Afro-American for inspiration. (427)

The Influence of Malcolm X. If there is a spiritual father of Black Power and a single major influence on BAM literary production, that person is Malcolm X, aka El Hajj Malik El Shabazz. Time after time, in essays, commentaries, autobiographical statements, and literary introductions, not to mention the hundreds of poems written by activists and artists from the sixties, the name and influence of Malcolm X jump off the page at you. Why? Why would a political leader have such a profound literary influence? In 1973 Dingane Joe Goncalves, the editor of *The Journal of Black Poetry* wrote:

> If you want to grasp the importance of Malcolm, compare the late writings of Sonia Sanchez or Imamu Baraka with their early, pre-Malcolm works. Bro. Imamu and Sis. Sonia would certainly acknowledge Malcolm's influence. Check out the change of tone and language, the irony and just plain dynamite that developed—and things will become obvious.
>
> The fact is, Malcolm X had a fantastic impact, like Garvey in his time, on all the Black Arts. Malcolm's influence on Black Poetry in particular is only too obvious—yes, and it is just as obvious in all the Black Arts. (Goncalves, "A Review" 89, 90)

To confirm Goncalves's observation about Malcolm's influence on Baraka and Sanchez, note the following: Amiri Baraka has written numerous articles, essays, and poems citing Malcolm's influence. Perhaps the most stellar example of Baraka's homage to Malcolm is the widely anthologized April 1965 poem, "A Poem For Black Hearts," which was first published in *Negro Digest* in September of 1965. In addition to her well known poem, "Malcolm," which is included in the 1969 anthology *For Malcolm X*, Sonia Sanchez also wrote an epic poem for multiple youth voices called "Malcolm/Man Don't Live Here No Mo" which was first published in *Journal of Black Poetry* in 1971.

Perhaps one of the most cogent statements about Malcolm's influence is contained in the introduction to *For Malcolm X*, a tribute anthology edited by Dudley Randall and Margaret G. Burroughs. They write:

> John Oliver Killens says in *Black Man's Burden* that if a black man walked with his wife in a southern country fair, and some drunken white slapped his wife on the buttocks, he had three choices. He could pretend he didn't see it, he could grin, or he could die. In such situations some black men have chosen to die, but many more have lived, but not without a diminution of spirit, of soul, of self-respect. What they admire in Malcolm is that he didn't bite his tongue, but spelled out the evil done by the white man and told him to go to hell. There is no black man, regardless of his agreement or disagreement with Malcolm's politics, goals, or racial theories, whether he's a serf in Mississippi, a cat on the corner in Chicago, or a black bourgeois in Westchester, who didn't feel a stiffening of his spine and pride in his blackness when he saw or heard Malcolm take on all comers, and rout them. (Randall and Burroughs xxi)

Larry Neal is quite specific in his citing of Malcolm as an aesthetic as well as political influence. He writes:

> What I liked most about Malcolm was his sense of poetry: his speech rhythms, and his cadences that seemed to spring from the universe of black music. Because I was not reared in the black church I was something of an anomaly among Northern blacks. I did not have ready access to the rhetorical strategies of Martin Luther King. My ears were more attuned to the music of urban black America—that blues idiom music called jazz. Malcolm was like that music. He reminded many of us of the music of Charlie Parker and John Coltrane—a music that was a central force in the emerging ethos of the black artistic

consciousness. Malcolm was in the tough tradition of the urban street speaker. But there was a distinct art in his speeches, an interior logic that was highly compelling and resonant. (Neal, "New Space" 125)

To fully appreciate Malcolm's impact we must keep in mind several factors. First, there is a natural confluence between BAM's performance orientation and Malcolm's widely admired oratorical skills. Second, during the BAM era, Malcolm's speeches were very popular and were widely circulated on records and cassette tapes, thus reinforcing the power of the spoken word. Finally, the impact of Malcolm's best-selling, and still widely available, autobiography, encouraged reading in general and also specifically encouraged an interest in Black Power-oriented literature. These factors significantly contributed to Malcolm's strong influence on BAM poets and writers.

Whereas some might argue that King was Malcolm's equal as an orator, no one can argue with the fact that Malcolm went far beyond King as a critical anti-establishment voice who offered new visions. Where King proposed civil rights, Malcolm proposed human rights. Where King proposed non-violence, Malcolm proposed self-defense. Where King proposed "integration," Malcolm proposed Black Power. Malcolm's voice was the embodiment of the Black Power sentiments both in content as well as in the stylistic flourishes of well-timed phrasing, non-Western references (especially Islam and Pan-Africanism), and audacious metaphors designed to appeal to grassroots sensibilities (e.g. "house negro"/"field negro"). Moreover, the majority of Malcolm's speeches were made on behalf of and directly to Black people. He seldom spent time trying to convert Whites. All of this was exactly what BAM poets strove to articulate in their Black Power-oriented poetry.

Larry Neal further defined Malcolm's impact and inspiration. He writes:

Then we began to hear Malcolm, the black voice skating and bebopping like a righteous saxophone solo—mellow truths inspired by the Honorable Elijah Muhammad, but shaped out of Malcolm's own style, a style rooted in black folk memory, and the memory of his Garveyite father. We could dig Malcolm because the essential vectors of his style were more closely related to our own urban experiences. He was the first black leader, in our generation, to resurrect all of the strains of black nationalism lurking within us.

> In the precise sense of the word, his stance was radical, rooted in a long strand of flesh-filled nights, and sea deaths, and cotton deaths, and revolutionary deaths; Malcolm was the Opener, the Son of the Word made flesh, and for the first time in our lives, we had a voice to offset the weaknesses and the temptations that we saw around us. (Neal, "New Space" 19)

Neal, more presciently than any other writer of his time, perceived the larger picture which connected BAM to Black Power and Black Power to Black history. "One thing is clear," Neal writes:

> As we move into the seventies, many of the things that concerned us in the early sixties are no longer as important as we once thought they were. We fought for the right to eat a meal in some cracker restaurant in the deep South, but now that that right has been assured by the Federal Government, black people are no longer interested in such things. Perhaps it was the victory itself that turned us off. Perhaps it was the acute awareness that finally what we wanted was not the cup of coffee in the cracker restaurant, but something more substantive than that. If we could get it, we wanted the land that the restaurant was built on. We wanted reparations. We wanted power. We wanted Nationhood.
>
> All the major activities that were directed towards the question of liberation and Black Power spring from an ethos, a group spirit. What we have to understand, I think, is that somewhere in the maw of this ethos which continuously manifests itself, are the techniques and means of our liberation. It is not a question of falling into one bag, tenaciously holding on to it as if there were no other. That would be the route to suicide. Rather, what we should be about is a meaningful *synthesis* of the best that our struggles have taught us. This is a more difficult task than feeling secure in our own particular, and often narrow, endeavors. What we need, above all, is a widening of our perceptions, especially in terms of our own history.

Neal continues:

> For example, take the concept of "Black Consciousness." When the thing got really going, black people in different places developed unique and often contradictory attitudes towards it; they operated out of the principle along a variety of different styles. Some people joined the Muslims. Some people stopped eating certain foods. Other people, just as sincere as the first group, began to relish those very same tabooed foods. Some people put on African clothing. Most wore naturals. Some wore brighter colors. Some raised hell in school. Some left their white wives and husbands. Some joined RAM or the Black

Panther Party. Some dug B.B. King, and some dug Coltrane. But shit. *It was all good and on time.* It was collective motion/ energy that could be harnessed and organized.

At times one would walk the streets and feel it in the air—black people asserting that they were each the bearers of an ethos. The beautiful became more beautiful; the black woman assumed more of her rightful place in the psyche of black artists; brothers greeted each other warmly. This was especially true after some catastrophic upheaval like Newark or Watts. Black people spoke to each other in strange tongues which they did not understand, but yet spoke well. Harlem, blighted and dope ridden, oozed an atmosphere of love and concrete spirituality. Black consciousness manifested itself collectively and resolutely upon large segments of the black community. (Neal, "New Space" 9, 11–12)

Although many BAM participants, as well as most detractors, were unaware of the depth and details of BAM's historic Black Power background, Black Power is nonetheless the foundation of BAM via the influence of Malcolm X, RAM organizers, and Karenga. Black Power came to be associated with a militant advocacy of armed self-defense, separation from "racist American domination," and a pride in and assertion of the goodness and beauty of Blackness, all of which was expressed in BAM art, poetry, music, and theater. In this sense, Black Power was both the content and the style of BAM expressions.

As Larry Neal, perhaps the leading theoretician/critic of the Black Aesthetic, proclaimed in "The Black Arts Movement," his major theoretical essay, "Black Art is the aesthetic and spiritual sister of the Black Power concept.... We advocate a cultural revolution in art and ideas. The cultural values inherent in Western history must either be radicalized or destroyed, and we will probably find that even radicalization is impossible" (Neal, 29). The commercialization and commodification of post-modern literary culture attests to the accuracy of Neal's reservation about the impossibility of radicalizing American culture.

Civil Rights vs. Black Power. Encouraged by the 1954 *Brown v. Topeka Board of Education* Supreme Court school desegregation ruling, the Civil Rights Movement organized and focused African American discontent with the status quo. Moreover, once this discontent was put into motion, the genie could not be put back into the bottle. There was no going back to the way things "used to be," back in the early fifties when the status quo was secure. The real question became, what next? After the desegregation of public accommodations, education, and, to a lesser extent, the desegregation of employment opportunities, the movement found itself at a crossroads as leader after leader attempted to provide a vision of the way ahead for the Black community.

With the signing of the Civil Rights legislation in 1964 and the Voting Rights Act in 1965, the Civil Rights Movement reached its zenith. After Civil Rights were enacted as the "laws of the land," politically active Black people realized we needed more than legal equality. We wanted freedom—freedom from White racism and freedom to determine our own destiny. Enter the Black Power era, 1966 to 1976.

Within the cultural sphere, BAM grew directly out of and voiced the widespread sentiment that independence rather than inclusion was the goal of the Black Power struggle. There were significant differences between the Civil Rights and the Black Power movements, differences that were directly reflected in BAM artistic expressions.

1. The Civil Rights Movement was Christian based and the Black Power movement was non-Christian oriented. This non-Christian orientation should not be construed to ignore the significant contributions of what was popularly called "liberation theology" by organizations and Christian people such as historian and theologian Vincent Harding, founding director of the Institute of The Black World and author of the insightful history *There Is A River* (1981). There is also the previously mentioned Rev. Albert Cleage, founder of Black Christian Nationalism and The Shrine of the Black Madonna. A third significant force was theologist James Cone, author of *Black Theology & Black Power* (1969). Nevertheless, the important contributions of Christian leaders such as those cited above notwithstanding, once the Black Power movement moved north and west and became Black Power-oriented rather than Civil Rights-oriented, Christianity was no longer at the cultural center.

Whereas gospel had been a major source for the "Freedom songs" of the Civil Rights Movement, jazz and R&B were the main musical forces of Black Power. Also, there was an ever increasing search for alternatives to Christianity which was widely perceived within BAM as being "the White man's religion." The two major influences in terms of non-Christian spirituality were traditional African religions (particularly Yoruba) and Islam.

Baba Oserjiman Adefumi of the Harlem Yoruba Temple directly influenced a number of the early BAM spiritual developments. For a brief time, Amiri Baraka adhered to the Yoruba faith. In Baraka's autobiography he specifically points to the Yoruba influence which lasted from 1965 to approximately 1967, when he went to California and became directly influenced by Maulana Karenga. In his autobiography, Baraka writes:

> Some of us were very much influenced by the Yorubas. When we first arrived in Harlem, Oserjeman's group was very political. They dressed as traditional West Africans from Nigeria, but upheld the right of black self-determination, declaring that Africans in Harlem must control it. We gave many rallies at which Oserjeman or some other speaker from the Yoruba Temple spoke. (Baraka 215)

Additionally, under the general influence of Malcolm X, as well as the specific broad influence of Elijah Muhammad's leadership of the Nation of Islam, Islam made significant inroads into the general Black consciousness of the sixties. After Malcolm's expulsion, a number of people turned to various denominations of orthodox Islam, chief among them the "Sunni" denomination.

2. There was a concurrent rejection of "non-violence," which was inextricably linked to the Civil Rights Movement and Christianity. Within the Black Power movement, armed self-defense at home and active support for Third World liberation movements became guiding principles. Expressions of militant outrage rather than the dignity of stoic suffering guided BAM aesthetics. This was the moment when Islam really took off within the Black community. It is interesting to note that with its "jihad," or "holy war" tradition, Islamic militancy in terms of fighting for one's beliefs was emotionally closer to Black Power than was Black Christianity's spirit of non-violence.

3. Black Power rejected interracial relationships. In hindsight, it is clear that much of the emotionalism surrounding "putting down Whitey" had its roots in the fact that some of the initial BAM stalwarts had previously lived integrated lifestyles. But regardless of its cause, Black separatism became one of the chief characteristics of BAM. During the Civil Rights Movement, "Black and White together" represented a direct threat to the status quo. A number of interracial relationships were consummated on both organizational and personal levels. For instance, until 1965, LeRoi Jones, who first cultivated his national reputation as a beat writer in New York's Greenwich Village, was married to Hattie Cohen, a Jewish writer. Beginning with the RAM-influenced expelling of Whites from SNCC in the mid-sixties, on through LeRoi Jones's symbolic move to Harlem in 1965 and Jones' subsequent divorce (both literally and figuratively) from his interracial past, "Black separatism" became a major force in BAM.

4. The Civil Rights Movement had emphasized "socially correct behavior" to prove that Blacks were ready for and deserving of assimilation into the mainstream. This emphasis necessarily validated White modes of cultural expression. BAM vehemently rejected this approach and instead focused on Black American and, eventually, African and African-heritage modes and manners of cultural expressions. "Black English" was validated and used extensively, especially in oratory and literature. All of this shaped and was in turn expressed by BAM, especially in BAM poetry which became known as the "New Black Poetry." The New Black Poetry was self-consciously anti-establishment in many of its techniques, themes and modes of delivery. The majority of BAM poetry actively "messed with" standard English through the use of alternative spellings, non-conventional grammar, and inventive and/or ambiguous use of word meanings.

5. The Civil Rights Movement had been primarily a domestic movement with a regional focus. Black Power saw itself as both a national and an international movement with Africa at the center of its consciousness. Such a centering of Africa

in the consciousness and expression of Black people had not happened in America since the Garvey era in the early twenties. African dance became instantly popular and dance troupes were started everywhere. As Black people searched for new ways to connect their lives in America with their African heritage, African languages and religions were investigated and, in some cases, adopted. Indeed, the intellectual current of eighties Afro-centrism is an outgrowth of BAM's cultural centering of Africa. Many of the leading Afro-centrists were either students during BAM's heyday or were, in fact, BAM participants.

6. Technological developments, particularly the expansion and maturing of the "newly integrated" (in the sense of Blacks on camera as well as behind the camera) communications technology of television, broadly disseminated the "news" that Black America was on the move. The sixties marked the first mass appearance of Blacks on television. Nationally broadcast programs such as *Black Journal* and *Soul*, plus numerous regional and local programs helped to rapidly spread BAM's example and message.

These were the major differences between a civil rights orientation and a Black Power orientation. All of these differences were directly reflected in BAM. Hoyt Fuller opens his 1971 essay, "The New Black Literature: Protest or Affirmation" with a paragraph that sums up BAM literary endeavors. He writes:

> There is a revolution in black literature in America. It is nationalist in direction, and it is pro-black. That means, in effect, that it is deliberately moving outside the sphere of traditional Western forms, limitations, and presumptions. It is seeking new forms, new limits, new shapes, and much of it now admittedly is crude, reflecting the uncertainty, the searching quality of its movement. But, though troubled and seeking, it is very, very vital. (Fuller "The New Black Literature," 346)

CHAPTER 3
The National Birth of BAM

BAM and BART/S. Immediately following the assassination of Malcolm X on February 21, 1965, LeRoi Jones moved from downtown Greenwich Village to uptown Harlem. That March 1965 exodus which culminated in the founding of BART/S (Black Arts Repertory Theatre/School), is considered the symbolic birth of BAM.

Jones was galvanized not only by the assassination of Malcolm X, but also by the fallen leader's political program, which pointed the way ahead and which Jones eagerly adopted. In what now seems to be a prophetic call, Malcolm X stressed the need for cultural development when he outlined the aims and objectives of his Organization of Afro-American Unity on June 28, 1964. In section VI, "Culture," the prophet of Black Power, Malcolm X, states that:

> We must work toward the establishment of a cultural center in Harlem, which will include people of all ages, and will conduct workshops in all the arts, such as film, creative writing, painting, theater, music, Afro-American history, etc. This cultural revolution will be the journey to our rediscovery of ourselves.
> (X 427)

LeRoi Jones and cohorts took up the challenge issued by Malcolm X. At that time, Jones was a highly visible publisher (*Yugen* and *Floating Bear* magazines, and Totem Press), a celebrated poet (Preface to a Twenty Volume Suicide Note, 1961 and The Dead Lecturer, 1964), a major music critic (*Blues People* 1963), and an OBIE Award winning playwright (*Dutchman* 1964) who, up until that fateful split from the Beat circles, had functioned in an integrated world. Other than James Baldwin, who at that time had been closely associated with the Civil Rights Movement, Jones was the most celebrated (by the literary establishment) and most widely published Black writer of his generation.

Of interest here is the mainstream's tendency to arbitrate who was the major "Negro" writer of the time period. Even though popular poet Langston Hughes was alive and Pulitzer prize winner Gwendolyn Brooks was actively writing and publishing, Black poets in particular, and Black writers in general at that time received very little national attention until BAM raised poets to the level of spokespeople for the emerging African American nation. Indeed, BAM's example of poetics engaged with community people is the springboard for a reinvigoration of American poetics, setting a trend which was taken up across the country, especially by other "minorities" or "ethnic groups" in America.

BAM aesthetics influenced many more poets of the period than is commonly credited. When BART/S opened, a gigantic poetry reading was held and Black poets from all over were invited to read at the new site in Harlem. The program included David Henderson, Calvin Hernton, and Ishmael Reed, who were not members of BART/S but who identified with the effort to assert a "New Black poetry." Incidentally, both Hernton and Henderson have poetry included in the seminal anthology *Black Fire*, and the work of both, "Jitterbugging in the Streets" by Hernton and "Keep On Pushing (Harlem Riots/Summer/1964)" by Henderson specifically, directly reflects the emphasis of BAM poetry in referencing Black music.

While founding the Black Arts Repertory uptown was symbolic, Jones' move to Harlem was short-lived. In December 1965 he returned to his home, Newark, and left BART/S in serious disarray. As a cultural institution, BART/S failed to sustain itself. However, as a catalyst for cultural activity, the Black Arts Repertory Theatre/School was wildly successful. Much like Bethlehem in Christian culture, BART/S was a birthplace of things to come, attracting national attention to BAM.

Baraka assesses the programs and impact of BART/S:

That one glorious summer of 1965, we did, even with all that internal warfare, bring advanced Black Art to Harlem. We organized, as part of HARYOU ACT, the nation's 1st anti poverty program, a summer arts program called Operation Boot Strap (under the overall direction of Adam Clayton Powell's point cadre, Judge Livingston Wingate). For eight weeks, we brought Drama, Poetry, Painting, Music, Dance, night after night all across Harlem. We had a fleet of five trucks and stages created with banquet tables. And each night our five units would go out in playgrounds, street corners, vacant lots, play streets, parks, bringing Black Art directly to the people.

Young Steve Young was the most trustworthy coordinator. He and my sister, Kimako (who was constantly attacked by certain negroes because she was an independent creative woman) ... dealt with drama and dance. Andrew Hill was music coordinator, Joe Gregory coordinated the painters, assisted by Joe Overstreet and William White who came to help us but refused to leave the Village.

One of my closest poet friends, in fact, pulled a pistol on me to emphasize his determination to stay downtown! It was that wild! But Sun Ra and Archie Shepp and Pharoah Sanders and Milford Graves and Don Pullen and Albert Ayler and at our benefits downtown, John Coltrane, Grachan Moncur, Bobby Hutcherson, and more. And uptown Larry Neal, Askia Toure, Bobb Hamilton, Sonia Sanchez, Ted Wilson, so many poets and black actors, directors, Jim Campbell, Rob Jackson, Kimako (who directed and did the lead role in Dutchman, Frank Adu, Barbara Montgomery, Yusef Iman (our stalwart classic Black Arts warrior artist) and his whole family.

That was an important, ideologically impacting and exciting time. Black artists came by constantly to talk, to argue, to join, to support, to learn, to teach. Harold Cruse taught politics, with two agents in his class. One night even Sammy Davis Jr. came uptown and did a benefit on 125th St. And from inside Harlem, artists like poets Clarence Reed and Clarence Franklin, Ojijiko, the Weusi Sanaa artists, Ademola, Rahman, Babatunde added strength to strength, Valerie Maynard, and so many others.

We had evolved through our practice a growing rationale for what we felt and did. We wanted Black Art. We felt it could move our people, the Afro American people, to revolutionary positions (See essay, "The Revolutionary Theater"). We wanted Black Art that was 1. Identifiably Afro American. As Black as Bessie Smith or Billie Holiday or Duke Ellington or John Coltrane. That is, we wanted it to express our lives and history, our needs and desires. Our will and our passion. Our self determination, self respect and self defense. 2. We wanted it to be a Mass

Art. We wanted it to Boogaloo (like them Deacons for Self Defense down in Boogaloosa, La., when they routed the Klan). Yeh, Boogaloo out the class rooms and elitist dens of iniquitous obliquity and speak and sing and scream abroad among Black people! We wanted a mass popular art, distinct from the tedious abstractions our oppressors and their negroes bamboozled the "few" as Art. We thought it was Ain't! White Ain't. And we wanted Black Art.

The last part of our eventual summation of the Black Arts Movement was that 3. We wanted an art that was revolutionary. We wanted a Malcolm art, a by-any-means-necessary poetry. A Ballot or Bullet verse. We wanted ultimately, to create a poetry, a literature, a dance, a theater, a painting, that would help bring revolution!

That was what it all was about. That's what the whole movement and essence of The Black Arts was raised and forwarded by, the desire by Black youth to make revolution in the U.S.. To resist and finally destroy the slave system of racism and national oppression.

The Black Arts Repertory Theater School lasted formally a little more than a year, but by the end of 1965, there were similar efforts rising all over the country.

What seemed most important about the BART/S was that it was a living paradigm of what many people had come to feel was the direction Afro American artists and the art with which they expressed the particular culture they reflected had to go.

(Baraka, "The Black Arts Movement" 6)

BART/S major influence was to establish the Black Arts Community Center as a model which could be replicated across the country. BART/S ideals included (1) linking artists and activists under the same roof; (2) using federal, state and philanthropic arts funding to support socially committed arts programs; (3) arts training geared to community youth; and (4) using community audience response as a validator of artistic worth. None of these were new concepts in and of themselves, but when combined and applied to the Black community, these were indeed revolutionary concepts that came to be identified with Black Arts centers nationwide.

Black Arts Centers. The Black Arts Center concept was irrepressible mainly because BAM was so closely aligned with the then burgeoning Black Power movement which was a national phenomenon whose time had arrived. The mid to late 1960s was a period of intense "revolutionary" ferment. Beginning in 1964, rebellions in Harlem and Rochester, New York, initiated four years of long hot summers. Watts, Detroit, Newark, Cleveland, and many other cities went up in flames, culminating in what seemed to be nationwide violence following Martin Luther King's April 1968 assassination. In the wake of these rebellions, government-funded "poverty programs" (as part of President Lyndon Johnson's "war on poverty") established community centers. Community activists and artists quickly transformed these centers into Black Cultural Centers.

While BART/S was formally the first of many Black Arts Centers, BART/S was short-lived. Infighting effectively crippled BART/S. In his autobiography, Baraka claims BART/S forces opposed to Baraka ransacked his apartment after he departed from BART/S and Askia Toure recalls that Baraka was also physically assaulted. Larry Neal was even shot as a result of getting caught in the middle of the split. Fortunately, Neal was only wounded in the leg. Eventually, Toure went south to work with SNCC, and Baraka reestablished himself in Newark.

One major source of constant internal conflict was that while the "revolutionary" forces often attracted those who were fearless, they also attracted elements that in less volatile times would easily be defined as socially unstable or "just plain crazy." BART/S was not the only instance, nor the only organization to degenerate beneath the weight of, to use Baraka's terminology, "nuts" running "amuck."

Although such infighting may seem "insane" when viewed out of context, the fact is that "fratricidal" infighting was one of the undercurrents of most liberation movements of the twentieth century, and the Black liberation struggle was no exception. In *Bitter Grain*, a popular history of the Black Panther Party, author Michael Newton sums up this tendency:

> Historically, militant groups have experienced trouble with two sorts of members. One group is composed of renegades, the criminals and mental defectives who cleave to a movement in hopes of furthering their own twisted ends; the other consists of police informers and agents provocateur, burrowing within the group like destructive parasites. Either faction, or both in unison, are capable of destroying a movement by inviting scandal and suspicion, bringing down the hammer of oppression through reckless violence or deliberate entrapment. (Newton 197)

Exacerbating this tendency was the ongoing feud between Muslim followers of Elijah Muhammad and movement activists who were inspired by and/or were followers of Malcolm X. Within BART/S, the anti-Baraka faction was associated with the Nation of Islam's "Black Muslims" and were ardently opposed to the teachings and honoring of Malcolm X. Ideological infighting would turn even more deadly on the West Coast, where the Black Panthers and Karenga's US organization literally engaged in shoot-outs, which were subsequently revealed to be instigated to a large degree by agents provocateurs in both organizations who were on the payroll of the federal government's COINTELPRO[1] anti-Black Power operation.

Another influential albeit short-lived BAM cultural center effort was Black House and Black Arts/West. This was a late 1960s formation that grew out of a coalition of Black political activity, Black Studies activity and BAM forces in the Bay Area of California. The famous 1968 Black Theatre issue of *Drama Review* carries this description of Black House:

> This photo shows a storefront on Fillmore Street, San Francisco, which Black Arts/West used briefly for their headquarters in Spring, 1966. The handbill on the right announces a showdown between Bay Area Black revolutionaries and the Oakland police, after the Oakland authorities had sent word to Laney College, where Black Arts was to perform Marvin X's Flowers for the Whiteman (next play in this issue, under its original title Take Care of Business) that "everyone will be arrested, even the audience."
>
> The confrontation never took place, because Black Arts/West had failed to establish operational relations with Black revolutionaries in the Oakland area.
>
> A lesson was learned from this incident, and the following Fall the Black House was formed as San Francisco headquarters of the Black Panther Party for Self Defense. Eldridge Cleaver, Minister of Information of the BPPSD, was Chairman; Ed Bullins, co-director of Black Arts/West and (with LeRoi Jones) the Black Arts Alliance, was Cultural Director; Marvin X, co-director of Black Arts/West, was Secretary. It was conceded by all that the Black political, economic, and social revolution must have a Black cultural revolution as its foundation.
>
> The handbill on the left announces a scheduled appearance of Julian Bond, after his failure to be seated in the Georgia legislature. (*Black Theater* 84)

Black House suffered a split between what became known as the Black Panthers and the Cultural Nationalists. But the splits and failure to keep the prototype cultural centers, BART/S and Black House, in operation did not stop the development of Black Cultural Centers in communities and on campuses across the nation.

Never again since those heady days of the late sixties and early seventies has community based arts activity been so vital to and influential on the daily social life of America's diverse Black communities. Moreover, BAM activities were not limited to formal cultural centers. People used their houses and apartments as meeting places and performance centers open to the Black community to participate in local BAM happenings and events. However briefly, most cities with large concentrations of Black residents or students had an active formal or informal cultural center.

The schisms and conflicts that beset BART/S and Black House, to one degree or another, were manifested in many other BAM institutions. Numerous issues were debated, among them were,

1. propaganda versus art
2. the appropriate uses (if any) of traditional Western art forms and aesthetic values
3. the merger or separation of topical and local political concerns with "timeless" and "universal" art themes
4. the appropriateness of using "cursing" and "derogatory" images for arts activity in which young people participated
5. the marketing and selling of art as entertainment versus the propagation of art as ritual
6. sources of funding and whether accepting government funds was detrimental to artistic and political self-determination.

Some of these issue have since been resolved by a general broadening of popular and accepted cultural tastes, and others have been subsumed into the mainstream by the relentless drive of the marketplace's appropriation of any and all arts activity for purposes of profit. For example, even though there is a debate about the content of today's rap music, the fact that rap is sold with only a sticker to warn of "explicit language" makes the BAM issue of "appropriate language" seem hopelessly dated. Nonetheless, Black Arts and Black Cultural Centers passionately raised and debated these, and many other, issues within the Black community as well as between BAM and the "establishment."

An archetypal example of the successful Black Cultural Center concept was "The East" in Brooklyn, New York, led by Jitu Weusi (Les Campbell), an educator who emerged out of the Oceanville/Brownhill demonstrations for community control of public schools. The East became the home of Weusi Shule, an independent school, and also the base of operations for *Black News*, a monthly news journal which was distributed throughout "nationalist" oriented organizations, businesses, and events nationwide. The East was also a concert hall/theater and featured many of the major Black musicians of the era. Their policy was "innerattainment" for "Afrikan people" which meant that Whites were barred from all activity. The East's cadre eventually joined the Congress of Afrikan People (CAP) and later resigned in 1974 when Baraka led CAP into Marxism.

Black Museums. Another far-reaching and often overlooked area of BAM's influence is its impact on the establishment of Black museums and art galleries. BAM's call for "Black institutions" with "Black directors" actively encouraged a number of people to consider careers as curators, art administrators, art historians and art critics. The DuSable Museum, founded in Chicago by Margaret Burroughs in 1961, is credited as the first major museum to focus on the art and culture of African Americans. The museum began as one floor of the Burroughs' spacious home and, some time during the mid 1960s, moved to a permanent home in Chicago's Hyde Park/Washington Park area. The founding and success of the DuSable lent credibility and support to BAM adherents and directly led to a call for a reinforcement of efforts to establish Black museums in other parts of the country. This is another example of BAM activity which took place outside of New York and, indeed, actually preceded the "official" national founding of BAM. Once again, it must be stressed that BAM represented the spirit of an era rather than any one or two specific thrusts by specific individuals and organizations.

BAM also served as a battering ram at the doors of philanthropy. Institutions such as the Studio Museum in Harlem, became a model of the Black museum movement, partly because of the publicity it received by being in Harlem, New York. Gaining this role model status would not have been possible without BAM agitation. In this new millennium, we would do well to remember that arts institutions did not just pop up out of the ground, nor were they founded and funded due to mainstream munificence. In order to start and maintain Black museums, art galleries, and other institutions, many of the early administrators, curators and producers of Black art gave up lucrative careers in establishment institutions, and dedicated themselves to bringing Black Arts institutions into existence.

BAM also spawned "Black caucuses" within professional organizations and institutions. As a direct result of the Black Power movement and the agitation of BAM advocates, Black caucuses appeared across the spectrum of professional and artistic activity, ranging from library and other academic associations to the United States Congress.

These and other related developments are not usually thought of or credited to either Black Power or BAM, but the historic fact is the roots of these organizations sprang directly from BAM, a dynamic, artistic movement that proudly had a political agenda whose goal was to effect change in the social order on behalf of Black people.

BAM's Collective Roots—Splitting and Reorganization Although LeRoi Jones is often cited as "the father" of BAM, that is an oversimplification of the historical process. While LeRoi Jones is responsible for coining the name "Black Arts" to refer to Black Power–oriented arts activity, he was neither the main theorist nor the sole force. Also, from a literary perspective, BAM's focus was on collectives rather than individuals. Finally, it is important to understand that BAM's geo-literary centers were based in California's Bay Area and along the Chicago/Detroit axis rather than in New York City, as is often assumed.

One of the seeds of BAM is found in the Umbra Workshop, a collective of young Black writers based on Manhattan's Lower East Side (1962–1965). Major members were writers Steve

Cannon, Tom Dent, Al Haynes, David Henderson, Calvin Hernton, Joe Johnson, Norman Pritchard, Lenox Raphael, Ishmael Reed, Lorenzo Thomas, James Thompson, Brenda Walcox, musician/writer Archie Shepp, and Askia Muhammad Toure (a.k.a Roland Snellings), who was also a visual artist.

Along with Larry Neal and other cohorts at RAM (especially Max Stanford, aka A. Muhammad Ahmed), Toure was a major shaper of "revolutionary nationalism" and a direct influence upon LeRoi Jones. Along with Umbra writer, Charles Patterson and Charles' brother, William Patterson, Toure joined Jones in founding BART/S. Although not usually directly identified as a lead or chief participant in BAM, the Umbra Workshop (which produced a self-titled magazine) was the first predominately Black literary collective to consciously identify themselves as "radical." Umbra was radical in the sense of wanting to establish their own voice distinct from and often in contradiction to the White literary establishment. That Umbra was primarily poetry and performance oriented designates a significant characteristic of BAM aesthetics.

Umbra was not the only formation of Black writers in the New York area at that time; John Oliver Killens was leading the Harlem Writers Guild, which included Maya Angelou, Jean Carey Bond, Rosa Guy and Sarah Wright among others. But the Harlem Writers Guild focused on prose, primarily fiction, which did not have the mass appeal of poetry performed in the dynamic vernacular of the time. Poems built around anthems, chants and political slogans, were used in organizing, making them more popular during this highly politicized time. This made poetry more suitable for promoting BAM ideology than other literary forms. Such was not generally the case with novels and short stories. Moreover, the poets could and did publish themselves, whereas greater resources were needed to publish fiction.

The attempt to merge a Black-oriented activist thrust with a primarily artistic orientation produced a "classic" split in Umbra—classic because Black writers have always had to face the issue of whether the thrust of their work was primarily political or aesthetic. In a study of twentieth-century Black periodicals, Abby A. Johnson and Ronald M. Johnson assert,

The literary materials in Afro-American magazines of the twentieth century weave into a rich narrative. The journals provide insight, not available in a comparable manner elsewhere, into the evolution of Afro-American literature. They trace the contributions made by major figures, including W.E.B. Du Bois, Langston Hughes, Charles S. Johnson, Alain Locke, and Richard Wright, among several others. They record the discussions over art and propaganda which have been long prominent in black literature. Decade by decade, black artists and intellectuals have debated the function of Afro-American literature: should it serve the aesthetic tastes of the individual writer, or should it advance the interests of Afro-Americans as a group. Some writers favored art-for-art's sake, or approximations of that emphasis; others articulated the need for art-for-people's sake, as they termed it. (Johnson xvii)

Umbra itself evolved out of this same type of split. In 1960, a Black Nationalist literary organization, On Guard For Freedom, was founded on the Lower East Side by Calvin Hicks. Its members included Nannie and Walter Bowe, Harold Cruse (who was then working on *Crisis of the Negro Intellectual*, published in 1967), Tom Dent, Rosa Guy, Joe Johnson, LeRoi Jones, and Sarah Wright, among others. On Guard activities included a famous protest at the UN of the American-sponsored Bay of Pigs invasion of Cuba as well as an endorsement of the Congolese liberation leader Patrice Lumumba. From On Guard, Dent, Johnson, and Walcott along with Hernton, Henderson and Toure established Umbra, a primarily literary organization.

In a 1995 interview, Baraka remembers, "Who the art was for, that was the issue. If it was for Black people then we thought we ought to live in the Black community with Black people and not just simply talk about Black people. That's what all the splits were really about, the politics of living the way you talked" (Baraka, "Interview").

When Umbra split, some members, led by Askia Toure and Al Haynes, moved to Harlem in late 1964 and formed the nationalist oriented "Uptown Writers Movement," which included poets Yusef Rahman, Keorapetse "Willie" Kgositsile from South Africa, and Larry Neal. They performed poetry all over Harlem accompanied by young "New Music" musicians. Members of this group joined LeRoi Jones in founding Black Arts Repertory Theatre/School (BART/S).

LeRoi Jones/Amiri Baraka's Role. It is impossible to ignore Jones/Baraka's role both as a literary figure and as a master propagandist/political activist. Shortly before moving to Harlem, establishment critics anointed Jones as "the New Negro Writer." This distinction led to Jones' work being followed and commented on in the major publications even as these same publications avoided even mentioning the work of other Black writers, including those who became identified as BAM writers. Jones was aware of his status as the "hand-picked Negro writer" and used it to call attention to BAM. Jones' ascendancy as a leading BAM figure was announced by his name change to Ameer Baraka, reflecting the Afro-centric BAM ideology. Within a year, "Ameer" was changed again to "Amiri" and the honorific "Imamu" (spiritual leader) was added. Imamu was later dropped when Baraka became a Marxist. Amiri Baraka has remained his name since the mid-seventies.

Although a number of others formulated ideologies and started major organizations, no one was better at "naming" than Baraka. His slogan "Nationtime" defined the Black Nationalist thrust for cultural and political self-determination and independence. As stated earlier, Baraka is also credited with branding the movement, "Black Arts." Few American writers could match Amiri Baraka's ability to coin timely phrases and produce work that captured and projected the zeitgeist of the era.

In addition to his propaganda prowess and his well-established success as a literary figure, Amiri Baraka was also the most successful political figure among Black writers during the period 1965 to 1976. Specifically, Baraka was a founder of the Congress of Afrikan People (CAP), a nationalist organization that he later transformed into a Marxist-Leninist organization. The CAP organization started off as a Black Power–oriented "united front coalition"—everyone from Whitney Young of the Urban League, to representatives of the Republic of New Afrika, to Minister Louis Farrakhan of the Nation of Islam were present in Atlanta in 1970 at CAP's founding. CAP quickly became a nationwide cadre-type political organization which effectively pushed Kawaida-styled Black Nationalism. CAP's success was largely a result of Baraka's prowess as a propagandist and organizer.

Baraka also founded a Black theatre company called the Spirit House Movers as well as Jihad, a publishing and recording company. Both companies were based in Newark, New Jersey. Additionally, Baraka was a major force in the National Black Assembly, which focused on electoral politics, and served as one of the chief organizers of the African Liberation Support Committee, which focused on solidarity activities with various African liberation movements. A 1968 survey of Black writers conducted by Hoyt Fuller for *Negro Digest* named Amiri Baraka as the most important living Black writer. Whether measured solely by literary output or by the combination of literary and political activity, no writer matched Baraka's success in the sixties and seventies.

BAM was a product of its volatile era, a focusing of social energy through an aesthetic lens. BAM was not the idea of one individual or even of one small revolutionary group. Indeed, with its "collectivist/community/African" focus, BAM was the very antithesis of the "great man" theory of historical development. The most important theoreticians initially were Neal and Karenga; however, very quickly other organizations and individuals, especially the Bay Area triumvirate of *Soul Book*, *Black Dialogue/Journal of Black Poetry* and the Chicago/Detroit axis of Hoyt Fuller, Haki Madhubuti and Dudley Randall, played indispensable roles in the founding and development of what became known as "the sixties Black Arts Movement." Baraka's contribution is certainly important, but even if he had not been present, there would have been a Black Arts Movement, especially in Chicago/Detroit and in the Bay Area of the West Coast.

BAM's West Coast and Midwest Focus. The two major locations of BAM ideological leadership, particularly for literary work, were California's Bay Area and the Chicago-Detroit axis. These formations provided both style and direction for BAM artists. Both locations acted as hubs for the cultivation of BAM ideological thought and for the production of BAM oriented poetry, journals and theater.

By 1966, the development of a trio of BAM journals, *Soulbook* (1964), *Black Dialogue* (1965), and *Journal of Black Poetry*

(1966), completed a monumental shift in BAM's national focus, moving from the East Coast to the West Coast. For the next two years through 1968, the West Coast was the spearhead of ideas and activities which would shape the course of BAM and of the Black Power movement in general.

In the Spring of 1965, "Black curriculum is introduced to San Francisco State University (SFSU) with one class titled Black Nationalism, instructed by Aubrey LaBrie," according to Dingane Joe Goncalves's correspondence ("Letters"). Then, in the Spring of 1967, "A Black Studies Program was proposed and formulated by the B.S.U. (Black Student Union). Nathan Hare will soon be called in by the Administration of SFSU to formulate a Black Studies Program which, however, when submitted by Hare, the Administration finds 'too political'" (Goncalves, "Letters"). Nathan Hare, the author of an explosive expose of Black academic conservatism entitled The Black Anglo Saxons, was a founding force behind the Black Studies movement, which, like BAM, was also an outgrowth of the Black Power movement. Hare had been expelled from Howard University in Washington, D.C., and in February 1968, had moved to San Francisco State University, where the battle to establish a Black Studies department was being waged by students and some faculty members. As with the establishment of the Black Arts Repertory Theatre/School, there was broad activity going on in California's Bay Area around the Black studies concept, including efforts led by poet and professor Sarah Webster Fabio at Merrit College (Black Panther founder Huey Newton's alma mater).

The Bay Area was also the "home" of the Black Panther Party, founded by Huey Newton and Bobby Seale on Oct. 15, 1966. On May 2, 1967, an armed group of thirty Black Panthers, including Eldridge Cleaver (unarmed at that time), entered the California capitol building in Sacramento and immediately made international headlines. On October 28, 1967, Huey Newton was involved in a shoot-out that left one policeman dead and also left both a second policeman and Newton seriously wounded. Over the next two years, the Black Panthers were the single most influential revolutionary organization in the Black community. Much of their popularity/notoriety was a result of a combination of popular community initiatives and media savvy (such as the Free Breakfast Program and the international Free Huey Campaign) led by Cleaver and Seale. Indicative of the tenor of the times was Cleaver's famous maxim: you're either "part of the solution or part of the problem."

Most Black artists of that period, regardless of discipline, regardless of whether they were community-based self-taught artists or professionally-trained entertainers and academics, chose to demonstrate in one way or another that they were part of the solution. By the late sixties, everyone in the Black community felt challenged to do something. This tendency toward movement and away from apathy infused the art world with a dynamism rarely evidenced before or since in the twentieth century.

The Black Power movement in the community and the Black Studies movement on the campus coalesced into a powerful dialectic. Confrontational demands on established institutions and organizing around community control gave both urgency and concreteness to the expression of BAM aesthetics. Such activities produced numerous rallies and meetings, and nearly every community-based rally included poetry. The emerging Black Studies programs and departments served as recruiting and training centers, while also providing financial support through lecture fees and visiting professorships for BAM leaders.

The initial thrust of BAM ideological development came directly or indirectly from the Revolutionary Action Movement (RAM), a national organization with a strong presence in New York. Both Toure and Neal were members of RAM. After RAM, the main ideological force shaping BAM was the California-based US organization, (as opposed to "them"/"wherever we are, US is") led by Maulana Karenga. US's California base is significant because it points to anchors of BAM ideological leadership development existing outside of New York. These formations provided both style and direction for BAM artists. The two major locations of BAM ideological leadership, particularly for literary work, were California's Bay Area and the Chicago-Detroit axis.

While a visiting professor at San Francisco State University, LeRoi Jones visited Karenga in Los Angeles and became an advocate of Karenga's philosophy of Kawaida in 1967. Jones also met Bobby Seale and Eldridge Cleaver and worked with a number of the founding members of the Black Panther Party (BPP). Additionally, Sonia Sanchez and Askia Toure were visiting professors at San Francisco State. Sanchez had preceded the others and was partially responsible for bringing Baraka to California.

Additionally, out west, Ed Bullins and Marvin X had established Black Arts/West and Dingane Joe Goncalves had founded *Journal of Black Poetry*. This grouping of Ed Bullins, Dingane Joe Goncalves, LeRoi Jones, Sonia Sanchez, Askia M. Toure, and Marvin X became a major nucleus of BAM leadership on the West Coast. Despite the absence of Larry Neal, this was the heaviest gathering of BAM luminaries in the decade-long history of that movement. The Bay Area proved to be an ideological and practical hothouse that germinated ideas and concepts later put into practice all across the country.

At the same time as these developments were happening on the West Coast, Chicago and Detroit were also jumping with important developments. The Detroit scene was spearheaded by Dudley Randall's Broadside Press while the Chicago scene was anchored by *Negro Digest* (which became *Black World*) magazine, edited by Hoyt Fuller, and Third World Press, founded by Don L. Lee (Madhubuti).

Chicago. Far, far more than New York and preceding the Bay Area, the Chicago/Detroit axis was the gravitational center of BAM. Of the two Midwest cities, Chicago offered a wider range of activities and organizations. Although the Nation of Islam was founded in Detroit, they moved to Chicago and that city became their stronghold. After the assassination of Malcolm X and with the subsequent rise of Muhammad Ali, as well as based on the media and economic impact of Johnson publications (particularly Ebony and Jet), Chicago was sometimes called The Mecca of Black America. In terms of both longevity and popularity, Don Cornelius' television program Soul Train successfully supplanted Dick Clark's American Bandstand. Although Detroit's Motown Records would surpass any musical activities in popularity and national impact, nevertheless, Chicago had a major impact on Black musical culture with a number of individuals and organizations. From Curtis Mayfield and Jerry Butler in popular music to the AACM (the Association for the Advancement of Creative Musicians), within the Black community Chicago was the place to be for the production of Black musical culture. The AACM is particularly important as it was founded in May of 1965 specifically to nurture, promote and produce Black creative music. AACM's goal was both to uplift jazz music and simultaneously to move beyond the term "jazz", which was considered a pejorative designation. The emphasis for most Chicago-based organizations and certainly for both Chicago's Third World Press and Detroit's Broadside Press was proudly and unapologetically on the up lift of the Black community both locally and nationally.

In terms of BAM the major significance of the Chicago/Detroit axis was their respective publishing enterprises. The significances of the Chicago/Detroit axis were their publishing enterprises. Nothing comparable in quantity or quality to the West Coast trio of journals or the Midwest publishing houses ever came out of New York. Broadside Press books and *Negro Digest/Black World* were more widely distributed than any of the West Coast publications or the later New York–based publications (i.e. *Black Theatre* and a revived *Black Dialogue*, which moved from the Bay Area to New York). Additionally, both the Chicago and the Detroit publishing apparatuses drew on writers from all over the United States, from all strata of Black society, and from widely diverse political backgrounds and viewpoints, including some writers who openly differed with or were hostile to BAM. Such diversity contributed to a healthy mix of ideas and styles of writing. To put the importance of Chicago/Detroit in terms of numbers, one to two years of the Chicago-based *Negro Digest/Black World* equaled the total output of the majority of other BAM publications. Moreover, with its 150,000-plus circulation, in one issue *Negro Digest/Black World* reached more Black readers than many other publications did in their entire lifetime. Furthermore, between the two of them, Broadside Press (Detroit) and Third World Press (Chicago) published more books during the BAM decade than the publishing output of all other BAM publishers combined.

The strength of BAM was its national scope. Nonetheless,

individual cities such as Chicago emerged as vibrant and influential sites of BAM activity. With its strong Black Muslim base, associated with the Nation of Islam headquarters located there, and the success of the Institute of Positive Education/Third World Press among a host of other activities and organizations, Black activists sometimes referred to Chicago as the "Black Nationalist headquarters" of the United States.

In the late sixties, a host of writers emerged out of Chicago. Among them were the Organization of Black American Culture (OBAC) writers Don L. Lee/Haki Madhubuti, Carolyn Rodgers, Angela Jackson, Johari Amini, Sterling Plumpp, Sam Greenlee, and Useni Eugene Perkins. Chicago also had a "re-emergent" Gwendolyn Brooks who not only mentored and supported but also openly aligned herself and her work with BAM activity. Brooks and other artists, such as Oscar Brown Jr., worked with members of the Blackstone Rangers and other gangs to develop a theatre piece.

Hoyt Fuller, editor of *Negro Digest/Black World*, was a founding advisor/mentor for the OBAC writers and had been actively engaged in the process of defining and defending the development of a Black aesthetic, a process that was integral to the propagation of the Black Arts. In a 1971 forward to OBAC's publication *NOMMO*, Hoyt Fuller writes:

> It is five years now since the Committee for the Arts, the precursor of the Organization of Black American Culture (OBAC), called together a group of interested Chicagoans in the main chamber of the South Side Community Art Center to launch a movement to encourage Black expression in the Arts.... It was the premise of the Committee that the apathy which seems always to be with us is a manifestation of the feeling of powerlessness and outsideness, which generates a sense of worthlessness, of nobodiness in Black people; and the Committee was convinced that, by releasing that natural, pent-up store of creativity within the community, by urging Black people toward an identification with and an acceptance of themselves and their images, their history, their humanity, art itself would achieve a fresh interpretation rooted in the lives, the aspirations—in a word, the experiences—of the community. The idea was revolutionary; it proposed that the usual approach to artistic expression which had been foisted upon Black people over the centuries had, of and in itself, inhibited when it did not destroy the Black creative impulse;

and it suggested that the seeds of liberation—political and economic and social, as well as aesthetic—would be planted in the Black psyche through this new approach to artistic expression. The interest then was primarily political; art for the sake of Black empowerment was the principle. (Fuller, "Foreword to *NOMMO*" 17)

Chicago was also the headquarters of Johnson Publications which published both *Ebony* and *Jet* in addition to *Negro Digest/ Black World*. Also from Chicago came the Africobra visual artist collective whose famous mural, "Wall Of Respect," inspired other community-based public murals. A precursor to the Africobra artists was muralist Bill White. In the area of music, between Sun Ra, Phil Corahn and his Afro Arts Theater, and the AACM (whose constituent members included Muhal Richard Abrams, Anthony Braxton, the Art Ensemble of Chicago, and Henry Threadgill and his trio Air), Chicago practically defined non-commercial, community-based, musician-produced, innovative directions in Black music between 1960 and 1975. Sun Ra would move from Chicago to New York in time to take up residence at the founding of BART/S influence on the New York scene. There was also a vibrant independent school movement that included the indefatigable Hannibal Afrik and his institution Watoto Shule and the Institute of Positive Education, and community-based adult education initiatives, chief among them The Communiversity, led by Anderson Thompson and Bobby Wright. No other single city could match Chicago in the quantity of institutional BAM activity and influence.

When we add all of the BAM manifestations that emanated from Chicago, we get an awesome panorama of literary, musical, visual, and performance arts. Indeed, a major study of the Black Arts Movement focused solely on the inspirational and instructive Chicago-based artists and institutions would be fruitful in grasping the full import and implications of BAM.

Thus BAM, which nominally started in New York, actually came to fruition in the Bay Area and in the Midwest. Additionally, many people frequently moved back and forth between the various locales. This significant diversification, diffusion, and decentralization of BAM leadership and activity insured that BAM became a national rather than a regional phenomenon.

1 COINTELPRO was the FBI's domestic counterintelligence program aimed at discrediting, disrupting and ultimately destroying opposition leaders and movements based in the United States, such as Malcolm X, and the Black Panther Party. The program was in operation from the Eisenhower through the Nixon Administrations.

CHAPTER 4
THEORY AND PRACTICE

BAM Manifestoes. Manifestoes, especially declarations of the new and condemnations of the status quo, are common in the arts and, in this regard, BAM is no exception. Although there were numerous documents created during the BAM era, two are significant as statements that sum up and present the main points. The first is Black Power activist and political theorist Maulana Karenga's "Black Art: Mute Matter Given Force And Function," which first appeared in *Negro Digest* (January, 1968) and was later anthologized in Abraham Chapman's *New Black Voices*. The second is Larry Neal's aforementioned "The Black Arts Movement," which appeared in the Summer 1968 issue of *Drama Review,* guest edited by Ed Bullins.

Karenga's essay, "Black Art," an expression of his Kawaida philosophy, articulated a position which was adopted and widely propagated by Baraka. Kawaida was the basis of what became known as Cultural Nationalism. Karenga's theory of Black Art was bold and unambiguous: "all Black art, regardless of any technical requirements, must have three basic characteristics that make it revolutionary. In brief, it must be functional, collective and committing" (Karenga, "Black Art" 478). This was a viewpoint diametrically opposed to "art for art's sake" and one that insisted that Black art, like everything else in the Black community, must respond positively to the reality of "revolution." This theory, of course, was widely and hotly debated. Although some of his assessments on art were ignored, such as his views of the blues,[1] his basic formulation of "functional, collective and committed" became the bedrock of BAM aesthetics.

This was a re-raising of the classic activist/arts argument that seems to be endemic to the African American literary tradition. Again, Karenga was unequivocal. He writes:

all art can be judged on two levels—on the social level and

on the artistic level. Let it be enough to say that the artistic consideration, although a necessary part, is not sufficient. What completes the picture is that social criteria for judging art. And it is this criteria that is the most important criteria. For all art must reflect and support the Black Revolution, and any art that does not discuss and contribute to the revolution is invalid, no matter how many lines and spaces are produced in proportion and symmetry and no matter how many sounds are boxed in or blown out and called music. (Karenga, "Black Art" 478)

Often lost in the debate over Karenga's formulation is the fact that he is focusing specifically on "revolutionary" literature and not on literature in general. Thus, Karenga would not argue that if a poem was not revolutionary then it was not a poem. Instead, the criticism would be that during a revolutionary period, a poem was not relevant if it was not revolutionary. Hence, Karenga succinctly sums up his arguments with this statement: "In conclusion, the real function of art is to make revolution, using its own medium" (Karenga, "Black Art" 479).

There was a slightly different, although complementary aesthetic position put forward by those who considered themselves "revolutionary nationalists." Larry Neal epitomized this position when he wrote

When we speak of a "Black aesthetic" several things are meant. First, we assume that there is already in existence the basis for such an aesthetic. Essentially, it consists of an African-American cultural tradition. But this aesthetic is finally, by implication, broader than the tradition. It encompasses most of the useable elements of Third World culture. The motive behind the Black aesthetic is the destruction of the white thing, the destruction of white ideas, and white ways of looking at the world. The new aesthetic is mostly predicated on an Ethics which asks the question: whose vision of the world is finally more meaningful, ours or the white oppressors'? What is truth? Or more precisely, whose truth shall we express, that of the oppressed or of the oppressors? These are basic questions. (Neal, "The Black Arts Movement" 30)

The differences between the two are subtle but significant. Karenga's thesis is basically inward looking, while Neal proposes an outward looking view. Karenga's view emphasized African history and traditions. Neal's view emphasized African liberation.

Kwanzaa is a good example of the Karenga focus. Participation in the African Liberation Support Committee and the Boycott South Africa movement are examples of the Neal focus. While these focuses are not mutually exclusive, and are in fact complementary, their differences accurately anticipated the internal split which wracked BAM: the nationalist versus Marxist split.

Of course, there were those who disagreed and actively attacked BAM aesthetics in general. BAM critics usually proposed one of two basic arguments. One argument rejected BAM's ideology of political and ethnic art, arguing instead that the purpose of art was "for art's sake." This criticism emphasized the importance of "technical expertise" as a given artistic discipline, as opposed to the importance of the message. BAM adherents dismissed "art for art's sake" as a "White orientation" unworthy of consideration for a people who were oppressed. The other argument was for the creation of art based on "commercial appeal" (art as entertainment strictly to make a buck). This "commercial" approach was condemned as "selling out" and "careerism." BAM countered with the formulation of concepts such as "inner-attainment," which argued that "message" was more important than "money."

Larry Neal and Maulana Karenga essentially defined BAM's general philosophy of a Black aesthetic. Although there were other BAM theoreticians such as Addison Gayle, Hoyt Fuller, Stephen Henderson, and Carolyn Rodgers, their main focus was in the area of literature as opposed to Karenga and Neal, who placed all of the arts into a larger political perspective.

Following Karenga and Neal, Haki Madhubuti, formerly Don L. Lee, was the major theoretician and, eventually, the major practitioner of the Black aesthetic. By the eighties Madhubuti became the leading practictioner of the Black literary aesthetic as both a publisher and practitioner. His controversial book *Dynamite Voices* (1971) was the first major critical evaluation of the "New Black Poetry." In his popular book *From Plan to Planet* (1973), Madhubuti outlined his intention to move into institution building as a way to actualize Black Power. He writes:

> Ideologically and politically we're trying to break our total dependence upon European and Euro-American publishers

and distributors. To publish our own books and to disseminate them in our own communities is one road toward self determination and self definition. It has become increasingly clear that if a book written by a black affronts the particular sensibilities of European or Euro-American publishers and distributors, one of several actions will be taken against that book: (1) the book will not be published; (2) the book will be published with a limited budget which results in the book being printed in limited quantities with few, if any, funds available for advertising—this in effect kills the book; if the book is published in this manner, there will be a deliberate attempt on the part of the distributor to systematically overlook the black bookstores and outlets. But the fact is, that if the book is published, no matter that it isn't pushed, the publisher uses its publication to ward off any criticism of racism or disregard for the black public and writer. This brings us to the political reality of publishing and distribution. We now understand that everything that involves human participation in this country is political from *My Fair Lady* to *Sweet Sweetback's Baadassss Song* to the air we breathe to the dangerous food we eat. The name of the game is control, and if we do not control our product from manuscript to book to readers we are, in the final analysis, just talking to the wind.

(Madhubuti, *From Plan to Planet* 115)

Although many others attempted to build long-lasting BAM publishing institutions, only Madhubuti's Third World Press has been able to stay the course as a major functional book publisher beyond the 1970s, and, of the aforementioned journals, only *Black Scholar* survives as a BAM publication.

Theoretically, Addison Gayle's anthology *The Black Aesthetic* (1971) was the most influential articulation of the controversial theory pertaining to a specifically "Black" aesthetic. Insightfully, Gayle connects the BAM's revolutionary aspirations to earlier developments of the Harlem Renaissance. While it is common to hear critics argue that the Black Aesthetic was never defined, seldom do those critics acknowledge or specifically critique Gayle's provocative, protean and powerful anthology. Following Gayle's anthology the most significant sourcebook on the Black Aesthetic was not a theoretical piece but an astonishing bibliography with a perceptive and far-reaching introduction offering an overview of the struggle to identify, define, and critique a "Black aesthetic." Painstakingly researched, Carolyn Fowler's *Black Arts and Black Aesthetics, A Bibliography* is a sine qua non BAM reference and research tool.[2] She writes:

> The following bibliography is an attempt to bring together studies of a general nature, or which contain statements of a general nature, on black arts and black sensibility, so that a tradition of black arts and black aesthetics in the United States may be delineated, its dominant and consistent features identified and its history traced. "Black arts" is here taken to mean the philosophy of art which can be inferred from works by Blackamericans. The term "black aesthetics" refers to the body of writings which touch on the issue of black creativity and human sensibility. Black aesthetics, then, alludes to a philosophical tradition within the Blackamerican community.

The term "the black aesthetic" also bears mention here. It is an attempt to describe how Black people respond to nature and to art. It maintains that certain qualities set Black people apart from other racio-cultural groupings. The term "the black aesthetic" can be subsumed under black aesthetics. The former is a philosophical stance; the latter attempts to trace the history of philosophical stances. Black aesthetics, because it is historical, is non-exclusive. Under its umbrella can be lumped not only those writers who have argued in favor of a black aesthetic, but also those who have wished, consciously or otherwise, to encourage black creativity along the lines of European art and are thus really advocating that Blacks become more proficient in and more assimilated into a Euroamerican aesthetic. Using black aesthetics as an organizing concept, we can also include as part of the Blackamerican philosophical tradition those who argue against the possibility in the future or the existence now of a specifically Blackamerican sensibility or tradition in art. Fowler continues:

> We cannot simply dismiss such nay-sayers. There does exist some basis for their point of view. To some extent, black sensibilities have been retrained in the United States. There seem to be two sets of aesthetic responses among Blackamericans who have been immersed in Euroamerican culture. Professor David Dorsey has spoken of the "dual aesthetic" of Blackamericans. But the phenomenon can also be schematized as a slide. That is to say, depending on the context, a Black person may respond according to one or the other set of values, or his responses may gradually shift to meet the gradual shift in

circumstances. All Blacks, for example, when speaking with great conviction or anger, seem to go gradually into the same distinctive intonation patterns, and those patterns seem to display the same sensuous values as black music. (Fowler, *Black Arts* v – vi)

No other book or publication even approaches what Fowler accomplishes in this book, first published in 1976. Largely unknown outside of BAM circles, this book, with 2,160 citations, culminates years of Fowler's research and active participation in BAM as both a critic and poet, in addition to her work as an educator.

The above mention writers must be prominently featured in any insightful assessment of BAM theoretical trends. A handful of other books of political theory and cultural criticism read by BAM adherents must also be considered if one is to get a grasp on the thinking behind BAM concepts. Chief among those books are *The Wretched of the Earth* by Frantz Fanon, *Crisis of the Black Intellectual* by Harold Cruse, *The Choice* by Sam Yette, *The Autobiography of Malcolm X* by Malcolm X and Alex Haley, and *The Destruction of Black Civilization* by Chancellor Williams.

BAM Writers. In the literary arena with respect to BAM, students are sometimes taught that there were only a handful of writers (e.g. LeRoi Jones/Amiri Baraka, Don L. Lee/Haki Madhubuti, Sonia Sanchez and Nikki Giovanni) whom everybody imitated and that older writers such as Langston Hughes, Robert Hayden, and Gwendolyn Brooks were dismissed by BAM. Such teachings are a gross oversimplification at best and at worst are outright lies. Yes, BAM often condemned the politics of some of the Black writers who preceded BAM, but a political rejection of assimilationist politics does not equate with a wholesale rejection of older writers.

Moreover, there did exist a very real aesthetic difference between BAM and earlier generations of writers. BAM could be understood to create new, alternative forms of writing which did not reject the work of older writers, but simply differed from it. Thus, more venues were available to Black writers of the period then ever before.

As with any literary movement, there were leading individuals who set the pace and often served as stylistic role models. Given the often cited criticism that BAM neglected women writers, it is interesting to note that of the four most important and popular BAM poets (Amiri Baraka, Nikki Giovanni, Don L. Lee/Haki Madhubuti and Sonia Sanchez), two were women. Moreover, one of the most famous and most widely anthologized BAM poems was Mari Evans' "I Am A Black Woman."

Madhubuti, who has sold over a million books and who was also an *Ebony* magazine honoree, was the most influential "Black poet" of the BAM era. He is a tireless lecturer and performance poet. Although he is a supporter of political activity, he chose to focus the majority of his energy on his writing (poetry and essays) and on building Third World Press and The Institute of Positive Education (an independent grade school), while continuing to work with the writers and artists of OBAC.

Haki Madhubuti is the leading BAM literary figure as a poet, theoretician, publisher and organizer. Not only was he the best selling BAM author, his books were aimed to and supported by a Black audience. Madhubuti exclusively published with Black presses. No one else is even close to the unparalleled accomplishments of Madhubuti. Perhaps one of the most significant aspects of Madhubuti's accomplishments is that he maintained a life-long commitment to BAM principles and practices many decades beyond BAM's sixties and seventies hey day. Moreover, Madhubuti published every major and countless minor BAM writers.

Other than Madhubuti, in terms of consistently publishing books of poetry, Sonia Sanchez has proven to be one of BAM's most prolific poets and continually innovative wordsmiths.

In terms of consistently publishing books of poetry, Sonia Sanchez has proven to be BAM's most prolific poet and continually innovative wordsmith. Sanchez is also one of the most dynamic performance poets in the history of America. Her use of music, song, and improvisational Black poetry is a marvel. She has the ability to rouse an audience to its feet with cheers and also to bring tears to the eyes of listeners. At less than five feet tall, Sonia Sanchez is diminutive in physical stature but is a towering literary giant as both a performance and textual poet.

Both Madhubuti and Sanchez maintain a consistent focus

on educating young college students, dating back to the late sixties. Madhubuti taught at Cornell during the 1968-69 academic year. That same year a group of armed students took over the campus. Madhubuti also taught at Howard University between 1970 and 1978. Sanchez, in addition to working at San Francisco State University in 1967 has had major stints at the University of Massachusetts and is now a tenured professor at Temple University. Their long stints as educators partially account for their continued popularity, high name recognition and busy schedules as lecturers and readers. But another important factor in their popularity among students is that both Madhubuti and Sanchez have stayed the course in their core beliefs in support of the empowerment of Black people and in their emphasis on ethical personal relations.

I cannot overemphasize the ethical aspect of BAM. Repeatedly BAM poets called for consistency in word and deed, for a new moral universe, for a "Black value" system that governed all behavior rather than simply applied to intellectual life or aesthetic production. In his unparalleled essay "The Black Arts Movement," Larry Neal declares:

> Further, national and international affairs demand that we appraise the world in terms of our own interests. It is clear that the question of human survival is at the core of contemporary experience. The black artist must address himself to this reality in the strongest terms possible. In a context of world upheaval, ethics and aesthetics must interact positively and be consistent with the demands for a more spiritual world. Consequently, the Black Arts Movement is an ethical movement. Ethical, that is, from the viewpoint of the oppressed. And much of the oppression confronting the Third World and black America is directly traceable to the Euro-American cultural sensibility. This sensibility, antihuman in nature, has, until recently, dominated the psyches of most black artists and intellectuals. It must be destroyed before the black creative artist can have a meaningful role in the transformation of society.
>
> It is this natural reaction to an alien sensibility that informs the cultural attitudes of the Black Arts and the Black Power movements. It is a profound ethical sense that makes a black artist question a society in which art is one thing and the actions of men another. The Black Arts Movement believes that your ethics and your aesthetics are one. That the contradictions between ethics and aesthetics in Western society is symptomatic of a dying culture. (Neal, *Visions of a Liberated Future* 64)

Many critics of BAM completely ignore the raising of ethical questions. Whereas BAM itself viewed ethics and aesthetics as the same thing, critics of BAM dealt with them as separate entities. This lead many BAM literary works to be dismissed because the writers were thought of as personally and ethically flawed.

Ignoring ethics and dismissing entire bodies of work based on the personal flaws of the writer is not sound criticism, yet that is how BAM literary work has generally been judged. If the fascism of Ezra Pound or the anti-Semitism of T.S. Eliot has not kept them from the pantheon of great poets, why should "Black Power," "anti-white," or "violent rhetoric" be cause to nearly universally dismiss BAM poets in general and the aforementioned four poets specifically. Note that, in Baraka's case, the majority of his anthologized work focuses on his "Beat" poetry period and ignores his BAM and socialist periods.

Baraka, Giovanni, Madhubuti and Sanchez were the defining voices during a poetically and politically revolutionary era. Their work (both as text and as performance) is a major example of the ethical and aesthetic nature of BAM poetics. I do not mean to exclude other BAM poets or to suggest that no other poets were of equal literary value; however, the fact is that these four were leaders and set the stage for being prolific, popular, and profound.

BAM'S MUSICAL INCLINATIONS

While the political opposition is usually clearly stated, BAM is often also opposed on a stylistic front. Many critics call into question BAM's use of music to shape poetic verse, as if to say "literary" can only be defined through Euro-centric ideals. Although "performance poetry" is widely recognized today and although there is a broad surge of newfound interest in "Beat" poetry and the Beat movement, there still remains a deep antipathy to the musicality of BAM poetry in critical and academic circles.

In an unusually prescient March 1973 *Black World* article, "Contemporary Afro-American Poetry As Folk Art," critic Bernard W. Bell offers not only a theory and analysis of Black music as a basis for the development of Black literature but also a historical analysis of the works of leading authors and demonstrates the commonality of folk art (specifically Black music) to the work of authors as politically and socially divergent as Paul L. Dunbar, Richard Wright, Ralph Ellison, Gwendolyn Brooks, Bob Kaufman and LeRoi Jones. Bell argues that one major element of commonality is the influence and use of Black music as a model for their literary constructs.

But Bell does more than simply demonstrate similarities; he also explicates a defining factor of "Black" literature. In essence, Bell attempts to demonstrate what makes "Black" literature distinctly "Black" as opposed to American literature in general. One element is the use of Black folk material as both theme and structure. Bell writes:

> I propose to demonstrate how the music of Black folk gets into a considerable amount of their poetry, especially poetry of the Sixties....The consensus of thinking by many Black writers and critics is that Afro-American folk art, music in particular, has provided a sound base for the development of a distinctive body of ethnic literature. ... Assuming that Black music is a synthesis of the Black American's African heritage and his American experience, and that it addresses itself to the needs, sufferings and hopes of the Black masses, Baraka is suggesting that the best, if not the only, means of judging the quality of Blackness in literature is by comparing it to the richness and vitality of Black music. "If there is ever a Negro literature," he concludes, "it must disengage itself from the weak, heinous elements of the culture that spawned it, and use its very existence as evidence of a more profound America." This was the revolutionary challenge for Black writers in the Sixties. (Bell 17, 20)

Bell adds a second cautionary element to the defining of Black poetry. He writes that:

> It is important to remember, however, that as products of a society in the state of ferment and flux, both Anglo-American and Afro-American folklore are marked by ambiguities. Insofar as both champion the values expressed in the American Creed, they are similar. But insofar as one is the lore of the oppressor, the white majority, and the other the lore of the victims of oppression, the Black southerner and his northern brothers, they are antithetical. On one hand, the basic values emanate from the preeminence of property, individualism and technology, while on the other, they spring from the

preeminence of the human spirit, social justice and physical freedom. (Bell 22)

According to Bell, the two major criteria for "Black" literature are the use of Black folklore in either theme or structure (or preferably both) combined with a validation of "the human spirit, social justice and physical freedom." Further on in the extensive twenty-five-page essay, Bell tackles the thorny question of "what is soul?" He eloquently answers that "soul power is the primal force of human nature, tempered by a common experience of suffering and struggle for survival that manifests itself through shared modes of perceiving and expressing that experience; it is, above all, the affirmation of the resiliency of the spirit—the inner experiences—in a world of insecurity and blues-like absurdity" (Bell 85).

Fortunately, Bell's observations were further developed in a small book published by Broadside Press as part of their *Broadside Critics Series*, with James A. Emanuel as general editor. The four works in the series were *Dynamite Voices: Black Poets of the 1960's* by Don L. Lee (Haki Madhubuti), *Claude McKay: the Black Poet at War* by Addison Gayle, Jr., *The Folk Roots of Contemporary Afro-American Poetry* by Bernard W. Bell, and *A Many-Colored Coat of Dreams: The Poetry of Countee Cullen* by Houston A. Baker, Jr. Although short-lived, the series brought BAM-oriented literary criticism to the foreground. Moreover, in direct contradistinction to the oft-repeated charge that BAM writers ignored or dismissed older Black writers, the *Broadside Critics Series* focused equally on both contemporary and traditional Black poets. BAM proponents evaluated the whole tradition of African American literature. Even though there were clear political differences and antagonisms, serious BAM critics recognized that the new Black poetry grew out of a tradition. Regardless of the particulars of political ideology, with respect to literature, "Blackness" (Black folk art) and "soul" (an assertion of the human spirit) remain constant as the core elements of African American literature, especially BAM literature.

BAM was not simply a status quo–accepted alternative, but a different species of literary/political animal altogether. This difference was not only disruptive of the status quo in that it undermined status quo "authority," but it also threatened, with its nationalist/separatist tendencies, to establish a permanent opposition to existing theories and practices of art. Not surprisingly, no effort was spared by the American arts mainstream in attempting to co-opt BAM artifacts, institutions, and history where possible, and to destroy and/or ignore BAM where co-option was not possible.

BAM Literary Critics. Although few cultural critics have delved deeply into BAM, attempts to define BAM aesthetics among the movement's own creative writers led to substantial analysis of BAM poetry. Chief among these critics are Carolyn Rodgers who wrote a series of four important and groundbreaking theoretical articles on Black poetry in *Black World* magazine (September 1969, June 1970, September 1970 and September 1971); Don L. Lee (Haki Madhubuti), who wrote BAM's first (and thus far, only) book of poetic literary criticism, *Dynamite Voices: Black Poets of the 1960's* (1971); and Stephen Henderson, who produced the seminal anthology *Understanding The New Black Poetry* (1972), which included a prescient and groundbreaking introductory essay.

Henderson's introductory essay is particularly important because it is the most extensive articulation of the aesthetic for "the new Black poetry" yet produced. Henderson proposes:

> There should be, of course, a way of speaking about all kinds of Black poetry, despite the kinds of questions that can be raised. In our attempts to clarify such a method, it might be wise to speak more specifically about the poetry itself, in addition to the critical premises stated above.
>
> Although it is an arbitrary scheme for the purpose of analysis, one may describe or discuss a "Black" poem in terms of the following broad critical categories: (1) Theme, (2) Structure, (3) Saturation.
>
> 1. By *theme* I mean that which is being spoken of, whether the specific subject matter, the emotional response to it, or its intellectual formulation.
>
> 2. By *structure* I mean chiefly some aspect of the poem such as diction, rhythm, figurative language, which goes into the total makeup. (At times, I use the word in an extended sense

to include what is usually called genre.)

3. By *saturation* I mean several things, chiefly the communication of "Blackness" and fidelity to the observed or intuited truth of the Black Experience in the United States. It follows that these categories should also be valid in any critical evaluation of the poem. (Henderson, *Understanding The New Black Poetry* 10)

Henderson goes on to detail the three categories. In later essays, he goes into more depth and provides subtle variations on his basic formulations. Carolyn Rodgers' stirring critical insights notwithstanding, there is no single essay as important as Henderson's introduction in specifically addressing the development of a comprehensive schema for critiquing the New Black poetry.

Literary Conferences. The BAM era was framed by a set of extremely important literary conferences which were held on the historically Black college campuses of Fisk and Howard Universities.

John Oliver Killens organized a series of Writer's Conferences at Fisk University, where poet Robert Hayden was located. Killens' conferences drew a line of demarcation between those Black writers from the Civil Rights and earlier eras who would accept (and even champion) the newly emergent BAM and those who rejected BAM. Killens was a well-respected member of the old guard who was enthusiastic, although not uncritical, in his support of BAM. Poet and critic Eugene Redmond notes in his book, *Drumvoices*, that:

> The 1967 conference (probably the straw that broke the camel's back for Hayden) is seen by some as a major juncture in the new black writing. Gwendolyn Brooks talked about it in her autobiography, Margaret Walker discussed it with Nikki Giovanni in their published "conversations," and Hoyt Fuller wrote glowingly of it in *Black World*. Writers attending the conference were David Llorens, Fuller, Ron Milner, [John] Clarke, [Lerone] Bennett, Margaret Danner, Nikki Giovanni, [Dudley] Randall, [Don L.] Lee, Margaret Walker, Sonia Sanchez, [LeRoi] Jones, and Margaret Burroughs. Probably held in the South for symbolic reasons, the conference provided the first real "new" national dramatic arena for old and young writers.

Gwendolyn Brooks (a "Negro" then, she has said) recalls being "coldly respected" after just having flown to Nashville from "white white South Dakota." However, she was among the first (with Randall and Fuller) to take up the banner of the black aesthetic and the causes of the young writers. Such action, of course, was displeasing to a number of white and black poets, not the least among them Hayden, who refuses to acknowledge the existence of a "separate" aesthetic for Blacks. (Redmond 380)

One of the most persistent, and yet totally undocumented, myths taught about BAM is that Robert Hayden in particular and other older poets in general were attacked by BAM adherents. Although this is repeated from classroom to classroom, the claim was never validated. The truth is complex but understandable. Simply put, there was a major ideological split on the issue of integration. The split was about content and not craft. Hayden was frequently published in *Negro Digest* and *Black World*, and was included in major BAM anthologies such as Henderson's *Understanding The New Black Poetry* and Randall's *Black Poets*. However, Hayden is not included in *Black Fire*, and the reason is simple: Hayden was not a Black Power advocate. The ideology of Black Power was then and remains today a major dividing line between supporters and detractors of BAM.

In addition to drawing a line of demarcation, Killens' 1967 conferences also provided an opportunity for writers to personally meet and get to know each other, to exchange books and contacts, and to debate and discuss BAM ideology and aesthetic ideas.

In "Broadside Press: A Personal Chronicle" Dudley Randall offers an anecdotal illustration of the excitement generated by Killens' 1966 Fisk conference:

In May 1966 I attended the first Writers' Conference at Fisk University, and obtained permission from Robert Hayden, Melvin B. Tolson, and Margaret Walker, who were there, to use their poems in the *Broadside Series*. I wrote to Gwendolyn Brooks and obtained her permission to use "We Real Cool." This first group of six Broadsides, called "Poems of the Negro Revolt," is, I think, one of the most distinguished groups in the *Broadside Series*, containing outstanding poems by some of our finest poets.

The first book planned (but not the first published) by Broadside Press was *For Malcolm: Poems on the Life and the Death of Malcolm X*. This book had its genesis at the first Fisk University Writers' Conference. As I was walking to one of the sessions, I saw Margaret Walker, the poet, and Margaret Burroughs, the painter, sitting in front of their dormitory. Mrs. Burroughs was sketching, and Miss Walker was rehearsing her reading, for she was to read her poems that afternoon. I sat down to watch and to listen, and when Miss Walker read a poem on Malcolm X, I said, "Everybody's writing about Malcolm X. I know several people who've written poems about him."

"That's right," Margaret Burroughs said. "Why don't you collect the poems and put out a book on Malcolm?"

I thought it over for a few seconds, snapped my fingers, and said, "I'll do it. And you can be my co-editor."

Thus the anthology *For Malcolm* was born.
Most conferences have much talk, but little action. Mrs. Burroughs and I decided to inject some action into this conference by announcing our book at the final session, and offering the writers there a concrete vehicle for their poems. David Llorens promised to announce it in *Negro Digest* (now *Black World*) and in a few days I received the first poem. This anthology is notable not only for the many fine poems it includes, but also because it brings mature poets such as Robert Hayden, Margaret Walker, and Gwendolyn Brooks together with younger poets such as LeRoi Jones, Larry Neal, Bobb Hamilton, Sonia Sanchez, Julia Fields, Etheridge Knight, David Llorens, and others. My editorship of the book acquainted me with many of the younger poets and with the periodicals *Soulbook* and *Black Dialogue*, and led to rewarding friendships with some of the poets. (Randall, "Broadside Press: A Personal Chronicle" 139–40, 141)

On the other end of the BAM timeline was the Howard University National Conferences of Afro-American Writers (November 1974) organized by Stephen Henderson, John Oliver Killens and Haki Madhubuti, all of whom were then working at Howard. There were five Howard conferences:

1. November 8-10, 1974.
2. April 22-24, 1976. "Beyond Survival: 200 Years of Black Literature, 1776-1976."
3. May 5-7, 1977. "Black Writers and Their People: Craft and Consciousness."

4. May 4-6, 1978 "The View of the 60s Through the Prism of the Present."
5. February 9-10, 1983 "The Human Resources of Afro-American Literature: Lessons from the Recent Past."

The Howard conferences were larger than the Fisk conferences and were almost entirely BAM oriented, although, again, not uncritically so.

Henderson was extremely conscious of the importance of the Howard gatherings and videotaped the proceedings, as well as videotaped oral histories and interviews with selected writers in attendance. As with the Fisk conferences, the Howard conferences were a cultural crossroads where writers gathered, exchanged ideas, information and publications, and renewed old and made new friendships.

By the 1970s there were many such conferences going on across the country. These gatherings inculcated a sense of kinship and espirt de corps among BAM writers that would have been impossible to achieve without physical face-to-face contact. The spirit of BAM encouraged "festivals" and "conferences," which in turn reinforced the sense of unity and purpose that was a major characteristic of BAM. The 1977 FESTAC Festival, a Pan-African festival of arts and culture, was held in Nigeria and featured over a hundred BAM or BAM-influenced writers, artists, and musicians. The event was a definitive example of BAM-oriented artistic conferences, festivals, and gatherings. A broad range of cultural workers attended, representing both the continent of Africa and the Diaspora.

The 1966 March Against Fear was resumed in Mississippi by Martin Luther King, Jr. and members of SNCC, including Stokely Carmichael, after James Meredith, the first Negro to be admitted to the University of Mississippi (Ol' Miss) and who had initiated the march, was shot by a Ku Klux Klan sniper.

CHAPTER 5
BLACK ARTS MOVEMENT PUBLICATIONS

The dissemination of Black Arts Movement ideology can be largely attributed to the national distribution of publications developed within BAM itself. Previous publications, Black or White, offered little space for creative, mainstream political expression. BAM publications attracted a great deal of young writers whose BAM-oriented message engaged new audiences.

In the early sixties, two New York-based, nationally distributed magazines, *Freedomways* and *Liberator*, began to introduce the world to BAM writers. Once given this initial push, BAM-oriented publications began to spring up across the nation. The following is a brief synopsis of influential BAM publications, as well as detailed accounts of the ideals they promoted.

Freedomways. Subtitled "A journal of the Freedom Movement" this journal was backed by leftists and receptive to young Black writers, but maintained a "Civil Rights" focus. One particularly important element of *Freedomways* was the annotated "Recent Books" column meticulously researched by bibliophile Ernest Kaiser. Kaiser's sharp-eyed, non-doctrinaire, Marxist-oriented comments buttressed by encyclopedic familiarity with Black books and related issues made his listing a must read for those attempting to follow the currents of Black and related literature. Published in *Freedomways* was the work of young emerging BAM writers, as well as commentary and critiques from more established academics and authors.

Liberator. Of the two BAM precursors, the more important magazine was Dan Watts' *Liberator*, which openly aligned itself with both domestic and international revolutionary movements. Many of the voices that later proved critical to BAM were first published in the *Liberator*. To a large degree, this development happened because of Larry Neal's tenure as an editor at

Liberator and Askia Toure's work as a staff writer. The magazine was the first post-fifties nationalist publication to have a national circulation and to showcase BAM writers. The first word people outside of New York received about BAM came through the pages of *Liberator*. Although both *Freedomways* and *Liberator* published BAM writers, neither publication identified itself as a strictly literary publication nor a strictly BAM publication.

Soulbook. (1964) *Soulbook* is the first nationally distributed, West Coast Black Power publication that had a strong BAM literary component. *Soulbook's* masthead promised "jazz, economics, poetry, [and] anti-imperialism" in announcing the premiere issue of *the quarterly journal of revolutionary afroamerica*. On its editorial board were Donald Freeman, Issac Moore, Ernest Allen Jr., Carroll Holmes, Kenn M. Freeman, and Bobb Hamilton, who was also the east coast representative.

Oakland-based *Soulbook* was mainly political but included poetry in a section ironically titled "Reject Notes." The editorial in the premiere issue announced:

> Black American literature has tended to be parochial simply because most Black writers did not actually believe that their experience and understanding of the world was valuable merely because it was theirs (and real), but rather because they were Black or half-Black or "passing" or even because they could pretend not to be any of these, and by such act make a display of "culture" in the White man's hopeless world.
> The Blackness of the best Black writing is not only in the fact of its creating myth and emotion that has legitimately been got by translating into art the peculiar emotional life of the Black man, but as world gesture that should be understood by any human being. (*Soulbook* 2)

The founding of *Soulbook* (1964) and the subsequent founding of *Black Dialogue, Journal of Black Poetry* and *Black Scholar*, all published out of the Bay Area, raises the question, why did this development take place here and not in New York? Aubrey LaBrie, a founder of *Black Dialogue* and long time activist in the Bay Area, responds to the question in a letter addressed to Dingane Joe Goncalves:

One answer is that writers such as Jones or Baldwin were published in established periodicals or literary reviews and had contracts with major publishers. My guess is that this may have put a damper on any plans by other Blacks to produce small, independent publications or diverted their focus to pursuing major publishers. Thus, the combination of limited physical, moral, and financial support and the daunting nature of the task may have discouraged the development of independent black journals on the East Coast. (Goncalves, "Letters")

LaBrie is essentially arguing that there was a greater need for BAM writing on the West Coast, and the potential to work un-co-opted by major publishers. California was also the home base of both the Black Panther Party and Karenga's US Organization, the two most influential Black Power organizations in terms of defining and influencing the practice of Black power in the Black community. The Bay Area of the 1960s is another fertile area of future research.

Black Dialogue. The first major BAM publication with a specifically literary focus was the California-based *Black Dialogue* (1965), which was edited by Arthur A. Sheridan, Abdul Karim, Edward Spriggs, Aubrey LaBrie, and Marvin Jackmon (later Marvin X). According to Ed Spriggs, *Black Dialogue* was initially going to be named Soulbook. But due to editorial differences that arose after Kenn Freeman and others became involved, the new publication split into two separate publications—*Soulbook* and *Black Dialogue*. Editor Spriggs recalls the initial group of people who produced *Black Dialogue* was Jim Aliniece, Marvin Jackmon, Aubrey LaBrie, George Murray, Marc Primus (Primus Devey), Belvie Harrison Rooks, Arthur Sheridan, Welton Smith, Edward Spriggs, and Duke Williams. The initial issue included work by LeRoi Jones, Marvin E. Jackmon, Al Young, Joe Goncalves, and Ed Bullins, among others.

The Kenn Freeman-led contingent lobbied for a specific political line. The original off-campus student group wanted an open forum, hence the title *Black Dialogue* instead of the originally intended title *Soulbook*. Art Sheridan's opening editorial announced, "This magazine is proudly dedicated to the late Malcolm X, a great leader and a greater MAN—a man who was able, better than anyone else, to articulate the deep frustrations and emotions of the oppressed and downtrodden Afro-American masses; and instilled in the Black people of this country a real sense of pride, dignity and identity" (*Black Dialogue* 1, No. 1, 1) *Black Dialogue* continued this sentiment by linking politics and aesthetics. In the third issue, the editorial board explicitly stated the journal's vision for Black literature.

> A new direction should be sought for the writing of Afro-American literature. The emphasis must be placed on Blacks as they relate to one another in the more positive and meaningful aspects of their environment. It should, above all, take into account the need to speak directly to our people in terms and symbols relevant to their experience.
>
> Presently too much attention is focused upon the prejudiced racial attitudes of white people and the consequent treatment accorded to black people. This concern is reflected in a host of writings underlined with protests, threats, and admonishments directed at white-folks. Actually it is nothing more than a complimentary plea to the consciences of white folks: "Come on baby, you're too intelligent to let yourself be subjected to all those irrational views and barbaric acts; straighten up and be the nice, reasonable person you've always taught us you were."
>
> We aren't suggesting that the use of invectives or moral suasion is of itself bad, just that it should be put into proper perspective. Even a righteous preacher would admit that a constant nagging at recalcitrant wrongdoers serves no real purpose: it either makes the conscience duller or turns people into neurotic masochists. Needless to say, it does nothing for the victims of this wrongdoing, but perhaps build up an abysmal reservoir of hatred and enmity in those who are fortunate enough to survive it. In our case, the oppressor, from his position of efficacious power, simply cast a contemptuous smile in response to the barrage of epithets and preachments hurled at him. This doesn't mean that he has no conscience; it simply means that his conscience is conditioned to respond only to certain things: (in most cases) the needs of his people – western white; and (in all cases) the preservation of his material interests. Consequently, our "telling him off" or "talking about him" does not elicit the desired response, nor does it give us any real sense of self-respect and human dignity. We are left in our same condition of psychological and cultural enslavement.

The editorial continues:

> By stating our case in this manner, we do not mean to imply that literary endeavors by blacks should be abandoned or

seriously curtailed. We are merely saying that Afro-American literature should be put into a more meaningful perspective. By aiming it at whites it has had little positive effect and only limited meaning. Therefore, it must be redirected.

It must be based on a thorough assessment of our cultural heritage and our present position in U. S. society. Moreover, it must be directed toward the establishment of a viable and distinct cultural base. In line with this objective it should (1) stress things like the strong feelings of spiritual kinship and brotherhood which help draw our people together; (2) extract objects and symbols from our already-existing culture, especially those which increase our sense of pride and self-respect; and (3) point out conditions, such as economic exploitation and discrimination, which give us cause for our unified action. Finally, it must make a conscious effort to promote attitudes and values which when put into practice will either correct or completely destroy all the oppressive conditions confronting us in this society. (*Black Dialogue* 1, No., 3, 3–4)

Black Dialogue was consistent in foregrounding an emphasis on the political. Significantly that issue included "Vietnam: An Eyewitness View From Hanoi," by Harold Supriano, in addition to articles by Lawrence Neal (Larry Neal), James T. Stewart, Eldridge Cleaver; artwork from Ramond Howell and Sargent Johnson; and a play by Marvin Jackmon and contributions from Ed Bullins, Abdul Karim, and C. H. Fuller, Jr.

In 1969 *Black Dialogue* moved to New York. In addition to Ed Spriggs, the editorial board now included: Nikki Giovanni, Jaci Earley, Elaine Jones, Sam Anderson, and James Hinton (photography); San Francisco/West Coast: Joe Goncalves; Mid-West: Ahmed Alhamisi, Carolyn Rodgers; Southern USA: Julia Fields, Akinshiju, A.B. Spellman; and in Africa: Ted Joans. K. W. Kgositsile (editor-at-large). The editors summed up the history of their journal as such:

A few years ago Black Dialogue was started as an off-campus publication by a few Black San Francisco State college students. The idea grew out of the NEGRO STUDENT ASSOCIATION, one of the first Black student groups on any campus (now known as BLACK STUDENT UNION). At the time, none of us had any journalistic experience to speak of, but we all felt the necessity for developing a platform from which the Black artists and political activists could speak to Black people. The year was 1965. The "civil rights movement" was being repudiated by many of us as a lost cause. Many Black Movement people were already returning home in disillusionment. EL-HAJJ MALIK EL-SHABAZZ (Malcolm X) had been assassinated just before we went to press (our first issue was dedicated to him). LeRoi Jones (AMEER BARAKA) had announced and was developing THE BLACK ARTS REPERTORY THEATRE SCHOOL in Harlem. Karenga's US organization was growing fast in Los Angeles. The teachings of such men as Malcolm, LeRoi and Maulana Karenga were still effectively reaching us thru the man's media. (Of late the man has gotten pretty tight with his media...except with his publishing houses. That should change soon and we don't mean by the Black-Capitalists publishing houses that will soon pop up.) A political and cultural revolution was beginning to ferment across this arcadia. Black people were beginning to feel themselves. Accept themselves. Want themselves. Love what they are—what was/is/will be theirs.

We have moved our editorial operations to New York City...and organized a new staff with broader national representation. Our determination is still Black. Our printer is still Black. We are still distributed and sold (where possible) Black. BLACK DIALOGUE remains "a meeting place for the voices of the Black community—wherever that community may exist."

(Black Dialogue 4, No.1, 2)

The Journal of Black Poetry. Dingane Joe Goncalves, a civil rights/black power veteran of CORE is one of the key linchpins of the BAM literary movement. During an interview with the author, Goncalves remembers traveling through the South with CORE on his way to the West Coast. He recalls:

We had our little .38, but we were met by brothers armed with shotguns and rifles. Black Power was all in the air everywhere at that time. No one person can take credit for it. Our people as a whole were on the move. This was in 1965. (Goncalves, "Interview")

Goncalves moved from Los Angeles to San Francisco the week before the Watts Rebellion in August of 1965. A self-effacing and very quiet individual, Goncalves quickly became the major literary editor of the revolutionary wing of BAM literary arts.

Goncalves had been selected as *Black Dialogue's* poetry editor, but as more and more poetry poured in he conceived the idea to start *Journal of Black Poetry*. Founded in San Francisco, the first issue of *Journal of Black Poetry* (1966) was a small magazine with mimeographed inside pages and a lithographed cover. The initial issues did not indicate a staff, but Issue #4 (Spring 1967) listed Editor, Joe Goncalves; Contributing Editors, LeRoi Jones, Newark, New Jersey; Clarence Major, New York, New York; Marvin Jackmon, San Francisco, California; and featuring artwork by Donald Patton (AUM) and a section of photography by Norman Brown.

Within a few months the staff expanded. Issue #5 (Summer 1967) carried the following names on the masthead: Contributing Editors: LeRoi Jones, Newark, New Jersey; Clarence Major, New York; Marvin Jackmon, San Francisco, California; Larry Neal, New York; Corresponding Editors: LeGraham, Detroit, Michigan; Ed Spriggs, Harlem; Editor: Joe Goncalves. That issue also featured drawings by Emory Douglas, who was the Black Panther Minister of Culture.

The inclusion of more and more writers and editors indicates not only the growth and the level of public interest in the magazine, but also the effort on Goncalves's part to reach out to the east coast and the Midwest. Issue number 4 is also instructive in demonstrating that Goncalves was a visionary. He focused on unearthing and propagating non-Western literary traditions as well as showcasing "new" directions for Black poetry. An editor's note reads, "The designs that appear on the first and final pages of *The Journal of Black Poetry* are taken from a Hausa book of proverbs, as is the proverb below," were written in Arabic script. Additionally, there is a special section, "On The Black Poet," featuring "statements" from LeRoi Jones, Marvin Jackmon and Clarence Major.

Jones evidences an ever-expanding vision. He writes that:

> The "Destruction of America" was the Black Poet's role... to contribute as much as possible to that. But now, I realize that the Black Poet ought also try to provide a "post american form," even as simple vision, for his people.
> We must study the present, and the past, and outline a maximum security and consciousness for our people's future. By past I mean, for instance "African and Arabic language, studies here would place our eyes on documents sacred to us. The study of hieroglyphs would open the mind of the Black man back into a time of his strength." Perhaps by studying and understanding Pre-american or Pre-white forms we will know

how to strengthen any Black post-american form. (Baraka, "Statement" 14)

Clarence Major concurs in his statement, titled, "A Black Criteria":

The black poet confronted with western culture and civilization must isolate and define himself in as bold a relief as he can. He must chop away at the white criterion and destroy it's hold on his black mind because seeing the world through white eyes from a black soul causes death. The black poet must not attempt to create from a depth of black death. The true energy of black art must be brought fully into the possession of the black creator. The black poet must stretch his consciousness not only in the direction of other non-western people across the earth, but in terms of pure reason and expand the mind areas to the far reaches of creativity's endlessness to find new ways of seeing the world the black poet of the west is caught up in

The nightmare of this western sadism must be fought with a superior energy and black poetic spirit is a powerful weapon.

With the poem, we must erect a spiritual black nation we all can be proud of. And at the same time we must try to do the impossible—always the impossible—by bringing the poem back into the network of man's social and political life.
Total life is what we want. (Major 15, 16)

Marvin Jackmon also sounded a clarion call for change:

THE BLACK REVOLUTIONARY POET MUST LISTEN TO THE MUSIC AND LANGUAGE OF HIS PEOPLE. HE MUST EXPRESS THEIR COLLECTIVE RHYTHM. THE POET IS THEIR SERVANT. HE RECORDS THE MYTHOLOGY OF HIS PEOPLE, HIS BROTHERS AND SISTERS. HE KNOWS THEIR HEARTBEAT. HE KNOWS WHAT THEY DO NOT KNOW: HE KNOWS THE LANGUAGE OF THE BEAST, THE JUNGLE TALK, THE GIBBERISH....SO THE POET IS A TEACHER OF TOMORROW, YESTERDAY, AND NOW, WHICH IS ONE MOMENT. ... THE POET IS A SCIENTIST, A LOVER, A JUDGE, A PRIEST, A LEADER OF THE PEOPLE. (Jackmon 17)

The *Journal of Black Poetry* was consciously fostering a completely different paradigm for poetic aesthetics, a politicized paradigm, an unapologetically Black paradigm. Jones, Major, and Jackmon would end up splitting into three different directions, but it is nonetheless important to note their common beginnings in a search for new directions for poetry. Because they equated poetry with life, they were searching not in the abstract for a new theory, but in the reality of their time for new directions for their lives. BAM in all of its myriad manifestations eschewed a mainly "arts-for-art's sake" orientation. BAM was about art for life. Goncalves understood that both practice and criticism (i.e. poetry and essays/manifestoes) were necessary if *Journal of Black Poetry* was going to be effective.

Up through the summer of 1975, *Journal of Black Poetry* published nineteen issues and grew to over a hundred pages. In the summer of 1974 *Journal of Black Poetry* changed its name to *Kitabu Cha Jua,* which means "book of the sun" in Swahili. *Journal of Black Poetry*'s editorial policy emphasized revolutionary struggle but was eclectic in including a wide range of writers.

Goncalves made a prophetic decision when he moved away from single editor leadership and began a policy of giving over the majority of editorial space to guest editors. The guest editor was responsible for selecting poetry, essays and other writings for each issue. Beginning with the Spring, 1968 (No. 8) issue, the guest editors were Ahmed Alhamisi of Detroit; Larry Neal of New York (Summer, 1968, No. 9), Marvin X, aka Marvin Jackmon, of the Bay Area, (No. 10), Ed Spriggs of New York (Spring, 1969, No. 11), Clarence Major of New York (Summer-Fall, 1969, No. 12), Askia Muhammad Toure of Harlem (Winter-Spring, 1970, No. 13), Don Lee of Chicago (Special Issue 1970–71, No. 15), Dudley Randall of Detroit (Fall-Winter, 1971, No. 16), and Sebastian Clarke (Special West Indian Issue, Summer, 1973, No. 17). These guest-edited issues not only insured that a broad range of writers were represented in the pages of the *Journal* but that fresh ideas and a variety of outlooks and aesthetics were represented.

During the publication's lifetime, over 500 different poets were published, embodying a broad range of cultures. Examples of international "revolutionary poetry" were presented by not only African American writers, but African, Caribbean, and Asian writers. Another significant aspect of *Journal of Black Poetry* was the copious use of photographs and graphic illustrations throughout the publication. The visual arts were closely aligned with the literary arts and were often presented as one. Even the first issue, which was mimeographed, had "revolutionary" and "cultural" images to complement the text, featuring a cover depicting a young African sister holding an M-1 rifle. The multi-disciplinary approach was also a salient characteristic of BAM. Consistent with its Black Power emphasis on both politics and art, *The Journal of Black Poetry* always carried historical and political articles, "roundups" (overviews of particular locales), interviews, and poetry.

"My real purpose was to change the world. I had the feeling that poetry had the power, and has shown the power, to make tremendous change in the world," asserted Goncalves in a 1995 interview. He continued, "People generally don't take poetry seriously and yet at serious moments—like death, marriage, births, or revolution—people call on the poets" (Goncalves, "Interview").

One of Goncalves's major objectives was to ensure that Marcus Garvey and Malcolm X would not be ignored or overlooked. Beginning with a full page photo of Malcolm X in issue number 3, every issue of *Journal of Black Poetry* thereafter carried quotes from both of the revolutionary leaders, along with photographs or drawings of Marcus Garvey and Malcolm X. Goncalves recalls that, "Some people thought I was a bit loony when I first started doing that but I knew it was important. Our enemies had tried to bury Marcus Garvey and just paint him as a 'back-to-Africa buffoon.' Plus, there were many people who wanted Malcolm to stay dead. I made a conscious decision to raise these brothers."

Although he seldom spoke in public and was never visible on the lecture circuit, Goncalves understood the importance of being a revolutionary communicator. Reflective of Goncalves's activist background, every issue of the *Journal* included an African Diaspora focused, city-by-city and country by country breakdown of who was doing what along with announcements about new publications (both individual books of poetry, as well as journals and anthologies), including contact information for subscriptions, purchase or further details.

Goncalves was serious about his commitment to

revolutionary literature and wrote about the catalytic and prodding role performed by the *Journal* along with *Soulbook* and *Black Dialogue*. In a penetrating review of Don Lee's *Dynamite Voices*, Goncalves corrects factual errors made by Lee and explains the historical background of the BAM literary movement, emphasizing the "intended" revolutionary impact of the West Coast trio of journals. He writes:

> The description of the growth of Black poetry on pages 13–14 presents that growth as some kind of spontaneous, spectacular miracle. Well, miracles went out with Jesus. Where was Don five years previous to this book (1971)? Where was he that he can say that in 1965–6 "Few brothers and sisters in-the-know foresaw the New Black press and Black bookstores, or for that matter, the concept of Black Power?" Well, there were people working day and night to make the things he mentions become realities.
>
> The story around the early 60's was that Black people did not read. In a way, that was true, because on the whole Black writers were not writing directly for/to Black people. *Soulbook* and *Black Dialogue* were very instrumental in bringing about a radical change in all that–they were perhaps the first magazines in the u.s. for Black people by Black people. At least the first we had seen in a long time. The early issues of *Dialogue* and *Soulbook* were bombshells. Naturally, the Negro establishment ignored the two magazines until it became obvious that this was the direction of the future. Then the move for co-option came in. People used to tell me, "Man, black people don't read poetry." I knew better–I knew we read some black poets, and it was obvious why we did not read more. If you flip through old issues of *Negro Digest* (now "Black World") you will get more than a clue of why we did not read more poetry. But the move towards co-option began. *Liberator*, perhaps first, which Don regards as important for the rise of Black poetry (and it was not) began to open its pages to Black (actually Black) writers, but lacking the adeptness (or money or whatever) of *Negro Digest*, *Liberator* could not pull the co-option off. Understand, by the way, that the writers, the editors of the small Black publications, among other things, meant to move *Liberator*, *Negro Digest*, etc. in the direction they moved. It was Ahmed Alhamisi who came down on Broadside Press for continually publishing "grey" poets, and not long after that Broadside moved into the "new Blackness." I say co-option, but I do not mean that in a derogatory sense. I am tracing sources, dealing with contexts. If you want to see where *Negro Digest* (now "Black World") was at the time, you need only look over some old issues.

Goncalves continues:

> You know, even as late as 1968, the *Digest* was still referring to
> what we regard as Black publications as "Non-mainstream"
> publications. You know, what does that mean? Marvin X a non-
> mainstream writer? Yes, I think so, and certainly Blackstream.
> "Non-mainstream" speaks a whole philosophy, a world-view
> that has not changed despite the name changes. The same
> philosophy that allowed a cartoon ridiculing Malcolm X to
> appear in the February, 1965 issue of *Digest*, and please note
> that date. The same philosophy that allowed, in the very
> same issue, poems written by a white girl—yes, where a Black
> poet (like Don) could have been. Yes, she must have been
> a "mainstreamer", along with white comedian-journalist Art
> Buchwald, white nuns, sundry white liberals and the rest. Yes,
> there was a need for "non-mainstream" publications then.
> (Goncalves, "A Review" 88–89)

Goncalves emphasized the positive value of struggle within
the movement to transform existing institutions as well as to
build new institutions. Basically, Goncalves believed, and I
agree, that the "revolutionary journals" had a major impact on
the substance and direction of BAM literature. In an important
November 1969 article in *Negro Digest*, critic Carolyn Gerald
(a.k.a., Carolyn Fowler) analyzes the growth and import of the
trio of revolutionary journals. She writes:

> The emergence of these journals and others similar to them
> was the literary enactment of the crisis of the Sixties: the Break
> With The West. Through them, black literature reorganizes itself,
> serving the cause of blackness by analyzing its suppression
> and recreating its images and its myths. Their role is thus
> revolutionary, and since the building of a black national
> consciousness is conceived of as urgent by those who write
> in the revolutionary journal, it must be accomplished on many
> levels. The immediate outer realities call for a reporting of the
> facts of oppression, for a mobilization of forces, for socio-political
> analysis. The soul within and the fragmented community require
> an image-making, myth-building symbolization of that reality.
> Political activism and poetry can thus complement each
> other. It is not the subject matter which distinguishes socio-
> political literature from esthetic literature here. The subject
> matter is really always the same: black survival through identity
> and strength. But the fiction or poetry of survival is rendered
> through imagery, through symbols, through experimentation
> with different rhythms, with different syntactical forms, with a

different vocabulary, through the indirectness of its statement about our condition. The revolutionary journals thus attest to an all-inclusive view of the black experience and it would be a mistake to pass them by in the vain search for evidences of the literary expression of a people neatly fractured off from life, as is too often the case in old, tired societies with nothing left to fight for; it would be a misreading of the times.

Gerald continues:

> ...Through these journals, and the many others which have sprung up since, current black literature is being grouped and diffused, digested and, in a sense, even created. The revolutionary black journal made its appearance at that moment in our history, somewhere in the mid-Sixties, when black people began to forsake civil rights and integration, and began to seek out a sense of self. They exist as one manifestation of that intense looking inward to see what we really wanted. The direction and developing quality of black literature can be but imperfectly seen if these journals are ignored. The revolutionary black journals attest to a growth toward nationhood in an ever-expanding harmony with the non-white universe. They are an important index of the measure and meaning of the sixties. (Fowler, "untitled" 24, 29)

BAM publications represented a triad of perspectives, forming BAM literary and aesthetic practices. *Journal of Black Poetry, Soulbook,* and *Black Dialogue* represented the Black Power-oriented, activist side of the triangle (thus, the reason to designate them "revolutionary"). The other two sides were the literary, represented by *Negro Digest/Black World,* and the scholarly, represented by *Black Scholar.* In the interest of accuracy, we must point out that neither the literary nor scholarly journals were "anti-activist" or even "un-activist." Rather one of the three elements (activist, literary, and/or scholarly) consistently took the lead in defining the character of individual journals. *Journal of Black Poetry* was clearly a literary journal, and both *Black Scholar* and *Black World* clearly had an activist focus. This tendency to focus on one particular area of the BAM agenda often makes it difficult to distinguish journals of the time as uniquely BAM. Nevertheless, these fine distinctions are important in conceptualizing how these journals worked together in the context of their times and also how they worked in concert with the BAM philosophy.

The Black Scholar. Founded in 1969 by Nathan Hare and Robert Chrisman, *Black Scholar*, "the first journal of black studies and research in this country," was seminal from a critical standpoint. All of the major theorists were represented in its pages. *Black Scholar* quickly became sensitive to what would become known as "feminist" concerns and by the third issue included women writers such as Yvonne R. Chappelle, Shirley Chisholm, Julia Reed, Sonia Sanchez, and Alice Walker. *Black Scholar* admirably fulfilled its editorial mission, which states:

> We recognize that we must re-define our lives. We must shape a culture, a politics, an economics, a sense of our past and future history. We must recognize what we have been and what we shall be, retaining that which has been good and discarding that which has been worthless.

> THE BLACK SCHOLAR shall be the journal for that definition. In its pages, black ideologies will be examined, debated, disputed and evaluated by the black intellectual community. Articles which research, document and analyze the black experience will be published, so that theory is balanced with fact, and ideology with substantial information. (*Black Scholar*, front matter)

In a 1995 interview, Chrisman attributed much of contemporary literary work by women writers to the groundwork laid by BAM.

> If we had not had a Black Arts Movement in the sixties we certainly wouldn't have had national Black literary figures like Henry Louis Gates, Alice Walker or Toni Morrison because much more so than the Harlem Renaissance, in which Black artists were always on the leash of white patrons and publishing houses, the Black Arts Movement did it for itself. What you had was Black people going out nationally, en masse, saying we are an independent Black people and this is what we produce. Take it or leave it. This had never been done before and it was both artistically and commercially successful. (Chrisman, "Interview")

Negro Digest/Black World. From a purely literary perspective, in terms of the overall publication of all genres of BAM creative literature, no publication was more important than *Negro Digest/Black World*. The publication actively propagated the second side of the BAM literary triangle, offering a full spectrum of the BAM "literary-oriented" material. Although *Negro Digest* (1942–

1951, revived 1961–1976) was the oldest of all the publications, it initially had a typically (for Johnson Publications) middle-class "imitation of life" orientation. When Hoyt Fuller became the editor in 1961 that orientation slowly began to change. By the spring of 1970, when the publication became *Black World*, the magazine was fully supportive of a BAM perspective and Hoyt Fuller emerged as a leading BAM proponent.

Because the monthly, ninety-eight-page journal was a Johnson publication, people were able to get *Negro Digest/Black World* on newsstands nationwide. According to a 1971 interview with Hoyt Fuller in the debut issue of *Black Books Bulletin*, the circulation for *Negro Digest/Black World* was approximated at an astounding 180,000 (42).

However, Johnson Publications often made distribution of the journal a low priority. Circulation was often suppressed in terms of newsstand distribution, mailing and promotions. In an interview, Hoyt Fuller acknowledged that:

> One of the problems, of course, is the circulation would be greater now if we were consistent in getting the magazine out on time. We have a great problem and have had a great problem with that. ... As it happens BLACK WORLD is the only one of the magazines that does not pay for itself and so it's the last one in terms of priorities. (Fuller, "*BBB* Interviews" 42)

Nevertheless, even with its problems, *Negro Digest/Black World* was not only the largest Black literary magazine in America's history, but probably the most widely circulated literary magazine in America period—Black, White, or otherwise—in terms of comparative absolute numbers, subscriber to subscriber, over the course of Fuller's editorship. By itself, *Negro Digest/Black World* illustrates BAM's reach and the depth of audience receptivity to its message. Given that America's Black population was then approximately twenty million, percentage-wise *Negro Digest/Black World* was more broadly circulated among its target population than almost any other literary magazine in existence.

The enormous impact and reach of this publication cannot be overstated; yet the fact remains, a majority of college students have never seen an issue of the publication and have probably only heard of its existence in passing.

One way to view BAM, especially with respect to *Negro Digest/Black World*, is not only as a literary movement but also as a major "literacy" movement which encouraged reading among a mass population. Percentage-wise, this population had far fewer college graduates (those who are mostly likely to be supporters of literary journals) than the general American population.

Originally patterned on *Reader's Digest*, *Negro Digest* became *Black World* in 1970, a change indicative of Fuller's view that the magazine ought to be a voice for Black people everywhere on the planet and that what Black people had to say should be of interest to the whole world. The name change also reflected the widespread rejection of the term "Negro" and the adoption of "Black" as the designation of choice for people of African descent. The name change was meant to indicate identification with both the Diaspora and Africa. Again, I must stress that BAM was an activist movement. One major reason that *Black World* moved from "Negro" to "Black" was because of a protest against Johnson Publications led by Haki Madhubuti and others in the Chicago area who insisted that Johnson be more sensitive to the rising tide of "Blackness" and less receptive to advertising and articles which promoted skin bleachers, hair straighteners, and other forms of literal, figurative and literary whitening-up.

When asked in the aforementioned 1971 BBB interview, "How would you describe BLACK WORLD: political, apolitical, cultural, what?" Hoyt Fuller responded:

> BLACK WORLD is not apolitical. BLACK WORLD is not political in the sense that it is directly concerned with political issues. I think that the best way to attack political problems is not always to get directly involved in them. I think that the role of BLACK WORLD, as I see it, is to arouse black people to their identity and to the commonality of problems that they have and to the necessity of acting to confront those problems, to do something about those problems. Now to deal directly or exclusively with political interests I think tends sometimes to be divisive and tends to invite a great deal of controversy in areas where controversy gets in the way of pointing out to people what they should be concerned with, what they should do. In that sense, we're not concerned so much with politics, that is political theories as political theories. We're more concerned

about drawing people's attention to their real situations and the necessity of dealing with them. (Fuller, "*BBB* Interviews" 20)

An unparalleled highlight of each issue of *Negro Digest/ Black World* was Fuller's perceptive column, "Perspectives (Notes on books, writers, artists and the arts)." In addition to providing succinct coverage of major literary developments, it informed readers of new publications and upcoming literary events. Fuller also produced annual poetry, drama, and fiction issues, as well as special issues on diverse subjects such as the Harlem Renaissance, Pan-Africanism and Black people in Brazil. The publishers of the journal also sponsored literary contests and gave out literary awards.

Many artists and scholars, Richard Long among them, credit Fuller with focusing attention on the concept of a Black aesthetic. Long writes:

In 1971, *The Black Aesthetic* edited by Addison Gayle appeared. The term by common consent had been used for a few years before by Hoyt Fuller in the magazine *Negro Digest/Black World*. The sentiment conveyed by the term was that there was a way of perceiving and valuing works of art that was appropriate to black people, particularly when such works derived from their group experience, and that this way of perceiving and valuing was not likely to be shared by non-black persons. A rapidly assumed corollary to this sentiment was that non-blacks ought not or should not be engaged in judging works by blacks. This rapidly assumed corollary is indeed sweeping and crude, but it was heard and echoed and therefore affected the climate in which discussions of the black aesthetic were held. Human discourse moves rapidly from the particular to the general, from concrete to the abstract, and the abstract discussions are frequently not at all congruent with the facts and circumstances to which they apply.

Mr. Fuller's creation of the term was in response to a rather specific set of circumstances. As editor, mentor, and social activist, he was much engaged with a group of younger writers whose products he esteemed, but who seemed to evince negative and unjust evaluations from non-black observers and from many blacks as well. His own judgment was that these evaluations were due to a lack of sympathy, resulting either from perversity or incapacity or perhaps both. This observation led naturally to a call for competent judges and judging. This situation is not at all uncommon in literary history, as the history of the English Romantic movement indicates.

This literary controversy, however, was embroiled in a much larger state of affairs. After all, we are talking about black writers writing mainly about black subjects in the United States, with its continuous historical tension between blacks and non-blacks. We are talking more specifically about a period, the '60s, of great tension occasioned by the transformation of the Civil Rights Movement, after some early apparent triumphs, into the Black Power movement. The Black Aesthetic, then, may be seen in its own historical context as emerging from a complex of events which seems to be far more momentous than judging a poem or a song. This, too, has historical precedent; we need only think of the French Revolution. (Long 5)

Within the pages of *Negro Digest/Black World*, Fuller shepherded the ever-increasing flock of BAM adherents, fellow travelers, interested spectators, and even the "doubting Thomases" by keeping the question of the development of both a Black Aesthetic and the intellectual development of Black critics the dominant concern of his magazine. Although he championed the Black Aesthetic, Fuller published a variety of viewpoints, always insisting on editorial excellence thereby making *Negro Digest/Black World* a first-rate literary publication.

The demise of *Black World* was swift and sudden, but in hindsight not inconsistent with the clash of its political philosophy with the realities of capitalism faced by its owner, John Johnson. When *Black World* published some pro-Palestinian/Anti-Zionist articles, some advertisers threatened to boycott Johnson Publications. *Black World* itself contained no advertisements other than for other Johnson publications and products. Therefore the journal continuously operated in the red. Johnson quickly decided to cut their commercial losses and shut down *Black World* in April of 1976.

Again, Haki Madhubuti, John Henrik Clarke, Val Grey Ward and numerous intellectuals, artists, activists and concerned readers protested the cancellation of *Black World*, yet this time to no avail. The economic guillotine suspended over John Johnson's head was too fatal for Johnson to ignore. The death of *Black World* is almost synonymous with the retreat of BAM. While *Black World* was alive, the measure of Black literature was defined and articulated by a Black publication under the control of a knowledgeable editor who was dedicated to the propagation of Black literature. After *Black World's* demise, there was a return to the status quo standard of the White establishment, through establishment publishing houses and establishment journals and newspapers, defining the standards of Black literature and choosing who were to be considered the leading authors of Black literature. Losing *Black World* was nothing short of losing a hard won literary independence. Over twenty years later, there is no Black-owned and edited journal that is even one tenth as influential and important to the development of Black literature as *Black World*. Moreover, in the entire history of African-American literature, there has been no comparable literary journal, not to mention one that is Black owned and Black edited.

Black Books Bulletin. Another major BAM publication was *Black Books Bulletin (BBB)*, published by the Institute of Positive Education (IPE) in Chicago. The inside front cover of the inaugural issue of *BBB* (Fall 1971) states that their goal was to present:

> Current, annotated listings of the newest writings by and about Black People. No subject area is excluded as long as the material deals with issues that affect Black People wherever they may be. BLACK BOOKS BULLETIN also contains critical reviews of current and future writings by and about Black People as well as social and political commentary by some of the most gifted minds among us. Black Publishing Houses world over will present news and announcements about their work and plans. (Black Books Bulletin 1, No. 1 inside front cover)

The initial masthead listed: Editor Don L. Lee (later known as Haki Madhubuti); Managing Editor Sterling Plumpp; Art Director Calvin Jones, Assistant Editors Johari M. Amini, Carol Easton, Rochelle Cortez, and Falvia Plumpp; and Contributing Editors James A. Emanuel, Sarah Webster Fabio, Hoyt W. Fuller, Addison Gayle Jr., Vincent Harding, Stephen A. Henderson, Catherine Hurst, George E. Kent, David Llorens, Richard A. Long, Dudley Randall, Darwin T. Turner. Staff included Lena Armistead, Virginia Johnson, Cecil Cartwright, Herschel Hunter, and Cleve Washington. This grouping of people represents the cadre of IPE/Third World Press and a number of their major supporters.

Editor Haki Madhubuti identifies the 1970 founding of the

Congress of Afrikan People in Atlanta as the inspiration for the founding of *BBB*. He conceded that, "I co-led a workshop with Larry Neal and the idea for a journal that would focus on our literature and review our books germinated out of the workshop. When we returned to Chicago, we decided to publish *BBB*."

Beginning with its first issue in Fall 1971, *BBB* published consistently for a while before becoming an occasional journal. *Black Books Bulletin* carried interviews with leading Black writers and editors such as Gwendolyn Brooks, Hoyt Fuller, Amiri Baraka, Chancellor Williams and Lerone Bennett, Jr. Additionally, the review section was extensive. Over the years a number of thematic issues were published which focused on a wide range of topics, including Pan-Africanism, food, music, politics, race, and technology.

Significantly, even a casual glance at the table of contents of early issues of *BBB* dispels the dangerously pernicious notion that BAM dismissed any concern for pre-sixties Black literature. For example, the first issue leads off with "Cultural Nationalism: The Black Novelist in America" by Addison Gayle Jr. Gayle's opening sentence reads, "We are familiar with the quest for Black Power in the political, social, and educational spheres of American life; however, few of us are familiar with the long struggle for Black Power or black nationalism in Afro-American letters" (Gayle 4). Gayle then proceeds to trace this development starting in 1859 with Martin Delaney's *Blake or the Huts of America* and taking his investigation through to DuBois, Locke, Hughes, Richard Wright, Ralph Ellison and James Baldwin. Issue number 3 (Spring/ Summer 1972) leads off with "Frank Yerby: Golden Debunker," by noted critic Darwin Turner. Turner is typically insightful. He writes:

> Frank Yerby has written more best-selling novels than any other Afro-American in history, more in fact than most writers regardless of race or nationality. From *The Foxes of Harrow* in 1946 to *The Dahomean* in 1971, he has sold more than twenty million hard-backed copies of twenty-four novels, retailed at a minimum of $3.95 each (the latest is $7.95). All but one of these novels have been book-club selections; most have been reprinted in paper-back editions; and several have been bought for motion pictures.
>   Like Paul Laurence Dunbar, the first nationally popular

Afro-American writer, Yerby immediately was judged as a symbol even before he had been evaluated adequately as a writer. Hugh Gloster boasted that Yerby had demonstrated the Afro-American writer's ability to shake himself free of the shackles of race. Then years later Robert Bone contemptuously dismissed Yerby as a "prince of pulpsters," who would not be considered seriously if he were not Negro.

Turner surmises that:

Yerby's actual merit lies between these extremes. He is considered to have transcended or ignored racial themes more than other Afro-American writers. He published twenty-two novels before he used a black protagonist. Bone accused him of sacrificing his race to "sheckles" paid for potboilers. But what matters is not so much Yerby's use of themes related to racial conflicts as the reactions of readers and critics towards Yerby's racial identity. Yerby is probably the first Afro-American fiction writer in America who is read neither because of his ancestry nor despite it. (Turner 5)

Frank Yerby is precisely the kind of writer that is a polar opposite from what is projected as a BAM prototype, yet *BBB* has a feature article on Yerby. If BAM was so insular, why would an article such as this appear? The trend of historic investigation combined with presenting the most current writers and critics was a hallmark of *BBB* and pointedly flies in the face of those who seek to dismiss BAM literature as a strident, one-note polemic. The Fall 1975 issue of *BBB*, for example, leads off with "The Forms and Focus of Black Literature: 1746–1860" by Hoyt Fuller. That same issue included "Of Flowers and Fire and Flowers," an essay by Gwendolyn Brooks, as well as an interview with internationally acclaimed Nigerian writer Chinua Achebe and an editorial statement on Black writing by Haki Madhubuti. Addressing Black writers, Madhubuti declares:

You are a reflection of your people—regardless of what anybody says. If you are Black, you will always be Black first and a writer second. Understand this. Writing is a vocation, a job, a weapon, a psychological necessity to be used in the best interest of our people, which also means the world's people. Always take yourself and your work seriously although not too seriously. Learn to smile and always listen to our people, especially the elders. Do more listening than talking. Your talking will be done with the pen, pencil or typewriter. Have patience with yourself and with life—it is going to be very, very difficult. I guarantee that. (Lee, "Black Writing" 26)

Along with literally hundreds of other short-lived or one-off literary journals, *Soulbook, Black Dialogue, Journal of Black Poetry, Negro Digest/Black World* and *Black Books Bulletin* created the largest Black reading audience for literature that has ever existed. Moreover, the BAM journals also pushed existing and newly founded literary and scholarly journals (such as *Phylon* and the *CLA Journal*) to be more receptive to BAM writers and viewpoints. This audience in turn produced an unprecedented number of writers, scholars and critics, many of whom would not blossom until the late seventies and early eighties. Even many of BAM's most ardent critics will concede that they were initially influenced by BAM writers, journals and events. Furthermore, through these journals, BAM had a major international impact, especially among African-heritage writers and scholars in the Diaspora and in Africa. Just as the Negritude poets in Paris acknowledged the influence of the Harlem Renaissance, equally if not more so, emerging Black writers throughout the world during the sixties and seventies were heartened and inspired by BAM. Indeed, many non-American born Black writers were published in BAM publications. This is another example of BAM's diversity that is often overlooked.

Yardbird and Other Publications: BAM's Baby. One most interesting and important observation about BAM literary publications is that the West Coast school of BAM publications provided the groundwork and became the hothouse for the development of what is now known as multiculturalism. Early issues of *Journal of Black Poetry* published not only Black, African and Caribbean writers; they also published Asian and South American writers. The first issue included poems from David Diop (West Africa), Aime Cesaire (Martinique) and Jacques Roumain (Haiti). The fifth issue advertised on its front cover, a Special 7 page supplement: Black Poets From Brazil, Cuba, Guyana, Martinique, Haiti: (i.e. Leon Damas, Jacques Roumain, Aime Cesaire, Nicolas Guillen, Jorge de Lima). The seventh issue included Chinese poets Ai Ching and Tien Ch'ien as well as Vietnamese poet and president Ho Chi Minh. Regardless of the popular characterization of BAM as a racially exclusive cabal, BAM documents evidence irrefutable proof of BAM's Third World inclusiveness. The conceptual model was the "Bandung world," which was an initiative of newly independent countries of Asia and Africa to chart a non-aligned and independent course in the 1960s.

Unlike the Chicago-based publications, which focused almost exclusively on racially Black writers, thereby following the Civil Rights/Black Power split on the issue of integration, the California-based publications championed a politicized anti-racialism which gave birth to multiculturalism. Umbra alumni David Henderson and Ishmael Reed moved to California and began publishing America's first self-avowedly multicultural publications. Henderson edited and published a Latin/Soul issue of the Umbra workshop's self-titled journal *Umbra* (*Umbra*'s fifth and final issue) in 1974 when he moved to California. In addition to a retrospective of seventeen poems by Cuban writer Nicolas Guillen and nine poems by Peruvian writer Cesar Vallejo, this issue also features a section of "Guerilla Poetry of South America" compiled by Carmen Alegria and two poems by Chilean writer and Nobel Prize winner Pablo Neruda, along with a host of U.S. based Black and Latino writers. The focus was not simply "color blind" interracialism but instead a prescient confluence of writings from communities of color whose commonality was struggle for self-determination and self-defense more than on behalf of a liberal sense of abstract humanism. The introduction refers to the Mission District of San Francisco as "totally Third World." It states that, "there is a special blend of unity that is displayed in the Mission in everyday life that could just as easily be formalized in terms of social justice." The editors of the Latin/Soul issue of *Umbra* even refer to "youths of the multi-culture." Nearly all of the former Umbra workshop members who continued to write and publish throughout the sixties and seventies were active in independent publishing efforts based on self-determination. So while writers such as Tom Dent, David Henderson, and Ishmael Reed are not normally considered Black nationalist/separatist in their political orientations, the reality of their life work has been to support the development of viable and self-determined Black writing and to emphasize the connection of that writing with a larger body of progressive writing worldwide. Ishmael Reed, along with Al Young and Cecil Brown, founded and edited *Yardbird* in 1972. Along with Reed, Young and Brown, the founding board of directors was: Ortiz Walton, Glenn Myles, Wayne Daniels, Doyle Foreman, Carl Thompson, Waverly Jenkins, and Lois Cunningham for the estate of Ted Cunningham.

Yardbird started as an explicitly BAM publication. In Introduction-I (Al Young and Cecil Brown also provided separate introductions), Ishmael Reed declared that:

> One day, early in 1971, a few of us living in Northern California were comparing notes concerning the treatment of Afro-American artists by callous publishers, editors and others. It was decided that we are treated as commodities; mute dictaphones recording someone's, often, ludicrous political and social notions—slaves, standing on an auction block as our proportions and talents are discussed.
>
> We are at the mercy of those who don't reply within a reasonable time about the status of our manuscripts, or art work (and often lose them), or who are out to lunch or in conference to our messages. Others are bent on proselytizing; they seek to edit our manuscripts until the manuscripts see it their way.
>
> We concluded that the best way we could alter this situation would be to begin a cooperative publishing company run by the victims: writers, painters, sculptors and their sympathizers in the fields of scholarship and business. We felt that our editorial and artistic judgment might be superior to our exploiters'.
>
> The first eleven Afro-American artists, writers, scholars and businessmen we approached, gladly provided us with funds. Our next step was to solicit work from writers and artists we respected. Most of the contributors we called upon, graciously responded with some of their best work.
>
> We call ourselves Yardbird Publishing Company, Incorporated, after Charlie Parker whose music and spirit best captures the international Afro-American genius; its sound and its brilliant prismatic light, flying into the 21st Century.
>
> Yardbird Publishing Company, Incorporated, will publish the finest work by Afro-American artists without regard to ideological or aesthetic affiliation. During the past decade, many of our best writers and artists received little or no recognition because they didn't belong to the right "club house" or didn't respond like sheep when some abstract, nebulous symbol was invoked. (Reed, "Introduction I" xix)

Although Reed and company had significant differences with many BAM writers, *Yardbird* was obviously a product of BAM. Indeed, the Chester Himes's preface to the initial issue of *Yardbird* reads like a BAM manifesto. He writes:

> YARDBIRD READER has thoroughly convinced me that we American blacks are the most inventive, creative and original people in the history of the world. We are a new force in the world's culture. We are a major influence in the world's civilization. and not least of all we are a guiding beacon in America's literature of tomorrow.
>
> We are the most imitated people in the western world. Gentiles imitate us, Jews imitate us, black Africans imitate us, Arab Africans imitate us, even the intellectuals and the escapists imitate us. Imitate our color, our speech, our hair, our dress, our gestures, our food, our poverty, our emotions, our sensations, our scatology, our sexology, and most of all our thoughts. Some are fascinated, some alarmed, some infuriated, some afraid. Our thoughts are like bullets or kisses; other races do not know whether we are assassins or lovers.
>
> We are a new people. Our thoughts influence the world. We are invisible leaders. We are the most exciting, the most advanced, the most complex, the most intelligent people who have ever lived.
>
> Inadvertently the institution of slavery created us into this super-race—we did not ask for it—and white Americans have been adding bits and pieces ever since our slave forefathers were freed. (Thank you, boss.)

Himes continues:

> We were made into a super-race by torture, death, rape, punishment—you name it, we've had it—by all of the harsh and subtle impacts of a crushing injustice. Fear taught us every device for survival; every nuance, speech, tone, expression, action and reaction to keep alive. Fear taught us how to read the white man's mind, how to think faster, how to anticipate all of his dangerous intentions and threatening actions. Why shouldn't we be more intelligent, inventive, creative, intuitive? We had to keep alive without friends or protectors, without wealth, arms or armor. We had to do it with our wit, our skin, our determination. In some instances we had to be holier than the white man's God, in others more depraved than the white man's lusts.
>
> YARDBIRD READER will give the uninformed a clue to why we have survived and excelled. Right on! YARDBIRD READER! (Himes xvii)

However, by the fifth issue, published in 1976, *Yardbird* was on the attack against a strictly "Black" orientation. That issue contained a scathing attack on *Black World* in which Amiri Baraka uses Marxist rhetoric to condemn Hoyt Fuller and the publication over which he presided:

> Black World, then, is simply the petit bourgeoisie at work, defending as usual, objectively, a bourgeoisie, which is classically their gig, whenst before it was defending it as integration against Black stuff, but now that "Black Stuff" can be filled with establishment values, they willst style theyseffs "nats," when all the time they never never dug no Black peepahs! Expose they sorry ass we say! (Baraka, "How Black Is *Black World*?" 17)

While some viewed the attack as scandalous, what was really happening was the birth of multiculturalism as a literary ideological construct which adamantly rejected "Black separatism" and what would later be known as "racial essentialism." I mark this as the birth of multiculturalism because this is the first major documented attempt to highlight the so-called minority cultures of America in a collective, or "rainbow," context. As with most births, it was bloody. In his introduction to volume 5, Reed is very clear when he writes:

> "Qualified" native missionaries unmindful of booby traps inherent in racist language, have begun to describe Yardbird's projects as "integrationist"; we reject this description of our efforts.
>
> How anybody can read *Yardbird* and come away with the impression that we believe that the culture of one people is superior to those of all others, and that everybody ought to be like them is a mystery to us.
>
> *Yardbird* reflects cultural exchange! A fact of everyday ordinary existence in the complex civilization in which we live. We feel that there are enough Black Worlds, Yellow Worlds, Red Worlds, Brown Worlds, and White Worlds for people who crave that.

Reed continues:

> There is room for all writing: feminist, third world, experimental, you name it, and we'll continue to provide space for it.
>
> *Yardbird* feels that the super-race phase of American art

whether advocated by yellows, blacks, browns or whites, men or women, is through! and our success proves that there is a growing readership which shares this point-of-view, a readership not satisfied with periodicals, magazines, reviews in which publishers, editors and contributors are of the same region, culture, or race. (Reed, "Integration or Cultural Exchange" 3)

Differences on the "race question" notwithstanding, *Yardbird* and the multicultural movement were a direct outgrowth of BAM, and demonstrate the influence that BAM had on the literary life of America, even within "multiculturalism," a movement which on first glance might seem to be diametrically opposed to BAM.

BAM Presses. While there were others, such as Naomi Long Madgett's Lotus Press in Detroit, Drum and Spear Press in Washington, D.C., Emerson Hall and Third Press both in New York, the two major BAM presses were Dudley Randall's Broadside Press in Detroit and Don L.Lee/Haki Madhubuti's Third World Press in Chicago. Again, it is significant to note that the two leading BAM publishers were not located in the northeast.

From a literary standpoint, Broadside Press, which concentrated almost exclusively on poetry, was the most important of the two major BAM presses. For a brief period, Broadside produced a literary criticism series that featured scholars such as Houston Baker and Addison Gayle, Jr. Founded in 1965, Broadside published over 400 poets, over 100 books or recordings, and was responsible for elevating established poets, such as Gwendolyn Brooks, Sterling Brown, and Margaret Walker. Broadside Press also introduced emerging poets, such as Nikki Giovanni, Etheridge Knight, Don L. Lee/Haki Madhubuti and Sonia Sanchez, who would all go on to become major BAM voices. There was an album, *Rappin' and Readin'*, by Don L. Lee and tapes (both cassette and reel) of poets James Emanuel, Nikki Giovanni, Lance Jeffers, Stephany Hodges, Etheridge Knight, Nancy Arnez and Beatrice Murphy, Sonia Sanchez, Jon Eckles, Marvin X, Don L. Lee, Keoropetse Kgositsile, Margaret Walker and Margaret Danner.

Although Dudley Randall was older than the young poets of the BAM generation and had been educated as a librarian as well as steeped in "traditional" or "classic" English poetry, he was an enthusiastic BAM supporter and also the most significant poetry editor in terms of mentoring emerging poets. He was both a valuable link to older traditions in literature and was a booster of the new iconoclastic BAM literature which sought to be an alternative to that which had come before. Without qualification, Broadside Press was the most important proponent of BAM poetry. In 1976, strapped by economic restrictions and a severely overworked/overwhelmed three person staff, Broadside Press went into serious decline. Broadside was later sold to Don and Hilda Vest who continue to operate the press, mainly reprinting and selling a backlist of selected titles. The rise and decline of Broadside is concurrent with BAM's life cycle.

Third World Press, founded in late 1967 by Haki Madhubuti (at that point still known as Don L. Lee), focused more on prose and political commentary, in addition to poetry from a broad range of emerging and established BAM writers such as Johari Amini, Amiri Baraka, Gwendolyn Brooks, Mari Evans, Keoropetse Kgositsile, Sterling Plumpp, Carolyn Rodgers, Askia M. Toure, and in later years Haki Madhubuti himself. Third World Press (initially through its affiliate organization, the Institute for Positive Education) also published the aforementioned *Black Books Bulletin*, a literary journal that focused on criticism and reviews.

BAM Anthologies. While a number of poets (e.g. Amiri Baraka, Etheridge Knight, Nikki Giovanni, Haki Madhubuti and Sonia Sanchez), playwrights (e.g. Ed Bullins and Ron Milner), and spoken word artists (e.g. The Last Poets and Gil Scott-Heron) are indelibly associated with BAM, one gets a much stronger and much more accurate impression of BAM literature by reading specific anthologies. Although there are a number of anthologies which focus on BAM, I have selected eight books which I believe offer a basic foundation for appreciating BAM literature.

Black Fire (1968), edited by Baraka and Neal, is an indispensable and massive collection of essays, poetry, fiction, and drama featuring the first wave of BAM writers and thinkers. Because of its impressive breath, *Black Fire* stands as a definitive BAM anthology.

For Malcolm: Poems On The Life And The Death Of Malcolm X (1969), edited by Dudley Randall and Margaret G. Burroughs, demonstrates the political thrust of BAM and the specific influence of Malcolm X. There is no comparable anthology in American poetry which focuses on a political figure as a poetic inspiration.

The Black Woman (1970), edited by the late Toni Cade Bambara, is the first major Black feminist anthology and features work by Jean Bond, Nikki Giovanni, Abbey Lincoln, Audre Lorde, Paule Marshall, Gwen Patton, Pat Robinson, Alice Walker, Shirley Williams, and others.

The Black Aesthetic (1971), edited by Addison Gayle, is significant because it both articulates and contextualizes BAM theory. Divided into sections on theory, music, fiction, poetry, and drama, Gayle's seminal anthology features a broad array of writers who are regarded as the chief BAM theorists/ practitioners. *The Black Aesthetic* also includes essays from Harlem Renaissance-era writers Alain Locke, Langston Hughes, and J. A. Rogers, as well as essays from W.E.B. DuBois and Richard Wright. Rather than an isolated Black Power-era phenomenon, Gayle proposed that BAM was a continuation of a movement for artistic self-determination which had deep historical roots. The BAM contemporaries and advocates included Hoyt Fuller, Larry Neal, Julian Mayfield, Ron [Maulana] Karenga, John O'Neal, Darwin T. Turner, Jimmy Stewart, Ron Welburn, Leslie Rout, Ortiz Walton, Sarah Webster Fabio, James A. Emanuel, Dudley Randall, Don L. Lee, W. Keorapetse Kgositsile, Loften Mitchell, Ronald Milner, Clayton Riley, Carolyn Gerald, John Oliver Killens, Adam David Miller, Ishmael Reed, and editor Addison Gayle. Taken collectively, their observations, opinions, theses, and analyses are indispensable to understanding the intellectual underpinnings of BAM.

Dudley Randall's *The Black Poets* (1971) is perhaps the mostly widely used anthology in high schools and university classrooms. With 132 of its 333 pages devoted to Black poetry of the sixties, this anthology offers a strong introduction to BAM poets, many of whom were just beginning to publish widely. Randall is fundamentally correct in asserting, as he does in the Introduction, that "the claim of *The Black Poets* to being at least a partially definitive anthology is that it presents the full range of black American poetry, from the slave songs to the present day."

Stephen Henderson's anthology *Understanding the New Black Poetry* (1972) is important not solely because of the poets included but also because of the insightful and unparalleled sixty-seven-page overview by Henderson. This is the most thorough exposition of the new Black poetic aesthetic. Insights and lines of thought now taken for granted were first articulated in a critical and formal context by Stephen Henderson who proposed a totally innovative Black poetics, a poetics reading which very precisely lived up to the anthology's title.

New Black Voices (1972) edited by Abraham Chapman (a White professor who also edited the popular *Black Voices* anthology) is significant because its focus is specifically on the emerging voices in addition to new work by established voices active in BAM. Unlike most anthologies which overlook the South, *New Black Voices* is geographically representative and includes lively pro and con articles side by side debating aesthetic and political theory.

The eighth book, *Drumvoices: The Mission of Afro-American Poetry: A Critical History* (1976), is actually not an anthology but rather a detailed survey by writer and chronicler Eugene B. Redmond. Given the magnitude (1746–1970s) of the survey, this surprisingly thoroughly researched book has been unjustly neglected. Although some of his opinions are controversial (note that in BAM, controversy was "normal"), Redmond's era-by-era and city-by-city cataloguing of literary collectives as well as individual writers offers an invaluable service in helping the reader appreciate BAM's national reach. Because the spirit of BAM was toward collectives rather than the elevation of one or two leaders, these eight books present a truer picture of both the impact and the breadth of BAM.

Fortunately, *Black Scholar* and *Negro Digest/Black World* are widely available on microfilm and at major public and college libraries. *Journal of Black Poetry* is more difficult to find but is available. *Black Fire, For Malcolm, The Black Woman, The Black Aesthetic, The Black Poets, Understanding the New Black Poetry, New Black Voices,* and *Drumvoices* are also available in libraries. Considered as a whole, these journals and books published well over a thousand Black writers during the

1965–75 BAM decade. In contradistinction to establishment literary circles, giving approval to only a handful of Black writers, BAM celebrated hundreds of Black writers and offered unprecedented publishing opportunities to both established and emerging Black writers.

Ishmael Reed believes BAM was one moment of originality. He states:

> You look at *Black Fire*, even though some of that stuff in there may not be well crafted, it's got energy. It's got heart. It's got fire in the belly. American literature has lost that. You see that in some of the Yiddish poetry from the turn of the century. You see some of that in the feminist poetry that is being written today; people have something to say instead of all this dull literary formalism. Now we're back to African American writers being lauded in proportion to how they imitate some white master. We're back in the fifties. (Reed, "Interview")

Carolyn Fowler's work appears under the names "Carolyn Gerald," "Carolyn F. Gerald," and "Carolyn Fowler"; all three are the same person.

CHAPTER 6
BLACK ARTS MOVEMENT RECORDINGS

The Sound of Black Poetry. With the exception of the Beat movement, the Black Arts Movement's performance orientation set it apart from all other American literary movements that came before it. BAM's emphasis on live performance makes it impossible to gain a full understanding of the movement simply by reading a few books. Attempting to confirm BAM'S influence solely by citing establishment-oriented, text documentation minimizes the national and international reach of BAM. The literary establishment more often ignored rather than critiqued BAM. In the 1990s, the availability of primary BAM materials and critical responses to the literary material became limited. The presentation power, the effect on the audience, and the diversity of BAM artistic expressions can only be fully appreciated through its recordings.

There has been little systematic propagation, informed criticism and scholarly investigation of BAM. Compounding this problem of inadequate criticism is the fact that BAM literary work consciously sought to directly incorporate musical influences, in terms of stylistic developments and in terms of collaborations. Again, Baraka is forthright in asserting the primacy of music in BAM poetry. He writes:

> Art Williams was running the Cellar just down the street from where I lived. He brought New York musicians in on the weekends. There were some very good sets. He also had poetry readings down there and I even read there myself one evening with a poet, Ronald Stone, who later changed his name to Yusef Rahman. Yusef's poetry was a revelation to me. He was like Bird in his approach to the poetry, seeming to scat and spit rapid-fire lines of eighth notes at top speed. It was definitely speech musicked. This was my first exposure to his work and I was mightily impressed. It confirmed some of the things I had learned in the first surge of the Black Arts movement, how different the black poetry was that emerged in that rush of new blackness that came upon us then.

Poets like Larry Neal and Askia Toure were, in my mind, masters of the new black poetry. Larry coming out of straight-out bebop rhythms, but actually a little newer than bop, a faster-moving syncopation. Askia had the song-like cast to his words, as if the poetry actually was meant to be sung. I heard him once up at the Baby Grand when we first got into Harlem and that singing sound influenced what I was to do with poetry from then on. To me, Larry and Askia were the state of the art, where it was, at that moment. Yusef was good, in some ways on a par with Larry and Askia, but Larry's syncopation was a little more elegant. Yusef was dead on a Charlie Parker bebop, straight ahead, blue wings flapping up a hurricane of funk. But Yusef was a definite new measure in the poetry, an innovative style that had to be absorbed by any who wanted to reflect where the word was ca. 1966.

The fact of music was the black poet's basis for creation. And those of us in the BAM were drenched in black music and wanted our poetry to *be* black music. Not only that, we wanted that poetry to be armed with the spirit of black revolution. An art that could not commit itself to black revolution was not relevant to us. And if the poet that created such art was colored we mocked him and his inspiration as brainwashed artifacts to please our beast oppressors!

Another poet I heard during this period had a great influence on me, Amus Mor (once David Moore) from Chicago. I heard him read his masterwork, "We Are the Hip Men." The way Amus put the music directly into the poem, scatting and being a hip dude walking down the street letting the sounds flow out of his mouth—putting all that into the poetry—really turned me on. We wanted to bring black life into the poem directly. Its rhythms, its language, its history and struggle. It was meant to be a poetry we copped from the people and gave them right back, open and direct and moving. Reading in the vacant lots and on the sidewalks and playgrounds of Harlem that summer of '65 had opened many of us all the way up. We had been able to reach deeper into ourselves than ever before. "We had been able to touch sometimes that dark brown feeling that is always connected with black and blues." (Baraka, *The Autobiography*, 236–37).

Essentially, "the new Black poetry" was indeed both. "New" in that it used Black music as a model rather than any English literary tradition, "Black" in that a measure of its worth included a political assessment of the poem's content vis-a-vis the general goals of Black Power, "self-determination, self-defense and self-respect."

In his introduction to *The Black Aesthetic*, critic Addison Gayle proposes a fundamental distinction between BAM aesthetics and Western-oriented aesthetics. He writes:

> A critical methodology has no relevance to the black community unless it aids men in becoming better than they are. Such an element has been sorely lacking in the critical canons handed down from the academies by the Aristotelian Critics, the Practical Critics, the Formalistic Critics, and the New Critics. Each has this in common: it aims to evaluate the work of art in terms of *its* beauty and not in terms of the transformation from ugliness to beauty that the work of art demands from its audience.
>
> The question for the black critic today is not how beautiful is a melody, a play, a poem, or a novel, but how much more beautiful has the poem, melody, play, or novel made the life of a single black man? How far has the work gone in transforming an American Negro into an African-American or black man? The Black Aesthetic, then, as conceived by this writer, is a corrective—a means of helping black people out of the polluted mainstream of Americanism, and offering logical, reasoned arguments as to why he should not desire to join the ranks of a Norman Mailer or a William Styron. To be an American writer is to be an American, and, for black people, there should no longer be honor attached to either position. (Gayle, "Introduction," xxiii)

The Black Aesthetic proposed change rather than the maintenance of tradition (i.e. the status quo) as its ideological sine qua non. Moreover, Black music was regarded as the artistic vanguard of the Black arts. Needless to say, many traditional mainstream critics were unfamiliar with "the music" and the Black vernacular of the street, as well as emotionally and rationally opposed to then current Black Power tenets (especially "separatism" and "violence"). Such critics predictably were not only affronted by militant "Blackness," they also failed to find much "poetry" in the "new Black poetry." But the poets understood and began not only to write books but also, and in some senses, more importantly, to release records which served to illustrate in practice what the Black Aesthetic proposed in theory.

New Black Poetry Recordings. On November 26, 1964, Amiri Baraka recorded a scathing poem, "Black Dada Nihilismus," with The New York Art Quartet, an avant-garde ensemble consisting of Roswell Rudd on trombone, John Tchicai on alto sax, Lewis Worrell on bass and Milford Graves on percussion. After his move back to "NewArk" (which is how Baraka spelled the name of his hometown) in 1966, Baraka recorded *Soul and Madness* on his own Jihad label, which featured Baraka with Yusef Iman and the Jihad singers featuring Freddie Johnson. This recording documents Baraka's early effort to mix blues, R&B, and modern jazz with his poetry. In 1967 Baraka recorded the famous poem, "Black Art," on a Jihad album called *Sonny's Time Now*, featuring Sonny Murray on drums, Albert Ayler on sax, Don Cherry on trumpet, with Henry Grimes and Lewis Worrell on bass.

Baraka was not the only poet to record. Chief among the others are Nikki Giovanni and Haki Madhubuti. Recorded with the backing of gospel music, Giovanni's three albums (*Like a Ripple On a Pond*, 1972; *Truth Is On It's Way*, 1973; and *The Way I Feel*, 1975) were very popular. Madhubuti had a solo album on Broadside Press's label, *Rappin' and Readin'* (1970). Later, he recorded two albums, *Rise Vision Comin* (1976) and *Medasi* (1984), which each sold over 15,000 copies. On those albums Madhubuti was joined by the Nationhouse Ensemble of Washington, D.C., led by Agyei Akoto. The albums were jointly produced by the Institute of Positive Education (Chicago) and Nationhouse Positive Action Center (D.C.), two independent Black educational institutions.

One of the most significant voices in the recording of Black poetry is Jayne Cortez, one of the four major writers who also recorded and originated out of sixties Watts/Los Angeles. The other three are: Stanley Crouch, who recorded *Ain't No Ambulances for No Niggers Tonight*; Quincy Troupe, who did not release a solo recording until the 1990s; and Wanda Coleman, who has recorded extensively in the 1990s. Also of note from the BAM era Los Angeles scene were the recordings *On The Streets in Watts* (1969), by Black Voices (Anthony Hamilton, Ed Bereal, Emmery Lee Joseph Evans, Jr. and Odie Hawkins), and *Rappin' Black in a White World* (1971), by the Watts Prophets (Dee Dee MaNail, Anthony Hamilton, Richard Dedeaux and Otis O'Solomon). Both of these groups were in the vein of the Last Poets.

Jayne Cortez, however, is one of the most important examples of a Black poet who consciously decided to actively pursue the "vocal" side of Black poetry. Although she does have books, Cortez is more widely celebrated and known as a performance poet. She recorded a duet with bassist Richard Davis on the LP *Celebrations and Solitudes* (Strata-East, 1974). Recorded on July 18, 1974, in White Plains, New York the majority of the poems focus on music and musicians or on political events (particularly the urban rebellions) or political figures (e.g. Kwame Nkrumah, Patrice Lumumba, Malcolm X, Amilcar Cabral). Although her style is very different from many others, Cortez's poetry specifically takes up the aesthetic and political challenges of BAM literature, especially in her innovative use of Black, folk-poetic techniques such as signifying ("name calling"), listing, and the vernacular. Cortez went on to form her own band, the Firespitters, which included Denardo Coleman, her son (with Ornette Coleman). Beginning in the late seventies Cortez recorded extensively with her band.

Another popular recording in the nationalist communities was the youth oriented *The Black Fairy*, a collaboration between two Chicago-based artists, writer Useni Eugene Perkins and saxophonist Chico Freeman. This album was broadly used by the independent Black schools that had sprung up in major cities across America.

There were numerous other recordings that featured poets or musicians performing poetry with their music. For example there was the innovative mix of electronic music, modern jazz and poetry called *Sing Me a Song of Songmy* (Atlantic Records, 1971), which was billed on the cover as "a fantasy for electromagnetic tape." It featured Freddie Hubbard and his quintet, with reciters, chorus, string orchestra, hammond organ, synthesized and processed sounds, composed and realized by Ilhan Mimaroglu. The poetry on this 1971 recording, including "Black Soldier" recited by Hubbard, was written by Turkish poet Fazil Husnu Daglarca. There were also excerpts from a wide variety of writers, including a poem by Che Guevara. Also of interest is the David Henderson recording "Science Fiction" with Ornette Coleman, which appears on the album *Science Fiction* (Columbia Records).

Finally, there is a very important, albeit hard to find, recording of James Baldwin reading his poetry with musical accompaniment. A *Lover's Question* (Crepuscule Records/ Austria), recorded in March of 1986, is not from the BAM period but it reflects the BAM influence and is notable because it includes "new music" musicians such as saxophonists Steve Coleman and Byard Lancaster along with Bob Stewart on tuba, Jimmy Owens on trumpet and other musicians who have been associated with innovation in both the aesthetics and the business of music. Baldwin's inclusion in this chapter notes the far-reaching effect of BAM.

The merger of Black poetry and Black music was not new—Hughes had actually been doing this in the twenties— nevertheless BAM was the first literary movement to foreground and popularize the effort to combine poetry and music. The recorded precursor of all of this was the collaboration of Langston Hughes with Charles Mingus on a historic recording called *The Weary Blues* (Verve), which was recorded in March of 1958.

Black Spirits/Nationtime. The years 1970 to 1974 are the high-water mark of many BAM activities. To get the best understanding of the poetry with music development, one should check out two major BAM poetry recordings, both produced by Woodie King on Black Forum Records, a division of Motown Records. For the poetry, *Black Spirits*, an anthology, and *It's Nation Time*, billed as "African Visionary Music" by Imamu Amiri Baraka, represent the pinnacle of what many poets were trying to do at that time.

Black Spirits, recorded live at the Apollo Theatre in Harlem in 1972, featured a virtual who's who of BAM poets. Hosted by Baraka, the lineup was Kali (the pre-teen daughter of Verta Mae Grovernor), Johari Amini, Clarence Major, David Henderson, Norman Jordan, Askia Muhammad Toure, the Original Last Poets (Gylan Kain, David Nelson, Filipe Luciano), Stanely Crouch, Jackie Earley, Amus Mor, and Larry Neal, all of whom are also included in the anthology *Black Spirits* (Random House, 1972). Listening to the musical and stylistic range of this poetry, as well as hearing the interaction of the poets with the audience, is instructive. The recording begins with African drumming and an invocation/introduction by Baraka. Afterwards, all of the music is in the reference, voices, and presentations of the various poets. The range of styles is extraordinary, ranging from the R&B inflections of David Henderson to the urban-toasts influenced Stanely Crouch; from the modern jazz inflections of Amus Moore to the reflective, Modern Jazz Quartet (MJQ)-like lyricism of Clarence Major; from the funky soul music scats of the Original Last Poets to a Sun Ra influenced, avant-gardish recitation by Baraka. A full appreciation of this poetry is impossible without a familiarity with Black music. This is a rare and important BAM document whose existence has gone largely unacknowledged in critical literary circles.

It's Nation Time, recorded in 1972, is better known but equally rare. Here Baraka pulled all of the tendencies together. He collaborated with the Spirit House Movers (Kaimu Mchochezi, Jeledi Katibu, Saidi Onaje, Muminina Sanamu, Muminina Furaha, Malaika Jaribu, Malaika Johari, Malaika Ibura, Malaika Hiba, Ndada Itabari), with New Music Group (Gary Bartz, alto sax; Lonnie Liston Smith, piano; Reggie Workman, bass; Herbie Lewis, bass; and Idris Muhammad, drums), an R&B group, Matchmakers 1619 (James Wheeler, alto sax; Phil Eley, tenor sax, along with Jerome McGoggle on trumpet; Khalid Ablal Shahid on electric paino; Ogden Lee Jr. on lead guitar; Lloyd Porter on drums; Gwendolyn Guthrie on vocals); and finally a group of African drummers (Akbar Bey and Pat Carrow on conga; Charles Jones on conga and shakari; Joe Armstrong on conga and cow bell). This recording demonstrated the full range of Baraka's poetics, including the avant-poetics of "Peace in Place," which is difficult, if not impossible, to appreciate on the page without having heard it performed.

Though it is criminal to think that these two recordings are nearly impossible to find, the mere fact that they got produced and released on Motown is inspirational. Just their existence on Motown, an overtly commercially-oriented label, demonstrates the profound influence that BAM had during the late sixties and early seventies in the Black community. Conversely, the disappearance of these recordings also demonstrates how thorough the effort to eradicate BAM has been. Black Spirits, for example, contains the only commercially available recording of Larry Neal and Amus Mor reading their poetry, and the fact that it is now unavailable to those interested in learning more about BAM is discouraging.

Even though BAM writers used (and often extended) all existing literary forms, the most effective and most influential revolution took place in poetry and drama. For example, the Last Poets introduced a form of chant poetry whose closest analog in English is Trinidadian "kaiso" or calypso. Gil Scott-Heron, after beginning as a Last Poets sound-alike, moved on to politicize the Top 40 popular/R&B song form by shifting the emphasis from romantic pursuits to political concerns. Although generally overlooked by the establishment and hardly ever mentioned by literary critics, both the Last Poets and Gil Scott-Heron would significantly influence subsequent generations, often to a much larger degree than many of the better-known "writers."

A major reason that the Last Poets and Gil Scott-Heron have been neglected by the establishment is because their work is steeped in Black Power politics and is unapologetically located within an oral tradition. Indeed, the recordings literally became books. The "texts" of the poems were printed on the album sleeves, which was only to aid in appreciating the "sounding" of the poetry. In fact, other than on the sleeves of their records, the Last Poets did not publish their poetry in traditional book form during the BAM era. Likewise, although Scott-Heron published two novels, *The Nigger Factory* and *The Vulture*, during the BAM era, the majority of his poetry was published on the sleeves of his recordings. The bulk of their work has gone unexamined even though numerous rappers give respect and praise to both the Last Poets and Gil Scott-Heron. Their music still appears on tracks like Kanye West's sampling of Gil Scott-Heron's "My Way Home," or the collaboration between the Last Poets and rapper Common. However, the combination of anti-establishment politics and grounding in an oral tradition of poetry (unpublished in book form) meant that these writers were not taken seriously by literary critics.

The Last Poets. The Last Poets had a split in the ranks early in their development. Founded on May 19, 1968 at a Malcolm X commemoration in Mount Morris Park in New York City, the initial Last Poets were Gylan Kain, David Nelson and Abiodun

Oyewole. A disagreement between Kain and Oyewole led to a split and the development of two different groups, both going by the name "The Last Poets." The split turned violent when Kain was physically attacked and beaten, but refused to agree to retaliatory violence directed at his former associates. BAM's immaturity was manifested in the recurring internal conflicts that dampened and sometimes disrupted forward motion.

"The Original Last Poets" are featured in *Right On*, a 1970 recording and film of the same name. The group consisted of Gylan Kain, Felipe Luciano and David Nelson. Their work was both politically and aesthetically challenging and complex, albeit uproarishly entertaining and cleverly captivating in their use of the vernacular of the times. The 1969 film *Right On*, produced by Herbert Danska and Woodie King, Jr., and directed by Herbert Danska, won Choice of Director Award at the 1970 Cannes Film Festival and the International Critics Prize at the 1970 Mannheim Festival. Unfortunately, the Original Last Poets only cut one record, the film's soundtrack.

The group more popularly known as "The Last Poets" consisted of poets Umar Bin Hassan, Abiodun Oyewole and Alafia Pudim (later Julaludin Mansur Nuriddin), plus percussionist Nilaja. Their first two recordings, *The Last Poets* (Douglas 3, 1970) and *This is Madness* (Douglas 7, 1971) catapulted them to the top ranks of what would now be called "performance poets." Although the Last Poets would again split into two factions, they continued to perform and record in the nineties. The effort to maintain unity, a political direction, and have a successful career in the entertainment industry is difficult if not impossible. Indeed, the industry has a knack for exploiting differences and breaking groups apart in order to package one individual superstar. The history of the Last Poets is replete with example after example of infighting and external exploitation.

The manager of "The Last Poets" sued the "Original Last Poets" and was able to win an injunction against them using the name "Last Poets." This legal action effectively halted any possibility of reconciliation and led to the breakup of one of the most innovative Black poetry ensembles ever recorded. Rather than hide or ignore these realities, we should learn from them so that in the future we will not be as prone to manipulation and co-option as a result of internal shortcomings. In any case, all of the early Last Poets and Original Last Poets recordings are available and not too difficult to locate.

Gil Scott-Heron. Gil Scott-Heron was even more influential than the Last Poets, largely because he was able to craft his poetic messages into a more popular musical style and consequently received wide airplay. He has proven to be an enduring influence on both the music and performance poetry scene. Some of his songs/poems, especially "The Revolution Will Not Be Televised," became not only hits but were also covered by other artists. Additionally, he wrote a series of "blues raps" which became signature selections: "H2Ogate Blues" (referring to the Watergate Hotel break-ins which eventually led to the resignation of President Nixon) and "Bicentennial Blues" were the two most popular. In the liner notes to his 1978 retrospective album *The Mind of Gil Scott-Heron*, subtitled "A Collection of Poetry and Music," Scott-Heron wrote:

> I am frequently asked which is my preference—music or poetry and prose writing. Different ideas call for different vehicles and the artist who limits himself or herself to one medium has lost a valuable opportunity for further growth. I generally use as my response and reference point to these questions the examples of Paul Robeson and Langston Hughes, men who used a range of artistic media—song, poetry, acting and oration—to convey in a variety of ways, contemporary social ideas and political circumstance. These ideas may have been common to most people on an individual level, but when placed in a creative context by the artist they dramatize, politicize and promote a group level of conscience and awareness.
>
> When I sat down to coordinate this introduction for an album and a book I was once again, as a recording artist and writer, straddling an artistic fence. I have tried to pursue the combined experiences of music, word rhythms and social ideas in all my work. (Scott-Heron, "Introduction")

Until recently there had been no book-length, critical treatment of either the Last Poets or Gil Scott-Heron, although their gigantic influence on the popularization of poetry and inception of hip-hop is obvious. I read this "silence" not simply as oversight and omission, but as systemically enforced narrowing and censoring by academia of what is considered "serious" poetry.

On the other hand, I understand that untangling the web of internal conflicts is no easy task. Consistent with the issues faced by BAM in general, the infighting of the Last Poets makes presenting an inclusive and accurate history exceptionally difficult. Thus, *The Last Poets: On a Mission* (1996), subtitled "Selected Poems and a History of The Last Poets," by Abiodun Oyewole and Umar Bin Hassan with Kim Green, actually offers an apology by Kim Green that explains why the "history" is not included. Essentially, when Green attempted to honestly research and write the history of the Last Poets, what she unearthed was an ongoing and seemingly irreconcilable blood feud and cover-up: the poets weren't talking to each other and both Oyewole and Hassan actively resisted what they viewed as "negative" commentary. Green decided to:

> ...be brutally honest. Paint the picture. Break it down. I hoped that when the Poets read it in their own private moments, they'd see their own chaos and want to rectify it. I do believe in the power of words.
>
> *The original introduction was political. It was harsh, I admit, but I was passionate about the implications of this. I was angry at what happened to these seven talented men who had, since their beginning, fought in the street, stolen from each other, turned on each other, and worse. I was angry that that always happens when success gets into the mix. Seemingly, a lot more often to Black people. (Green xxv)*

After an intense confrontation about the content of the history section, Green sums up the difficulty of writing the history:

> After the argument I had lost my will to fight for what I believed, which is what happened to the collective Last Poets,
>
> *This group is an example of an important phenomenon in America that makes our leaders fall beneath the pressure of getting theirs in a country that is so insincere in its giving to people of color. The Last Poets show that we all collectively and individually must rise up. (Green xxvii)*

The task of writing our history is complex and often frustrating. The problems that Green had in trying to do an honest history of the Last Poets partially illustrates the problems one encounters when writing about BAM in general. First, the surviving participants are sometimes bitter and often still harbor grudges and feuds that grew out of conflicts in the past, conflicts that sometimes involved unethical interpersonal behavior and thus are conflicts which are not easily forgiven nor forgotten. Second, survivors are often distrustful of scholars and researchers, especially if the interviewers and writers are unknown to the subjects being examined. Third, there is no easy way to write about a difficult period within which reversals, conversions, conflicts and internal contradictions were an ineradicable part of the process of making history. Fourth, in dealing with "cultural nationalists," this research cannot adequately be done by non-Blacks or by assimilated Blacks because some key BAM participants still consider them either the enemy or traitors and refuse to talk to them. These realties, as well as restraints such as limited research resources, all contribute to the absence of critical work. Regardless of the obstacles, as the non-history of the Last Poets demonstrates, there is a critical vacuum of research and informed criticism that cries out to be filled.

Furthermore, I believe there is another factor contributing to the ignoring and undermining of the importance of BAM. Most establishment-oriented critics are unequipped emotionally and aesthetically to analyze the "what, how, and why" of the type of poetry developed by the Last Poets and Gil Scott-Heron. One could read the majority of academic assessments of BAM and these artists; yet these artists influenced thousands to pick up the pen and write. In this regard, BAM encouraged people to write out of an alternative tradition, a tradition which valued street language and social engagement over technical expertise and traditional poetic forms.

Before BAM, American poetry and most African American poetry had been viewed as a highly intellectual and primarily textual art form which had a long tradition in classical Euro-centered poetry. BAM poetry was different; it was musically inspired and drew on the vernacular of the day. BAM took poetry off the page and emphasized performance that in turn created Black, community-based audiences for poetry and drama. Although James Weldon Johnson, Langston Hughes and Sterling Brown were clearly predecessors in this regard, by the fifties most poets were "writing" in a highly educated and formal style. BAM reintroduced and popularized the performance of poetry. By the early seventies America's Black community closely resembled the traditional African homeland described by ex-slave Olaudah Equaino, or Gustavus Vassa the African, in 1789 when he wrote of his native society that "we are almost a nation of dancers, musicians and poets."

CHAPTER 7
BLACK THEATRE

FOLKLORIC TROUPE. The two hallmarks of Black Arts Movement activity were (1) the proliferation of Black poetry—both performance and text—and (2) the development of Black theatre groups. BAM poetry and theatre had close ties to community organizations and issues. Black theatres served as the focus of artistic activities which included the performance of poetry, dance and music in addition to presenting both formal or traditional, Western-oriented drama and newly developed Black ritual drama. The traditional dramas were usually realistic, slice-of-life presentations that presumed the audience as onlooker. Black ritual drama, on the other hand, was usually non-linear, music and dance-based performance that included the audience as participant in the presentation. Black theaters were also venues for community meetings, lectures, study groups and film screenings.

Marc Primus' Afro-American Folkloric Troupe, founded in San Francisco in 1962, was the precursor to BAM developments in Black theatre and in dramatized presentations of the New Black Poetry. The six founding members of the Afro-American Folkloric Troupe were Stella Beck, Belvie Harrison, Norman Jacob, Charles Columbus Thomas, and Duke Williams. Beck (1962–1966), Jacob, Thomas and Primus remained with the group throughout the majority of its lifetime (1962–1971).

In 1965, California-born and, at that time, New York-based actress/director Kelly Marie Berry convinced LeRoi Jones to invite the Folkloric Troupe to perform at BART/S. That short summer stint led to a long running stay at a small, approximately 50-seat; space called Bro Herrod's 13th Street Theatre. On February 19, 1966, at Town Hall in New York City, The Afro-American Folkloric Troupe participated in "The Souls of Black Folk," a tribute to W.E.B. DuBois sponsored by *Freedomways* magazine. Also in 1966, the troupe performed for the Free Southern Theatre in New Orleans, Louisiana. Under the auspices of SNCC, they worked the summer in the tri-state area of Georgia, Alabama, and Mississippi—including performances in Lowndes County Alabama for the original Black Panther Party of Lowndes (which was later to be an inspiration to Huey Newton, the founder of the nationally known, Oakland-based Black Panther Party).

Primus judges that the San Francisco scene was far more politically sophisticated in the early sixties than was New York. Primus was decisively influenced by the San Francisco Negro Historical and Cultural Society. Writing to Goncalves, Primus outlines their beginnings:

> There was a branch of Carter Woodson's National Association for the Study of Negro Life in San Francisco from the 1930's on and when that (rather conservative) branch combined with the DuBois Club (Marxist) in 1955 to form the S. F. Negro Historical and Cultural Society, things began to happen. The Communist Party was influential in San Francisco for a long time. It evidently had a substantial number of Black members. It kept a very low profile as it went about its work in the fifties and sixties. And it was allied to the Historical Society, though the alliance was never openly discussed. Norman, Belvie and I were certainly courted, though we never joined. We even attended classes of the cadres, without a full understanding of the association. We simply wanted to be involved in some action that would change the plight of Black folks. So we picketed with Harry Bridge's longshoremen, and we picketed the House Un-American Activities Committee, and some where along the way we were radicalized. Our close association to Jim and Shirley Herndon, Ada Holly, Frank Alexander, Carl Bloice, et al, helped the process. And the philosophical schism which developed in The Afro-American Association helped clarify where we stood in the debate on economic systems. All this was before the 60's. By the time the Black Muslims injected the idea of nationalism into the debate, we were already Black Nationalists, having rejected international communism from the instruction in Ralph Ellison's *Invisible Man*. We knew that "The Brotherhood" was not to be trusted because it had no clearly defined "Negro program." So the 1960's arrived, The Black Panther Party of Lowndes County arrived, Malcolm X arrived (and The Muslims), and we were prepared to be engaged. (Goncalves "Letters")

As was often the case, Primus and the founding members of the Folkloric Troupe were unapologetic activists as well as artists. In an article in *Freedomways*, troupe founder Marc Primus clearly stated:

We have a quest. We search for ourselves. We have discovered that we are stolen men. We know that we are covered in lies. In spite of that we feel our beauty, we see it every day reflected, in the conversation, in the movement, in the faces of our people. And it is *because* we know that control of our own destiny is dependent upon the knowledge of ourselves and our situation that The Afro-American Folkloric Troupe exists.

The Troupe's function is the examination and the demonstration of the reaches of beauty and poignancy, the humor, the bite, the music of the folk forms of black people in the old and new world. So, we sing a little—the blues and the spirituals together. We protest, and pray, curse, preach, swear, moan, grunt, scream. And all of this is done in the words of our traditional and contemporary poets and folklorists. The reservoir of materials seems limitless.

Primus continues:

Because the tradition of the American theatre is such that the commercial theatre has continually usurped Afro-American forms, while the essence of the material escaped it, it becomes a novel thing to see black men in the theatre, working without artifice to be themselves—to restore the essence to the form.

In a full program the format of the Folkloric Troupe's presentation always includes: (1) A Langston Hughes suite; (2) Folktales, both African and Afro-American; (3) Blues and spirituals; (4) Sermons; (5) Protest poetry (overt) and contemporary poetry and (6) dialect poetry. (Primus 31–32)

In many ways, unbeknownst even to succeeding BAM poets, the Folkloric Troupe set the standard. Certainly they influenced Baraka and others in the New York area as well as members of the Free Southern Theatre (FST) in the Deep South. The Folkloric Troupe pioneered the now accepted format of a theatre program of poetry. In the late sixties, FST would produce BLKARTSOUTH, a troupe of poets who dramatized their work with stage movements and music. Also, the popular Broadway theatre piece, *A Hand Is On The Gate*, was directly influenced by the Folkloric Troupe. Primus recalls: "They came down and saw our show and then used the material we were doing with some big name actors and called it their show. I remember some of us were very upset about that" (Primus, "Interview").

As influential as it was, the Afro-American Folkloric Troupe is relatively unknown precisely because the performers were never lauded by the establishment media and because they disbanded before they could be promoted by Black student unions and Black Studies departments that developed nationally on college campuses in the seventies. Moreover, because it had a "nationalist" thrust and actively sought Black audiences, the Folkloric Troupe is under documented in that the performers neither sought nor encouraged establishment reviews. "We just wanted to do our work," Primus states, "We didn't worry about becoming stars." So although it may seem like an obscure footnote, the Folkloric Troupe nevertheless established a foundation for BAM dramatic poetry. Moreover, Primus pointed out that they were conscious of the profound psychological issues they were addressing. In the *Freedomways* article, he writes:

> We are in great danger, if, in our rush into the American mainstream, we neglect to honestly examine ourselves and our heritage. We run the risk of becoming psychological white men. To be such is not only to suffer existential fear, but more importantly, it means the assumption ourselves of their awful heritage of destruction and inhumanity. How ironical it would be to discard in ignorance the majesty of an Afro-American heritage in order to assume that which bears the seeds of a self-hatred which will ultimately cause our psychic destruction.
>
> The past presses us more than we know. And we have made a mistake in accepting the delineation given our history by white men. We have been told that our history began with our American experience. And very often we insist that any past beyond that is nonsense, as if our sojourn in America has not been demeaning enough to deny *that* Negro history and claim only an *African* one. The truth is, we are creatures of two cultures. And honest men must accept both. That is why we called ourselves The Afro-American Folkloric Troupe; we sought to be whole men by accepting a whole heritage. To agree to a slave past and deny that we are also descendants of kings and chiefs and free men is a matter of lunacy. (Primus, "The Afro-American" 33)

It is criminal that a development as forward looking and dynamic as the Afro-American Folkloric Troupe is relatively unknown. The Folkloric Troupe is a prime example of a BAM precursor whose vision and actuality was far in advance of others who became better known and more extensively documented. Symptomatic of its obscurity, the Folkloric Troupe was neither featured nor mentioned in what became the major and most popular documentation of BAM theater, the Black Theatre issue of *Drama Review*.

A National Black Theatre Movement. The summer 1968 issue of *Drama Review* offered a special issue on Black Theatre that was edited by Ed Bullins. The special issue featured essays and/or plays by Bullins himself and most of the major movers in BAM theatre, such as Larry Neal, Ben Caldwell, LeRoi Jones, Jimmy Garrett, John O'Neal, Sonia Sanchez, Marvin X, Ron Milner, Woodie King, Jr., Bill Gun, and Adam David Miller. BAM theatre proudly emphasized its activist roots and orientations as a distinct, and sometimes antagonistic, alternative to traditional theatres, both Black and White.

By 1970, BAM theatres/cultural centers were active throughout America. The New Lafayette Theatre with Robert Macbeth as executive director and Ed Bullins as writer-in-residence and Barbara Ann Teer's National Black Theatre led the way in New York. Baraka's Spirit House Movers held forth in Newark and traveled up and down the East Coast. Val Grey Ward's Kuumba Theater and the ETA theatre group, led by Abena Joan Brown, spearheaded activity in Chicago. David Rambeau's and Woodie King's Concept East Theatre in Detroit, which premiered the work of playwright Ron Milner, was particularly important. Milner went on to become one of the most enduring of BAM playwrights and Woodie King became BAM's leading theatre impresario. In Cleveland there was Karamu House, whose existence actually predated BAM. BLKARTSOUTH, led by Tom Dent and myself, was an outgrowth of the Free Southern Theatre in New Orleans and was instrumental in encouraging Black theatre development across the south from the Theatre of Afro Arts and M Ensemble in Miami, Florida to Sudan Arts Southwest in Houston, Texas. In California there was the Watts Writers Workshop, the Watts Poets, InnerCity Theatre and PASLA (Performing Arts Society of Los Angeles) led by Vantile Whitfield. Later, in the 1980s, Whitfield founded the influential "Expansion Arts Program" through the National Endowment for the Arts. Expansion Arts was responsible for funding many non-traditional arts organizations. In addition to those mentioned and numerous other community-based theatre groups across the country, there were literally hundreds of BAM theatres on college campuses.

Art vs. Politics. As was true in all other realms of BAM activity,

BAM theatre practitioners debated the classic "art vs. politics" divide. What distinguishes the BAM take on this century-old debate is the fact that many of its artists were also committed activists. Some even came to "art" after becoming activists. In the Black Theatre issue of *Drama Review*, John O'Neal, co-founder, along with Doris Derby and Gilbert Moses, of the Free Southern Theatre, philosophically addressed the issue in his article, "Motion in the Ocean: Some Political Dimensions of the Free Southern Theatre." He wrote:

> It surprised me to notice, after the theatre moved from Jackson to New Orleans, in 1964, how much we were dependent on Movement activity. The theatre depends on its relationship to the activists for relevance and perspective. The awareness of that activity is extremely important for the orientation of new people who had not previously been engaged, and the dialogue is important to all. On our arrival in New Orleans, we felt less relevant because there was very little Movement activity going on in the city. Since that time things have begun to change; several programs and organizations have emerged. I think the presence and activity of the FST has been a little bit responsible for that.
>
> The relationship between the FST and Movement people is important also because it opens up the question of arts as propaganda. It is important to distinguish between the inevitable political function of the arts and propaganda. Propaganda is legitimate, a necessary function of political partisans. The artist has license not available to the propagandist, however. A given work of art may have the qualities of propaganda, if a given partisan position is made clear or illuminated by the artist's work. But the propagandist has the additional responsibility for shaping information to meet political priorities.
>
> It is possible to have good propaganda and not have art at all. At the same time, the artist can speak quite sharply to a specific political situation without sacrificing to propaganda. The artist operates at the vanguard of man's cultural consciousness. In that role his responsibility becomes to inform men's judgments; from this principle he derives aesthetic license. Dereliction of the duty to inform judgment deprives the artist of relevance and leaves him defenseless against history's indictment. The commercial entertainment theatre business is not relevant to Black theatre; but most Black artists have been taken away from the cultural basis of their own development by the lure of "success." Only recently, since the shift in political circumstances has pulled the Blacks into center-stage, has it become possible for the commercial Black artist to retain a bit of integrity without jeopardizing his commercial option too seriously. Even so, most of the commercial markets include Blacks to no significant degree.

O'Neal continues:

> In the creation of a relevant theatre the development of an active and critical rather than a passive audience is the most important task. It is not enough that a particular theatre group be composed of Black people or even that it be physically located where Black people live, if the theatre is not addressed to the needs of Black people and grounded in their experience. "Exposure" is not only a patronizing concept—it does not develop an audience. Being in Ireland is not what made the Irish theatre Irish—it was the positive search for the theatrical forms which comprehend and speak to that ineluctably Irish soul. When one finds the essence of an Irishman one finds the same truth that binds all men. Yet the statement remains distinctively Irish. And so with any man or culture.
>
> If the "Irish" theatre could have been distinguished from an English theatre only because it had Irishmen and was in Ireland, then it would have been an English theatre in Ireland. The distinction is largely political. A theatre run and operated by Negroes that can be distinguished from other theatre in this country only by the complexion of the cast is not a Black theatre, it is a white theatre with Negroes.
>
> The inescapable fact remains. There is no truth that speaks so clearly to me as the truth of my own experience. If I cut to the essence of my own truth there will lie a truth for all men. One can only achieve that kind of statement, however, in the context of specific historical, cultural, political, economic circumstances. The work, regardless of whether it deals directly with them, must comprehend such problems. As the truth of Black people finds expression in theatrical forms, new forms will be created. As that truth finds expression, it will be political. It will be opposed to the ruling powers because history (and the ruling powers) makes it so. The Free Southern Theatre is one part of the process in the larger context of that struggle. (O'Neal 76–77)

Critical thinking and evaluation had been going on from the founding of FST in 1964. In the 1966 Winter issue of *Freedomways*, FST member Tom Dent addressed the critical issue of "audience" in "Free Southern Theatre: An Evaluation." He wrote:

> To say that the Negro writer writes for a white audience does not mean he always writes to *appease* that audience. On the contrary. Today one might say instead that the Negro writer because he lacks a substantial readership among his own people may be forced into bitterness. Forced, because when he writes for a society patterned after and dependent upon the very denial of his humanity it is only natural that he be bitter.

Contrast this increasingly self-defeating situation with that of the Negro jazz musician. The Negro jazz musician creates a music for an audience of and out of the travail, joy, hope of his own people. No matter how inventive his technical development or how suffused in his own vision, he can relate back to something real in people who share his experience and situation. And no matter how commercial he becomes if he really has something to say he relates to his own audiences *first*. This is why Negro jazz musicians dominate American music, and have for some time. Art is not an ivory tower exercise but always, basically, an act of communication. And a subtle, sophisticated, complex creation becomes possible if the creator is assured of the possibility of communication. The first step (for the Negro writer) out of this trap, is the development of a responsive audience of his own people. (Dent, "Free Southern Theater" 28–29)

This emphasis on audience, on developing and interrelating to a critical audience, is simply a variation of call and response, which is itself a manifestation of the value placed on reciprocity (i.e. acknowledging and responding to one's environment, one's history, one's culture). BAM theatre measured itself not by how the productions compared to classic productions, nor by how "critics" received the work, nor by how many tickets were sold, but rather by the audience's composition and response, (i.e. who was the audience and how the work affected their thoughts and actions.)

Internal Diversity. Within BAM there were heated debates and ongoing ideological struggles. *Black Theatre* was a drama-oriented BAM journal edited by Ed Bullins and founded in September 1968. The journal published a total of seven issues, the final one appearing in 1971. Bullins molded *Black Theatre* into an extremely open forum which published sometimes diverse and sometimes even conflicting points of view. The publication also had a policy of directly addressing internal struggles. In issue number 4 (1969), 12 of 44 pages are devoted to a discussion of the play *We Righteous Bombers*. A two-page introduction by Larry Neal is followed by a ten-page transcription of a forum held on the play. Larry Neal charges out of the gate stating that: "The real controversy underlying this symposium has little to do with *We Righteous Bombers* itself. Behind the discussion lay fundamental questions concerning the role and the direction of the Black Arts Movement" (Neal, "Toward a Relevant Black Theatre" 14). After briefly describing the participants in the forum and some of his own particular objections, he continues, "I myself perceived the same anarchistic thrust that upset Askia and Ernie but supposed that this was an intentional device on the part of the playwright. I was especially concerned with the play's form, which appeared dead and informed by European concepts of play craft" (14). Neal went on to directly confront aspects of Kawaida thought. He wrote:

> What concerns me now, and what concerned me during the symposium is this: The broad lack of understanding of the dynamics of Afro-American culture that abounds in many sectors of the Black Arts Movement. The most serious manifestations of this lack of understanding is exemplified by Maulana Ron Karenga's sincere, but misguided statements about the blues. In his book of quotations, he accuses them of "teaching resignation." This statement is so awesomely erroneous that we wonder how a man of Maulana's intellect could have made it. Doesn't he know that the blues are the fundamental source of *all* relevant Black music? Ask Leon Thomas or Pharoah Saunders. *A cultural revolution that does not include and absorb blues feelings and modes of sound will surely fail.* The blues sound is the blackest part of the Black man's voice; this sound is the essence of our existence here in this land of the beasts. Further, the blues are the creation of a collective sensibility. (Neal, "Toward a Relevant Black Theatre" 14)

Neal next addresses the New Lafayette Theatre, the institution which published *Black Theatre* and which was considered the leading Black revolutionary theatre.

> The New Lafayette Theatre is one of the most important groups in the Black Arts Movement. But it is beginning to slip. One reason is that the theatre's physical space is not being used enough. Aside from a very beautiful memorial to Malcolm X, and a concert by Pharoah Saunders, the theatre has presented nothing but plays. Further, and this is the case of most of the black theatrical groups, the organization is badly afflicted with the disease of "cliquism." All of the plays, except *Goin' A Buffalo*, have been directed by Bob Macbeth. Thus one man is overworked, and no new directorial talent is being developed. And it is finally the Black community that suffers.
> Open your doors, Bob, stop going through changes... My

remarks, on this occasion, are being addressed specifically to the New Lafayette, but it pertains to all the other theatre groups who call themselves Black. (Neal "Toward A Relevant Black Theatre" 14–15)

Neal concludes his article, "Toward A Relevant Black Theatre," with a major criticism of the play which was originally billed as having been written by Kingsley B. Bass, Jr. Subsequently, it was revealed that Bass was actually a pseudonym for Ed Bullins, the editor of *Black Theatre* and the writer in residence at New Lafayette. Bullins was the most published, most produced, and most awarded playwright of the BAM era. The transcription of the forum on *Bombers* opens with Marvin X announcing: "First of all, Brother Ed Bullins is the author of WE RIGHTEOUS BOMBERS... Brother Ed wrote the play, he said, in an attempt to suggest the type of play that a brother killed in the Detroit Revolution would have written. And he wrote it in an attempt to suggest some of the rhetoric that is used, you know, among so-called revolutionaries" (Panel 16). In the article, Neal responds to Bullins's penning the play under a pseudonym.

> Brother Bass, whoever he was or is, is a poor literary thief. The whole play is abstracted from Albert Camus' *Les Justes*, which was translated into English by Stuart Gilbert as *The Just Assassins*. "Abstracted" is a mild word. In many places, Brother Bass has stolen Camus' play word for word, situation for situation, conflict for conflict; in short, the whole thing. If we wanted to get academic about it, we could lay both texts side by side and compare them, but the textual correspondences are too numerous to illustrate. You can check for yourselves by comparing the text of the two plays. This is serious shit. What we have on our hands is the first literary hoax of the Black Arts Movement. Bad scene. We have all lost something. (Neal, "Toward a Relevant Black Theatre" 15).

In a footnote Bullins responds to Neal's assertion about "loss" with two words: "Our innocence." A different take on Bullins' "adaptation" of the Camus play is offered by Leslie Catherine Sanders in her book, *The Development of Black Theater in America*. After admitting that "essentially he retains the original text," Sanders notes:

Bullins reorders its sequence and adds a twist to the plot that reveals his additional intent. In Bullins' play, Murray Jackson (his version of Yanek) discovers that the man he thought was the Grand Prefect (who represents Camus' Grand Duke) is an imposter, and that the chief of police who interrogates him is actually the Grand Prefect. Moreover, he is informed that all the people his cadre has assassinated are actors; thus it has accomplished only useless murder. Furthermore, one of the women terrorists persists in speculating that all the killings have been manipulated by whites since all their targets have been black people and since the orders they have carried out were from an unknown superior.

A further alteration of Camus' plot elaborates and articulates the question of illusion versus reality raised by the woman's doubts...

We Righteous Bombers challenges every aspect of plays dealing with revolutionary violence. Not only does it, through Camus' text, comprehensively raise the ethical issues that must be confronted if the new society emerging after the revolution is to approach those ideals in whose name it has been won, but, further, it suggests that the black revolution envisioned on American soil most likely will result in even greater repression of blacks than they previously experienced, and in a genocide cruelly manipulated so as to appear self-inflicted. For Bullins, whenever blacks talk of killing other blacks or actually kill them, for any reason, only the oppressor is served. In The Reluctant Rapist his hero sadly observes, "The world prepares the black man in a single skill: treachery to his fellows." For Bullins, internecine revolutionary acts fall into that category. (Sanders 190)

Any suggestion that BAM was a mindless purveyor of violence is flat out wrong. As the controversy surrounding Bullins' play demonstrates, questions were constantly asked, doubts raised. Moreover, given the long history of infighting that was exacerbated, when not outright originated, by covert establishment activities (for example, COINTELPRO especially), questioning the source and use of internal violence was not an abstract issue. Facile characterizations of BAM are easy to make, but the truth is that BAM writers and thinkers were grappling with hard ethical and practical issues that arose out of the context of active struggle against dominant and dominating establishment forces. The New Lafayette forum was far more than simply a drama critics roundtable talking about the latest theatrical sensation.

A transcript of the forum revels the volatile and confrontational tone of the event. Interestingly, especially when one considers how BAM is characterized as being virulently sexist, the following exchange is noted:

> TOURE: Other detrimental points about this play are: One. In my opinion, it completely degrades the revolutionary Black sister by portraying her as a whimpering, paranoiac coward wishing to escape from life into death and asking her comrades to execute her, for she lacks personal courage (Sissy); or by portraying her as a vacillating, schizophrenic character, at one time tenderly and idealistically affirming life with her man and at another becoming a bitter, howling matriarchal figure, castigating her brothers, cynically putting down the revolutionary struggle in favor of her ego by asking her man, Murray, to place her before the struggle and the people; and finally she is shown wallowing in the arms of another brother, screaming shouts of self-doubt and self-pity, before her former lover is even dead.
>
> This play portrays the revolutionary Black sister as a neurotic, loose slut rather than the queen she really is.
>
> (Several voices: "Right." Applause.)
>
> TOURE: At this point, too, I would like to make a suggestion to Mr. Chairman, like in terms of this panel. Since in this play two sisters are main characters, I ask that we be truly revolutionary and ask some of the sisters to come sit up on the panel.
>
> (Applause.)
>
> We got (like) Sister April Spriggs, Helba [sic—refers to "Melba"] Kgositsile in the audience.
>
> MACBETH: I think that we would have enough to talk about at this point. I—(Laughter.)
>
> I—with all due respect to the sisters—I think that we five brothers have a great deal to talk about right now. The sisters are our friends, but let's us try to get to what we've got to talk about right now, and then we can go home. Okay?
>
> MARVIN X: We have a panel—
>
> TOURE: Yeah, brother, but maybe the sisters might want to sit on the panel. What's wrong with that?
>
> (Applause; banging of gavel.)

TOURE: Sisters are main characters in the play. Also the sisters are part of the Black revolution—

(Voice: "That's right.") (Break in continuity of tape.)

TOURE: I don't want to make this much longer.

(Break in continuity of tape) (Macbeth gets two extra chairs and places them at the table. There is a wait. When no sisters come up to take the seats Toure continues. (Panel 1)

Criticism, sharp polemics, debate and, sometimes, even hostile confrontation were the norm of exchanges in BAM. In its pages, *Black Theatre* consistently reflected this reality. In issue #6 (1972), Los Angeles-based poet Wanda Coleman criticizes BAM publications. She wrote:

Lots of Black Brother/sister artists/writers all over the Black kingdom from Detroit to Watts to Jackson to Harlem are singing the blues because they have been rejected.

The phenomenon of rejection has grown wider and deeper with the establishment (the nebulous forming of) a Black clique that is perpetuated by so-called "Black" publications. This phenomenon is the direct result of certain Brothers and Sisters selling an image of what "Black" is really supposed to be. Not only have they sold it to the white establishment, but to the Black masses as well and shame on the Black masses 'cause they should know better.

Magazines like all of Johnson's publications (and particularly *Black World*), the *Liberator* (who ignores any cries of help outside New York), and *Essence* (a fatuous piece of shit that exploits Black womanhood) leech on particular segments of the "blood community" and then sell them as representatives of all Blacks.

Equally frustrating is the cold shit of capitalizing on Blackness. "Groups" of Black artists/writers have cropped up over the past six years, after mass Black revolts, to sponge off the social momentum created. True, a beginning is necessary and the beginnings of places like the Douglas House (part of Watts Writers' Workshop, Los Angeles) are fine until they turn into Black meat-chewing cliques and exclude all but the mediocre and enforce upon everyone (who attempts something new and creative) their idea of what Black writing/art is. (Coleman 23)

The characterization of BAM as insular, uncritical and monolithic is easily disproved simply by reading the BAM publications that are now historical documents. Unfortunately, some of the most important of these publications are not widely available to the casual reader. Thus, I have quoted at length from *Yardbird* and *Black Theatre* not only to illustrate the breadth and depth of BAM but also to give the full picture of the dynamic critical back and forth that was a BAM hallmark.

There were literally hundreds of other small BAM publications, most of them lasted less than a decade and some of them for only a year or two. However, each individual publication contributed to the larger BAM sentiment of encouraging a new literature and a new form of criticism which was avowedly Afro-centric and anti-Western.

CHAPTER 8
BLACK ARTS MOVEMENT AND BLACK MUSIC

The Cutting Edge. Although all of the fields of artistic production were deeply affected by the Black Arts Movement, Black music remained the cutting edge and in many ways predated BAM in its revolutionary stance. During the BAM era, Black music (gospel, blues, jazz and popular), which consistently has been referred to as the "leading" African American cultural expression, also introduced major innovations and developments which affected all of popular culture in America.

For example, gospel music was revised and popularized by artists such as Rance Allen, Edwin Hawkins, D.J. Rodgers, Andrae Crouch and above all, The Staples Singers, who completely revolutionized the form and content of contemporary gospel. During the BAM decade, gospel music could be heard on the soul and Top 40 radio stations right next to the popular music of the day.

On the blues scene there was the development of a bevy of progressive young blues artists who were knowledgeable of and often proficient in traditional as well as contemporary blues styles. Chief among such blues artists was the charismatic Taj Mahal, who eventually combined blues with reggae. Perhaps the most inspirational of the blues trends was epitomized by B. B. King's highly political anthem, "Why I Sing the Blues."

In jazz the developments are too numerous to mention. Suffice it to say that artists such as John Coltrane, Pharoah Sanders, Gary Bartz, Doug and Jean Carn, Max Roach and Abbey Lincoln, McCoy Tyner, and literally thousands of others produced music that explicitly commented on current political events and consciously infused non-Western and African elements into the new jazz.

In rhythm and blues, or "funk" as it was then called, one could not miss the message in the music—a message that was implicit in the double entendre of a number of lyrics, for example, Issac Hayes' remake of "Our Day Will Come." The double entendre was also explicit in songs like Sam Cooke's "A Change Is Gonna Come," Aretha Franklin's "Respect," Curtis Mayfield's "We're A Winner" and "Keep On Pushing," the Isley Brothers's "Fight The Power," the O'Jays's entire album *Ship Ahoy* (which opened describing the Middle Passage), and James Brown's anthem of the period "Say It Loud, I'm Black and I'm Proud."

James Brown is key to appreciating the radical changes that took place within music during the BAM era. He was the most popular artist during this period. His string of sixteen number one R&B hits was matched only by Aretha Franklin. Although some may argue that Ms. Franklin was personally more popular, no one can seriously argue that she established an entire genre of music as Brown did in establishing funk; moreover, Franklin's music is not copied and sampled as copiously as Brown's.

Writing in the epilogue to Brown's autobiography, *James Brown: The Godfather of Soul,* critic Dave Marsh proffers a strong case for Brown's supremacy. He asserts that as a singer, James Brown found his métier in the shout, not so much the gospel kind as the field holler. His cracked and rasping yell in "Papa's Got a Brand New Bag," "I Got You (I Feel Good)," "Night Train," "Cold Sweat," "I Can't Stand Myself (When You Touch Me)," "Please Please Please," "Out of Sight," and "Get Up, I Feel Like Being Like a Sex Machine" doesn't just declare a man exulting in his search for and discovery of a new identity, but proclaims a new order of American popular music, one based on the triumph of polyrhythm over the restrictions of conventional Western harmonics and melodies. Marsh writes:

> I once joked that one day in 1967, James Brown grew weary altogether of the tyranny of chord changes and so he banished them and thus begot "Cold Sweat." Looking back over his career now, I fail to see the humor. It's no joke, just the truth, the bare facts of what the man did—and if you don't think it amounted to much, try turning on the radio. You will hear a myriad of recordings in which everything is subordinated to beats—beats generally far less complex and subtly interwoven than those in the great James Brown hits (of which there are far more than those listed in the previous paragraph, perhaps three or four times as many). Beats heard today are often fragments taken directly from James Brown records a decade

or more old.

...By critical acclimation, he is now quite clearly seen as the most influential American popular musician of the second half of the twentieth century. (My only qualm is whether "American" is too restrictive.) I would argue that as a radical innovator within popular music, only Louis Armstrong indisputably stands before him in the century's first half. (Marsh 277)

As is frequently the case in African-American history, Brown was aesthetically progressive, radical even, and politically conservative. On the one hand, Brown produced a rhythm-based music which offered an explicit and widely influential challenge to existing standards of popular music. On the other hand, Brown endorsed Richard Nixon for president and was a strong advocate of assimilation as a solution to our people's problems. A particularly poignant example of Brown's view is contained in his autobiography which states:

A lot of people at that time besides Rap [Brown] and me were looking for ways to get justice. Not too long after that Apollo engagement [where James Brown and Rap Brown had a brief meeting] Otis Redding called me in Cincinnati.

"Bossman"—Otis always called me that—"I've got an idea I want you to help me with."

"What's that, Otis?"

"I want us to form a union of all black entertainers. We can start by getting all the singers and musicians that we know, and then we can get actors and dancers and the rest later on."

"What do you want to do that for?"

"Well, it would give us all more leverage in the business. No more getting messed over by the white promoters and managers and people in the record business."

"Naw, Otis," I said. "I don't want to go that way. You remember when the musicians union was like two separate unions, one for white and one for black? We just wound up second-class citizens. I don't think we ought to risk going back to that."

"It wouldn't be like that, Bossman. If the big stars stuck together, they could see to it that a lot more black entertainers got work and got treated fair."

"I can't do it, Otis. I don't believe in separatism. I think that's going backwards, and I don't want to be part of that." (Brown 176)

Brown acknowledges that his conservative political views, particularly his endorsement of Richard Nixon, often made him a target of severe criticism from the Black community.

> The attacks on me and on other Afro-Americans who endorsed Mr. Nixon became vicious.... Less than a week after I endorsed Mr. Nixon I did a show in Baltimore. There were pickets outside the arena discouraging people from coming to see my show. Usually I sold out all thirteen thousand seats there, but that night only about two thousand five hundred people showed up. I was disappointed. People just didn't understand. Even Mr. Neely, a Republican himself, said to me one time, "I don't think endorsing Nixon was a very smart thing to do." (Brown 230)

The BAM era was not a period when one could divorce art from politics and simply be an entertainer—what side you were on, vis-a-vis the struggle, was a major question of the day that affected everyone. Brown's political conservatism notwithstanding, his peerless musical innovations stand as a major development incorporating BAM aesthetic principles and even, occasionally, political principles consistent with BAM objectives, such as in the case of "Talkin' Loud and Sayin' Nothing" or "Say It Loud, I'm Black and I'm Proud." Even a cursory review of Black music from the BAM era reveals a spirit of innovation in the aesthetic realm and lyrics of spiritual and political uplift.

Catalyst for Change. The focus of this study is on the Black Arts Movement with specific attention to Black literary production, but it would be impossible to understand BAM literary production without giving specific attention to the importance of music, particularly the developments in jazz of the era where the musicians not only were innovative in their aesthetical developments, but also took on the production and business side of the music world to demand self-determination. One particularly important example, which undoubtedly influenced Baraka, was the so-called 1964 "October Revolution" in jazz. A 1996 Evidence Records press release concerning a tribute recording of *October Revolution* gives this background:

> In mid-1964 fluegelhornist/trumpeter Bill Dixon decided to organize a series of presentations of what was at the time being called the "new thing," a music too new to be named or defined, but which was audaciously emerging in the face

of the recent folk embattled jazz mainstream. Having been closed out of conventional jazz clubs and concert halls and told by record companies that there was no interest in this music, Dixon set out to prove that there was an audience for the next phase of jazz, and to demonstrate how musicians might further their own cause. He booked the Cellar Cafe, a small coffee house on West 91st Street, for four days and nights, and scheduled 40 musical events and panel discussions on the state of the music with people like Paul Bley, Jimmy Giuffre, Cecil Taylor, Steve Lacy, Andrew Hill, Milford Graves, Shelia Jordan, John Tchicai, Sun Ra and Roswell Rudd. Though there was no advance publicity, the concerts were a huge success and played to a packed room. And even though there were no reviews in the New York press, word slowly filtered out that jazz had announced the arrival of its modernism, what was to become its seemingly permanent avant garde. Out of this event was to come ESP Records, which was created to document the music, as well as the Jazz Composers Guild, a group designed to take over many of the functions normally handled by clubs, agents and lawyers. The Guild inspired other musicians to begin using every conceivable New York City space for staging their own concerts—coffee houses, churches, museums, basements, lofts, the streets. The music would never be the same. (October Revolution Press Release)

Within a year, BAM artists were following the example set by "new music" musicians. When we consider how influential jazz musicians were on BAM artists, there can be no doubt that this event influenced the thinking of Baraka, Neal, Toure, and others who were then active in New York. Indeed, Baraka would later recruit some of the *October Revolution* musicians to perform a benefit to support BART/S. But before BART/S, before Black House, before the coining of the term "Black Arts," there was the "October Revolution" in jazz—concretely establishing the principle and practice of self-determination.

John Coltrane. The most influential jazz musician of the period was undoubtedly John Coltrane. Coltrane's influence was so far-reaching that he even influenced James Brown. Some of Brown's band members were jazz musicians who also played R&B, such as Pee Wee Ellis who was one of Brown's band directors during the BAM era. On some of his recordings, Brown employed wailing saxophone solos over funk beats. On "Super Bad," Brown can be heard telling tenor saxophonist Robert

127

"Chopper" McCollough to "blow me some Trane, brother" and Chopper responds with a whirlwind, avant-garde solo. Also noteworthy is the fact that "Super Bad," which was recorded June 30, 1970 in Nashville, Tennessee, almost exactly three years after Coltrane's death on July 17, 1967, shot to the top of the R&B charts on November 21, 1970. It is extraordinary that Coltrane had such an impact on James Brown, a musical entertainer whose popularity, record sales and ticket sales far exceeded Coltrane's. However, even more extraordinary is Coltrane's impact beyond the field of music.

Coltrane had a major impact on BAM poets. He inspired numerous poems of tribute. Additionally, Coltrane's musical innovations encouraged literary innovation. He released the influential and trend-setting recording, *A Love Supreme*, in 1965, the same year as the assassination of Malcolm X and the founding of BART/S. The album had been recorded the previous December 1964. Coltrane was reaching his peak at precisely the moment BAM was coming out of its formative eggshell and emerging as a nationally self-conscious phenomenon.

The most widely known example of Coltrane's musical innovation directly leading to literary innovation is Don L. Lee's famous poem, "Don't Cry, Scream," in which he employs the rhythms and the actual "cry" (sound) of Coltrane's saxophone as a literary device:

> your music is like
> my head—nappy black/a good nasty feel with
> tangled songs of:
>> we-eeeeeeeeeee
>> WE-EEEeeeeeeeeee
>> WE-EEEEEEEEEEEEEEEEEE
> (Lee, *Don't Cry* 28)

There are numerous other examples, including "JuJu" by Askia Muhammad Toure, an "epic" poem which recreates John Coltrane's long lines and intricate cross-rhythms:

> His horn cascading fountains of blood and bones and stormy
> rainbows firedarts purple blue-song tear-stained
> channels of love.
> Past green beast-eyes and the carnal lear of lust and hate
> we wander sad in our soul song, big as life and warm as
> throbbing Earth
> loamy in the crystal rain of Spring.
> (Toure, "Juju" 35)

Then there's the title poem of Michael Harper's well-known book *Dear John, Dear Coltrane*, in which Harper exclaims:

> Why you so black?
> cause I am
> why you so funky?
> cause I am
> why you so black?
> cause I am
> why you so sweet?
> cause I am
> why you so black?
> cause I am
> a love supreme, a love supreme:
> (Harper 75)

If one is not aware of the musical model that Harper is using, then the poem might easily be misread as filled with redundancies, instead of being emphatic in its use of rhythm, tension, and release, which was such an integral part of Coltrane's explorations with drummer Elvin Jones.

Another interesting point of convergence between Coltrane and the New Black Poetry is that the reigning critics initially considered both Coltrane's music and BAM poetry to be far beyond the pale. Coltrane's music was even referred to as "anti-jazz" and many BAM poets were dismissed as political rhetoricians and sloganeers masquerading as artists. In both cases, the aesthetic in question was a prima facie radical departure from the status quo.

Again, this is not the place to do a critical reading of BAM poetry. Suffice it to note the intentional and innovative uses of Black musical influences in the development of a BAM literary style. Other than Malcolm X, the Black musicians of the BAM era were undoubtedly the strongest influence on BAM poets, stronger even than any particular literary influence.

The Malcolm X/John Coltrane Connection. At this point, allow me a brief digression that will hopefully illuminate and/or indicate an area for further study. There is a relationship between Malcolm X and John Coltrane in terms of who they were, the social milieu which produced them and their efforts to escape status quo confinement. This interesting intersection of major influential forces is addressed in Frank Kofsky's analysis of Black music, *Black Nationalism and the Revolution in Music*, which concludes with an overview of "The Career of Malcolm X." Kofsky's book includes this tantalizing footnote: "Although to my knowledge it has not been remarked upon by any reviewer, the same milieu which gave rise to Malcolm had also generated the most vital forms of contemporaneous jazz; Malcolm's *Autobiography* reveals him to have been an intimate friend of many of Harlem's leading jazz figures of the forties and fifties" (Kofsky 256).

I am suggesting that while it is common knowledge that the music influenced artists, and it is generally accepted that political leaders through influencing the social climate thereby influenced musicians and artists. One should also look at the influence of musicians on specific political leaders, especially those political leaders of a radical Black temperament. In an interview published in *Journal of Black Poetry* and conducted at the Pan African Cultural Festival in Algiers in July 1969, Don Lee raises the question of "musician's influence on political leader[s]" with Stokely Carmichael, who was then living in Africa.

> DL: What relaxes you these days, if that's possible?

> SC: My wife and Nina Simone, Wes Montgomery. I dig Wes Montgomery cause he's good for relaxing, you know. The blues. This time I didn't bring too many like
> T. Bone. I dig some T. Bone. Get dead into that—yeah!

> DL: Have you heard Pharoah's new record, *Karma*?

> SC: No, I've had no new ones, you know. I ask people to send them, but you know. (Lee, "Don L. Lee Interviews Stokely Carmichael" 72)

Lee's question about *Karma* is significant because that recording, which contained the important composition, "The Creator Has a Master Plan," was one of the most popular and widely listened to recordings of the BAM era and Lee wanted to know Carmichael's opinion of it. Unfortunately, Carmichael had not heard the recording. Nevertheless, it is interesting that Carmichael lists two women vocalists (his wife, Miriam Makeba, and Nina Simone) who were known for their overtly political lyrics and two blues-steeped guitarists (Wes Montgomery and

T-Bone Walker), neither of whom is usually thought of as overtly political. I think Carmichael's tastes in music are consistent with his politics. Carmichael has a deep concern and love for African people, specifically African Americans (blues) and an equally deep commitment to Pan Africanism and political activism (politicized songs).

As for the political importance of blues, I agree with Larry Neal who emphasized that:

> The blues, with all of their contradictions, represent, for better or for worse, the essential vector of the Afro-American sensibility and identity....
>
> The blues are the ideology of the field slave—the ideology of a new "proletariat" searching for a means of judging the world. Therefore, even though the blues are cast in highly personal terms, they stand for the collective sensibility of a people at particular stages of cultural, social, and political development. The blues singer is not an alienated artist attempting to impose his view of the world on others. His ideas are the reflection of an unstated general point of view. Even though he is a part of the secular community, his message is often ritualistic and spiritual. Therefore, it is his ritual role in the community which links him to the traditional priests and poets of Africa. (Neal, *Visions of a Liberated Future* 107, 113)

This leads me to the linking of John Coltrane and Malcolm X. Malcolm articulated and popularized the "house slave/field slave" analysis. John Coltrane consciously reintroduced old blues elements into the sound of his modern music, specifically recalling the work of Bessie Smith and Sidney Bechet. Could it be that Neal's identifying of the blues as "the ideology of the field slave" helps explain the nexus of Coltrane and Malcolm, both of whom were directly influenced by the culture produced by "field slaves"?

While I am sure that the poets and political figures had some influence on the musicians, especially in Malcolm's case, I think it is important for us to realize that the musicians arrived at concepts such as Pan Africanism and Black Power before the currents were politically popular in the Black community, and certainly before they were articulated by any of the BAM writers.

Whereas Islam became popular in the fifties among Black intellectuals, by the sixties, African American musicians had been investigating and adopting Islam for well over a decade. The ascendancy of bebop in the forties was paralleled by an interest in Islam among musicians such as Abdullah ibn Buhaina (Art Blakey), Ahmad Jamal, Yusef Lateef, and Liaquat Ali Salaam (Kenny Clarke), among many.

Overtly African and Black Power-oriented recordings by artists Sonny Rollins (*Freedom Now Suite*, 1958), Max Roach and Abbey Lincoln (*We Insist: The Freedom Now Suite* 1961), Randy Weston (*Uhuru Afrika*, 1961, which included text by Langston Hughes), John Coltrane (*Africa/Brass*, 1961), and Oliver Nelson (*Afro-American Sketches*, 1962), just to name a quick handful, preceded BAM. The musicians were ahead of Amiri Baraka, Larry Neal, Askia Muhammad Toure, and any other BAM writer in creatively acknowledging Africa's influence on African American culture. These musicians centered the then developing Black social movement as content and inspiration for aesthetic work, and explicitly advocated Pan Africanism.

Once again, John Coltrane is particularly important in this regard because his explicitly acknowledged interest in African aesthetic and political influences began around 1957. In the informative and eye-opening *A Night in Tunisia: Imaginings of Africa in Jazz*, Norman C. Weinstein offers the following assessment of Coltrane's recording career as a leader. He writes:

> Whatever one thinks of the plausibility of demarcating his career in this fashion, consider alternatively segmenting Coltrane's career in terms of the nature of his imaginative identification with Africa. Although Coltrane never visited Africa, it was a presence in his musical imagination at exactly the same time that he began leading his own bands in 1957. He began collecting recordings of African music during this time, and, from these recordings, began to try on various bits of African musical ornamentation for two years: the recording sessions with trumpeter Wilbur Harden are dusted with sparse African colors; a recording of Watusi drum rhythms inspired the rhythmic underpinnings of "Dial Africa"; "Oomba" has horns soloing over a one-chord vamp; "Bakai's" (meaning "cry" in Arabic) horns rigorously repeat call-and-response patterns; "Dakar" uses an Eastern-sounding mode, perhaps inspired by Yusef Lateef. (Weinstein 61, 63)

And that was only the beginning. Coltrane went on to more

specific involvements with African music and aesthetics. At the end of his life in 1967, he had partnered with Nigerian drummer Olatunji to establish an African-centered cultural arts center.

My supposition is that Coltrane is more than a popular jazz musician. Indeed it is arguable that Coltrane was not as popular as Miles Davis, who sold more records. The whole arc of Coltrane's career reflected his serious investigations of African American blues culture and African musical aesthetics—blues and Pan Africanism—the two root aesthetics of BAM. I believe that BAM artists deeply responded to Coltrane because of these roots.

Moreover, I contend that within Black culture, the musicians have always preceded other artists simply because the music is the area of the arts that African Americans have first mastered in mass numbers. In Weinstein's prodigiously documented book, Max Roach is quoted as declaring:

> It is my duty, the purpose of the artist to mirror his times and its effects on his fellow man. We American jazz musicians of African descent have proved beyond all doubt that we're master musicians of our instruments. Now, what we have to do is employ our skill to tell the dramatic story of our people and what we've been through. (Weinstein 118)

Many writers have said this, but how often has the literature been delivered in a style that was addressed to and understandable by the masses of African Americans?

The confluence of Malcolm X and John Coltrane as the chief inspirations for BAM artists is no accident, but rather is reflective of the deep nexus between social commentary and Black music that is generally overlooked by establishment critics. Stephen Henderson, however, cleanly hit the bull's-eye when he noted: "What Coltrane signifies for black people because of the breadth of his vision and the incredible energy behind his spiritual quest, Malcolm X signifies in another way—not as musician, but simply and profoundly as black man, as Black Experience, and that experience in process of discovering itself, of celebrating itself" (Henderson, *The Militant Black Writer* 110). In an article on BAM publications which focuses on what she called "the revolutionary journals" (i.e. *Soulbook, Black Dialogue* and *Journal of Black Poetry*), literary critic Carolyn Gerald (aka Carolyn Fowler) specifically points out the importance of these two Black men as inspirations for BAM. She writes that: "In the work of the poets to give us back our heroes and to provide us with new ones, two types of black men are always sung: Jazz and blues musicians (Otis Redding, Ornette Coleman, Charlie Parker, and above all, John Coltrane) and political activists (Chaka, Nat Turner, Marcus Garvey, Patrice Lumumba and, more than any man any time anywhere, Malcolm)" (Fowler, "untitled" 28).

Both Malcolm X and John Coltrane represented the combination of an innovative articulation of a blues people sensibility and an avowedly anti-Western/pro-Africa stance, inherent not only in the meaning of their message/music but also in the aesthetics they employed. At the same time, it must never be overlooked that both were self-taught masters of American oratorical rhetoric/Western music theory. Malcolm went so far as to study the dictionary word by word. Coltrane studied western music in great depth and was widely known among his musical peers as someone who was always practicing, except when he was performing. These two individuals who represented the Blackest of the Black, were paradoxically two of the most ardent students of the Western aspects of their particular disciplines. What distinguishes them from other students of the Euro-traditions, however, is that their study of Western traditions was not a goal but rather part of a means to an end, an end which either swept aside or significantly transformed the very traditions they so ardently studied. Additionally, rather than directed by Euro-centric teachers, both men were self-directed seekers of knowledge, autodidacts whose broad and deep investigations were intended to facilitate the making of revolutionary change within their respective disciplines of politics and music.

Malcolm X and John Coltrane embody the two chief elements of BAM, Black Power politics and non-Western/pro-African aesthetics. Indeed, the politics and the aesthetics are twins, and Black music offered the most developed and strongest examples of both.

The Commercialization of Black Music. I do not mean to mystify the music into a contradictionless fount of soul and inspiration because musicians are also susceptible to exploitation and commodification. Especially in the immediate post-BAM era, when there was the birth and championing of so-called "fusion" jazz. During the fusion heyday, the emphasis of the music shifted from the head to the butt—from raising consciousness to shaking booty.

On the liner notes of a reissue of music from the seventies, pianist Herbie Hancock, who took the Swahili name Mwandishi (teacher) for a period and produced highly "spiritual" music, comments on his decision to change directions and begin producing "fusion" music. You don't have to read between the lines to understand that the commercial influence on the music turned many artists away from the "heavy" Black consciousness direction that BAM advocated. The liner notes, written by Bob Blumenthal in 1994, state that:

> By the close of 1970, when Hancock recorded his next session, only Williams remained in the sextet. With the exception of the bassist [Buster Williams] and trombonist Julian Priester, the personnel was made up of younger and less familiar figures, and everyone in the band had taken a Swahili name. Hancock was Mwandishi, the horn players were Mganga Eddie Henderson, Pepe Mtoto Julian Priester and Mwile Benny Maupin; and the rhythm section was completed by Mchezaji Buster Williams and Jabali Billy Hart. An affinity quickly arose among these musicians, which Hancock described with great enthusiasm during a June 1971 interview with this author shortly after the album Mwandishi was released.
>
> "I've played with some fantastic soloists," [Hancock] went on, "but there's a thing that I think is more important than solos. I think music is supposed to make you high, to give you an experience so that you can transport yourself from wherever you are and that whole physical contact with the world so that you can gain a little more consciousness—inner consciousness. I think it would be impossible for most of my early music to do that, just from the very nature of the material; but my new music is set up to do just that. It's set up to make you high."
>
> Hancock called Mwandishi "my favorite record of all the records I have ever made, and the loosest I've ever done. None of the tunes have chords. After we play the melody, then we can go where we want to. Usually the structure of the melody leads you in a certain direction, so at least you're not walking off of a cliff... Albums like Mwandishi fit into what I think

might be considered the new mainstream of jazz," Hancock said at the time. "The new avant-garde has finally found a direction, but it's like a spectrum. It's not one direction; there are many directions and they all have to do with giving people an experience rather than just giving them a bunch of notes." (Blumenthal 9, 11, 14)

Mwandishi was recorded December 31, 1970 and released in 1971. This was at the height of BAM, but afterward there was a sharp swing rightward. Hancock is forthright in articulating his change of direction, a change which reflected the demise of BAM and the ascendancy of a marketing mentality rather than an elevating mentality in the music. Blumenthal writes that:

> Hancock sustained this approach briefly after signing with Columbia in 1973 and recording Sextant—but not for long. "One thing became apparent to me last year," he explained in a 1974 interview that explained the change in perspective that led to this ultra-funky and enormously successful Headhunters album. "I'd go to friends' homes and see my albums on the shelves with lots of other people's records, and they'd play all the others except mine. My intention at the time was to play music to be listened to with undivided attention; but how many people have the time to approach music that way? Before, I was so interested in spirituality that I didn't recognize that a person puts on a record with his hands and not his spirit." So the emphasis shifted from "heavy musical trips that try to expand people's minds" to "making people feel like getting up in the morning and going to work." (Blumenthal 16)

BAM was an all-encompassing arts movement that strongly influenced popular and the so-called "high" art. In the parlance of the times, BAM was about raising "Black consciousness."

CHAPTER 9
BLACK FILM AND TELEVISION

Blaxploitation Movies. While BAM had an extraordinary impact on the live performance arts (e.g. music, poetry, theatre, dance) within America's Black communities, BAM probably had its greatest impact on general American culture in a completely unexpected area. Perhaps the most dramatic change in popular culture happened in the movies with the development of what became known as "Blaxploitation movies." These movies were a Hollywood response to independent Black cinema in general and particularly to Melvin Van Peebles' hit film *Sweet Sweetback's Baadasssss Song*.

Writing in his trenchant analysis of Black movie making, *Black Film/White Money*, cultural critic Jesse Algeron Rhines succinctly summarizes Blaxploitation. He writes:

> Sex, violence, and dope are the hallmarks of the blaxploitation film. In *Coffy* (1973), full-figured Pam Grier sets the female mold as she wields a shotgun in retribution against the gangsters and politicians who hooked her younger sister on drugs. In *Welcome Home, Brother Charles* the Black star's penis takes on a life of its own and, stretching to more than twenty feet long, creeps across rooms to invade the bodies of sleeping women. In *Mandinga*, set during slavery, a white woman visiting a plantation is so aroused at a slave's whipping that she sneaks back to the place where he remains chained, standing with arms and legs outstretched. She seduces him, kissing and rubbing her hands all over his wounded, bleeding body.
>
> But despite the black hipsters and "foxy" women on screen, the blaxploitation period was not an example of African American filmmaking. Much more often than not, whites were in control behind the camera reproducing their own point of view. In fact, of the hundred or so films featuring significant numbers of African American characters and/or an African American-derived story line and produced during the blaxploitation period, roughly 1970 through 1974, fewer than one-fifth were under African American control. Even fewer came from Black-owned production houses, and fewer still were financed and/or distributed by African Americans.

Films aimed at an African American audience, featuring significant numbers of Black characters and/or an African American-inspired story line, but controlled by non-Blacks may more properly be called Black-oriented films. Bogle says that "many of the new Black-oriented films were written, directed and produced by whites.... Worse, many of the new movies were often shot on shoestring budgets, were badly directed, and were technically poor. The film industry hoped simply to make money by indeed exploiting an audience need." These films were released during the height of the civil rights/Black liberation movement, yet their subject matter of sex, violence, and "super-cool" individualism was the antithesis of what contemporaneous black political organizations, like SNCC, the NAACP, or SCLC supported for Black people; hence the name "blaxploitation," a term coined by *Variety*. (Rhines 45 – 46)

Significantly, *Sweetback* was a challenge to Hollywood in two critical ways. First, the movie was produced with Van Peebles' own money and without financial backing from the Hollywood system. Second, Van Peebles refused to submit his film to the Hollywood infrastructure for rating and instead advertised that the film was "rated X by an all white jury." After *Sweetback* proved to be a commercial success, Hollywood quickly moved to co-opt Black filmmakers, including Van Peebles. Incredulous as it may seem in hindsight, before making *Sweetback*, Van Peebles directed a satirical Hollywood comedy starring comedian Godfrey Cambridge called *Watermelon Man*, about a White man who turns Black over night. Shortly to follow *Sweetback* were the Shafts, Superflys and Foxey Browns.

The difference between *Sweetback* and the "Blaxploitation" films which followed was the difference between "Black Power" and "assimilation" into or "co-optation" by the system. Again, Rhines is fundamentally on point in his analysis. He writes:

Although Gordon Park's direction of *The Learning Tree* for Warner Bros. marked a milestone in Hollywood feature production, it was Melvin Van Peebles who best captured the new attitude in African America and made most creative use of structural imperfection in the 1970s film industry. Stating that what major studios like Columbia Pictures, which had offered him a three-picture contract, called a little control he called extreme control, Van Peebles dropped the contract to make a "revolutionary" and independent film. Produced for $50,000—the money he had earned as director of Columbia's *Watermelon Man*, a loan of

$50,000 from Bill Cosby, and funds from non-industry sources—Van Peebles's $500,000 production, *Sweet Sweetback's Baadasssss Song* (1970) changed the course of African American film production and the depiction of African Americans on screen.

Sweetback champions a "'bad Nigger' who challenges the oppressive white system and wins," says film scholar Ed Guerrero, "thus articulating the main feature of the Blaxploitation formula."Political scientist and professor of African American studies Charles Henry says of this African American folk type: "From the slaves' Br'er Rabbit and Slave John to the more recent Great MacDaddy, John Henry, Railroad Bill, Dolemite, Shine, and Stackolee, the 'bad Nigger' or black 'bad man' tradition is characterized by the absolute rejection of established authority figures." (Rhines 43)

BAM's militant pressure for empowerment coupled with an unequivocal opposition to the White-dominant status quo introduced new cultural expressions and, as a byproduct, resulted in the inclusion of Blacks in mass media expressions. Johnson and Johnson conclude their study of the "literary politics of African-American magazines" with this limited but nonetheless accurate bottom-line assessment of BAM's effect on the American social landscape:

The black arts movement initiated in the 1960s encouraged nationalism among blacks who felt alienated from the cultural mainstream, but it did not foment revolution or radicalize the broader Afro-American population. The movement did, however, aid in altering the status quo. By adopting a revolutionary stance in their magazines and elsewhere, writers of the black aesthetic drew attention to the unresolved questions of racial and social caste in the nation. In the process, they advanced the civil rights movement, even though they did not support its tenets and leadership. Their extreme statements pushed many whites into accepting the positions articulated by relatively moderate blacks, such as Martin Luther King, Bayard Rustin, Roy Wilkins, and Whitney Young. Talk about "assassin poems" and "the Conquest of White Eye" made the historic black call for full civil liberties seem quite reasonable. By urging revolution, the black arts movement of the 1960s and early 1970s dramatized the need for change and helped secure long-needed reforms. (Johnson 200)

Thus, BAM had both a direct and an indirect impact—with the indirect impact being often far broader than the direct impact.

Independent Black Cinema. Just as most young people in the 1990s have never seen any of the actual BAM publications and are unfamiliar with the more politically oriented BAM recordings of that era, similarly, most Blacks who are under forty know only about the "Blaxploitation films" and have not seen the many independent films which were a product of that era. Films by Haile Gerima (*Bush Mama*), Larry Clarke (*Passing Thru*), Robert Van Lierop (*A Luta Continua*), and Kathleen Collins (*Losing Ground*), among many, many others are virtually unknown today outside of film studies classrooms and small coteries of Black film fans. If you judge Black film only by the Blaxploitation movies, you entirely miss the cutting edge of independent Black cinema, the cinema which was an active and popular part of BAM.

The new Black independent cinema, like much of BAM literature, first came to light on the West Coast. In a perceptive article, critic Ntongela Masilela describes the development of this movement:

> Only with the passage of time is it possible to reconstruct the conditions under which a Black independent filmmaking movement emerged in Los Angeles in the early 1970s. Founded at the University of California, Los Angeles, by African and African-American students, most of whom were completing a film degree in UCLA's Theater Arts Department, the movement had two distinct waves. The first included Haile Gerima, Charles Burnett, Larry Clark, John Reir, Ben Caldwell, Pamela Jones, Abdosh Abdulhafiz, and Jama Fanaka; among those in the second were Bill Woodberry, Julie Dash, Alile Sharon Larkin, and Bernard Nichols.
>
> The arrival of Charles Burnett at UCLA in 1967, two years after the assassination of Malcolm X and the Watts Rebellion, and the arrival of Haile Gerima from Ethiopia, via Chicago, in 1968, the year of the assassination of Martin Luther King and the launching of the Tet Offensive in Vietnam, were generative events in the formation of the Black independent movement in Los Angeles, a school of filmmaking that would last approximately a decade. By 1978, when Teshome Gabriel, a distinguished scholar of African film and Third World Cinema, conducted a series of fascinating discussions with Brazilian film director Glauber Rocha at UCLA, the group had disbanded, as members moved in different directions even while remaining in close contact with one another.
>
> The intellectual and cultural coordinates of this Black independent film movement are inseparable from the political

and social struggles and convulsions of the 1960s. For these African and African-American filmmakers, imagination was inescapably wedded to political and cultural commitment. The Civil Rights Movement, the Women's Movement, the anti-war movement, and activities in America in support of national liberation struggles in Africa, Asia, and Latin America informed the political consciousness of the members of the group....

For African-American filmmakers, Fidel Castro's maxim that "the duty of a revolutionary is to make a revolution" prompted a concrete question: how might they establish an independent Black film enterprise that was true to their cultural roots and contested the falsification of African-American history by Hollywood. ... The challenge facing this generation of independent Black filmmakers was to find a film form unique to their historical situation and cultural experience, a form that could not be appropriated by Hollywood.

The search for such a form led them to the family dramas of Oscar Micheaux from the 1920s and '30s. The revolutionary breakthrough of the UCLA school was to draw on Micheaux's work, yet shift its social subject matter from a middle-class to a working-class milieu in which Black labor struggled against White capital. (Masilela 107–108)

Through the efforts of the UCLA-based, initial wave of BAM independent Black filmmakers combined with the Hollywood-driven Blaxploitation era, film actually became the second (after music) most far reaching area of BAM influence on popular American culture.

Black Journal. BAM influence on television actually preceded film. While some critics focus on the integration of sit-coms such as *I Spy* and *Mod Squad*, the real news was the advent of *Black Journal*. In his write-up for "The L.A. Rebellion: A Turning Point in Black Cinema," noted critic Clyde Taylor contextualizes the BAM-oriented efforts in both television and film presented by the Whitney Museum of American Art, January 3-19, 1986):

By the turn of the next century, film historians will recognize that a decisive turning point in the development of black cinema took place at UCLA in the early 1970s. By then, persuasive definition of black cinema will revolve around images encoded not by Hollywood, but within the self-understanding of the African-American population.

The latest black independent film movement (roughly from 1964 to the present) represents the most concerted effort to establish black cinema and to distinguish it from "images of blacks in films." Among the independents determined to make films outside the Hollywood orbit, two episodes of creative collaboration stand out. Both reveal all the marks of cultural movements—the efforts to establish definitions, the drafting of manifestos, the excited exchange of ideas and techniques, the revisionist review of historical legacies, and the self-conscious awareness of being players on a new historical stage.

One of these episodes was the activity around *Black Journal*, a PBS television magazine program regularly produced by a team of black directors under the leadership of William Greaves from 1968 to 1971. There, the contours of black documentary, aimed at exploring the self-definition of African-Americans, were effectively laid out. But even these revisionist documentaries understood the vital role of dramatic narrative for the full expression of black cinematic possibilities.

Narrative films were also the focus of a second group of talented, resourceful cinema interventionists who came together as students in the 1970s at UCLA. Energized by the momentum of the Black Power movement, the growth of Pan-African and cultural-nationalist organizing in post-Watts rebellion Los Angeles, and the dozens of cultural, artistic, and educational ventures of the second Black Reconstruction, these young filmmakers made a commitment to dramatic films—a commitment fired by the discomfort of dwelling in the belly of the beast: minutes away, Hollywood was reviving itself economically through a glut of mercenary black exploitation movies. (Taylor)

Note that *Black Journal* was a precursor to the independent Black films. That the breakthrough happened in television is significant. Filmmaker St. Clair Bourne, one of the original *Black Journal* staff people, recalls that:

...by and large, the films that we did on *Black Journal* we could not make without the cooperation of the community. That's what really made our films distinctive from others. The white guys could go in and they could report on a situation, but what we were able to do was to go in and get the people who were involved to say what the situation was, which often was different from what others reported. Because we had a framework of national broadcasts every month it gained legitimacy. People saw it on television, and since everybody knows television is truth (ha ha), they bought it. Even though we were in the minority in many ways of Black film activities, we set a tone.

Then a lot of other Black current-affairs shows began to evolve in local cities. That's one of the ways that I think that we effected change. I was able to make films, and I was able to see that the people you serve are also your protection. (Bourne 51)

Black Journal is another important example of BAM era arts activity changing the terrain of cultural life within the Black community and American society as a whole. Of course, the effect on American cultural life is not often acknowledged. Most of us can immediately relate to the number of "magazine" format, Black-oriented, community affairs programs that were produced in urban television stations across the nation, but what about the national media itself? Bourne insightfully notes the important influence *Black Journal* exerted. He states:

> In the treatment of Black people in the media, overall, with a couple of exceptions, we were victims and the subject of a problem. Sometimes they romanticized that, but basically we were the problem—the "Negro problem"—that's what they called it. Also, we could never really talk for ourselves. We had to have somebody, usually a hip white boy, to say, "This is what they think, and this is why they feel that life is unfair, blah, blah, blah. There may be some racism in this." That kind of stuff. We said, "Wait a minute. We don't want people to speak for us." So we always allowed the people to speak for themselves, number one. Number two: we always had them advocating something rather than just "Woe is me." We always took somebody who represented a way.
>
> The other thing that we did, even more than was recognized, is create the magazine concept for television, like *20/20*. We did that back then. The reason that we did it was we only had an hour, so we had to get in as much regional stuff as we could. The way we could do it was just to compress things and have a magazine. *60 Minutes* actually started about a year after we did, and that was the technique that they used. I always felt that the *60 Minutes* style was basically what they saw us do. Overall, then, I would say that during that time *Black Journal* had a major influence on the treatment of Black images and people in the media. I think what's happened is that that contribution got moved back, and the whole victim thing is coming back now. They haven't gotten others to talk for us yet, totally, but they have Black versions of that. (Bourne 51)

Again and again, the concept of self-determination became the basis for aesthetic developments. During the BAM era, the link between politics and aesthetics was not only clear but, this link was also causal in the sense that the opportunity to present one's aesthetics usually was the result of political activity. Again Bourne is articulate in defining the linkages.

> In those times Black people were still protesting. This was
> in the '70s, and Black Power was still happening, and self-
> determination was happening, and the mainstream institutions
> had to relate to that. They could no longer just treat us like
> victims, because we could always threaten to burn down the
> city, and literally some cities were burned down. I believe to this
> day that *Black Journal* came into existence because too many
> brothers threw too many bricks at some rich white people's
> house, and they said, "Okay, let's cool them out somehow.
> One of the things that they are always screaming about is not
> being on TV other than in the roles of criminals. Let's give them
> their own show for an hour a month." I really believe that's what
> got us the *Black Journal* experience. It wasn't benign charity,
> but it was self-interest on the Establishment's part. (Bourne 52)

CHAPTER 10
DANCE

Popular Dance. The leading role of Black Arts Movement-oriented music, and to a slightly lesser extent, BAM-oriented film and television, in no way diminishes the impact of BAM in other areas of popular and performing arts.

Dance critic and former editor of the now defunct Black dance quarterly newsletter, *Dance Herald*, contextualizes the impact of Black dance on American society. William Moore writes that:

> Very few dance people know of the role that African Americans have played in the formation of dance aesthetics in the United States. There are many facts on this subject coming out of research being done at Duke University [American Dance Festival's "Black Traditions in American Modern Dance"]. One of them is the fact that from the time slaves performed in New Orleans' Congo Square until the beginning of minstrelsy—and later of vaudeville—when Americans went to see dance, they did not see Europeans dancing; they saw mostly African Americans dancing.
>
> Imagine the impact of being influenced by another culture's type of dance for a lifetime. We still don't appreciate the value of the Black contribution to the fields of music and dance. (Moore 85)

Admittedly, the influence of Black dance on American culture has been less than the influence of Black music, and in the post–Civil Rights era, less than film and television. However, dance's influence has exceeded that of Black literature or the visual arts. The difference, however, is that dance's influence has occurred much more on a vernacular/mass level rather than a concert/professional artistic level.

Black popular dance has influenced everything from ballet and modern dance companies to Broadway musicals and television music programs. From the often-venerated, White-oriented *American Bandstand* to the Black-oriented *Soul Train*, what is called Black "vernacular" dance as practiced by non-professional dancers from various communities has been a major source of influence and artistic inspiration for professional choreographers and dancers. Additionally there were people such as Chubby Checker, who popularized the twist, and Major Lance, who popularized the monkey. The Checkers and Lances notwithstanding, the Fred Astaire syndrome, i.e: a White expert practicing a dance form pioneered or extensively influenced by Blacks, is usually in effect. Hence, we had the success of disco era icon John Travolta. The popularity of the Astaires and the Travoltas notwithstanding, the most significant dancer of the era was James Brown.

During the BAM period, James Brown achieved a unique amalgamation of rhythm and blues whose driving rhythms gave us the music commonly known as "funk." Brown's music had a heavy emphasis on rhythm, so much so that all of the instruments were often played as though they were percussion instruments. Moreover, there was no one—professional concert dancers included—who could match James Brown's dancing abilities in the arena of vernacular dance. Many, many popular music groups and individuals were well known for their flashy and complex choreography. Nonetheless, no one matched Brown's mastery of Black popular dance. Brown explains:

> I stayed on top of all the latest dances—the slop, the funky chicken (even before it was called the funky chicken), the alligator, the camel walk. I guess the camel walk is a dance people associate with me. I first saw people dance it around 1940 and I heard Louis Jordan sing about it a little later, but I put the pizzazz into it. Really, I developed my own camel walk so that it would eventually become the James Brown. It shouldn't be confused with the moon walk that Michael Jackson does, which is really the bicycle, a move Charlie Chaplin used to do. You know how you get on a bicycle and ride it backwards? That's the moonwalk—the Charlie Chaplin bicycle done backwards. (Brown 55)

Black popular dance has had a larger influence on American dance culture than professional Black dancers have had. Moreover, Black professional dance companies have been relatively few in number and all of them have been dependent on philanthropic funding for their continued existence. Unlike other areas of the arts, the dependency on dance companies is near total. This dependency has, of course, shaped the direction of Black professional dance. Such a shaping influence from White culture is unknown in Black popular dance. This then is the major contradiction of dance as a performing area: the prevalence and effectiveness of Black popular dance and the dependency of professional, Black concert dance on mainstream largesse.

Concert Dance. Although there was a phenomenal rise in African dance troupes during the BAM era, Black professional dance continued to lag. Partly because some Black choreographers and professional dancers wanted to be considered "dancers" rather than "Black dancers" and were also interested in dance as pure movement rather than dance which makes a sociological, political or ethnic statement. Noted cultural critic Richard A. Long sums up the post-Civil Rights development of concert dance. In *The Black Tradition*, he writes:

> While constraints continue to operate, attributable largely to racist institutions and attitudes, the manifestation of Black talent after fairly open access to training, the impact of the Civil Rights Movement of the 1960s, and the virtual explosion of Black creative and organizational talent in the 1970s, all assure a strong and obvious Black presence in American dance in the last third of the century.

> The leading choreographers who had emerged in 1960 were Alvin Ailey, Talley Beatty, Donald McKayle, and Louis Johnson. Hard upon their heels came Eleo Pomare, Gus Solomons, Jr., and Rod Rodgers. In the next two decades the ranks expanded to include Garth Fagan, Diane McIntyre, Bill T. Jones, Ulysses Dove, and a host of others. Most of the choreographers began as outstanding dancers and their respective companies and works revealed to the dance world a thrilling assemblage of brilliant and accomplished dancers. (Long, *The Black Tradition* 129)

In terms of cultural impact judged by reviews, touring, and the opinion of dance contemporaries, the four major dance companies active during the BAM era were the Alvin Ailey American Dance Company, Arthur Mitchell's Dance Theatre of Harlem, the Eleo Pomare Dance Company, and the Rod Rodgers Dance Company. These companies were the most influential, especially Ailey who traveled extensively, specialized in Black themes and often used Black music, particularly the jazz of artists such as Duke Ellington and Charlie Mingus. Indeed, Ailey is considered the dean of modern Black concert dance. The Dance Theatre of Harlem was notable in its success at cracking the then prevalent notion that Black bodies could not fit into nor be trained to adequately perform in the European classical dance tradition. However, neither Ailey nor the Dance Theatre of Harlem advocated BAM aesthetics or political principles. In this regard, Pomare and Rodgers were leading figures, especially the outspoken Pomare.

In her definitive survey, *Black Dance: From 1619 to Today*, dance scholar Lynne Fauley Emery wrote an enthusiastic assessment of Pomare which included a number of quotes from '70s-era interviews and profiles of Pomare in which he was forthright about his "Blackness." Emery draws from Pomare's own words given in several interviews:

> They have called him angry, to which Eleo Pomare has replied:
> I'm labeled...angry...because I will not do what they want from a black dancer. They want black exotics...I have something to say and I want to say it honestly, strongly and without having it stolen, borrowed or messed over.
> Questioned about discipline, he responds, "How many critics really understand the discipline it takes to erase all white influences, and yet dramatize precisely the world the black artist is struggling to escape from?"
> Of the classic ballet he wrote:
> They say the classic ballet is superior but they're dancing about fairies running around in gardens. They repeat these ancient, ancient rituals to death when there is so much life, so much art around them in everyday life.
> He formed his own company in 1958, toured Europe— where the group received rave reviews—and made his major New York City debut in 1966. (Emery 298, 300)

Pomare's ascendancy parallels BAM's development. He clearly had no qualms about combining politics and aesthetics. He proclaimed, "Our role is to break the ethnocentric thinking patterns which have led these people—drunk with power—to believe that theirs, although dead, is the superior art" (Emery 300).

Rod Rodgers, who formed his integrated dance company in New York in 1966, was also forthright in upholding Black culture as a source for both techniques and inspirations.

>...the theatrical manifestation which we call Black dance is as real and relevant as the uniquely diverse Afro-American culture that it represents. As long as Black Americans have reason to be concerned about the specialness of our identity and as long as we see evidence that our interpretation of our own experience is significantly different from the depictions of our heritage and culture by the establishment media and arts, there will be a justification for continuing to cultivate and support separate Afro-American arts generally and dance artists specifically. (Emery 303)

Emery notes that, "In 1965 Rodgers became director of the dance project of New York's Mobilization for Youth..." (Emery 303). This is the same year that BART/S, which was also a Mobilization for Youth program, was founded. While I will not argue that one was the result of the other, nevertheless, there is a confluence of ideals and direction towards Black self-determination in the arts.

Though both Pomare and Rodgers maintained a high profile and were recognized as important creative forces even by those who might disagree with their politics, like BAM in general, attempts have been made to write them out of history. Edward Thorpe—a dance critic for *The Evening Standard* in London and the author of several books including *Kenneth MacMillan: The Man and the Ballets* and *Ballet Genius*—wrote a survey overview called *Black Dance*. Thorpe's coffee table book, which is replete with photographs and extends through the 1980s, devotes pages to numerous choreographers but does not even mention either Pomare or Rodgers. In fact, Thorpe's book virtually skips over the BAM era as if BAM, as well as the leading choreographers of that era, did not exist.

Thorpe's attempt at erasure notwithstanding, both Pomare and Rodgers were major inspirations as choreographers, dancers, and directors of professional dance companies. There were many other choreographers and company directors active in Black concert dance including Garth Fagan, whose Rochester, New York-based company debuted in November 1977, and Chuck Davis. Emery writes that Davis founded the Chuck Davis Dance Company in 1968 "to present works that portray the complete range of black dance heritage, from its origins in African dance to contemporary forms" (Emery 330). Commenting on BAM era dance, Emery notes that:

> Throughout the United States companies led by black dancers and choreographers have appeared, many of them in connection with a sponsoring group, such as the Elma Lewis School in Roxbury, Massachusetts, where Talley Beatty, for example, organized a repertory company. Fred Benjamin, who began his dance study at the Lewis School, organized his own company under the sponsorship of Clarck Center. The Inner City Cultural Center in Los Angeles developed a repertory company under the leadership of Donald McKaye, Janet Collins, and Jaime Rodgers, while the Jones-Haywood School of Dance in Washington, D.C., presented several ballet performances throughout the city during the summer of 1970. Cleveland's Karamu House has been the starting place of many fine dancers and the influence of Gloria Unti's San Francisco Performing Arts Workshop has been felt. (Emery 308)

A plethora of Black concert dance companies notwithstanding, Black vernacular dance remained the wellspring and major force. Popular dance was overwhelmingly Black in that the techniques and creators overwhelmingly originated in Black working class communities across America without the benefits of formal training or direction from non-Blacks. Professional concert dance, on the other foot, although certainly influenced by Black culture, maintained a Euro-centric influence both aesthetically and politically. This dichotomy prevails today.

Black Dance Aesthetics. Even more so than literature, dance (especially concert dance) raises the question: is there really a Black aesthetic? Dr. Sandra Richards, an associate professor of theatre and African American studies at Northwestern University, addresses the question at a 1989 symposium, "Black Choreographers Moving Toward The 21st Century." She states:

> One of the things that has been apparent to me from these

panels is that it seems that at least in the dance world we can make a distinction between a "Black Aesthetic" and "Black Choreographers." I am not saying that is a negative distinction, but it seems to me that it is apparent that some Black choreographers do not necessarily practice a Black aesthetic.

Allow me to briefly define my use of the term. A Black aesthetic is rooted in an African matrix, yet, in some of its specific elaborations, modified by the disapora experience of the Americas. As in most cultures, performance serves a variety of social functions: it entertains, teaches the moral vision of a given community, and enhances community cohesion. What seems to be particular about African and African disaporic performance is the high value placed upon the moment of transcendence, when the performer "catches a spirit," so to speak. That is, the moment when the performer goes beyond the rehearsed to an improvised or spontaneous testing of his/her earthboundness (in dance) in order to explore the previously unexplored. The writer Ralph Ellison offers the analogy of jazz, wherein the audience expects the improvisatory moment in which the musician solos, pushing against his known limits towards new discoveries and is supported in his efforts by the rest of the ensemble, who offer a way back into the safety of the known, i.e., of the social unit.

I think we can also speak of a Black aesthetic in terms of a kind of "democracy of the sense." That is, "good" art within this aesthetic is art that is also polyfocal, polyrhythmic, tolerates contradiction, does not necessarily sublimate "minor" to "major" points of view, and has an open-ended quality in its challenge to audiences to figure out the meaning(s) of the artwork. (Richards 53)

In a moment of revelatory candidness, modern choreographer, Donald Byrd, responded to Richards's statement with a confession that precisely spells out the difference between Blacks who are practitioners of a Black aesthetic and Blacks who practice either a "gumbo" aesthetic (in that it is a mix of many specifics) or a Eurocentric aesthetic in their artwork. Byrd states:

It is a fact that I'm Black and that I grew up having certain cultural experiences and that is always in what I do. However, this is my particular issue here. I don't know if this is true for everybody. If you are Black and you end up at a school like Stanford or Yale or Harvard, something happens to your relationship with the community that you came out of, if you came from a predominantly Black community. It changes. That's the experience that I had. And I would say that affects the work that I do. So there is an aspect of the work that I do that I would say is Black aesthetic and then there is a part of it that isn't. In the generation that I'm from, the whole point was assimilation. To assimilate into mainstream American culture, I worked hard. (Byrd 53)

Here we directly confront one of the major controversies raised by BAM: is a Black aesthetic the result of nature or nurture? Richards and others argue essentially that a Black aesthetic is a learned aesthetic and, as choreographer Byrd clarifies, Blacks may choose to use or not use that learned aesthetic.

Choreographer Jawole Willa Jo Zollar, founder and artistic director of the Urban Bush Women dance/theatre company, proudly affirms her BAM roots. She asserts, "one of the important things for me was reading the critical work of Larry Neal and Amiri Baraka" (Zollar 89). Informed by BAM ideals, Zollar states:

> When I hear choreographers say, "I'm a choreographer who happens to be a Black person," I understand what they are saying, but it's an unfortunate choice of words. Something about that statement is very painful because what I hear them buying into is, "Yes, I see Black as limited, too, so I don't want to be defined by that," rather than saying, "I am an African or Black American choreographer, and I choose to work with this aesthetic, or I choose to work in a culturally specific aesthetic based on growing up as an African or Black American person and everything that means."
>
> It doesn't mean any limitations. It hurts me to hear people say, "I'm colorless." I had that experience with some choreographers in England who were under attack, specifically Ralph Lemon, who was told, "You shouldn't be on this program; you're not a Black choreographer because you're using a Eurocentric or ballet-based aesthetic." In response, his choice of words was, "I'm colorless and I just..." For me, this was an unfortunate choice, because it means we are buying into the thing we say we don't want. (Zollar 79)

This is precisely an issue raised by BAM which argued for a break with the Western tradition because, as Zollar says:

> Racism is part and parcel of this culture. No one escapes it. Racism is institutionalized. It's in every nook and cranny of our society and of our existence. No one can escape. Racism has its own dynamic that we all are subject to. I think we have to be honest about this and say, "I have grown up in America,

I am racist, sexist, and homophobic." That is what we are programmed to be. Then we've got to challenge ourselves to, at every turn, deal with these issues and really try to overcome them. They're in all of us. As a Black person growing up in America, I've been trained to be a victim; I've been trained to be oppressed, so I've got to overcome all of that. (Zollar 73)

In the American context, racism has ruled, creating an adversarial context for Blacks in the arts and limiting the options open to professional Blacks. Dr. Brenda Dixon, an assistant professor of dance at Temple University and board member of the Dance Critics Association, delineates the historical confrontation as such:

Redefinition, reversal, and irony practiced by Afro-Americans are survival tactics. So if a postmodernist like Douglas Dunn performs or quotes ballet but doesn't straighten his legs or show heroic energy, he is redefining the idiom; he parallels traditional Afrocentric redefinition which is recognized by most Americans, be they white or Black. It's ironic, it's paradoxical, and it contains double entendres rather than linear logic. And all of those values are inherent in African-based folklore, music, and dance.

The United States resists the integration of the Black dancing body with Eurocentric body codes and, of course, we know that those body codes, which are based on a ramrod straight torso and articulation of limbs in relationship to this center, is very different than a technique which is based on isolations, asymmetry, torso articulation, and of course syncopation, polyrhythms, and polymeters. That's pretty difficult for a culture to accept which was based, in its initial premise, on a minimalist Protestant ethic. Eurocentric body codes were totally on the other side of the spectrum and an African American like Dunham was made to believe that her dances did not even belong on the concert stage.

African Americans aspiring to do ballet have been told that they have been trying to achieve a Eurocentric form which their bodies can't really learn to do. The career of Arthur Mitchell and others before him disproves this contention, although choreographers and critics saw to it that his ballet roles in the New York City Ballet remained jazzy or exotic according to the standard stereotypes. So Mitchell has taken Balanchine's americanization of ballet a step further, and this isn't recognized at all. By creating a ballet company composed principally of dancers of African lineage, he has institutionalized the final taboo in ballet, the Black dancing body.

> The Afrocentric influence is the defining ingredient which
> sets American ballet apart from its European counterpart.
> (Dixon 23–24)

The significance of BAM is that it not only offered an
alternative, but also forced open doors to options. BAM made
it possible for Black professional artists to reject Black advocacy
and to pursue careers as assimilated artists. This is one of the
richest results of BAM: even as BAM encouraged artists to be
Black, it also made it possible for artists to ignore or downplay
their "Blackness" and to assimilate into the dominant culture.

Again, Donald Byrd is amazingly candid in confronting these
issues. Here Byrd addresses the issues that continuously swirled
around BAM. He states:

> In regard to our responsibility to the community, I would say I have
> been negligent. My concerns have been about myself, and not
> about giving something back and putting something in, even
> though that's been in the back of my head. Given the economic
> state of things right now, the primary concern for most artists is just
> being able to do the work; we have not felt supported enough
> that we could actually go back [into the community]. One of the
> remarkable things, for me, from participating in this festival, is that
> I notice how much I need the approval of the Black community.
> That's become an issue for me, and I never knew how much that
> need was there.
>
> Now, the thing about Black dancers doing classical
> movement...My company, at the moment, has only one Black
> dancer in it. The kind of Black dancers that I need are very much
> in demand, and I can't afford them. I can't compete with the
> well-funded, well-organized, well-established companies for those
> dancers. Obviously, I would love to have them. The obvious solution
> to that is if I can't get them, go into the community and create
> them, and that will ensure that I have a long, ongoing relationship
> with the Black community. One of the things that happens in our
> culture, in America, is that most of us are basically existing, and
> we haven't thought of some of the larger social issues. (Byrd 94)

This was and continues to be a major theoretical contribution
of BAM: it forced one to contemplate the larger social issues
and the relationship of whatever one does to these larger
issues. Moreover, BAM didn't just abstractly contemplate these
questions, BAM called for involvement and movement, and also
inspired people and gave them a sense of confidence that they

could confront and overcome whatever were the obstacles.

We have addressed some of these philosophical questions in the context of a discussion of dance because it illustrates the far-reaching implications of BAM. Whereas most of us do not associate the Black Arts Movement with dance, as the foregoing discussion has demonstrated, the movement affected every aspect of Black culture and continues to be relevant.

Nontsizi Cayou, chair of the department of dance at San Franciso State University, author of *Modern Jazz Dance*, and founder of Wajumbe Cultural Institution, Inc., offers a summary assessment of BAM. Cayou writes:

> The greatest influence on any member of the Black dance community during this period, however, was the great consciousness movement. A great collective consciousness affected all Black people in the United States. This movement was so pervasive that no Black person could escape, not even those who tried. The issues were centered on political and human rights, cultural identity, and "doing our own thing."
>
> Historically, there has always been a relationship between times of high collective consciousness and the development of art and culture in the Black community, a development which always begins at the grassroots level and moves upward to and through cultural artists. From 1960 to 1970 there were 70 or 80 social dances which were created as an act of collective consciousness.
>
> It was a time of high vibration, a fertile time for the expression of creative energy in all aspects of Black life, including dance...In concluding this segment on the Sixties and its historical significance to the Black choreographer, I would like to forward the possibility that the impact and value of the historical occurrences are yet to be understood and appreciated by both scholars and artists. (Cayou 13)

CHAPTER 11
VISUAL ARTS

The visual arts, mainly painting and sculpture, but also craftwork, of the Black Arts Movement took on a fiery form not seen since the heyday of the Harlem Renaissance. In the 1920s artists such as Aaron Douglas, Richmond Barthe, Sargent Johnson and Agusta Savage introduced African icons, imagery and inspiration in their two- and three-dimensional works. During the Black Arts Movement era, Africa and the African influence took prominence as an aesthetic. The triad of BAM concerns—Black leadership and mass involvement in the arts, the development of a Black Aesthetic, and the creation of socially engaged art which openly advocated Black struggle—were directly presented in the artwork of individuals and collectives. The move to form collectives consisting of artists who shared a BAM outlook was a significant development in the visual arts. This move was noteworthy since it occurred in an area which has consistently emphasized artists working as isolated individuals, often at odds with their peers and predecessors.

Weusi and Africobra. Of the BAM collectives, the two major forces were Africobra and the New York-based Weusi group. In *Black Art: Ancestral Legacy*, leading art critic/curator/artist Edmund Barry Gaither assessed Weusi as "the most important and abiding" of "Afrocentric artist organizations" which emerged during the BAM era in New York. He explains:

> Founded in Harlem in 1965, Weusi was organized as an association of artists which sought "to preserve, develop, promote and project African and African-American culture through the visual sciences," and to make available to ordinary people fine art at affordable prices. In 1969 the group expanded to become the Weusi Ya Sanaa Gallery and Academy of Fine Arts and Studies...Among the artists who are/were members of Weusi are: Otto Neals, Abdullah Aziz, Kay Brown, Falcon Beazer, Taiwo DuVall, Abdul Rahman, James Phillips, Ademola Olugebefola, Bill Howell (deceased), Oko Pyatt, Jim

Sepyo, Milton Martin, Rudi Irwin and Gaylord Hassan. (Gaither 29)

Gaither asserts that, "AfriCobra, though only one of many Afrocentric visual movements in the Americas, is nevertheless the oldest and most consistent artist group in the United States which espouses a synthesis of African and Afro-American stylistic elements in the service of an ideology of socio/political liberation" (Gaither 28).

In "Heading for a Black Aesthetic," Wadsworth A. Jarrell gives both the history and philosophy of Africobra. He writes:

> In 1967, on Chicago's South Side, a group of artists formed an organization called OBAC, Organization of Black American Culture. These artists became the visual voices of the civil rights struggle. They were on the cutting edge, slicing through aesthetic sounds in search of a new direction. The OBAC artists' energies and efforts culminated in the *Wall of Respect*, in search of a black aesthetic. The names and images of black militant leaders screamed from the face of a Chicago tenement building in the heart of the black community, exploding in brilliant expressive colors. This brought only partial fulfillment to the OBAC artists, and later the group disbanded.
>
> A splinter group of OBAC artists continued to explore the possibilities of articulating black art that speaks to black people. There was a strong need for a specific direction in art that would encompass black lifestyles and enlighten the black race about their history.
>
> COBRA, the Coalition of Black Revolutionary Artists, was born in Chicago in '68.... To support the ideology of a black aesthetic, it became obvious that we should adopt a sound philosophy that expressed aspects of black existence in America... The subject matter must be clear and easy to understand by the viewer, with words stating the theme and initial idea the artist is attempting to convey. The words were to be an integral part of the total composition yet convey messages like a billboard, and this was to be a step towards a new dimension in art. Our art was to be categorized to keep others from imposing a category upon it. We agreed on the name "Poster Art" because it was direct and clear.

Jarrell identified:

The following principles were adopted as part of the philosophy of COBRA:
   a. *Open Color*: integration of the subject and background

where in some instances they form a synthesis to stress freedom.

b. *Free Symmetry*: the syncopated rhythm pertinent to African dance, walk, and song; repetition with change, as in the blues.

c. *Arbitrary Use of Light and Line*: lost and found line that is used to accent and delineate specific areas. Reverse the direction of light to reject the concept of single source light coming only from one direction.

d. *Positive Images*: images committed to humanism inspired by black people and their experiences. Images that enlighten the dignity of black people by accentuating the positive. Art that reflects and relates to African people, with which African people can identify.

e. *Programmatic*; art that teaches, preaches, and embraces concepts that offer positive and feasible solutions to our collective problems, local, national, and international.

f. *Mimesis at Mid-Point*: composition which marks the spot where the real and the unreal, the objective and the non-objective, the plus and the minus meet.

g. *Shine*: a lustre that is apparent in black life styles—gold and silver threads in clothing, shiny cars, shoes, hair and furniture.

h. *Written Statements*: direct, unequivocal statements incorporated in the composition to clarify the concept. Art that carries the visual impact of a billboard, but with sophistication; art that speaks to African people, Poster Art.

i. *Cool-Ade Color*: a variegation of bright intense colors with sensibility and harmony. Colors in dress worn by black people everywhere.

j. *Visibility*: clarity of form and line based on the interesting irregularity one senses in a freely drawn circle or organic object, the feeling for movement, growth, changes, and human touch.

k. *Expressive Awesomeness*: that which does not appeal to serenity but is concerned with the eternally sublime, rather than ephemeral beauty. Art which moves the emotions and appeals to the senses.

Jarrell continues:

We became AFRICOBRA, African Commune of Bad Relevant Artists, and moved from national to international philosophical concepts. Our concepts were Pan-African. After meeting and working for two years, our artistic efforts culminated in the exhibition "Ten In search Of A Nation" at the Studio Museum of Harlem in 1970. Our exhibition was a knock-out; AFRICOBRA was born. AFRICOBRA appeared on the horizons in a vivid blaze of cool-ade colors, sending out warm vibes from compelling positive images, clarity of form, free symmetry, shine, syncopated rhythm, and expressive awesomeness. The exhibition was unprecedented. No other group of artists had attempted to work collectively towards a philosophy with such a compelling direction. (Jarrell 16–18)

I have quoted at length because it is important for us to understand that Akili Amabenemu, Michael Auld, Adger Cowans, Jeff Donaldson, Michael Harris, Napoleon Jones-Henderson, Wadsworth Jarrell, James Phillips, Murry DePillars, Frank Smith, Nelson Stevens and Gerald Williams (and other members at various points) were collectively, actively and consciously working to develop the Black Arts Movement. Although much of this history has been ignored, misrepresented, lost, and/or intentionally buried, AFRICOBRA offers instructive illustration of the far reaching implications of the Black Arts Movement—an arts movement which profoundly altered the production and perception of "art" in America.

Fortunately, Samella Lewis, an artist from an earlier generation, understood the importance of documenting the ongoing developments in the visual arts. In 1970 she founded *International Quarterly of The Black Arts*, which still continues today. As has been the case with other BAM era publications, *International Quarterly* has not received the acclaim due it as a repository of images, criticism, interviews, and explication of Black art creators, trends and major developments. Nonetheless, Ms. Lewis has steadfastly maintained her journal and has thereby provided a concrete and ongoing institutional presence for Black visual arts. *International Quarterly* is, in fact, one of only two BAM-born journals (*Black Scholar* is the other) to survive into the nineties and continue publishing on a regular schedule.

Outdoor Festivals. In conjunction with the predominately White "counterculture" movement, a whole era of massive outdoor cultural events was inaugurated that included the vending of art, handicrafts, and food. Although people may not realize it, this model harkens back to New Orleans's Congo Square, where enslaved Africans gathered on Sundays to sing, dance, make music and sell their wares and food, and to fellowship. This became an ongoing model for arts and social activities.

Moreover, as is the case with people of African descent worldwide, every social event—from a church service to a political prisoner rally, from a college homecoming weekend to an impromptu neighborhood block party, regardless of its politics or purported purpose—has a cultural vector, a celebratory tone, and an aspect of collective performance associated with the event. The visual arts traditionally has been a major part of all of these activities, although in many cases the specific artwork was the clothing, the handicrafts, and, indeed, the sense of style of our people themselves. To their credit, BAM adherents picked up on and amplified this African-based aesthetic of incorporating art into every social activity. In this regard, BAM was woven into the social fabric of everyday Black life.

The Black Arts Movement also had far-reaching implications on the professional arts and arts administration because BAM opened doors to positions which had previously been closed to Blacks, regardless of the qualifications and experience a Black applicant or potential applicant might have. Today, the many Blacks who function as curators, administrators, executive directors, senior producers and consultants in major and regional arts organizations, in commercial arts enterprises, in non-profits, and in philanthropic and government agencies (such as state and regional arts organizations) hold those positions as a direct result of the foment and struggles of the sixties and seventies. Participants in the Black Arts Movement led the charge for Black empowerment, encouraging Blacks to take charge of the propagation and preservation of our culture, especially in public and quasi-public funding agencies.

CHAPTER 12
BAM'S CRITICS

Given its Black Power pedigree, vociferous and sustained criticisms of the Black Arts Movement are not surprising—even when that criticism comes from Black literary figures. While many critics have simply ignored and/or wholesale dismissed BAM, some critics, such as the influential Henry Louis Gates, Jr., cannot resist slipping a negative reference to BAM politics and/or aesthetics into whatever subject matter they happen to be writing about. Such continuing sniping suggests just how formidable and negative some critics consider BAM.

Clearly we are dealing with more than literary differences. Much of the criticism has an emotional/psychological vector that has as much to do with the background of the person delivering the criticism as it does with BAM itself. In his autobiography, Baraka relates an incident that partially illustrates the point. He writes, "Fifteen years later, a white woman came up to me in a bar and talked to me in a bitter accusing tone about how I had personally estranged her black husband away from her. With my wife, Amina, sitting there listening to her. It was sad" (Baraka, *Autobiography* 218). Critics who are involved in intimate interracial relationships, as is Gates, often have emotional investments which are diametrically opposed to—indeed outright attacked by—a significant portion of BAM literature. But the psychological dimension is not just psychosexual, there is also an element of bourgeoisie propriety that frowns on "impolite rhetoric" and certainly abhors violence. The sippers of tea versus the crude, beer-drinking revolutionaries.

In the conclusion to his book *Afro-American Poetics: Revisions of Harlem and the Black Aesthetic*, critic Houston A. Baker, Jr., in a confessional tone, offers a criticism of BAM, specifically pinpointing Baraka. Baker writes:

> In *private*, Baraka, who was a foremost public advocate for the Black Arts is: The Artist as Thug. The tough guy stands in seamy opposition to the idealistic, revolutionary culture worker.

The criminal and asocial private aspects of the sixties could, perhaps, be held in abeyance. But such a suppression would prevent us from arriving at that second sign in an American equation called "Black Power." Having reread the twenties under the sign of blackness or race, it is now incumbent to read the sixties under the sign "power." ... [P]articipants in the Black Arts often failed, I believe, to negotiate the intricacies of "power." Principal confusions of Black Arts workers and critics—myself included—involved a failure to distinguish between bullying militarism and revolutionary organization, between cults and interest groups, between verbal throwaways designed for political rallies and carefully articulated Afro-American expressive texts. Bullet words and paramilitary posturing were read as signs of black "power," and a rhetoric of hard facts was mistaken for a realization of genuine expressive power... In the Black Arts, loudspeaking resulted in a plethora of drumlike, monotonous, and sometimes silly utterances passed off as the "New Black Poetry." Black critical complicity emerged as a Black Aesthetic which sometimes proclaimed: "If it's too loud, you're too old!" Which is to say, anyone (especially *white* ones) who had reservations, questions, or criticisms was deemed too pedantic, bourgeois, or unrevolutionary to comprehend the excellence of *all* black works.

I surely must seem uncharitable in this assessment. For, as I have acknowledged, the sixties gave birth to me as an "Afro-American" and as an Afro-American critic. I believe the present assessment is necessary, though, as a release and relief of the spirit. (Baker 175–176)

But Baker's "criticism" is tame compared to Baraka's own criticism of himself and the BAM era. Baraka pulls no punches and speaks clearly against militarism and adventurism even as he acknowledges his complicity in the events and movements he criticizes. But in Baraka's criticism there is no apologizing to the status quo, for Baraka remains at odds with, rather than comfortable within, the American status quo. In the final analysis, for many people who were there at the time but who were not active "off-campus," Black Power was a phase one went through in one's youth rather than a lifelong commitment made to struggle.

One key to understanding the difference is very simple. The Black Arts Movement was about independence rather than inclusion. BAM saw itself as a revolutionary movement and agreed fully with Chairman Mao[1] when he said, "A revolution is not a dinner party, or writing an essay, or painting a picture, or doing embroidery; it cannot be so refined, so leisurely and gentle, so temperate, kind, courteous, restrained and magnanimous. A revolution is an insurrection, an act of violence by which one class overthrows another."

This actual emphasis on revolution is then the crux of a great deal of BAM criticism. Of course, BAM made mistakes and some actions were outright stupid, but the errors along the way do not negate the goal of self-defense, self-determination, and self-respect, the achievement of which, BAM advocates argued, would require nothing less than revolutionary action. Baker's heartfelt comments may be characterized as the neocolonial misgivings of a reluctant fellow traveler petitioning the academy for admittance as a "humanist" who, mainly interested in literature (i.e. "Afro-American Spirit work"), now rejects the use of violence.

Baker goes on to indicate what he felt was important about BAM. He writes:

> I have indicated the seamier sides, the thuggish and nonhumanistic sides of Afro-American aggressive resistance during the sixties. On the more positive side of such resistance is the actual empowerment that it provided. It is indisputably the case that had there been no aggressive Black Power offensive during the late sixties and early seventies, whites surely would have felt free to continue to whip black heads and to kill black leaders on prime-time television. The entrance of the "tough guys" changed all of that.
>
> At Yale, for example, the president and his men became aggressively willing to talk to black "intellectuals" after the Black Panther party organized in New Haven. Malcolm X, with his usual perspicacity, realized years ago that when he emerged as a militant and charismatic national black leader, white people were suddenly eager to hear the integrationist rhetoric of Martin Luther King.
>
> The doors of business, the academy, and the professions opened more as a direct function of Afro-American street therapy than as a response to beneficent changes of white American hearts. (Baker 177–178)

There in a nutshell is the Black petit-bourgeois interest fully unveiled, i.e. access to "the doors of business, the academy, and the professions." Access for the Gates and Bakers of the Black world may have been a byproduct of BAM, but, as reggae artist Bob Marley so presciently warned, "equal opportunity" was never the goal. Indeed, once one becomes comfortably ensconced within "business, academy and the professions," one necessarily defends one's comfort and criticizes any and all threats to that comfort, especially "militant" threats such as BAM.

If the personal psychosocial and professional attachments were not enough, there is also an element of cultural ignorance implicit in much of the criticism. While giving lip-service to Black folklore and music, the lifestyle of some BAM critics is so far removed from "Blackness" that except for their dark skins they could easily be mistaken for any other upper-middle class Americans in their manifestations of cultural values and behavior. They dispassionately study Black culture but have no direct emotional involvement in its production, propagation or preservation, except in so far as writing about and being an expert on Blackness serves business, academy or their profession.

Scholar David Lionel Smith has written one of the most insightful theoretical assessments of BAM in an essay titled, "The Black Arts Movement and Its Critics." In this essay, Smith correctly assesses the ideological thrusts directing the critical assault on BAM. He writes:

> The relationship of criticism to the Black Arts Movement is complicated. Some of the most knowledgeable and discerning critics of the movement, such as Neal, are also important figures within the movement. This is true even of many academically oriented critics, such as Stephen Henderson. On the other hand, some influential recent black critics have been openly hostile to the Black Arts Movement—most conspicuously Henry Louis Gates, Jr. The activists of a movement are not necessarily the ideal persons to assess the actual achievements of that movement, though their comments can be illuminating. Similarly, the ideological opponents of a movement are not the most reliable sources of careful and dispassionate analyses. Unfortunately, most criticism regarding the Black Arts Movement has been deeply partisan, for or against. The fierce polemics surrounding the movement have discouraged careful and balanced scholarship. Yet without such scholarship, the achievements and failures of the movement can never be clearly understood.
>
> A conspicuous difference between Black Arts writing and the work of previous black writers such as Wright and Baldwin is that Black Arts writing directly addresses a black audience. Thus, it immediately demands of its reader (or listener) a

sympathy and familiarity with black culture and black idioms—and in many cases, with black nationalist cultural politics as well. In particular, since such writing addresses common black people, it demands that the critic be familiar with the common experience of black people—or more precisely, that the critic share the kind of knowledge that such an audience would likely possess. Finally, since the Black Aesthetic claims to reject European literary models, it requires the writers to develop new forms, new techniques, and new conventions. Therefore, the critic must be prepared to recognize, understand, and assess these new literary forms and experiments. Needless to say, an education in conventional literary studies does not prepare a critic to face these challenges. Consequently, a critic who wishes to study Black Arts Movement writing must be prepared to move beyond university training, which can entail both establishing new criteria and rejecting established ones. (Given the familiar set of incentives, rewards, and punishments within the academy, such boldness could prove very costly to a member of an English department—especially an untenured one.) (Smith 102)

Smith addresses two seminal complications: (1) the motive and methodologies of the critics, and (2) the positives and negatives of BAM. On the critics, Smith is succinct and deadly when he writes:

> In a very direct sense, Gates' difference with the Black Aesthetic critics is summed up in his comment: "[W] e write, it seems to me, primarily for other critics of literature" (Figures 56). This expresses the conventional, academic understanding of criticism as the specialized discourse of a professional elite, in direct opposition to the Black Arts vision of a populist, communal discourse. Though Gates often assaults Black Aesthetic critics for having an ideological agenda, the real struggle is between one ideology that rejects the institutional status quo and another that embraces it. (Smith 106)

As we will see when we consider Charles Rowell's criticism of BAM, Smith accurately articulates the fundamental contradiction surrounding criticisms of BAM, i.e. contending ideologies demarcated by opposition and alternative versus embraced by and absorbed into the literary status quo. Smith is also very accurate in assessing the direction BAM strove to go. He concludes:

Neal wants poets to sing or to scream like James Brown.

In addition to music, he proposes oratory ("Malcolm's speeches") as another paradigm. The emphasis on vernacular performance implies that literature should become an immediate, communal form to be experienced in public, contrary to the private experience of reading a text. Indeed, much of Black Aesthetic theorizing, especially Neal's seems to want to replace reading as the dominant mode of literary reception with listening. Theater and poetry readings, once again, represent movement in this direction. Consequently, writers attempting to take "the Black Aesthetic" seriously would be inclined to reject formalist aesthetics and to think most seriously about the sound of their work and its effect upon a listening audience. They would be more concerned with rhythm than with stanzaic form, more with rhyme sound than with the formal pattern of rhyme, and, in particular, they would be concerned with diction based upon conversational norms rather than upon literary conventions. The use of allusion as a device would not vanish from such an aesthetic, but its focus would shift away from bookish references and into the realm of black historical experience and popular culture. An obvious area for literary exploration would be modes in which verbal effect and narrative converge. A striking example of the latter kind of innovation is Baraka's ritual drama, *Slave Ship*. Thus, if Black Aesthetic theorizing proscribed writers' use of existing literary traditions, it also opened up exciting new possibilities of artistic experimentation, and it sought to redefine the relationship between writer and audience. In effect, this meant both liabilities and opportunities for writers, audiences, and critics. Neither the liabilities nor the innovations have been adequately understood. Regardless, the commitment to ground literature in black vernacular culture was a definitive characteristic of Black Aesthetic theory. (Smith 101)

The task yet to be completed is a critical assessment aimed at absorbing BAM strengths and discarding and/or strengthening BAM weaknesses. This task is complicated by BAM's inherent "oppositional" stance to the status quo. In many ways, BAM has suffered similarly to jazz, in that the majority of the critics have been people from outside the culture—except in BAM's case, the outsiders are not only Whites but also Blacks who have chosen to cast their lot with "business, academy and professions" rather than with the masses.

The final critic I will consider is Charles Rowell. He was publisher and editor of *Callaloo* magazine at the time of this writing. Unfortunately, Rowell is the quintessential anti-BAM black critic—unfortunate because he is also a major spokesperson for and publisher of Black literature. *Callaloo* was founded by Tom Dent, Charles Rowell and Jerry Ward in 1976. Dent was based in New Orleans, Rowell was teaching at Southern University in Baton Rouge, Louisiana, and Jerry Ward was teaching at Tougaloo College located on the outskirts of Jackson, Mississippi. The avowed aim of *Callaloo* as spelled out on their founding masthead was direct and unequivocal: "*CALLALOO* is a non-profit, tri-annual journal devoted to the creative and critical writings, arts, culture and life of the Black South." Unfortunately, shortly after its founding, Rowell moved to Kentucky and took over as editor. He dropped Dent and Ward, acquired funding from various sources and liquidated the "Black South" emphasis. *Callaloo* became what it is today, an academic oriented, literary journal focusing on Black writers worldwide.

> In the preface to the debut issue, Tom Dent asserts: "*CALLALOO* was born out of a specific desire to give expression to the new writers in the Deep South area. It appears at a time when we are suffering the demise of *BLACK WORLD* and many of the community-based literary magazines, which sprung up in the late sixties & early seventies. This paucity of supporting outlets for our growing literature underscores the need for a new journal as it does the need for journals like *HOO-DOO* and *OBSIDIAN*, to which we feel a brotherly relationship" (Dent v). Now a juried publication, *Callaloo* is no longer receptive to emerging Black writers in the South. This is part and parcel of the shift in emphasis away from community and toward the upper reaches of professionalism, which is characteristic of those who abandoned BAM once they entered the newly opened doors of "business, academy and the professions."

Rowell's major contribution to the premier issue was "Diamonds in a Sawdust Pile: Notes to Black South Writers," an anti-BAM tirade that masquerades as cultural criticism. First, because he cannot deny that BAM opened many doors, Rowell gives an obligatory and brief genuflection to BAM's accomplishments. He writes:

> Let it not be construed that I view the Black Arts Movement as a failure. On the contrary, I see the Movement as a historical necessity and an achievement. As a historical necessity, it once and for all issued a statement to White critics that their unwarranted negative criticism of Black literature is founded

on the racist myopia of their culture, and that, therefore, their pontifications are predicated on anti-humanist intentions. For the achievements of the Movement, one has only to point to its capturing of a Black audience for the literature, its encouragement of Black creativity, its teaching self-affirmation and validity within the framework of all African peoples—the list could go on and on. But to rearticulate again and again these and other achievements is to become racially self-congratulatory and, hence, stagnant. Therefore, with the hope of giving directions for Black South literature to come, I want now to focus on what I consider some of the shortcomings of the Movement to which, I hope, writers and critics here will not fall prey. (Rowell 5)

Afterwards Rowell goes on the attack. With three main criticisms, first he writes, "as a non-South urban phenomenon, the Black Arts Movement not only neglected the Southern experience; it also ignored many Black South critics, writers and other artists. And those critics [it] could not ignore—like Alice Walker, Albert Murray, Robert Hayden, and Ernest Gaines, for example—they often attacked because these writers did not readily subscribe to the rigid prescriptive political dictum of the Aesthetic" (5–6). This is an ironic criticism in light of the fact that once Rowell shook the red clay off his boots and ascended the ivory tower of academe, he committed the same infractions for which he criticized BAM. He "neglected" and "ignored" Black southern writers and critics.

One of the unaddressed aspects of the absence of Black southern literature is the fact that few of the Black South writers, Rowell included, have been interested in writing primarily about the South. If one examines the body of Rowell's literary work (especially after he went to Kentucky and began his escape from the South and "southern parochialness"), it becomes clear that an emphasis on Black southern themes and substance is absent. Part of this lack is undoubtedly that the establishment publishing circles are not interested, but the other part is that the writers themselves have not been interested in examining these issues. The Black Aesthetic's chief architect, Addison Gayle was completely honest when he opened a 1974 article with this statement:

"We are a Southern people," John Killens had said, "because

that is where our people are closest to Africa. But our literature does not show this." I thought immediately about my own writing and discerned an almost purposeful absence of my Southern experiences, as if, somehow, what I had known there and endured there and hated there and loved there had been obliterated by my experiences in the North; I thought, too, of my contemporaries—novelists, essayists, poets, critics—and, with the exception of Killens and Ernest Gaines, I could recall none who dealt with the South in a significant way, though a great many of them, like myself, were Southerners. (Gayle "Reclaiming" 20–21)

The absence of southern themes was caused as much by self-censorship and self-rejection as by any penchant of BAM or any other literary movement to suppress "southerness." Additionally, the hard news of America's literary life is that the overwhelming majority of publishing interests are in the northeast. Indeed, had it not been for BAM, a significant number of those Black southern writers who did get published, more likely than not, would not have been published at all.

The truth is that while each had its own regional interest, all of the BAM publications were receptive to Black southern writers. Rowell does acknowledge that in the same critique when he writes, "Thanks to Dudley Randall of Broadside Press and Hoyt Fuller of *Black World* our Southern voices were occasionally heard." But Rowell is being less than candid. The other journals were also receptive and Rowell knew this first hand because his poetry was published in *Journal of Black Poetry* along with numerous other Black southern writers. Certainly, Black southern writers were not published commensurate with their talent or numbers, but to assert that they were ignored and locked out is a direct contradiction of the evidence of the publications themselves.

Rowell is flat out wrong when he contends, "most non-South advocates of the Black Aesthetic closed their ranks at the border of the Mason-Dixon line and shut their eyes and ears to the creative and critical fervor in the making in the South" (6). The proof is in the publications, not in assertions by a professor trying to make a name for himself by accusing BAM of ignoring an entire region. When one goes back through BAM publications, even a casual researcher will note that the Black south is represented.

A final ironic note is that early in his article Rowell quotes Addison Gayle, the editor of *The Black Aesthetic* and the literary critic most prominently identified with the Black Aesthetic. Rowell points to "an article in the September, 1974, issue of *Black World*," however he does not give the name of the article he quotes. Significantly, the title was "Reclaiming the Southern Experience: The Black Aesthetic 10 Years Later."

The September 1974 issue of *Black World* was also the annual poetry issue. It included a poetry feature on Alvin Aubert of Louisiana, poetry by southern poets Tom Dent and Julia Fields, a Charles Rowell review of a poetry book by a Black southern writer, plus a "Report on A Poetry Festival, Third Annual Melvin A. Butler Memorial," which was written by Jerry Ward. The festival in question was held at Southern University in Baton Rouge, and the featured story ran three and a half pages, including photos of Pinkie Gordon Lane and Eugene Redmond; a panel consisting of Charles Rowell, Dudley Randall and Jerry Ward; a reading featuring Ahmos Zu-Bolton, Irma McClaurin, and Larry Neal; and a reading featuring Alvin Aubert. The question must be raised: who was Rowell attacking and why? The evidence is clear that far from being ignored, Black southern writers were featured. Moreover, the leading champion of the Black Aesthetic, Addison Gayle, had issued a 1974 statement calling for more attention to be paid to Black southern literature. Rather than pretend he is breaking new ground and saying something that the architects of the Black Aesthetic were unwilling to hear, why didn't Rowell acknowledge the source of some of his thinking and point out that over a year earlier, Gayle had raised and directly addressed the very question of Black southern inclusion? Unsubstantiated attacks, such as Rowell's December 1975 lecture, smack of deep-seated envy and a massive inferiority complex.

Rowell's second criticism is that, "while the writers of the Movement declared they were writing for the people, and while they argued they were part of the community, they made this distinction: the artist-the man in the street" (6). Rowell does not offer one quote to demonstrate that this dichotomy is indeed generally reflective of BAM writers. Moreover, Rowell's real target was not the difference and tension between the artist and the audience, but rather a perceived shunning of the middle class. Here again, similar to Baker, we get the special pleading of the petit bourgeois for understanding of their goals and aspirations. Or as Rowell articulates:

> For the advocates of the Black Aesthetic it was always "the masses." The advocates often ignored the Black middle class or professionals, who probably more than "the masses," needed to hear. The Movement's dictum on audience was too restricting. And it, no doubt, frustrated and/or silenced many of those writers whose sensibilities were not entirely shaped by a folk community, but who, with study, could have made invaluable contributions to the systematizing of the Black Aesthetic. The Movement did not tolerate the notion that we should as a people develop many kinds of writers whose voices reflect what is positive in the entire spectrum of the Black American community. With its romantic emphasis on "the masses," the Movement caused many writers and would-be writers to speak in cracked and shrilled voices not their own and to write down, as it were, to "the masses" as if they could not comprehend the multiple nuances of the English language. (Rowell 6)

Again the proof is in the publication. One need only read any recent issue of *Callaloo* to see what type of "English language" Rowell was actually interested in publishing. Much of what he publishes is aimed strictly at a literati cognosti who are well versed in the latest literary theories of academe. Clearly "the masses" need not even crack a cover of *Callaloo* for they will seldom find anything they can understand, not to mention poetry or fiction that they like. This pleading for diversity is really a rallying around the old art-for-art's sake flag by proposing that the artwork in and of itself is more important than connecting to its audience, as if art exists in a vacuum.

Third and finally, Rowell charges that:

> ...at times the Black Arts Movement created an anti-art atmosphere, and, encouraged the creation and publication of much that was less than art. Young ranting poets wrote poems with thoughtless slogans and inarticulate screams that were frequently passed off as art by literary pimps.... The overemphasis on politics in the Black Arts Movement created two major problems: 1) the architects of the Black Aesthetic failed to articulate a clear concept of aesthetic; and 2) they

misinterpreted the concept of functionalism in Black art. ...As far as I can tell that "shared standard or ideal" for a Black Aesthetic has not yet been adequately articulated. And this, it seems to me, is what the architects of the Black Aesthetic should have been about. That is, the articulation of shared standards by which Black people judge beauty should have been the central focus of that plethora of critical treatises on the Black Aesthetic. ...advocates of the Black Aesthetic began to judge all creations by Black artists on that dictum, especially as to whether they had immediate political or practical uses. If the creations of our authors did not fulfill these intentions, then, their poems, their plays, and their novels were, to such critics, invalid. (Rowell 7–8)

In what seemed to be a preemptive response to Rowell, Hoyt Fuller offers a perceptive perspective on the criticism that there was a serious lack of "quality" and "craft" in BAM literature. In his 1968 article "Towards a Black Aesthetic," the *Negro Digest/ Black World* editor writes:

During any year, hundreds of mediocre volumes of prose and poetry by white writers are published, little noted, and forgotten. At the same time, the few creative works by black writers are seized and dissected and, if not deemed of the "highest" literary quality, condemned as still more examples of the failure of black writers to scale the rare heights of literature. And the condemnation is especially strong for those black works which have not screened their themes of suffering, redemption and triumph behind frail facades of obscurity and conscious "universality." (Fuller, "Towards a Black Aesthetic" 202)

The truth of Black literature is the truth of all literature; it takes a long time to develop a tradition of writers. Sometimes we forget that universal literacy for African Americans is little more than a hundred years old. Whatever else BAM did or did not do, it established the precedent that African Americans could write as well as read and that in the literary sphere, we could innovate as well as emulate. Thanks to BAM, it was possible for the average brother and sister to believe that they could be a writer regardless of whether they were college educated or a high school drop out. In much the same way we did with the music, BAM writers ranged from the totally self-taught, untutored "instinctive" writer to highly educated, mentored craftspeople.

The trick was that for most of the hundred years or so

that constituted the post-bellum period of Black literature, the majority of Black writers had been middle class and Euro-American educated. These writers tended to reflect not only the views and values of the middle class, but they often avoided dealing with the experiences of "the masses of Black people." BAM opened literature to the unlettered and in so doing an entirely different set of views and values was introduced into Black literature. So different, in fact, that the work produced by these non-middle class writers seemed—well actually was—"unliterary." By conventional literary standards, much of the BAM literature was technically ordinary, even mediocre, albeit psychologically liberating.

Of course, we are dealing with two factors. First, BAM produced a literature that required a different set of criteria to judge it. Although criteria such as that put forth by Stephen Henderson was rejected by establishment oriented critics, BAM writers often took the same position vis-a-vis establishment oriented critics that jazz musicians took vis-a-vis establishment oriented jazz critics. That is, they paid no attention to what the critics had to say because they believed that most of the critics had little understanding and very little empathy for the work.

The second factor is that the best stand on the shoulders of the rest. The majority of material is not the best but is the fertile ground out of which the best is produced. As Hoyt Fuller sagaciously noted, we need not be embarrassed because there is more sand than gold—that's just the way life is.

That Rowell and other BAM critics continue to traffic in the tired assertion that BAM adherents never developed an adequate literary theory of a Black Aesthetic is a travesty. Ignoring or downplaying the monumental work of critic Stephen Henderson is criminal. Henderson consciously and calmly offered a theoretical framework, made adjustments to the framework over the years, and successfully offered a paradigm that both explained what the New Black Poetry was and what it meant. He also pointed out areas that needed further study and development. In the June 1975 issue of *Black World*, Henderson offered "Saturation: Progress Report On a Theory of Black Poetry," in which he stated:

In *Understanding The New Black Poetry* (Morrow, 1973), I attempted to sketch a critical framework which would help make the poetry accessible to a larger number of people. I tried to do this in a serious, nonpolemical fashion because, although some of the attacks on the poetry deserved to be simply blasted away by polemic, other attacks and misunderstandings were more challenging. And much of this misunderstanding was, frankly, in the minds of the Black people to whom the poetry was addressed. Not all of them were over 30, or reactionary, or brainwashed. Many of them were young, bright men and women who wanted to know more fully what was going on. Some of them were even poets themselves. I conceived the book with them in mind, and, to be honest, in order to clarify some things for myself. The book has been generally well received, but like most attempts to explain or explicate or verbalize art, it also raised questions which need some systematic response.

These questions revolve mainly around one of the three categories that were basic to my discussion—*saturation*. The other two categories are *theme* and *structure*. Before I address those questions, however, I shall summarize briefly the entire argument. It says that there are two traditions or levels of Black poetry—the folk and the formal—which must be seen as a totality, since they often intersect and overlap one another, and since the people who create them are one people. It says further that the overriding theme of Black poetry is the idea of Freedom and/or Liberation, expressed in various ways and on various levels. This, of course, is not to deny the existence and importance of other themes—both public and personal; but the poetry reflects the concerns, the consciousness of the people—and Freedom/Liberation has been, and still is, obviously, the main objective of Black American life, and as a theme it virtually leaps from the pages of our poetry. (Henderson "Saturation: Progress Report" 4–5)

Henderson went on to make a detailed and lengthy exegesis concerning the issue of "blackness" in poetry. He continued:

If the critic is half worth his salt, then he would attempt to describe what occurs in the poem and to *explain*—to the extent that it is possible—how the "action" takes place, i.e., how the elements of the work interact with one another to produce its effect. And if one of those elements is "Blackness"—as value, as theme, or as structure, especially the latter—then he is remiss in his duty if he does not attempt to deal with it in some logical, orderly manner. Finally, he must place some value judgment on the work, on the totality of the work—not just its theme, its sociology, or its ideology, but also its structure. And if the theme involves Blackness as value, and if the structures are

Black, whether in a traditional sense or not, then the judgment must involve that Blackness as well. (9)

Essentially Henderson was doing exactly what Rowell charged had not been done. Moreover, there were others, albeit not many others and none who were as comprehensive as Henderson. That Henderson's post-1974 work either went unpublished or was obscurely published speaks volumes about the difficulties BAM critics had in getting their work published. My contention is not that the critical work didn't exist but rather that after 1976 there was nowhere to publish and encourage the production of BAM critical theory. Broadside Press was in hiatus, *Black World*, *Journal of Black Poetry*, and *Black Dialogue* were all gone. Most of the journals which were left were either academically oriented or antagonistic to BAM, or (more likely) both. Only *Black Scholar* offered any opportunity for informed, proactive BAM literary criticism, but since the journal was not primarily a literary magazine, those opportunities were also very limited.

Finally, there is a spurious contention that the Black Aesthetic was monolithic and condemned anyone who did not toe the party line. The assumption was that there was one definition of "Blackness" to which everyone had to adhere if they wanted their work to be considered truly "Black." This charge is easily refuted by going to the major anthology on the Black Aesthetic, which Gayle appropriately titled *The Black Aesthetic*. In the introduction Gayle is unambiguous when he writes:

> To paraphrase Saunders Redding, I have been enclothed with no authority to speak for others. Therefore, it is not my intention, in this introduction, to speak for the contributors to this anthology. Few of them may share my views; a great many may find them reprehensible. These are independent artists who demand the right to think for themselves and who, rightfully so, will resist the attempt by anyone—black or white—to articulate positions in their names.
>
> Each has his own idea of the Black Aesthetic, of the function of the black artist in the American society and of the necessity for new and different critical approaches to the artistic endeavors of black artists. Few, I believe, would argue with my assertion that the black artist, due to his historical position in America at the present time, is engaged in a war with this nation that will determine the future of black art.

> Likewise, there are few among them—and here again this is only conjecture—who would disagree with the idea that unique experiences produce unique cultural artifacts, and that art is a product of such cultural experiences. To push this thesis to its logical conclusion, unique art derived from unique cultural experiences mandates unique critical tools for evaluation. Further than this, agreement need not go! (Gayle, *The Black Aesthetic* xxii–xxiii)

The Black Aesthetic was not a strict and restricting concept. Indeed part of the strength of the Black Aesthetic was its flexibility and its ability to contain not only diversity but also contradiction—the both/and Afrocentric approach rather than the either/or Eurocentric approach. However, by the mid-seventies, whether BAM was understood or not, appreciated or vilified, life went on. Black Aesthetic soon took a major shift in focus with the advent of literature presented from the perspective of Black feminist eyes.

The Black Feminist Critique. As much as BAM was an outgrowth of the Civil Rights era with significant differences, Black women's literature of the feminist era of the 70s was a direct outgrowth of BAM with significant differences. Ntozake Shange's *For Colored Girls Who Have Considered Suicide/When the Rainbow is Enuf* was, in terms of national perception, perhaps, the opening salvo in the blast of Black women's writings which would completely transform Black literature.

A significant, yet generally unknown, aspect of *For Colored Girls* is that the New York Equity debut and development of the stage production was produced by BAM's leading theatre producer, Woodie King, Jr. *For Colored Girls* was King's third major attempt at producing Black poetry as a form of Black theater. His first two efforts had been *Black Spirits*, built around Baraka, and *Right On*, built around the Original Last Poets.

In a 1980 interview, King spoke about the process of developing the New York version of *For Colored Girls*. He stated:

> I had read pieces of Ntozake Shange's work in the *Black Scholar* and a lot of other poetry publications for about three or four years, and I really liked what I read. We had originally produced a play by her sister Efa, and we presented it here

at the playhouse and she came in and talked to us about it and introduced Ntozake to us. *Colored girls* was brilliantly put together by stage director, stage manager, O.Z. Scott.

So, when he brought *Colored Girls* to us I jumped at it because it had been a project I had been trying desperately to put together for some time, something that made a statement directly to women in general and about poetry. We put the play on here at the New Federal Theater—and it was a blockbuster. We had lines around the block. We hooked up with Joseph Papp in a co-production deal and we moved the play to Broadway. It ran for two years and went on tour. I have produced it in Australia and three or four months ago in London to a tremendous success—in addition to the national company which toured the United States. (King 99)

Shange had first presented *For Colored Girls* in December of 1974, at the Bacchanal, a woman's bar just outside Berkeley, California, with Paula Moss and Elvia Marta, Nashira Ntosha, Jessica Hagedorn, and Joanna Griffin. Shange and Moss motored to New York in 1975, hooked up with Oz Scott who, according to Shange, "offered to help me with the staging of the work for a New York audience, since Paula & I obviously didn't understand some things." Work at a bar, DeMonte's, turned into an incubator. Shange continues, "By this time, December 1975, we had weaned the piece of extraneous theatricality, enlisted Trazana Beverley, Laurie Carlos, Laurie Hayes, Aku Kadogo, and of course, Paula & I were right there. The most prescient change in the concept of the work waz that I gave up directorial powers to Oz Scott" (Shange, *See No Evil* 16). Although the rest, as the proverbial saying goes, is history, the important point not to be forgotten is that *For Colored Girls* was a transitional BAM theater piece which heralded the politics of gender concerns and related matters. This development was both profound and timely.

Consider the dates: *For Colored Girls* came to life in 1974; in September 1976 it hit Broadway. By 1976 BAM adherents were forced to take stock and to assess what had gone wrong with the political emphasis on power, an emphasis which, as I have pointed out earlier, produced numerous opportunities for mainstream inclusion, even though inclusion was not its original goal. On the other hand, BAM had produced either distorted or negligible opportunities for long lasting and stable independent and alternative institutions. This failure led to a reassessment of goals, objectives, and methodologies. Black feminism led the way in this regard.

In essence, gender politics questioned the nature of relationships, which was a significant shift from the Black Power emphasis on opposition to the status quo and the seeking of political power. Whether they had abandoned or clung to Black Power, whether they had been supporters or opponents of a Black Aesthetic, whether male or female, the shift in emphasis forced people to take stock and take sides. *Black Scholar* featured a number of forums around these issues. Everyone had an opinion. The debate was often vociferous and contentious, but regardless, again, just like when BAM burst on the scene, the debate was unavoidable. My contention concerning this shift of emphasis is simply that with the dispersal of Black Power as the political focus, feminism became the "new political focus." Thus, it also became the major theoretical/political concern of the Black Arts Movement, which was now a movement focused on gender and race.

The criticism of BAM by Black feminists actually marked a maturing rather than a dissolving of BAM. Whether we saw and understood the shift at the time is irrelevant. *For Colored Girls* and novels such as *The Color Purple* were "Black," as Black as Baraka's play *Slaveship* or Sam Greenlee's novel *The Spook Who Sat By The Door*—the emphasis on the politics of gender and intracommunity relations of women's literature notwithstanding. Black women's literature offered both the correction as well as the completion of a conception of blackness that returned humanity and relationships to the center.

BAM started off by seeking power, but Black women's literature taught us that true power was not "political" power but rather the power of human relationships—from the elemental embrace of two people, to the multi-member extensions of family, friends, comrades and the world community. Of course, the establishing of this radical redefinition of power took massive struggle and the majority of men (both within and outside of BAM) were often vociferously antagonistic. But opposition notwithstanding, eventually most, if not all, BAM adherents expanded their vision to embrace Black women's literature. It was a literature which forever shattered the nostalgic and romantic image of "Black queens" and "wives, mothers and lovers" by replacing such romanticized but nonetheless restrictive roles with the reality of women as social equals, comrades in the struggle and whole human beings who think for themselves.

This shift in the definition of Black womanhood is reflected in the literature, especially the fiction of Black women such as Toni Morrison, Gayl Jones, Alice Walker, and Ntozake Shange. Moreover, during the transition period of 1975 to 1980, the critical work of BAM male critics such as Addison Gayle, Stephen Henderson, Larry Neal, Maulana Karenga, and Amiri Baraka, just to name a few, broadly acknowledged and often welcomed the rise of Black feminist literature.

Undeniably there were differences and disagreements, sometimes even seemingly unresolvable contradictions between what was characterized as BAM's male chauvinist emphasis and the militant anti-sexism of emerging Black women writers. Some of these contradictions were not just theoretical, such as, for example, the issue of utilizing Black and independent publishers. A great deal of Black women's literature was published by mainstream publishing presses, the same presses which either had ignored or were themselves boycotted by BAM writers. But such contradictions do not negate the fact that the majority of Black women writers had either been associated with BAM or considered themselves influenced by BAM. Commenting on both her BAM roots and her different focus, Ntozake Shange says:

> I'm a daughter of the black arts movement (even though they didn't know they were going to have a girl!). Previously, the self was very much negated: there was a black man or a black woman and the black masses, all of whom were fairly two-dimensional but very powerful. Enough to risk home and family for, even though you might not know who these people were. So generationally, as a descendant of this, I was very suspicious of this two-dimensionality. I have to feed the people but when I feed the people I can't give them rations, I have to give them a meal that's nurtured with love and that has particular spices for particular tastes. I'm very involved in the specific child, the specific black man and how he or she appears to him or

herself. (Shange, "Artists' Dialogue" 159)

Because Black women's literature was very critical of BAM's faults and shortcomings, there is sometimes a tendency to define the two literatures as entirely separate, yet aesthetically Black women's literature of the era is very much an extension of BAM. Black women's literature often emphasized the basic BAM triad of concerns, except that a focus on gender struggles now replaced or superceded the racial focus. Black women's literature emphasized (1) Black female leadership and involvement of the masses of Black women in a struggle for self-determination, self-respect and self-defense, (2) a Black feminine aesthetic, and (3) social engagement.

One of the founding manifestoes of this movement was the April 1977 "The Combahee River Collective Statement." The Combahee River Collective was, according to founding members, "a Black feminist group in Boston whose name came from the guerrilla action conceptualized and led by Harriet Tubman on June 2, 1863, in the Port Royal region of South Carolina. This action freed more than 750 slaves and is the only military campaign in American history planned and led by a woman" (272). This influential statement succinctly analyzed the divergences and convergences between BAM and the Black feminist movement. This statement affirms that:

> Many of us were active in those movements (Civil Rights, Black nationalism, the Black Panthers), and all of our lives were greatly affected and changed by their ideologies, their goals, and the tactics used to achieve their goals. It was our experience and disillusionment within these liberation movements, as well as experience on the periphery of the white male left, that led to the need to develop a politics that was anti-racist, unlike those of white women, and anti-sexist, unlike those of Black and white men. (Combahee 273)

The collective's self-definition is a defining break with the Black Power, and hence the Black Arts Movement, formulation of Black womanhood. The women of the collective claim, "We reject pedestals, queenhood, and walking ten paces behind. To be recognized as human, levelly human, is enough" (Combahee 275). Moreover, there was a clear call in the statement for both unity and struggle:

Although we are feminists and Lesbians, we feel solidarity with progressive Black men and do not advocate the fractionalization that white women who are separatists demand. Our situation as Black people necessitates that we have solidarity around the fact of race, which white women of course do not need to have with white men, unless it is their negative solidarity as racial oppressors. We struggle together with Black men against racism, while we also struggle with Black men about sexism. (Combahee 275)

This two-line declaration was fiercely debated both within and between BAM organizations and individuals. Some saw the advent of Black women's literature as bringing about the decline of BAM literature. But in hindsight, during those transitional years, 1975 to 1980, when Black women's literature was then eclipsing a waning male-dominated BAM literature, the fact is that Black women's literature maintained the focus on the conditions of Black people, albeit through the experiences of Black women.

BAM may have been born out of Black Power, but BAM was transformed by Black feminism and this transformation marked the point when the literature ceased to be generally referred to as "the Black Arts." So, yes, there was a shift in both focus (from male-dominant political power to female-led tri-focused struggles around sexism, racism and classism) as well as a shift in nomenclature (from "Black Arts" to "women's literature" or "Black women's writing"). However, this shift actually expanded and extended Black literature.

Chairman Mao Zedong was the head of the ruling Chinese Communist Party. In 1966 he launched the Great Proletarian Cultural Revolution.

CHAPTER 13
A CRITICAL ASSESSMENT

BAM's Decline. The Black Arts Movement's decline began in 1974 when the Black Power movement was co-opted. Black political organizations were hounded, disrupted and defeated by repressive government measures such as COINTELPRO and IRS probes. Black Studies activist leadership was gutted and replaced by academicians and trained administrators who were unreceptive, if not outright opposed, to BAM's political orientation. Black community-based organizations and community centers were disbanded, defunded and drastically "downsized" when Richard Nixon became president in 1974. These disruptions significantly undercut the economic and political viability of BAM organizations.

Key internal events in the disruption were: (1) the split between nationalists and Marxists in the African Liberation Support Committee (May 1974), (2) the Sixth Pan African Congress in Tanzania where race-based struggle was repudiated/denounced by most of the strongest forces in Africa (August 1974), and (3) CAP officially changing from a "Pan Afrikan Nationalist" to a "Marxist Leninist" organization (October 1974).

As the movement reeled from the combination of external and internal disruptions, commercialization and capitalist co-option delivered the coup de grace. Nixon's strategy of pushing Black capitalism as a response to Black Power ("Black Power is Green Power") epitomized mainstream co-option. As major film, record, book, and magazine publishers identified the most marketable artists, BAM's already fragile independent economic base was completely undermined.

A particularly poignant exposé of one case of co-option was written by Cleveland poet Norman Jordan, of the Muntu Poets Collective. It was published in issue number 11 of *Journal of Black Poetry*, as well as in *Black Art Black Culture*, an anthology of articles that originally appeared in the *Journal*. Jordan was both insightful and sarcastic in his critique:

> Brothers who had been working together beautifully lost contact with each other, brothers divided up into little cliques, and started calling each other "Uncle Toms." Then the root of the evil, money, became the final wedge. In the beginning we had agreed to do the reading under one (so-called) condition. That condition was: We would use the money to open a Black Theatre. Here's how the brothers copped out of this: one group of brothers called the other group "the police", and said they didn't want to open *nothing* with The Man. After it was agreed we could split the money, the shit really started to fly. Brothers took it into a competition thing. Brothers started negatively judging other brothers' works to decide who deserved the largest share of the money. Brothers took it into a pride-and-honor thing, carrying guns and talking about assassinating each other. That was the end of the MUNTU POETS. Since then, the police have been keeping a closer watch on the Black artists here in Cleveland. (Jordan 35)

Time and time again, funding would prove to be a weak spot. Marc Primus identifies money as the cause of the Folkloric Troupe's 1971 demise. In an interview, he said, "Initially we all worked because we wanted to and not for a salary. And when some grants first came, everyone got paid the same amount. But eventually, as we performed more and more, and received salaries and grants, an element of working to get paid took over" (Primus, "Interview"). Primus believes that part of the problem was that no art in this country exists without support from outside of itself.

All of the arts are subsidized. BAM made the garnering of such support almost impossible because it actively separated itself from white audiences and white patronage. Further, the Black audience which was most responsive to BAM was also the poorest sector of the community and thus was in no position to financially support BAM. The question of how to fund the revolution, whether cultural or political, was never satisfactorily answered. The paucity of financial support not only forced many BAM organizations to close, it also made many organizations and individuals susceptible to establishment co-option.

In 1975, *The Wiz*, a Black version of *The Wizard of Oz*, opened on Broadway. In the same year, *The Jeffersons* premiered on network television, and a Motown-produced movie, *Mahogany*, starring Diana Ross and Billy Dee Williams had its Hollywood release. BAM was experiencing government disruption and severe economic restrictions caused by outside forces and internal fighting. Additionally, a great loss to the movement was the defections of major figures such as Amiri Baraka (a nationalist who became a Marxist) and Eldridge Cleaver (a Marxist who returned from exile on November 18, 1975, surrendered to the FBI, denounced his previous "revolutionary" positions, and declared himself a capitalist).

At the same time, the establishment was promoting and profiting from books, music, movies, and other Black entertainment. This entertainment was either White controlled or mediated by White institutions, or both. Internal contradictions, combined with external repression and commercial commodification, sealed BAM's fate.

Corporate America (both the commercial sector and the academic sector) once again selected and propagated one or two handpicked Black writers. During the height of BAM activity, each community had a coterie of writers with publishing outlets for hundreds. However, once the mainstream regained control, Black artists were once again tokenized. Although BAM activity continued into the early eighties, by 1976, the year that Gil Scott-Heron called the "Buy-Centennial," BAM was without any sustainable political or economic bases in the Black community. Most of the BAM theatre groups/cultural centers were either defunct or significantly downsized.

BAM's Deficiencies. Although criticized for its virulent sexism, homophobia and crow jimism (i.e. "reverse racism"), important distinctions and contextualizations need to be understood. First, although some BAM adherents were not flagrantly anti-White, sexist and homophobic, many, if indeed not most, were. There can be no denying of that fact. But let us more closely examine the context.

BAM's anti-White stance was in specific opposition to the traditional behavior of American Whites toward people of color both here and abroad. Moreover, we must remember that during this period, America was engaged in an unprovoked war against Vietnam; was actively supporting apartheid and colonialism in Africa, and was supportive of repressive regimes throughout Central and South America. These repressive political realities were either actively or tacitly supported by the majority of the American population. Where there was opposition, the influence of the Black struggle was evident. For example, the opposition to the war in Vietnam was spurred by the Civil Rights movement and led by Whites such as Tom Hayden of SDS, who had been active in Civil Rights work. So then "White" was not strictly a racial definition, it was first off a political description of those who actively opposed or tacitly supported the opposition to freedom, justice and equality for peoples of color both in America and elsewhere.

Second, there was an ongoing debate within BAM about the participation of Whites at any level—the positions ranged from no participation whatsoever to operational and tactical unity on an issue by issue basis. Indicative of this range is the inclusion of John Sinclair in the Broadside anthology on Malcolm X. Sinclair was a founder of the White Panther Party and considered a revolutionary "John Brown" type poet.

While BAM is generally defined in practice as a separatist, anti-White movement, its growth and development—especially in terms of collaboration with African, non-U.S. American (particularly Cubans), Asian and other Third World liberation struggles—mitigated charges of racial exclusivity or racial essentialism. Thus, even the hardcore, fundamental Chicago school of Black nationalism admitted that in particular international contexts, people of European descent functioned as revolutionaries.

Although there was a great deal of antagonism between BAM adherents and White Americans, BAM's international vector kept it from falling completely into a "skin" trap. For example, Don L. Lee, in guest editing an issue of *Journal of Black Poetry*, included Palestinian poets Mahmoud Darwish, Sameeth Al-Qassem, Salem Jubran and Tawfeeq Zeyad—whom Lee notes in the introduction, "are certainly in prison in their homeland, occupied Palestine, and their works were smuggled out and passed on to their people and the world. They call their poetry 'poetry of necessity.'" (Lee, "Why This Issue?" 2). Furthermore, there was not only a broad range of shifting attitudes about race over time, BAM was also the progenitor of multiculturalism.

The charge of being anti-White is valid but only in a domestic context and, even then, not over the entire span of BAM's lifetime.

As for the charge of sexism and homophobia there is no doubt that they were correct. Yet, BAM was no more sexist or homophobic than American society in general, and, in specific cases, much less blatant. Moreover, there was a great deal of struggle against sexism and much of that struggle is documented in BAM and Black Power publications, especially *Black Scholar*.

Again, contextualization is important. At no time in the history of BAM were women excluded. Moreover, while most BAM men were undoubtedly patriarchal, few of them were overtly misogynistic. Also, as dubious as the notion may seem in hindsight, Black Power—the elevation of the Black man—was proposed as a corrective to the historic emasculation of the Black male. Abbey Lincoln eloquently professes in *Freedomways*:

> The image of the female African-American in music is one of the realist. The man she sings of is a flesh and blood man, a man with positive and negative aspects, of a give and take relationship, of responsibilities to that relationship and of the resulting rewards. She has not demanded that he be the "ideal man." Recognizing her own human frailties, she candidly acknowledges his, and loves him none the less for all that.
>
> ...It was no accident that Gershwin's Porgy was a cripple, without legs. It was no accident that Harold Arlen's *Cabin in the Sky* featured a song called "Happiness is just a *thing* called Joe." It has been no accident that the hostile, racist-oriented white poet could find no excellence or worth to portray in the black man. It has been no accident that the white poet has *always* portrayed the black male image as a Step'n Fetchit, ne'er do well, Joe, irresponsible and helpless. Still there was always that certain something that had to be conceded, and that was that the "Negro" woman loved her man . . . that he was the source of her fulfillment and happiness. There's a lot to be said for a man who can inspire that kind of vilification on one hand and so much devotion on the other. (Lincoln 12–13)

While it is easy to say that BAM was dominated by sexists, the truth is far more demonstrative. At one point, there was a conference in San Francisco during the late sixties, at which Askia Toure recollected it was "time to put the pants back on the Black man. It was time for him to stand up, be a man, be a warrior, a fighter for his people, a protector of Black women."

Additionally, one would do well to consider whether there was any development over the course of BAM's lifetime. In all cases, the record will show growth and development rather than a simple-minded adherence to a limited view of women or race. In particular, Maulana Karenga, whom BAM critics often cite as the epitome of BAM male chauvinism, moved from the adoption of traditional African views and values of gender roles to a nuanced progressive and revolutionary view. Karenga responds in a statement written in 1976 and published in 1977:

> The so-called "woman question" is imposed incorrectly and reveals the extent to which our theories of liberation begin and end with a male perspective. It is not a woman question, but rather a woman-man question; in a word, a human question, a question of how to *rescue* and *redefine* our history and humanity from alien, anti-human hands. The real question is what kind of new relationships and human beings we want to build and become and the structure and content of the new world we want these new people to live in (Boggs and Boggs, 1974).
>
> It is undialectical and in brutal contradiction to the needs of our struggle and development to divide the question of how males should be from how women should be, and what women should do and become from what men should do and become. For the question posed thus becomes itself part of the ideological arsenal of the established order is employed to further hack humanity and our people in half, to foster false and deforming relationships between female and male and in the process, pervert the human image and human essence.
>
> What is at stake here is the negation of exploitative, repressive *values* and *structures* produced, enforced and reproduced by a capitalist, racist and sexist society. And the struggle to change structures must begin with the struggle to change ourselves, our basic views and values and the negative ways we organize and live our daily lives. It can never be just a struggle to change social structures. For the values of society are an equal and simultaneous threat and obstacle to human freedom and fullness and thus, must be transcended and transformed into their opposites. (Karenga, "Beyond Connections" 74–75)

My point is not to dismiss BAM chauvinism, but to simply point out that over time, based largely on internal struggle and international contact, BAM transformed itself. Indeed, change is a basic principle of life. If we don't change, we die. If we don't transform ourselves, we become reactionary. As Karenga posits:

> The cultural revolution remains a central concern, for progress in struggle is directly dependent on progress in thought. In other words, the battle is still first for the minds and hearts of our people and the theoretical addition is simply this: it is not a one-way process, for through actual struggle, our thoughts and values change also. So let us keep what is good for us, reject that which is not and be audacious and wise enough to determine the difference. (Karenga, "Reaffirmation and Change" 18)

It is one thing to argue that BAM was anti-White, sexist and homophobic in the beginning years, it is quite another to argue that there was no struggle within BAM on those issues or struggle between BAM and other forces around those issues. Certainly it is totally incorrect to argue that BAM views and practices did not change for the better over the decade or so of its existence.

So, yes, there were glaring defects in BAM, but those defects cannot be used to either define or dismiss BAM as a totally reactionary movement. In truth, BAM was a tremendous force for positive change that transformed the cultural face of America.

Ishmael Reed, who is not considered a BAM apologist or advocate ("I wasn't invited to participate because I was considered an integrationist"), in a 1995 interview, asserts that BAM:

> was mostly a performance thing and many of the people who put down Black Arts never saw any of the performances. I think what Black Arts did was inspire a whole lot of Black people to write. Moreover, there would be no multiculturalism movement without the Black Arts. Latinos, Asian Americans and others all say they began writing as a result of the example of the 1960s. Blacks gave the example that you don't have to assimilate. You could do your own thing, get into your own background, your own history, your own tradition and your own culture. I think the challenge is for cultural sovereignty and Black Arts struck a blow for that. (Reed, "Interview")

BAM's Power. BAM was a vibrant and exhilarating movement. For all its seriousness, high drama, and the often very real threats of imprisonment, death and/or physical/ideological struggles, there was zest, good humor, and a vitality that made the movement attractive. In his 1980s poem, "Courageousness,"

Baraka remembers:

> In the 60's there was enough feeling
> enough emotion to go round.
> There was no reason to be square,
> that's what we felt. We could do
> anything, be anything, even free.
> That's how young we were. That's
> now long ago, that was.

Baraka declaimed in his famous 1960s poem "Black Art" that "We want 'poems that kill.'/Assassin poems, Poems that shoot guns." He was not simply speaking metaphorically. Baraka was highlighting the politically engaged side of BAM. During that period, slogans such as "Arm Yourself or Harm Yourself" and "Off the Pigs" established a social climate which promoted "confrontation" with the White power structure, especially the police. Indeed, Baraka had been arrested and convicted on a gun possession charge during the 1967 Newark "rebellion" (or, according to the power structure, Newark "riot"). His conviction was later overturned on appeal. Armed struggle was widely viewed as the only effective means of liberation.

Following King's assassination in April 1968, Nikki Giovanni responded to her own rhetorical question—What could a "poor Black woman" do to "destroy America?"—with the stunning statement, "There is one answer—I can kill." The power of BAM was precisely that it was politically partisan. BAM was militant, and supportive of armed struggle in its opposition to the forces of oppression. Unlike "protest" literature which complained to and petitioned Whites for relief, BAM spoke to and for Black people in the language of the "folk," the people Malcolm X called the "field negroes," the ones who, given the chance, would burn down the big house.

In a 1977 *First World* article, critic Addison Gayle summed up the Black Arts Movement:

> Certainly, the young Black writers who gathered around
> Baraka and the Black Arts Theater in 1964 [sic] and who had
> earlier begun to write for Liberator and Black World Magazines,
> would find little support among the Black literary establishment.
>   The reason was that their view of the nature of art and
> its function was based upon a political premise—Black

Nationalism—which was and is anathema to both some Black and white Americans. These new writers rejected not only the idea of an integrated America, but even the value of it. In the words of Etheridge Knight, they denounced protest literature designed to change the attitudes of whites:

Now any Black man who masters the techniques of his particular art form, who adheres to the white aesthetic, and who directs his work towards a white audience is, in one sense, protesting. And implicit in the art of protest is the belief that a change will be forthcoming once the masters are aware of the protestor's "grievance" (the very word connotes begging, supplication to the gods). Only when that belief has faded and protesting ends, will Black art begin.

The new art would be devoted to explaining the world in which Black people lived, to bringing about a new relationship between one Black person and another, to redefining the definitions handed down by Western philosophers and intellectuals concerning the Black experience. The essence and importance of a work of art, argued the proponents of the new Black Art, resided in its ability to move men towards changing the oppressive conditions under which they lived. In this sense, with this view in mind, Maulana Ron Karenga writes that a work of art must be committed and committing, must "expose the enemy, praise the people and support the revolution."

Against the noninvolvement, static notion of art as defined in the critical articles of the American academicians, the Black Aestheticians demanded an art that was involved, that was dedicated to change. (Gayle "Blueprint for Black Criticism" 42–43)

One of BAM's avowed goals was to inspire and help organize the Black masses. Much of BAM's aesthetic dynamism, impact and effectiveness was precisely because BAM was insistent on advocating both artistic and political freedom "by any means necessary." America had never witnessed such a broad and, militant and artistic movement.

BAM'S Legacy. By 1980 very few, if any, Black writers were referring to themselves or their work as part of the Black Arts Movement. Nevertheless, the spirit of BAM didn't just disappear—that spirit was transformed and reappeared in the work of Black women writers and other artists who replicated the BAM emphasis on "socially engaged" content and "doing for self" independent development. Moreover, BAM's long term impact on the direction and substance of cultural life, both domestically and internationally, was profound.

Aesthetically, BAM reintroduced speech, music and performance/drama as major orientations in the articulation of literary creations. In his *Black Fire* afterword, Larry Neal notes: "Our music has always been the most dominant manifestation of what we are and feel, literature was just an afterthought, the step taken by the Negro bourgeoisie who desired acceptance on the white man's terms." This led to the innovative use of language that has not since been matched.

Inherent in BAM performances was a sense of ritual that required an active interchange with the audience unmediated by commercial forces, which always attempted to tone down the political orientation and overemphasize the entertainment aspects. BAM successfully validated, as well as popularized, the cultures of Black people in America, the Diaspora, and in Africa. Although primarily through music, but also through literature, BAM encouraged various people to both accept the validity and importance of their own cultures, and to challenge all forms of cultural commodification and/or imperialism.

Tom Porter, a chief of the Traditional Mohawk Nation and founder and leader of the Mohawk Valley Community in upstate New York, writes in an article published in *Lapis* magazine (1995):

> About 25 years ago, we made a revival of who we were as native people, for the first time in 200 years. For the first time we began to speak Mohawk in public, without shame. For the first time, in 1960. And you know what—I have to say this—I have to stand, and I have to salute the Black man. Because the black people woke me up as a Mohawk. Before, I was scared to say anything. But when I seen the newspaper, and the television, Black people were sitting down, and they were confronting, because of racism. And because of inequalities. My grandmother and I began to talk: "The Black man is fighting for his rights. And he comes from another country, he doesn't even belong here really. This is not his homeland. But it's our homeland. We are the original. How come we're not fighting?" (Porter 35)

Black struggle in general, and BAM cultural struggle in particular, served as inspiration various ethnic, gender and other related social struggles in the United States and throughout the world. For example, Marc Primus of the Afro-American Folkloric Troupe

191

worked in Australia during the summers of 1973 to 1975. He vividly remembers the BAM influence down under. He said, "They modeled themselves on what we had done. They had a Black Panther Party and a Black Arts Movement" (Primus, "Interview"). Even though many subsequent social movements were critical of BAM shortcomings, we should never overlook the fact that despite whatever shortcomings, BAM was both catalyst and genesis of cultural struggle in modern America and worldwide.

BAM aesthetics emphasized orality (which includes the ritual use of call and response between artist and audience) as opposed to written text. This same orientation is apparent both in rap lyrics and in 1990s "performance poetry" (e.g. the Nuyorican Poets). Amiri Baraka, Jayne Cortez, Nikki Giovanni, Haki Madhubuti, Sonia Sanchez, The Watts Poets, and many other poets began recording as well as writing books. The Last Poets and Gil Scott-Heron merged their poetry so thoroughly with music that they produced records rather than books. Despite the popularity of their recordings and the broadly acknowledged impact as an inspirational force in the development of rap music, both the Last Poets and Gil Scott-Heron have been largely ignored by mainstream oriented literary critics who viewed them as vulgar entertainers and/or extremist politicians. Nevertheless, the success of BAM poets proved that a socially engaged content and an imaginative style could be both artistic and economically feasible. This process effectively broadened and deepened popular culture by making it simultaneously popular and socially significant. In the final analysis, the enlargement and elevation of popular culture is another major legacy of BAM.

BAM led directly to an increase in the number of people who wanted to be publishers, producers, entrepreneurs, writers, artists and entertainers. Although twenty years later, there are no surviving major independent Black record labels, Black presses, though bookstores have increased in number, size and quality. I am aware of the numerous hip-hop record labels, but almost all of these, particularly the so-called successful ones, are aligned with major record companies through distribution deals—deals in which much of the so-called independence of the labels are circumscribed. Cultural commodification and the influences of the marketplace are directly opposed to "independence" and "self-determination" as envisioned by BAM.

While right-wing cultural trends and relentless commercialization attempt to push America's cultural clock back to the 1950s, the lessons, the literary work and the ideological inspiration of BAM continue to show tremendous resiliency in the Black community and among other marginalized sectors. Even twenty years after it's demise, when people encounter BAM, they are delighted and inspired by the most audacious, prolific, and socially engaged literary movement in America's history. As we enter the second decade of twenty-first century, the Black Arts Movement's legacy of self-determination, innovation, and conscious alternative to the status quo continues to be relevant to daily existence and spiritual rejuvenation.

STUDY GUIDE
FOR THE MAGIC OF JUJU
DEVELOPED BY JITON DAVIDSON

PREFACE:

1. When did the goals of the Black Liberation Movement shift from Civil Rights to Black Power? What facilitated that change? xiv

2. Why does the author, Kalamu ya Salaam, focus on Black Arts Movement publications? xv

CHAPTER 1: DEFINING THE BLACK ARTS MOVEMENT

1. How does ya Salaam define the Black Arts Movement (BAM)? 1.1

2. What did the Black Power perspective call for? 1.1

3. What was the unforeseen result of the Free Southern Theatre's production of LeRoi Jones' (later known as Amiri Baraka) play *Slaveship*? 1.2-3

4. According to author, ya Salaam, what was the major internal contradiction of the Black Arts Movement? 1.4

5. What were some of the external contradictions of the Black Arts Movement? 1.5

6. What was Ed Spriggs goal for the boycott of Black writers/ white publishers? 1.6-7

7. Why did Askia Muhammad Toure call for a boycott of *Essence Magazine*? 1.8

8. How did the advent of the Black Arts Movement strain personal relationships? 1.9

9. Why did the Black Panther Party believe that the Student Nonviolent Coordinating Committee (SNCC) was obsessed with excluding Whites? 1.10

CHAPTER 2: BAM'S HISTORICAL BACKGROUND

1. Why is it difficult to establish the dates of the Black Arts Movement? 2.13

2. What was the event that propelled the Black Arts Movement forces into action? 2.13

3. How is the end of the Civil Rights Movement marked? 2.13

4. How does ya Salaam mark the beginning point of the Black Arts Movement? 2.13

5. According to ya Salaam define the political mission of the Black Arts Movement? 2.14

6. When and how does the term "Black Power" become established? 2.14-15

7. Identify the two camps of the Civil Rights Movement. 2.16

8. According to Muhammad Ahmed, what does RAM (Revolutionary Action Movement) have to do with Black Power? Who are the ideological leaders of the Black Arts Movement, and what caused the shift to Black Power? 2.16-17

9. Who helped to author SNCC's Black Power position paper and what was his significance? Who were key ideological figures? What made them important to the movement? 2.17-2.20

10. Who was Robert Williams and why is he significant? 2.19-20

11. On the religious front, who had the greatest Black Power impact on Christianity? How does he (and others) manifest the articulations of Malcolm X? 2.20

12. How does Malcolm X articulate the tasks of Black Power?

2.20

13. What are some examples of Malcolm X's influence as captured in the introduction to Dudley Randall and Margaret G. Burroughs 1969 anthology, *For Malcolm X*? 2.21

14. How does Larry Neal describe Malcolm X's influence on the Black Arts Movement? 2.21-22

15. How does ya Salaam describe Malcolm X's influence on Black Power literature? What is the difference between Martin Luther King, Jr. and Malcolm X? 2.25

16. How does ya Salaam connect Black Power to the Black Arts Movement? 2.24

17. What events mark the zenith of the Civil Rights Movement? What were the new goals? 2.25

18. List and briefly describe the difference between the Civil Rights Movement and the Black Power, as well as its cultural arm, the Black Arts Movement? 2.25-28

CHAPTER 3: THE NATIONAL BIRTH OF BAM

1. What founding marks the symbolic beginning of the Black Arts Movement? Explain. 3.30

2. What was prophetic about Malcolm X's call for cultural development as outlined in the aims and objectives of the Organization of Afro-American Unity (OAAU)? 3.29

3. According to the author, what poet/writer was the most celebrated by the literary establishment before and during the Black Arts Movement? Why? 3.30

4. Explain some of the accomplishments of BART/S. 3.32

5. In Amiri Baraka's essay presentation titled "The Black Arts Movement," what was needed of Black art before the

Black Arts Movement got underway? What seemed most important? 3.31-32

6. The author writes that "BART/S major influence [upon the Black Arts Movement] was to establish the Black Arts Community Center as a model which could be replicated across the country." List the other major influential ideas ya Salaam attributes to BART/S. 3.32

7. Explain the downfall of BART/S. 3.33

8. According to *Drama Review*, explain what "lessons" led to the creation of Black House in 1966. 3.34

9. List and explain the six issues that were highlighted as a result of the "schisms and conflicts that beset BART/S and Black House." 3.35

10. Chicago's DuSable Museum's role in the Black Arts Movement was significant, according to the author. What was that role? 3.36

11. What were the Black Arts Movement "geo-literary" centers? 3.37

12. How does the organization UMBRA, as well as its workshops and publication, contribute to the Black Arts Movement? Who are some of the members who are known today as important Black writers? 3.37-38

13. Explain the focus of the Harlem Writers Guild? Who are some of the members who are known today as important Black writers? 3.38

14. In the author's analysis, why was poetry more successful during the Black Arts Movement than fiction? 3.38

15. Major publications tended to acknowledge and at times even focus on the works of LeRoi Jones (Amiri Baraka), why

does ya Salaam think this is the case? What were the affects of this mainstream attention upon the movement? 3.40-41

16. How do the multiple name changes symbolize Jones/ Baraka's political transformation? 3.40

17. Briefly explain Jones/Baraka's impact upon the Black Arts Movement. 3.41

18. According to the author, explain the two major locations of BAM ideological leadership, particularly for literary work. What caused the "monumental shift in BAM's national focus...from the East Coast to the West Coast?" 3.41

19. The Black Panther Party was an important influence upon the Black Arts Movement in the assessment of ya Salaam. Explain. 3.42-43

20. How did emerging college Black Studies programs and departments serve as recruiting and training centers for Black Arts Movement participants? What other support did these academic centers offer to young Black writers? 3.41-42

21. List the "major nucleus of BAM leadership on the West Coast." 3.42-44

22. Explain the importance of Chicago and Detroit to the Black Arts Movement. 3.44-45

23. How did mid-west publishing venues contribute to a healthy mix of ideas and styles of writing? 3.45

24. What city carries the distinction of being the "'Black nationalist headquarters' of the United States?" Explain. 3.45

25. How does poet Gwendolyn Brooks contribute to the Black Arts Movement? What was her distinction before the

movement? 3.46

26. Explain how the "decentralization of BAM leadership and activity insured that BAM became a national rather than a regional phenomenon". 3.47

CHAPTER 4: THEORY AND PRACTICE

1. Which two Black Arts Movement manifestos does ya Salaam consider significant statements that sum up and present the main objectives of the movement? 4.49

2. List and explain the "three basic characteristics which make [Black art] revolutionary, according to Maulana Karenga. What must all Black art do? 4.49, 4.50

3. According to Karenga, what is the motive behind the Black Aesthetic? 4.50

4. Describe the "subtle but significant" differences between the approaches of Karenga and Larry Neal. 4.50-51

5. Who does ya Salaam consider the third major Black Arts Movement theoretician after Karenga and Neal and what is his contribution to the shaping of BAM literature? 4.51

6. According to Don L. Lee/Haki R. Madhubuti, what is the mission of the revolutionary Black writer? What is one thing the Black writer can do to lead his community toward self determination and self definition? 4.51 – 52

7. Explain the significance of Third World Press. 4.52

8. Explain what the author considers the most influential [theoretical] articulation of the Black aesthetic. Why? 4.52

9. Explain Carolyn (Gerald) Fowler's analysis of the Black aesthetic. 4.52 – 53

10. Name the two erroneous assumptions that students are often taught regarding the Black Arts Movement, as listed by the author. 4.51

11. Who were the four most important writers of the Black Arts Movement, according to the author? Who is the best-selling poet/author of BAM? List some of his books and explain his contributions to BAM. 4.54-55

12. Who is Sonia Sanchez and what is her significance to the Black Arts Movement? What makes her and Madhubuti popular even today? 4.55-56

13. How does Larry Neal address the ethical aspects of the Black Arts Movement? 4.56-57

14. As analyzed by critic Bernard Bell, how does folk art, especially Black music, tie together the works of writers "as politically and socially divergent as Paul L. Dunbar, Richard Wright, Ralph Ellison, Gwendolyn Brooks, Bob Kaufman and LeRoi Jones?" 4.58

15. According to Bell, "what makes 'Black' literature distinctly 'Black' as opposed to American?" What are the two major criteria? 4.58-59

16. How did the Broadside Critics Series help to shape the writings of the Black Arts Movement? 4.59

17. Explain the core elements of African American (especially BAM) literature as articulated by the author. 4.59-60

18. How does Stephen Henderson articulate the aesthetic of the new Black poetry? How does he define theme, structure, and saturation? 4.60-61

19. What was one major accomplishment of John Oliver Killens series of Black Writer's Conferences at Fisk University? 4.61-62

20. According to Eugene Redmond, author of *Drumvoices,* how was Gwendolyn Brooks received at the 1967 Black writer's conference at Fisk University? 4.62

21. What was the nature of Robert Hayden's ideological split from Black Power poets? 4.62

22. Explain the genesis of the anthology *For Malcolm: Poems on the Life and the Death of Malcolm X.* 4.62-63

CHAPTER 5: BAM PUBLICATIONS

1. Explain how the Black Arts Movement ideology was disseminated. How were the publications *Freedomways* and *Liberator* beneficial? Specifically, what made *Liberator* so important? 5.65

2. Describe *Soulbook's* distinction out of all the BAM publications. 5.66-67

3. How does Aubrey LaBrie, a founder of *Black Dialogue,* address the question of why the Bay Area (rather than New York) became so important as far as the founding and publication of Black Arts Movement literary publications? Why is California so significant? 5.67

4. What was the major distinction and aim of *Black Dialogue?* According to an editorial in this journal's first issue, why must Afro-American literature be redirected? 5.67-70

5. Explain the genesis of *Black Dialogue.* 5.67-70

6. What is LeRoi Jones' ever-expanding vision as expressed in *Journal of Black Poetry?* How does Clarence Major echo this vision? 5.71-72

7. According to an article in *Journal of Black Poetry* by Marvin Jackmon (Marvin X), what is the role of the Black revolutionary poet? 5.72

8. Why was (founding editor of *Journal of Black Poetry*) Dingane Joe Goncalves' decision to moved away from single editor leadership and the use of guest editors prophetic, according to ya Salaam? 5.73

9. What two Black revolutionary leaders did Goncalves pay tribute to in each issue of *Journal of Black Poetry* and why? 5.74

10. What were Goncalves major problems with *Negro Digest*? How does he address these issues in *Journal of Black Poetry*? 5.75-76

11. According to Carolyn (Gerald) Fowler, what is the importance of Black revolutionary journals? 5.76-77

12. What was the editorial mission of *Black Scholar*? 5.78

13. Why was *Negro Digest/Black World* so important to the Black Arts Movement? What was Editor Hoyt Fuller's role and contribution to the Black Arts Movement? 5.78-81

14. When and why did *Negro Digest* become *Black World*? What became the role and dominate concerns of *Black World*? According to ya Salaam and to Fuller, why was *Black World* such a low priority for Johnson publications? 5.80; 5.82

15. Who coined the term Black aesthetic? What was the significance of the sentiment? 5.81; 5.83

16. How did the death of *Black World* affect the Black Arts Movement? 5.82-83

17. What group founded *Black Books Bulletin* and what was its goal? According to ya Salaam, what was significant about it? 5.83-84

18. What was the major accomplishment of Black literary journals of the Black Arts Movement? 5.86

19. Explain how the Black Arts Movement "became the hothouse for the development of what is now known as multiculturalism" as stated by the author. 5.86

20. Explain the connection between the 1971 founding of the literary journal *Yardbird* and multiculturalism. Why did Ishmael Reed and other founding editors of the publication start a cooperative publishing company? 5.88-89

21. How does Chester Himes define Afro-Americans in the preface to the initial issue of *Yardbird?* Why does ya Salaam state that Himes' preface reads like a BAM manifesto? 5.89-90

22. The author states that, "by the fifth issue, published in 1976, *Yardbird* was on the attack against a strictly 'Black' orientation." What was the journal's new direction and how does Amiri Baraka contribute? 5.90

23. Name the two leading Black presses of the Black Arts Movement. What is the significance of their physical locations? 5.91

24. Explain the connection between the two presses and their founding publishers. What did these men and their publishing efforts contribute to the Black Arts Movement? 5.91-92

25. What is Third World Press' distinction? 5.92

26. Explain the impact of the 1971 anthologies, *The Black Aesthetic* and *The Black Poets,* as well as the 1972 anthologies, *Understanding the New Black Poetry,* and *New Black Voices.* Define the Black Arts Movement presents of each of the editors. 5.93-94

CHAPTER 6: BAM RECORDINGS

1. Why were Black Arts Movement audio recordings important to the cause? 6.96

2. According to Amiri Baraka, how did Larry Neal and Askia Toure influence his presentation style? Why does he believe Black music was so important to Black Arts Movement poetry? 6.97

3. Who is Jayne Cortez and why is she a significant figure of the Black Arts Movement? 6.99-100

4. What important writer of the Harlem Renaissance is the precursor to the merger of Black poetry and Black music? Explain. 6.101

5. What Black Arts Movement poetry album was recorded "Live at the Apollo"? Explain the importance of the recording, and list the "who's who" of BAM poets." 6.101

6. Explain the impact of the 1972 recording, *It's Nation Time*. 6.102

7. Why have Last Poets and Gil Scott-Heron been neglected by "the establishment?" Why were they not taken seriously by literary critics? What was their lasting contribution to Black poetry? How is that impact apparent today? 6.103

8. What cause the rift within the group, the Last Poets? How was the conflict resolved? How does the conflict within the Last Poets illustrate some of the problems one encounters when writing about BAM in general? 6.103-105

9. Why was Gil Scott-Heron more influential than The Last Poets? 6.105

10. How was Black Arts Movement poetry a departure from traditional American and African American poetry? 6.107-108

CHAPTER 7: BLACK THEATRE

1. In the assessment of ya Salaam, what are the two hallmarks

of Black Arts Movement activity? Explain the function of Black theatres within the movement. 7.109

2. Why does Marc Primus believe San Francisco became more politically sophisticated than other major cities involved in the Black Power and the Black Arts Movement? 7.110-111

3. What important African American literary work inspired Primus' Afro-American Folkloric Troupe to reject international communism? Explain. 7.110

4. According to Primus, what was the function of Afro-American Folkloric Troupe? What was the troupe's significance to the Black Arts Movement? 7.111

5. According to ya Salaam, why is the Afro-American Folkloric Troupe relatively unknown today? How does Primus address this issue? 7.111-112

6. As stated by *Drama Review* co-founder John O'Neal, why was Black theatre dependent upon its relationship to Black Power and Black Arts activists for relevance and perspective? How does he describe the relationship between art and propaganda? 7.114-115

7. Why is audience important, according to Tom Dent? What theatre troupe was he involved in, and why was that group significant to the Black Arts Movement? 7.115-116

8. Within the context of the controversy surrounding the play *We Righteous Bombers,* what was the real issue? How does Larry Neal articulate this issue? 7.118-119

9. What is Neal's response to Maulana Karenga's statement about the blues? 7.117

10. How does Leslie Catherine Sanders, author of *The Development of Black Theater in America*, explain the difference between Ed Bullins' *We Righteous Bombers*

and Albert Camus' *Les Justes?* According to Askia Toure, what were some other major problems with *We Righteous Bombers?* 7.118-120

11. How does Wanda Coleman critique Black Arts Movement publications? 7.121

CHAPTER 8: BAM AND BLACK MUSIC

1. According to the author, why was Black music so important to the Black Arts Movement? How did Black music (gospel, blues, jazz and popular) introduce major innovations and developments which affected all of popular culture in America? 8.123-124

2. What was James Brown's significance to the Black Arts Movement? What were some of his contributions to Black music? 8.124-125

3. Explain some of James Brown's contradictions. What was the Black Power proposal that Otis Redding made to Brown? Why did Brown reject that proposal? 8.125-126

4. Explain the "October Revolution" in jazz. What is the significance of the 1966 album titled *October Revolution?* 8.126-127

5. How did John Coltrane impact Black Arts Movement music and poetry? How was the poet Don L. Lee (Haki Madhubuti) inspired by the music of Coltrane? Explain Lee's use of the rhythms and the actual "cry" (sound) of Coltrane's saxophone as a literary device. 8.127-129

6. How does ya Salaam describe the relationship between Malcolm X and John Coltrane? What are the two chief elements of the Black Arts Movement that both Malcolm X and John Coltrane embody? 8.129-130

7. What is significant about Stokely Carmichael's musical

choices and inspirations? How did they affect his work as a leading Black Power revolutionary? 8.130-131

8. What is Larry Neal's sentiment on the blues? How is jazz linked to the traditional priests and poets of Africa? 8.131

9. How does an African aesthetic inform Coltrane's music? 8.132-133

10. According to Max Roach, what is the duty or purpose of the Black artist in general and the Black musician in particular? 8.133

11. How does ya Salaam define the shift to jazz fusion? What was its effect on Black consciousness? 8.135

12. According to Bob Blumenthal, how does Herbie Hancock explain his "change in perspective that led to [his] ultra-funky and enormously successful *Headhunters* album?" How does this "change in perspective" symbolize the shift in Black consciousness in the mid-seventies? 8.135-136

CHAPTER 9: BLACK FILM

1. What does author ya Salaam consider the Black Arts Movement's greatest impact on American culture? 9.137

2. How does Jesse Algeron Rhines summarize Blaxploitation? How was Blaxploitation the antithesis of Black Power? 9.137-138

3. Why was Melvin Van Peebles' hit film *Sweet Sweetback's Baadasssss Song* a challenge for Hollywood? How did the film stand outside of the Blaxploitation genre? 9.138-139

4. How is the folk type of the "bad Nigger" characterized and how does it challenge the oppressive white system, according to Rhines? 9.139

5. What was the Black Arts Movement's effect on the American social landscape, as concluded in the study by Abby Arthur Johnson and Ronald Maberry Johnson? 9.139

6. Describe the two distinct waves that characterize the Black independent filmmaking movement that emerged in Los Angeles in the early 1970s, as articulated by Ntongela Masilela. How does Cuban president Fidel Castro's maxim on the duty of the revolutionary inspire the drive within that movement? 9.140-141

7. What is the significance of *Black Journal*, a PBS television magazine? How did it help to shape mainstream American television news magazine format and programming? 9.141-144

CHAPTER 10: DANCE

1. How does Black dance impact American culture? How does ya Salaam define Black vernacular dance? 10.145-146

2. What does James Brown contribute to Black vernacular dance? How does Brown characterize his innovations in dance? 10.146

3. What is the major contradiction of Black dance as a performing area? Why did Black professional dance lag behind the rest of the arts during the Black Arts Movement? 10.146-147

4. According to Richard A. Long, what assures Black presence in professional dance? 10.147

5. List the four major Black dance companies of the Black Arts Movement and the distinction of each. 10.147-148

6. As stated in interviews, why was dancer Eleo Pomare labeled angry by White dance critics? How does his ascendancy

parallel Black Arts Movement development? 10.148

7. According to Rod Rodgers, what justifies continuing cultivation and support of separate Afro-American arts generally and dance artists specifically? 10.149

8. What example does ya Salaam give of the mainstream professional dance community's attempted erasure of the contributions of the Black Arts Movement to Black dance? 10.149

9. How does popular dance prove to be overwhelmingly Black? Explain the dichotomy that prevails today. 10.150

10. How does Sandra Richards characterize the distinction between a Black aesthetic and Black choreography? How does she use Ralph Ellison's analogy of jazz to explain her thesis? What is "good art" within the Black aesthetic? 10.150-151

11. What does dancer/choreographer Donald Byrd confess in response to Richard's analysis? How does his sentiment illustrate the difference between "Blacks who are practitioners of a Black aesthetic and Blacks who practice either a 'gumbo' aesthetic (in that it is a mix of many specifics) or a Euro-centric aesthetic in their artwork?" 10.151-152

12. What two important Black Arts Movement literary figures inspired Jawole Willa Jo Zollar, founder and artistic director of the Urban Bush Women dance/theatre company? According to Zollar, how do some Black dancers buy into the perceived limitations of Blackness? How must Black dancers challenge themselves? 10.152-153

13. How does dance critic Brenda Dixon define Eurocentric body codes? How do Protestant ethics influence these codes? What is the "final taboo" in ballet, according to Dixon? 10.153-154

14. In ya Salaam's assessment, how did the Black Arts Movement also make it possible for artists to ignore or downplay their "Blackness" and to assimilate into the dominant culture? How does Donald Byrd confront this issue? Why does he have problems getting Black dancers for his dance troupe? 10.154

15. What does ya Salaam believe continues to be a major theoretical contribution of the Black Arts Movement? According to Nontsizi Cayou, what was the Black Arts Movement's greatest influence upon the Black dance community? 10.154-155

CHAPTER 11: VISUAL ARTS

1. What connects the visual arts of the Harlem Renaissance and the Black Arts Movement? What were some of the themes of the art work of the Black Arts Movement? 11.156

2. According to critic/curator/artist Edmund Barry Gaither, why was Weusi "the most important and abiding [of] Afrocentric artist organizations" within the Black Arts Movement? What was the other major Black arts collective of the era? 11.156-157

3. What was the stated mission of COBRA (Coalition of Black Revolutionary Artists)? Explain the philosophical principles that guided the production of their art. 11.157-158

4. Explain AFRICOBRA's contribution to the Black Arts Movement. 11.158-159

5. Who is Samella Lewis, and what is her lasting contribution the Black arts? 11.159

6. Explain the African-based aesthetic that adherents of the Black Arts Movement picked up on and amplified. 11.159-160

CHAPTER 12: BAM'S CRITICS

1. How does ya Salaam classify some of the Black Arts Movement critics? 12.161

2. How does literary critic Houston A. Baker classify Amiri Baraka? According to Baker, "participants in the Black Arts often failed" to do what? How does ya Salaam characterize Baker's criticism? 12.161-162

3. How does Chairman Mao define revolution? What was his influence upon the Black Arts Movement? 12.162-163

4. What were some of the positives of the Black Arts Movement, according to Baker? 12.163

5. According to ya Salaam, how does Baker's criticism illustrate the interest of the Black petit-bourgeois? Those interests are? 12.163-164

6. Explain the cultural ignorance implicit in much of Black Arts Movement criticism. 12.164

7. Why is the relationship of criticism to the Black Arts Movement so complicated, as stated by David Lionel Smith? 12.164-165

8. Explain what Smith believes is a conspicuous difference between Black Arts writing and the work of previous black writers such as Wright and Baldwin. 12.164

9. What are the demands set upon would-be critics of the Black Arts Movement? How can honest criticism of the literature of BAM be costly to those within the academy? What are two of the seminal complications? 12.165

10. According to ya Salaam, how does Smith accurately articulate the fundamental contradiction surrounding criticisms of BAM? 12.165-166

11. Why does Smith state that, if Black aesthetic theorizing proscribed writers' use of existing literary traditions, it also opened up exciting new possibilities of artistic experimentation? Explain. 12.166

12. What is the connection between Black Arts Movement critics and jazz critics? Why is this a problem according to ya Salaam? 12.166

13. How does the journal *Callaloo* illustrate the shift in emphasis away from community and toward the upper reaches of professionalism? 12.167

14. Explain what *Callaloo* editor Charles Rowell means by the statement, "I see the Movement as a historical necessity and an achievement." What were Rowell's three main criticisms of the Black Arts Movement? 12.167-168

15. How does author ya Salaam turn Rowell's criticism against him? Explain Rowell's argument about southern Black writers. 12.167-172

16. According to Black aesthetic critic, Addison Gayle, why have some Black writers ignored their southern past? 12.168-169

17. What Rowell statement does ya Salaam believe is flat-out wrong? Explain. According to ya Salaam, who and/or what is Rowell's real target? 12.169

18. What does Rowell see as the problem with the Black Arts Movement dictum on audience? 12.171

19. What is ya Salaam's major criticism of the journal *Callaloo*? 12.171

20. How does Rowell define the so-called "anti-art atmosphere" that was sometimes created by the Black Arts Movement? How did an overemphasis on politics create a problem?

What does he believe should have been the central focus of the Black aesthetic? 12.171-172

21. What was Hoyt Fuller's response to the criticism that there was a serious lack of quality and craft in Black Arts Movement literature? 12.172

22. What was the result of the Black Arts Movement's opening up of literature to the unlettered? 12.173

23. According to ya Salaam how does Stephen Henderson offer a theoretical framework that both explained what the New Black Poetry was and what it meant? How does Henderson summarize his argument? 12.173-174

24. Explain Henderson exegesis concerning the issue of "Blackness" in poetry. 12.174-175

25. Why is it so hard to find critical work on the Black Arts Movement published after 1976, according to ya Salaam? 12.175

26. How does ya Salaam describe the erroneous contention that the Black aesthetic was monolithic and condemned anyone who did not toe the party line? 12.175-176

27. Explain what ya Salaam considers part of the strength of the Black aesthetic. 12.176

28. Describe the major shift in the Black aesthetic that took place in the mid-seventies. 12.176

29. Who produced the New York Equity stage debut of Ntozake Shange's choreopoem *For Colored Girls*? Why is that significant? Why was the development of the stage production timely? 12.176-177

30. Explain the shift in the ideological and political focus of the Black Arts Movement, according to ya Salaam. 12.177-178

31. What did women's literature have to teach about true power? Explain the shift in the image of Black women as illustrated in Black woman's literature. 12.178

32. Explain the seemingly unresolvable contradictions between what was characterized as Black Arts Movement male chauvinist emphasis and the militant anti-sexism of emerging Black women writers. 12.179

33. Explain the triad of concerns that Black women's literature often addressed. 12.180

34. From where did the Combahee River Collective take their name? Explain the symbolism. 12.180

35. According to the "Combahee River Collective Statement" what led to the need to develop a politics that was anti-racist, unlike those of white women, and anti-sexist, unlike those of Black and white men? 12.180

36. How was the Combahee River Collective definition of Black womanhood a break with Black Power? How did the collective see themselves as different from white feminists? 12.180-181

37. How is the Black woman's movement in literature an extension of the Black Arts Movement, according to ya Salaam? 12.181

CHAPTER 13: A CRITICAL ASSESSMENT

1. List some of the external factors that led to the decline of the Black Arts Movement. What were some of the key internal events that were disruptive? How does Black capitalism figure in? 13.182

2. How does Cleveland poet Norman Jordan describe the conflicts over money that hastened the end of the MUNTU Poets Collective? How is that situation symbolic of the monetary conflicts that crippled the Black Arts Movement?

13.183

3. In what way did the Black Arts Movement make subsidized support almost impossible for Black arts? 13.183

4. How did defections of major Black Arts Movement figures mark the coming end of the movement? 13.184

5. Explain the Black Arts Movement's anti-White stance. What kept the movement from falling into the "skin trap?" 13.184-185

6. How does ya Salaam explain charges of sexism within the Black Arts Movement? How does singer Abbey Lincoln defend Black men? 13.186

7. How does Maulana Karenga address the "woman question?" What does he believe the struggle to change structures entails? 13.187

8. According to Ishmael Reed, how did the Black Arts Movement strike a blow for cultural sovereignty? 13.188

9. Explain the difference between protest literature and Black Arts Movement literature. 13.189

10. Why did "young Black writers who gathered around Baraka and the Black Arts Theater in 1964 [sic] and who had earlier begun to write for *Liberator* and *Black World* Magazines... find little support among the Black literary establishment," according to Addison Gayle? 13.189-190

11. To what, does Gayle believe, would the new Black art be devoted once protesting ended? What were the avowed goals of the Black Arts Movement? 13.190

12. How did the actions of the Black Power and Black Arts Movement inspire Tom Porter, founder and leader of the Mohawk Valley Community in upstate New York? 13.191

13. According to ya Salaam, how does the influence of the Black Arts Movement live on today? 13.193

WORKS CITED

Ahmed, A. Muhammad. "Black Cultural Revolution." *Kitabu Cha Jua* (Formerly *Journal of Black Poetry*) 1, no. 19 (Summer 1975).

Baker, Houston A., Jr. *Afro-American Poetics, Revisions of Harlem and the Black Aesthetic*. Madison: University of Wisconsin, 1988.

Baraka, Amiri [LeRoi Jones]. *The Autobiography*. New York: Freundlich Books, 1984.

---. "The Black Arts Movement." National Black Arts Festival. Atlanta. August 1994.

---. "How Black Is *Black World*?" In *Yardbird Reader* 5 (1976). Edited by Ishmael Reed. Berkeley: Yardbird Publishing Incorporated.

---. Interview with Kalamu ya Salaam. November 1995.

---. "Negro Theater Pimps Get Big Off Nationalism." In *Raise Race Rays Raze*. New York: Random House, 1971.

---. "Statement." In *Journal of Black Poetry* 1, no. 4 (1967). Edited by Dingane Joe Goncalves. San Francisco: The Journal of Black Poetry, 1967.

---. "The Wailer." In *Vision of a Liberated Future*. Edited by Michael Schwartz. New York: Thunder's Mouth Press, 1989.

Bell, Bernard W. "Contemporary Afro-American Poetry as Folk Art." *Black World* (Mar 1973).

Black Books Bulletin 1, no. 1 (Fall 1971). Chicago: Institute of Positive Education, 1971.

Black Dialogue 1, no. 1. San Francisco: Black Dialogue 1965

---. (Volume 1, no. 3). San Francisco: Black Dialogue, 1965.

---. (Volume IV, no. 1). New York: Black Dialogue, 1969.

Black Scholar 1, no.1 (November 1969). San Francisco: The Black World Foundation, 1969.

Black Theatre/The Drama Review 12, no. 4. Edited by Ed Bullins. New York: School of the Arts, NYU, 1968.

Blumenthal, Bob. "Liner notes." *Mwandishi: Herbie Hancock: The Complete Warner Bros. Recordings.* New York: Warner Bros. Records, 1994.

Bourne, St. Clair. Interview by Clyde Taylor. In *Artist and Influence* XV. Edited by James V. Hatch, Leo Hamalian, and Judy Blum. New York: Hatch-Billops Collection, Inc., 1996.

Brown, James, and Bruce Tucker. *The Godfather of Soul, an Autobiography by James Brown.* New York: Thunder's Mouth Press, 1986.

Byrd, Donald. "Untitled Article." In *Black Choreographers Moving.* Edited by Halifu Osumare and Julinda Lewis-Ferguson. Berkeley: Expansion Arts Services, 1991.

Carmichael, Stokely. "We Are Going To Use The Term 'Black Power' and We Are Going To Define It Because Black Power Speaks To Us." In *Black Nationalism in America.* Edited by John H. Bracey, Jr., August Meier, and Elliott Rudwick. Indianapolis: The Bobbs-Merrill Company, Inc., 1970.

Cayou, Dolores Kirton Nontsizi. *Modern Jazz Dance.* Palo Alto, California: National Press Books, 1971.

Chrisman, Robert. Interview with Kalamu ya Salaam. November 1995.

Combahee River Collective. "The Combahee River Collective Statement." In *Home Girls: A Black Feminist Anthology.* Edited by Barbara Smith. New York: Kitchen Table Women of Color Press, 1983.

Coleman, Wanda. "The Cruel Papa Really Put Me Down-Blues." In *Black Theater* 6. Edited by Ed Bullins. New York: The New Lafayette Theatre Publications, 1972.

Dent, Tom. "Free Southern Theater: An Evaluation." In *Freedomways* 6, no. 1. Edited by John Henrik Clarke. New York: Freedomways Associates, Inc., 1966

---. "Preface." In *Callaloo 1, no. 1.* Edited by. Charles Rowell. Baton Rouge: Charles H. Rowell, 1976.

---. *Southern Journey.* New York: William Morrow and Company, 1996.

---. Interview with Kalamu ya Salaam. November 1995.

---. "Letters." (Private correspondence.) Various dates.

Dixon, Brenda. "Untitled Article." In *Black Choreographers Moving.* Edited by Halifu Osumare and Julinda Lewis-Ferguson. Berkeley: Expansion Arts Services, 1991.

Emery, Lynne Fauley. *Black Dance: From 1619 to Today.* Hightstown, NJ: Princeton Book Company, 1988.

Fowler, Carolyn (Gerald). *Black Arts and Black Aesthetics, A Bibliography.* Privately printed, 1976. (Available from Carolyn Fowler, 513 Spinnaker Lane, Fort Collins, CO 80525).

---. "Untitled." In *Negro Digest* (November). Edited by.Hoyt Fuller. Chicago: Johnson Publications, 1969.

Fuller, Hoyt. "BBB Interviews." In *Black Books Bulletin* 1, no. 1 (Fall 1971). Edited by Haki Madhubuti. Chicago: The Institute of Positive Education..

---. "Foreword to NOMMO." In *NOMMO: A Literary Legacy of Black Chicago*. Edited by Carole A. Parks. Chicago: OBAhouse, 1987.

---. "The New Black Literature: Protest Or Affirmation." In *The Black Aesthetic*. Edited by Addison Gayle, Jr., editor. Garden City, New York: Anchor Books, 1971.

---. "Towards a Black Aesthetic." In *Within The Circle: An Anthology of African American Literary Criticism from the Harlem Renaissance to the Present*. Edited by Angelyn Mitchell. Durham: Duke University Press, 1994.

Gaither, Edmund Barry. "Heritage Reclaimed: An Historical Perspective And Chronology." In *Black Art: Ancestral Legacy: The African Impulse In African-American Art*. Chief Curator Alvia J. Wardlaw. Dallas: Dallas Museum of Art, 1989.

Gayle, Jr., Addison. "Introduction." In *The Black Aesthetic*. Edited by Addison Gayle, Jr. Garden City, New York: Anchor Books, 1971.

---. "Blueprint for Black Criticism." In *First World 1, no. 1 (Jan/ Feb 1977)*. Edited by Hoyt Fuller. Atlanta: First World Foundation.

---. "Cultural Nationalism the Black Novelist in America." In *Black Books Bulletin* 1, no. 1 (Fall 1971). Edited by Haki Madhubuti. Chicago: The Institute of Positive Education.

---. "Reclaiming the Southern Experience: The Black Aesthetic 10 Years Later." In *Black World* (Sept 1974). Edited by Hoyt Fuller. Chicago: Johnson Publications..

Goncalves, Dingane Joe. "A Review of *Dynamite Voices*." In *Journal of Black Poetry* 1, no. 17 (Summer 1973). Edited by Dingane Joe Goncalves. San Francisco: Journal of Black Poetry..

---. "Letters." Private collection.

Green, Kim, Abiodun Oyewole and Umar Bin Hassan. *Last Poets on a Mission: Selected Poetry & A History of the Last Poets*. New York: Henry Holt & Co., Inc., 1996.

Harper, Michael S. *Dear John, Dear Coltrane*. Urbana: University of Illinois Press, 1985 (original copyright 1970).

Henderson, Stephen E., and Mercer Cook. *The Militant Black Writer in Africa and the United States*. Madison: University of Wisconsin Press, 1969.

Henderson, Stephen E. "Saturation: Progress Report on a Theory of Black Poetry." In *Black World* (June 1975). Edited by Hoyt Fuller. Chicago: Johnson Publications..

---. *Understanding The New Black Poetry, Black Speech and Black Music as Poetic References*. New York: Williams Morrow, 1973.

Himes, Chester. "Preface." In *Yardbird Reader* 1, no.1. Berkeley: Yardbird Publishing Cooperative, 1972.

Jackmon, Marvin. "The Black Revolutionary Poet." In *Journal of Black Poetry 1, no. 4 (Spring 1967)*. Edited by Dingane Joe Goncalves. San Francisco: The Journal of Black Poetry..

Jarrell, Wadsworth A. "Heading For A Black Aesthetic." In *Art Papers* (Nov/Dec 1985). Edited by Xenia Z. Zed. Atlanta: Arts Papers.

Johnson, Abby Arthur and Johnson, Ronald Maberry. *Propaganda & Aesthetics: The Literary Politics of African-American Magazines in the Twentieth Century*. Amherst: University of Massachusetts Press, 1979.

Jones, LeRoi. [Amiri Baraka] "Statement." In *Journal of Black Poetry* 1, no. 4 (Spring 1967). Edited by Dingane Joe Goncalves. San Francisco: The Journal of Black Poetry.

Jordan, Norman. "News from Cleveland." In *Black Art Black Culture*. Edited by Dingane Joe Goncalves. San Francisco: The Journal of Black Poetry Press, 1972.

Karenga, Maulana. "Black Art: Mute Matter Given Force and Function." In *New Black Voices*. Edited by Abraham Chapman. New York: New American Library, 1972.

---. "Beyond Connections: Liberation In Love And Struggle." In *NKOMBO*. Edited by.Kuumba na Kazi and Kalamu ya Salaam. New Orleans: Ahidiana, 1977.

---. "Reaffirmation and Change: A Modest Contribution to the Council of Kawaida Elders." In *NKOMBO*. Edited by Kalamu ya Salaam. New Orleans: Ahidiana, 1975.

King, Woodie, Jr. *Black Theatre: Present Condition*. New York: Woodie King, Jr. and National Black Theatre Touring Circuit, 1981.

Kofsky, Frank. *Black Nationalism and the Revolution in Music*. New York: Pathfinder Press, 1970.

"Lafayette Theatre Reaction to Bombers." In *Black Theater*, no. 4. Edited by Ed Bullins. New York: The New Lafayette Theatre Publications, 1969.

Lee, Don L. [Haki Madhubuti] "Black Writing: A Subjective View." In *Black Books Bulletin* 3, no. 2 (Fall 1975). Edited by Haki Madhubuti. Chicago: The Institute of Positive Education.

---. "Don L. Lee Interviews Stokely Carmichael." In *Journal of Black Poetry* 1, no. 14. Edited by Don L. Lee. San Francisco: The Journal of Black Poetry, 1971.

---. *Don't Cry, Scream.* Chicago: Third World Press, 1969.

---. "Why This Issue." In *Journal of Black Poetry* 1, no. 14. Edited by Don L. Lee. San Francisco: The Journal of Black Poetry, 1971.

Lincoln, Abbey. "The Negro Woman in American Literature." In *Freedomways* 6, no. 1. Edited by John Henrik Clarke. New York: Freedomways Associates, Inc., 1966.

Long, Richard A. "A Note on the Black Aesthetic." In *Art Papers* (Nov/Dec 1985). Edited by Xenia Z. Zed. Atlanta: Arts Papers.

---. *The Black Tradition in American Dance.* New York: Rizzoli, 1989.

Madhubuti, Haki R [Don L. Lee]. *From Plan to Planet.* Chicago: Third World Press, 1973.

Major, Clarence. "A Black Criteria." In *Journal of Black Poetry* 1, no. 4 (Spring 1967). Edited by Dingane Joe Goncalves. San Francisco: The Journal of Black Poetry, 1967.

Marsh, Dave. "Epilogue: Prisoner of Race." In *James Brown: The Godfather of Soul, an Autobiography.* Edited by James Brown and Bruce Tucker. New York: Thunder's Mouth Press, 1986.

Masilela, Ntongela. "The Los Angeles School of Black Filmmakers." In *Black American Cinema.* Edited by Manthia Diawara. New York: Routledge, 1993.

Moore, William. *Black Choreographers Moving.* Edited by Halifu Osumare and Julinda Lewis-Ferguson. Berkeley:

Expansion Arts Services, 1991.

Neal, Larry. "The Black Arts Movement." In *Black Theatre/The Drama Review* 12, no. 4 (Summer 1968). Edited by Ed Bullins. New York: School of the Arts, NYU.

---. "New Space / The Growth of Black Consciousness in the Sixties." In *The Black Seventies*. Edited by Floyd B. Barbour. Boston: Porter Sargent Publisher, 1970.

---. "Towards A Relevant Black Theatre." In *Black Theater*, no. 4. New York: The New Lafayette Theatre Publications, 1969.

---. *Visions of a Liberated Future: Black Arts Movement Writings*. New York: Thunder's Mouth Press, 1989.

Newton, Michael. *Bitter Grain: Huey Newton and the Black Panther Party*. Los Angeles: Holloway House Publishing, 1980.

October Revolution. "Press Release, Evidence 22166." Conshohocken, PA: Evidence Records, 1996.

O'Neal, John. "The Motion In The Ocean: Some Political Dimensions of the Free Southern Theatre." In *Black Theatre/The Drama Review 12, no. 4 (Summer 1968)*. Edited by Ed Bullins. New York: School of the Arts, NYU.

Panel (Baraka, MacBeth, Mkalimoto, Neal, Toure, Marvin X). "Lafayette Theatre Reaction to *Bombers*." In *Black Theater*, no. 4). New York: The New Lafayette Theatre Publications 1969.

Porter, Tom. "The Mohawk Nation." In *Lapis* (Summer 1995). Edited by Ralph White. New York: New York Open Center.

Primus, Marc. "The Afro-American Folkloric Troupe." In *Freedomways* 6, no. 1 (Winter 1966) New York:

Freedomways Associates, Inc.

---. Interview with Kalamu ya Salaam. January 1997.

Randall, Dudley. "Broadside Press: A Personal Chronicle." In *The Black Seventies.* Edited by Floyd B. Barbour. Boston: Porter Sargent Publisher, 1970.

---. and Margaret Burroughs. *For Malcolm X: Poems on the Life and the Death of Malcolm X.* Detroit: Broadside Press, 1969.

Redmond, Eugene B. *Drumvoices: The Mission of Afro-American Poetry: A Critical History.* Garden City: Anchor Press/ Doubleday, 1976.

Reed, Ishmael. "Integration or Cultural Exchange?" in *Yardbird Reader 5.* Edited by Ishmael Reed. Berkeley: Yardbird Publishing Incorporated, 1976.

---. Interview with Kalamu ya Salaam. November 1995.

---. "Introduction." In *Yardbird Reader 1*, no. 1. Berkeley: Yardbird Publishing Cooperative, 1972.

Rhines, Jesse Algeron. *Black Film/White Money.* New Brunswick: Rutgers University Press, 1996.

Richards, Sandra L. "Untitled Article." In *Black Choreographers Moving.* Edited by Halifu Osumare and Julinda Lewis-Ferguson. Berkeley: Expansion Arts Services, 1991.

Rowell, Charles H. "Diamonds in a Sawdust Pile." In *Callaloo 1*, no. 1. Edited by Charles Rowell. Baton Rouge: Charles H. Rowell, 1976.

Sanders, Lelie Catherine. *The Development of Black Theater in America—From Shadows to Selves.* Baton Rouge: Louisiana State University Press, 1988.

Scott-Heron, Gil. *The Mind of Gil Scott-Heron*. (Recording with 24-page booklet of poetry.) New York: Arista Records, 1978.

Shange, Ntozake. "Artists' Dialogue." In *The Fact of Blackness: Frantz Fanon and Visual Representation*. Edited by Alan Read. Seattle: Bay Press, 1996.

---. *See No Evil*. San Francisco: Momo's Press, 1984.

Smith, David L. "The Black Arts Movement and Its Critics." *American Literary History* 3, no..1 (1991).

Soulbook 1, no. 1. Berkeley: Afroamerican Research Institution, 1964.

Spriggs, Ed. "On the 'Boycott'." *Black Art Black Culture*. San Francisco: Journal of Black Poetry Press, 1972.

Taylor, Clyde. "The L.A. Rebellion: A Turning Point in Black Cinema." *The New American Filmmakers Series, Exhibitions of Independent Film and Video*. New York: Whitney Museum of American Art, 1986.

Toure, Askia M. "Report on the *Essence* Magazine Affair," In *Black Art Black Culture*. Edited by Dingane Joe Goncalves. San Francisco: The Journal of Black Poetry Press, 1972.

---. "Juju." In *Journal of Black Poetry 1, no. 7*. Edited by Dingane Joe Goncalves. San Francisco: The Journal of Black Poetry, 1968.

---. Interview with Kalamu ya Salaam. November 1995.

Turner, Darwin. "Frank Yerby: Golden Debunker." In *Black Books Bulletin 1, no. 3 (Fall 1972)*. Edited by Haki Madhubuti. Chicago: The Institute of Positive Education..

Weinstein, Norman C. *A Night in Tunisia: Imaginings of Africa in Jazz.* New York: Limelight Editions, Books of the Performing Arts, 1993.

X, Malcolm. "The Organization of Afro-American Unity: For Human Rights and Dignity." In *Black Nationalism in America.* Edited by John H. Bracey, Jr., August Meier, and Elliott Rudwick. Indianapolis: The Bobbs-Merrill Company, Inc., 1970.

Zollar, Jawole Willa Jo. "Untitled Article." In *Black Choreographers.* Edited by Halifu Osumare and Julinda Lewis-Ferguson. Berkeley: Expansion Arts Services, 1991.

PHOTOGRAPHS, DOCUMENTS AND HISTORICAL ARCHIVES

Here is a selection of images from the period of the most productive decade of the Black Arts Movement (1965 – 1975). The bulk of photos are of books, magazines and journals. These images illustrate the wide and diverse range of BAM. For example, some people accuse BAM adherents of disrespecting Detroit-based poet Robert Hayden who served as United States poet laureate (1976 – 1978). The reality is that Hayden was published by Broadside Press and his poems "Runagate" and "Frederick Douglass" were celebrated. Hayden was politically at odds with the nationalist emphasis of BAM but he was never disowned.

There were many other writers who were published during the BAM decade, some of whom were white, whose work focused on Black literature. Although it would be incorrect to say that they were all members of BAM, there is no denying the fact that their work not only focused on Black people and the struggles associated with Black people, a number of them did not published outside of the BAM period. BAM opened doors for a wide variety of writers including a significant number who were not U.S. citizens.

International writers were embraced by BAM and additionally, internal connections to Latino/a, Asian, and Indigenous American individuals and movements were developed, mainly but not exclusively on the west coast and in New York. Once again, rather than argue this point in text, photographs of BAM era publications prove the case.

One final note is that there was a multi-generational aspect to the BAM decade that is too often completely overlooked. The two leading BAM publishers, Dudley Randall (b. 1914) of Detroit's Broadside Press, and Haki Madhubuti, aka Don L. Lee, (b. 1942) were a generation apart. They both published writers who were over fifty years old, particularly Gwendolyn Brooks, Margaret Walker Alexander, Sterling Brown, and George Kent among numerous others. This sampling of book covers amply illustrates just how far reaching and effective BAM was.

This selection of BAM era photos is from the tremendous body of work collected by BAM photo-griot Eugene Redmond who is also a widely celebrated poet and educator.

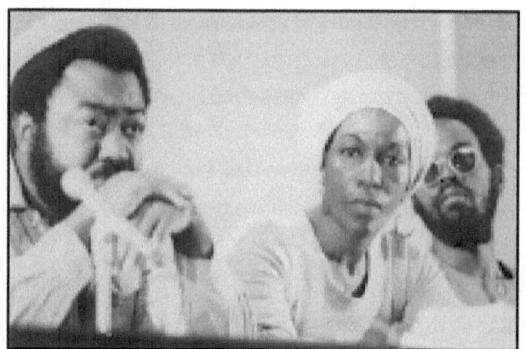

Askia Muhammad Toure,
Mari Evans, and Kalamu ya Salaam

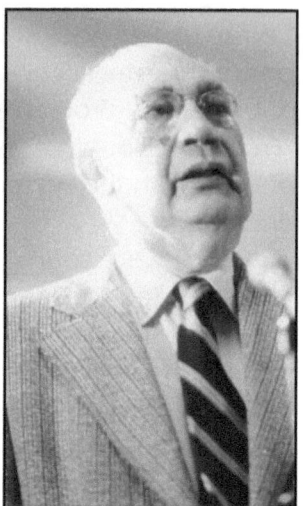

Sterling Brown

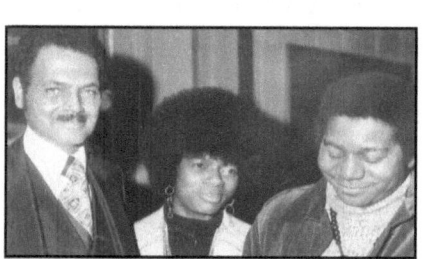

Mr. Officer
and Eugene B. Redmond

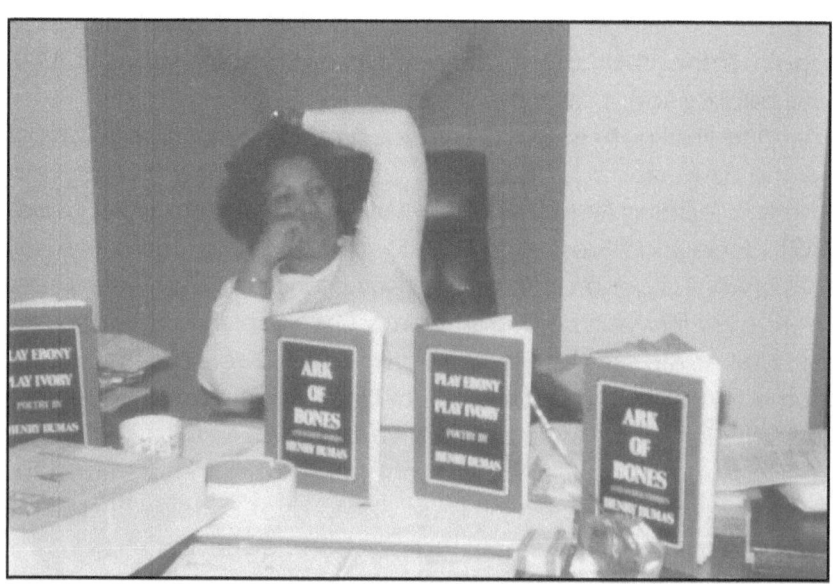

Toni Morrison

234

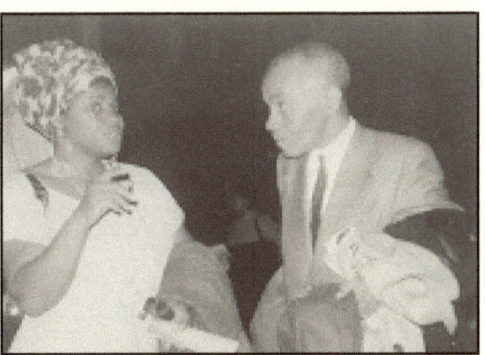

Bernice Reagon
and Leon Dumas

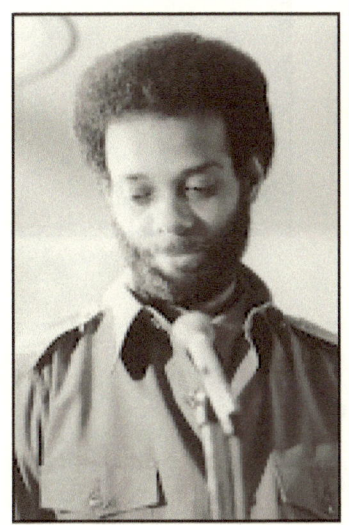

Haki Madhubuti

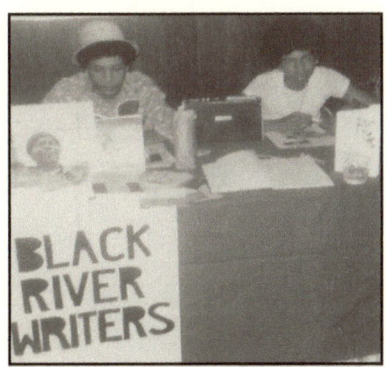

Black River Writers

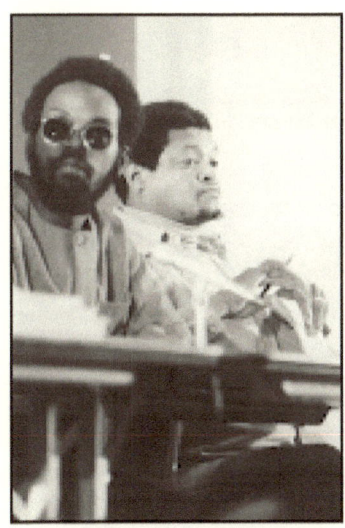

Kalamu ya Salaam
and Quincy Troupe

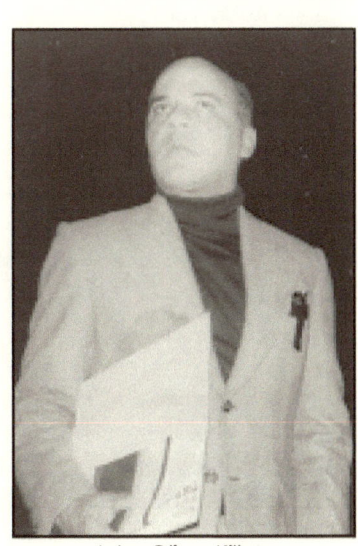

John Oliver Killens

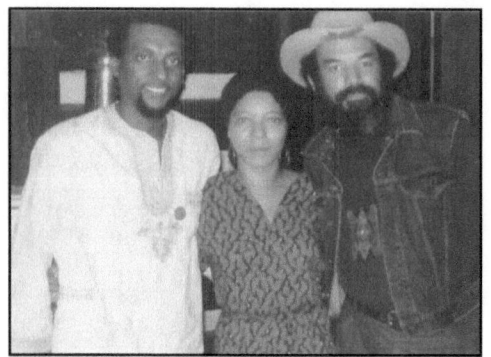

Kwame Ture

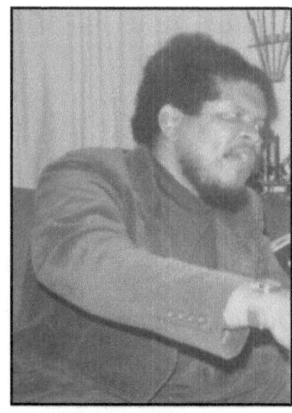

Ishmael Reed

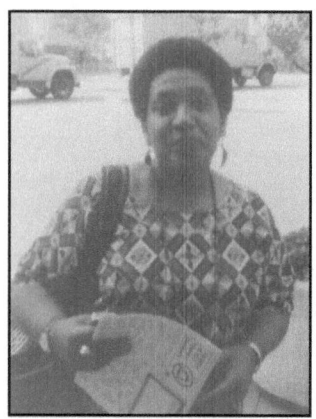

Audre Lorde

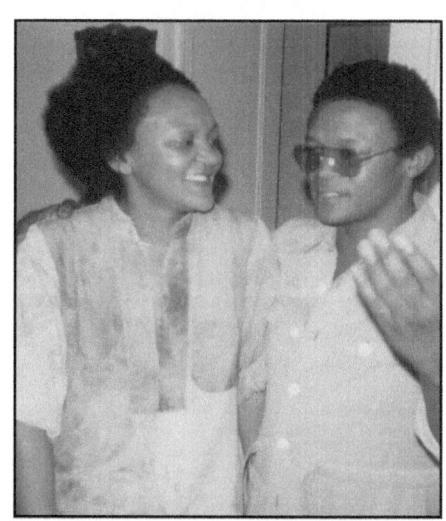

Barbara and Hugh Masakela

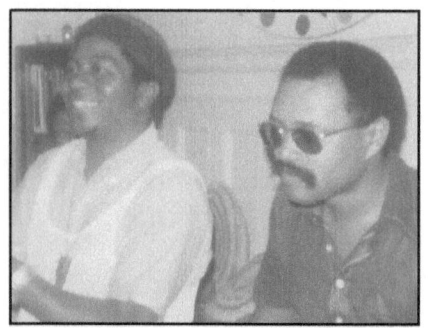

Redmond and Larry Neal

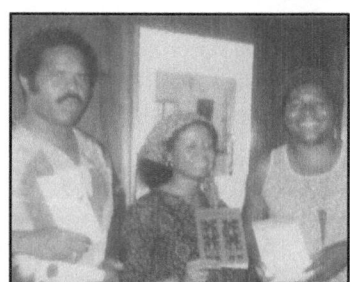

Mel Edwards, Cortez,
and Redmond

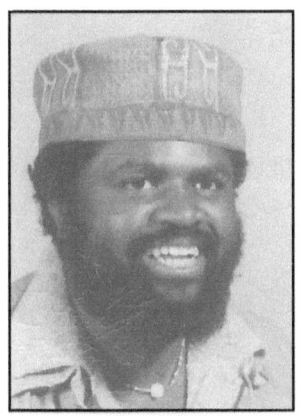

Keith Jefferson

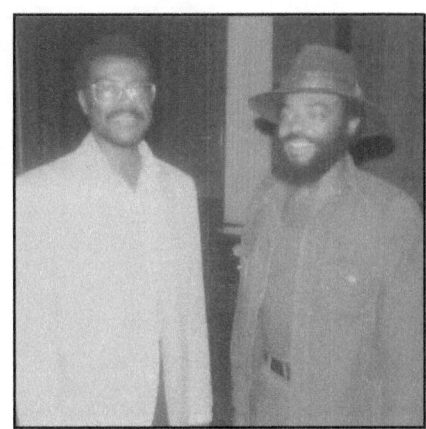

Allan Gordon and John King

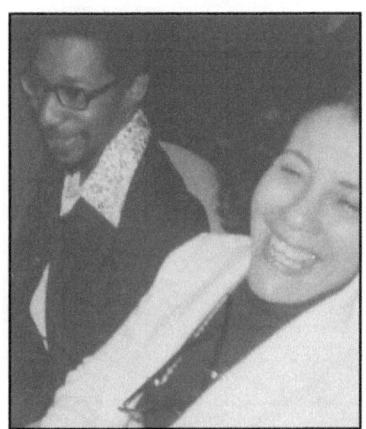

Charles H. Rowell
and Pinkie Gordon Lane

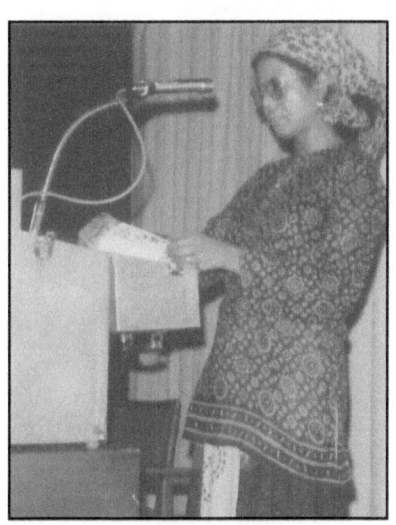

Jayne Cortez

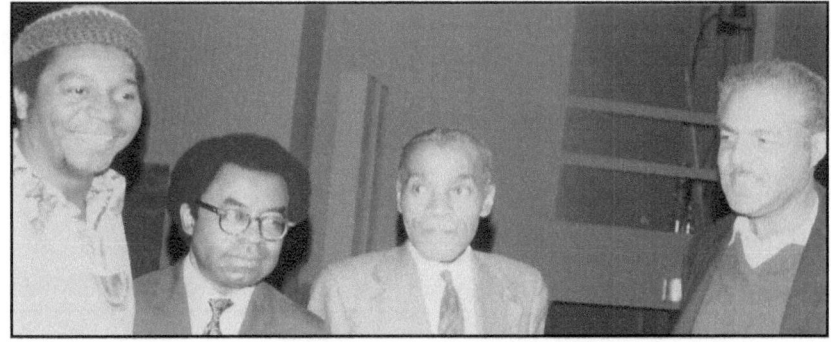

Redmond, Henderson,
Damas, and Allen

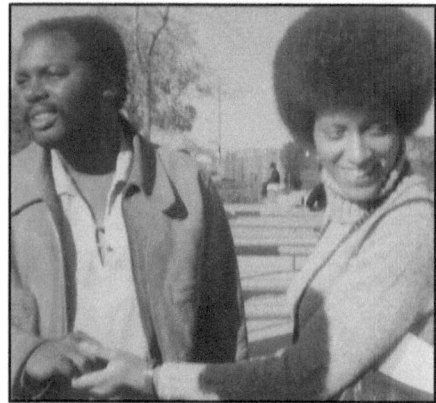

Clay Goss and Paula Giddings

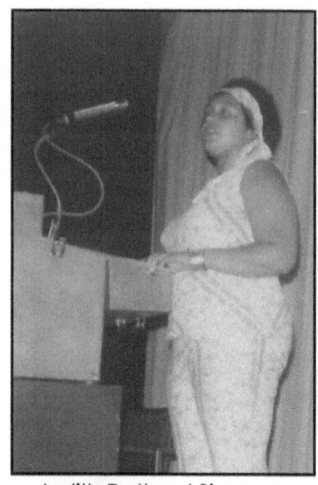

Judith Dothard Simmons

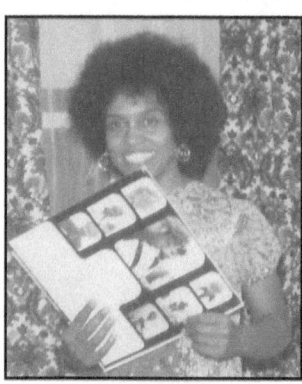

Loretta Dumas

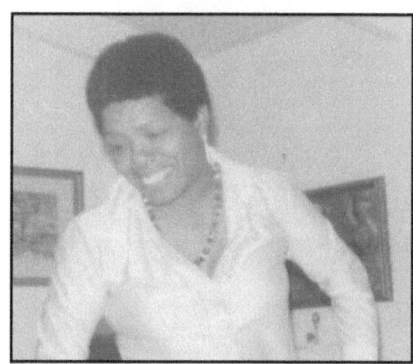

Maya Angelou

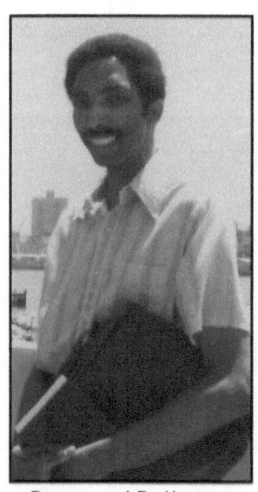

Raymond Patterson

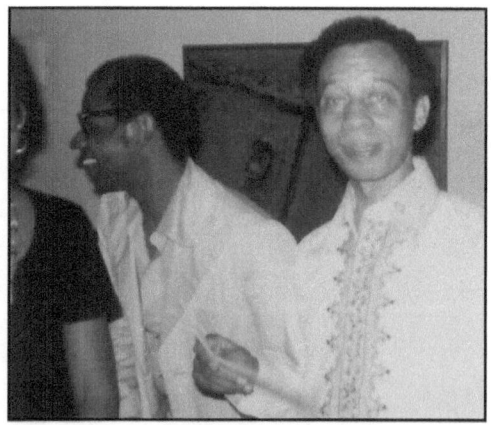

Richard Long

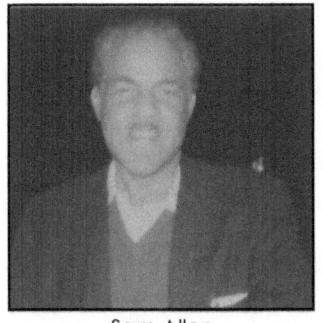

Sam Allen

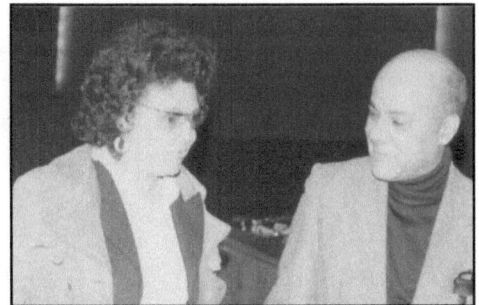

Sarah Webster Fabio and Killens

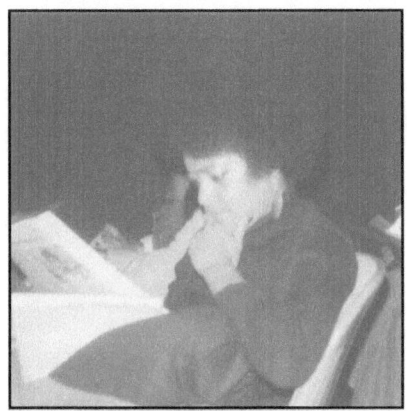

Toni Cade Bambara

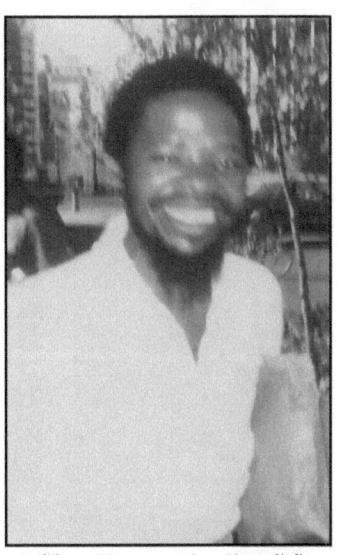

William Keorapetse Kgositsile

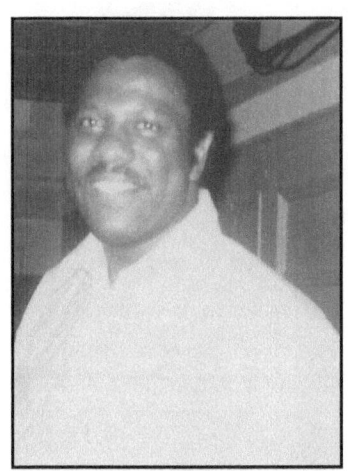

Woodie King

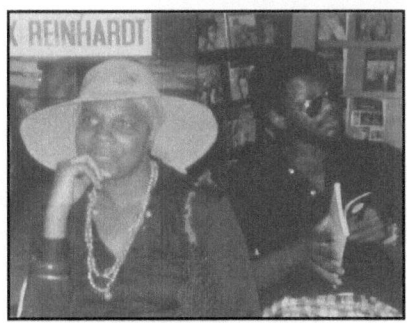

Vertamae Grovesnor

BLACK RIVER WRITERS BOOKS

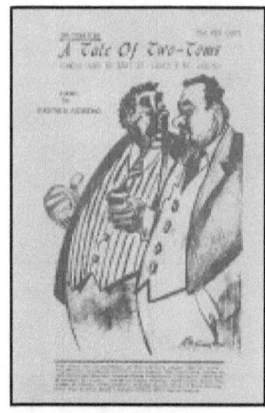
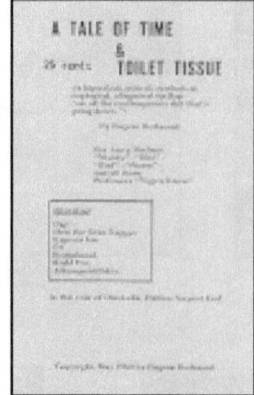
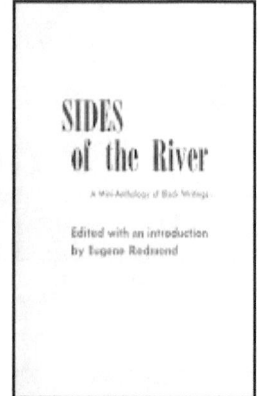

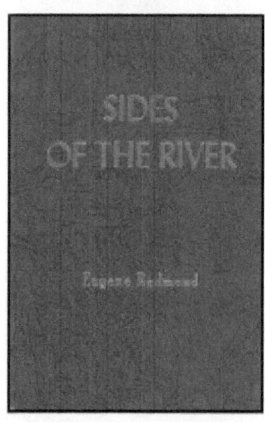
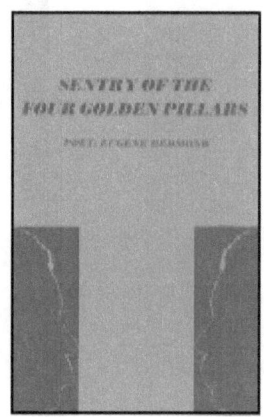
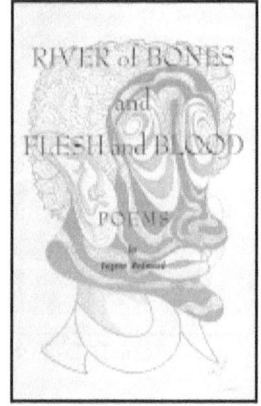

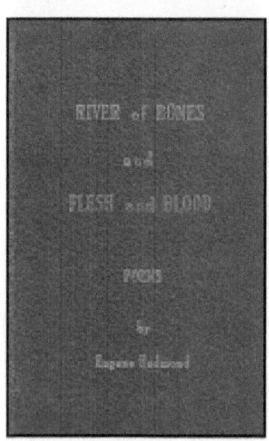
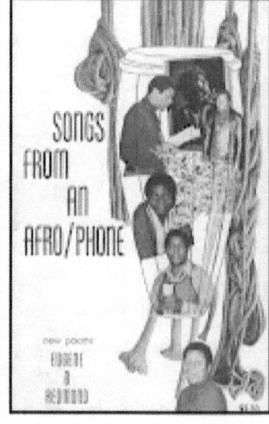
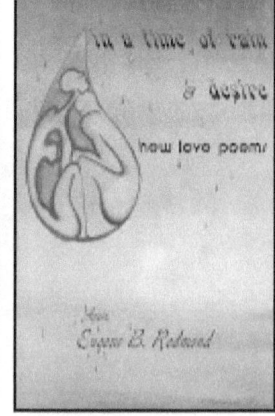

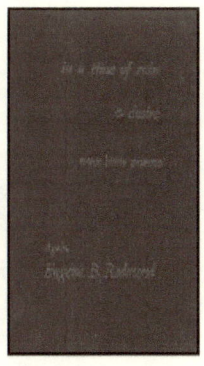
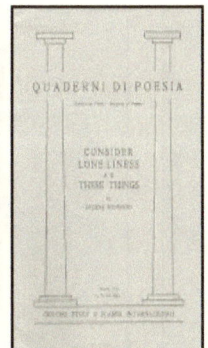
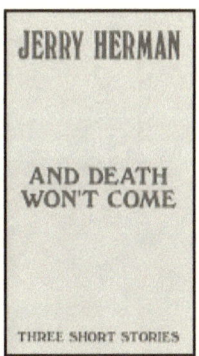

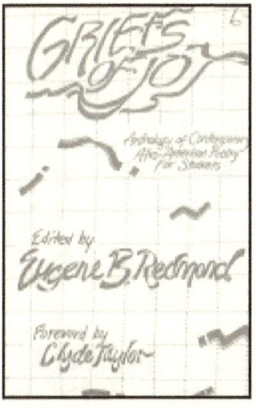
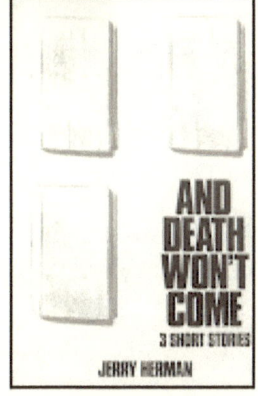
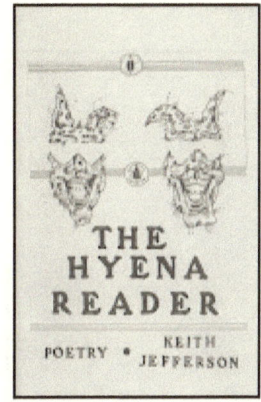

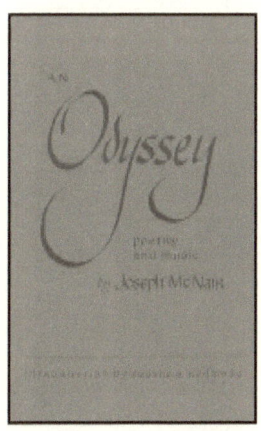
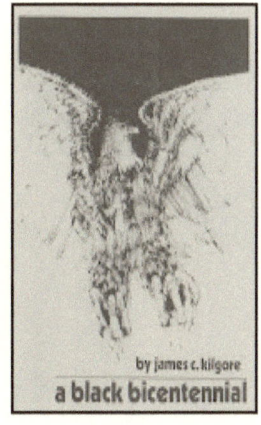
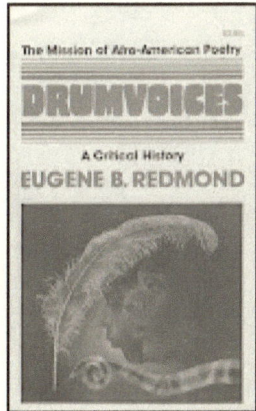

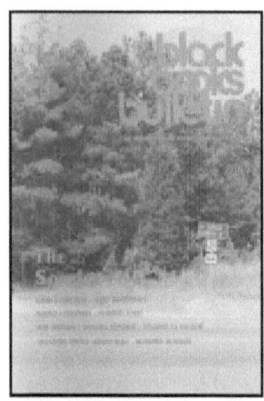
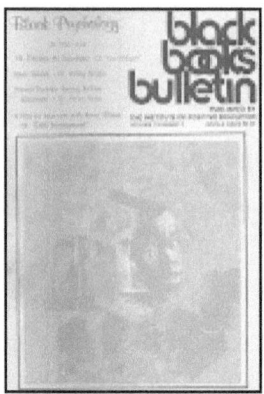
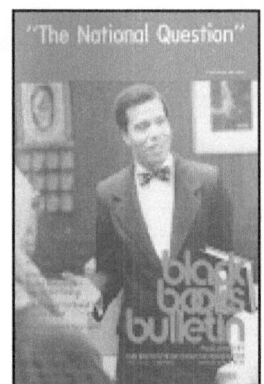
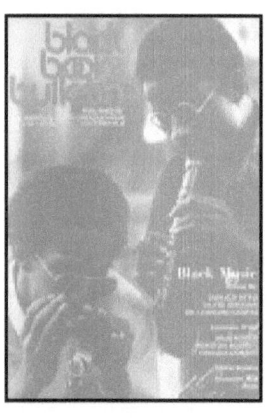
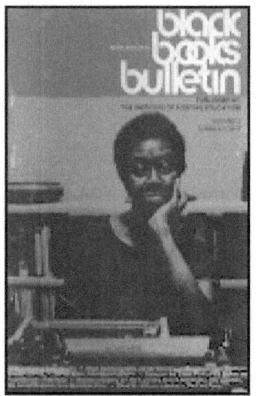
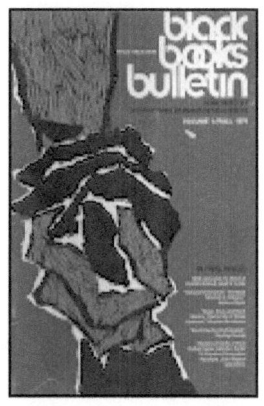
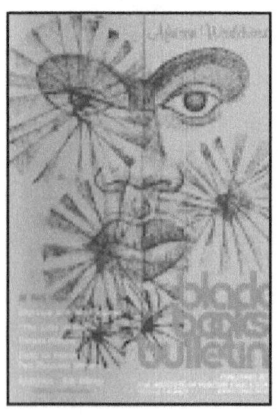
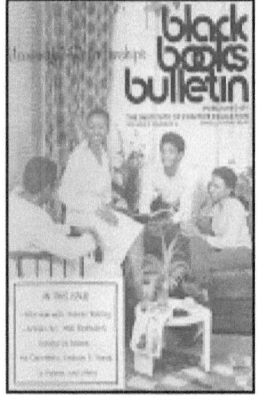
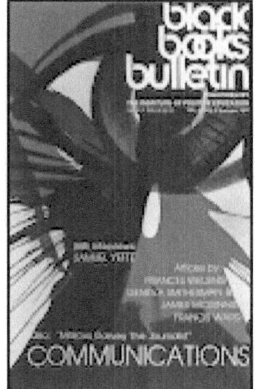

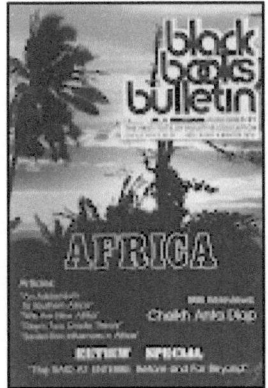
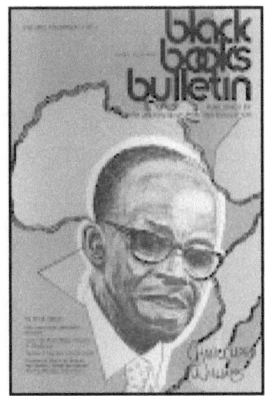
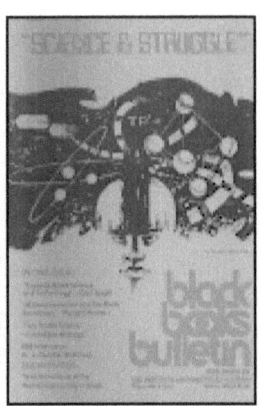
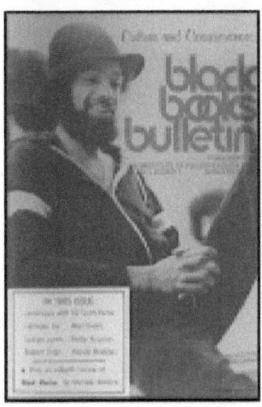
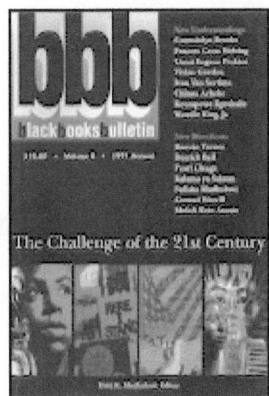
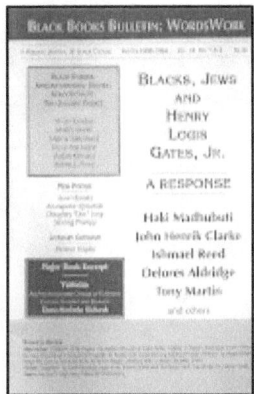

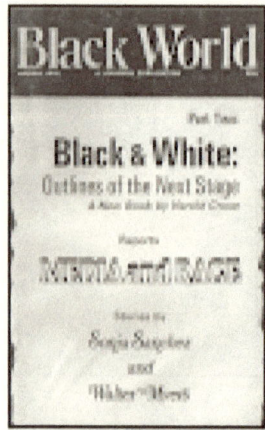
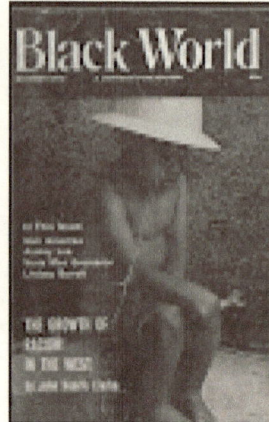
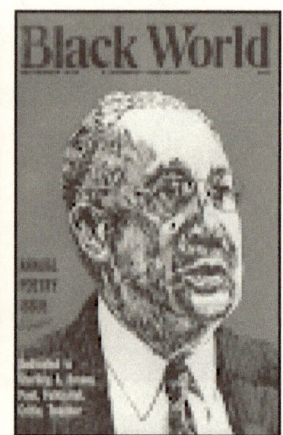
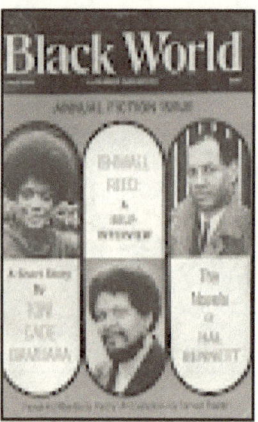
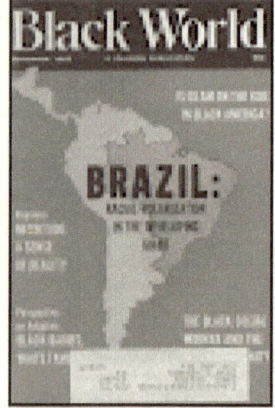
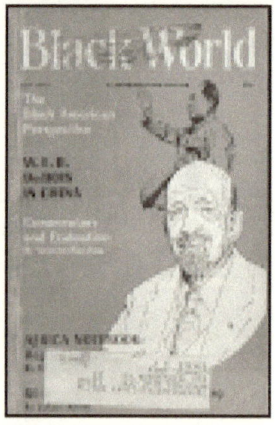
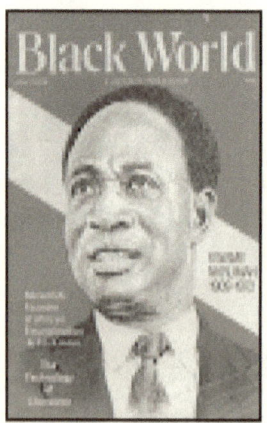
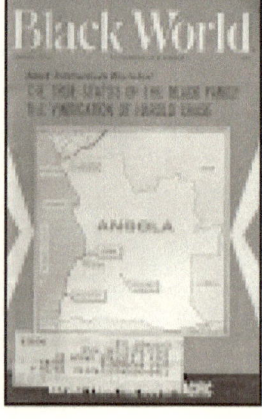
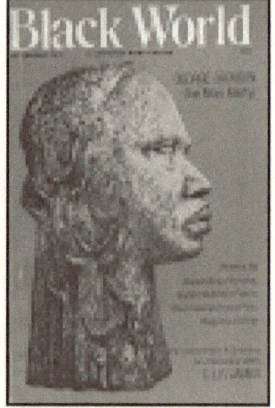

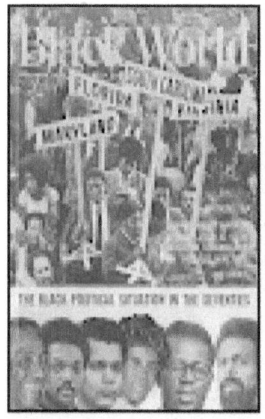
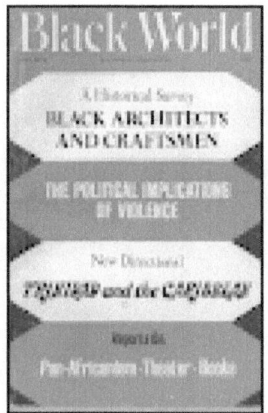
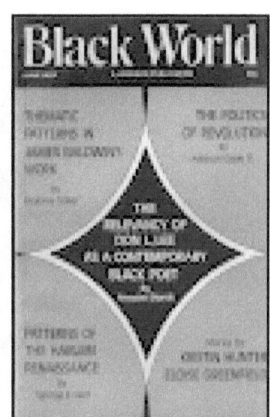
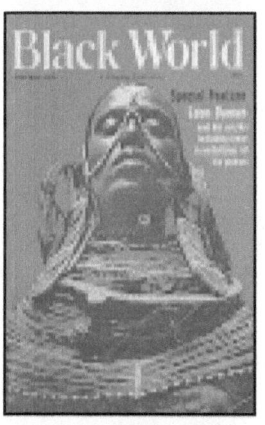
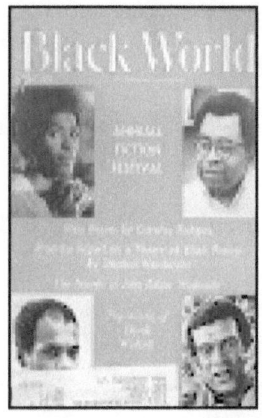
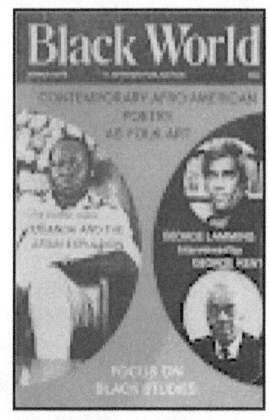
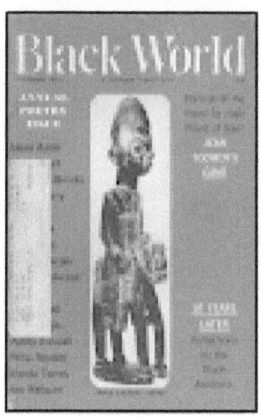
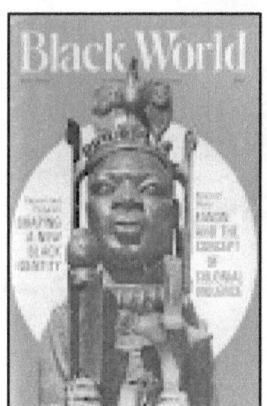
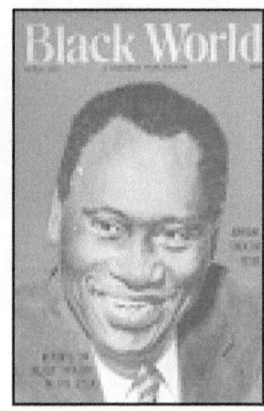

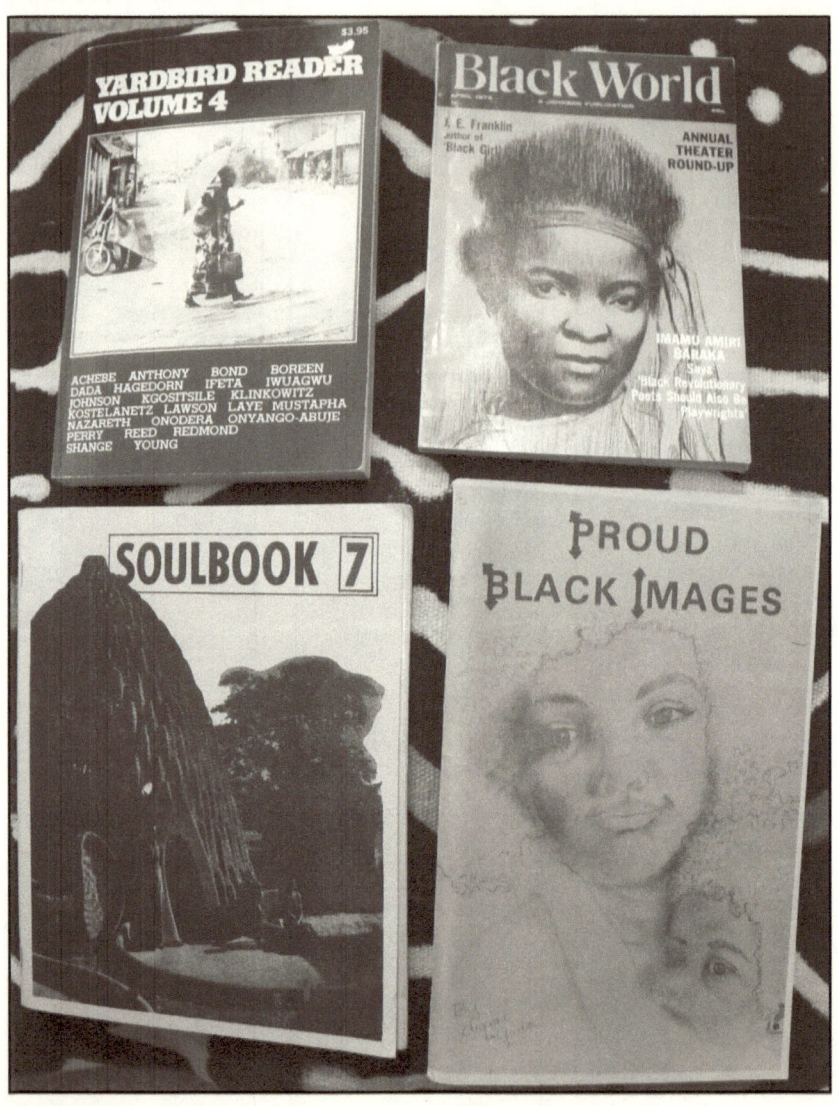

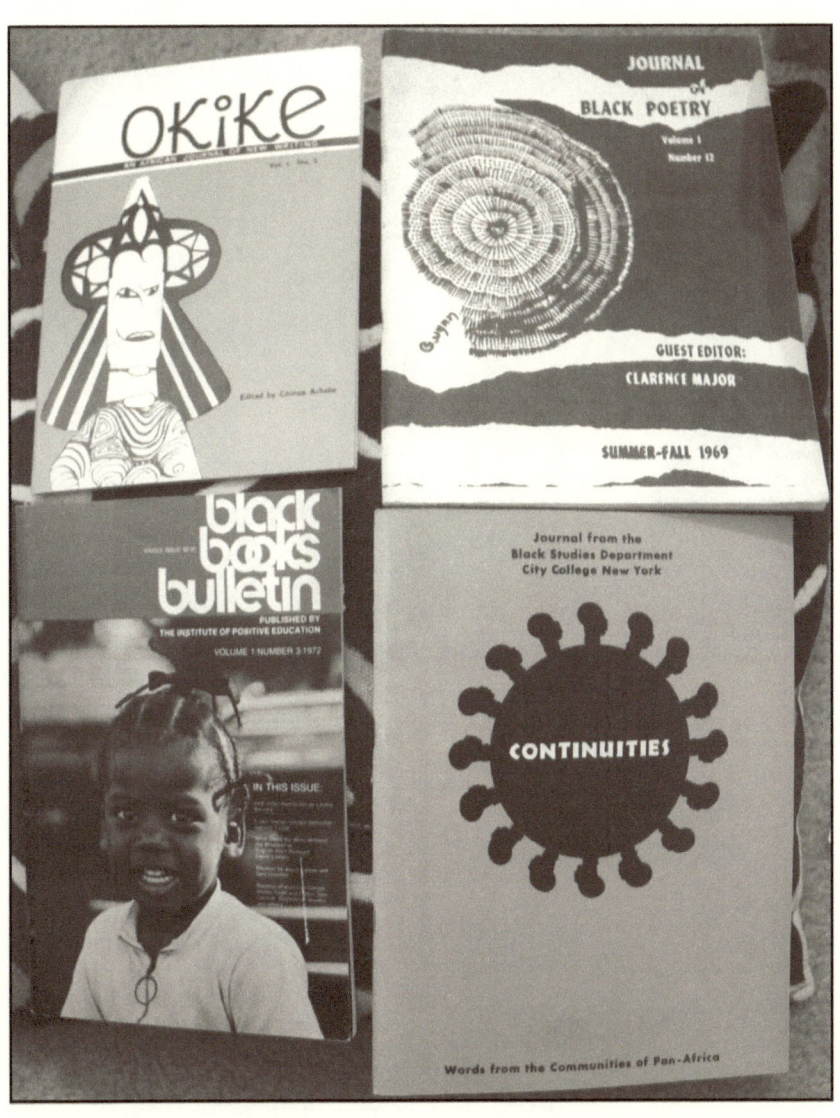

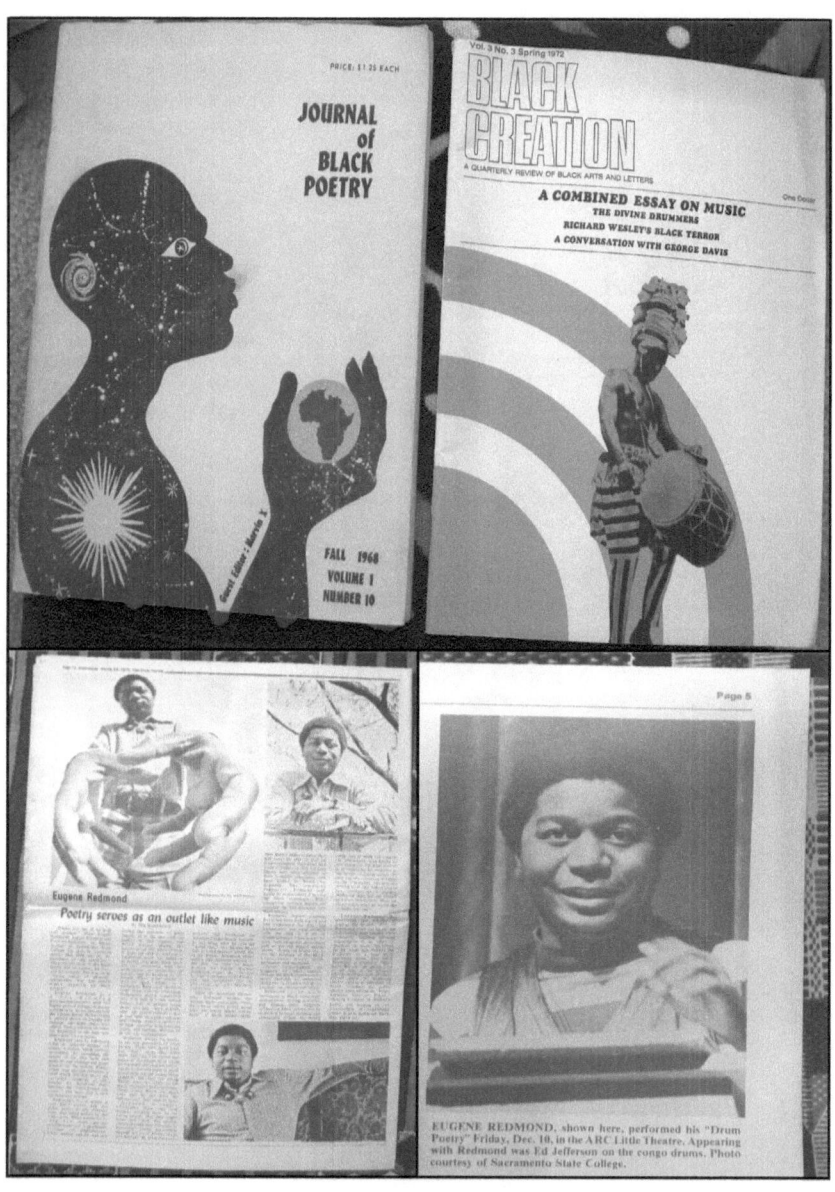

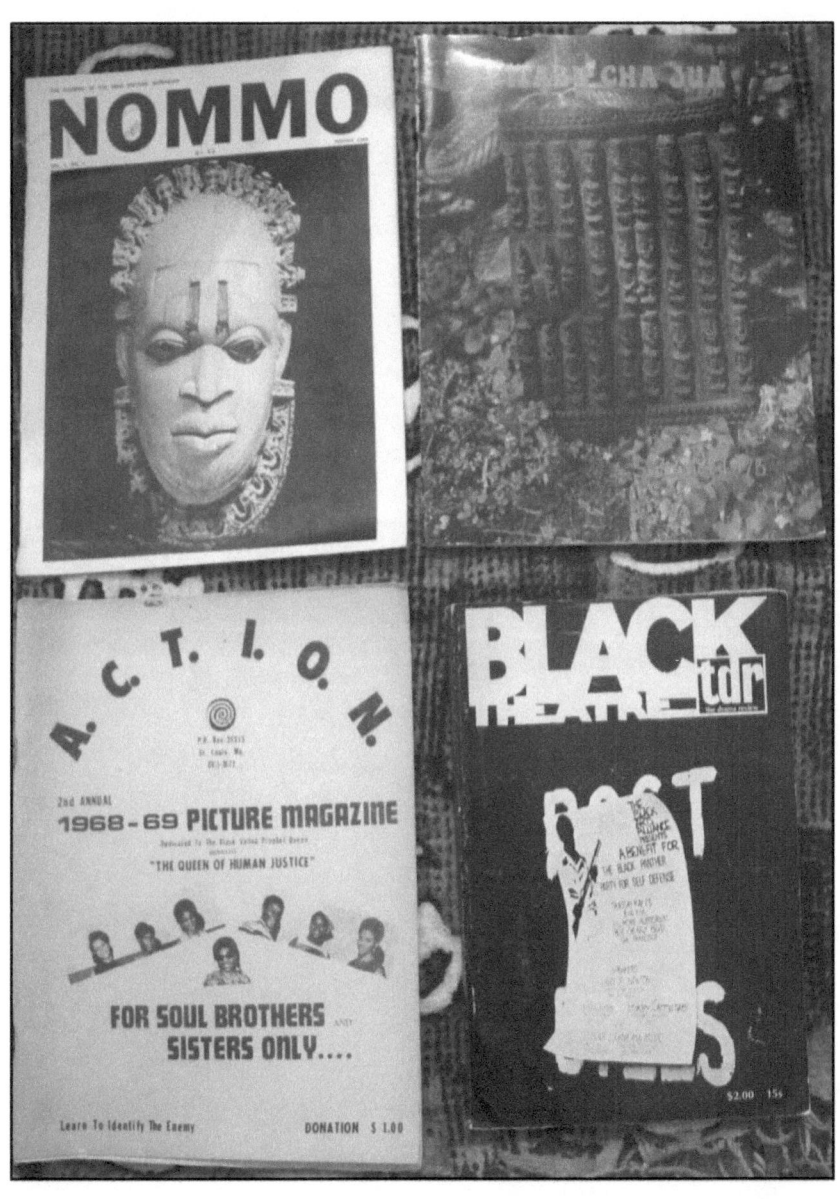

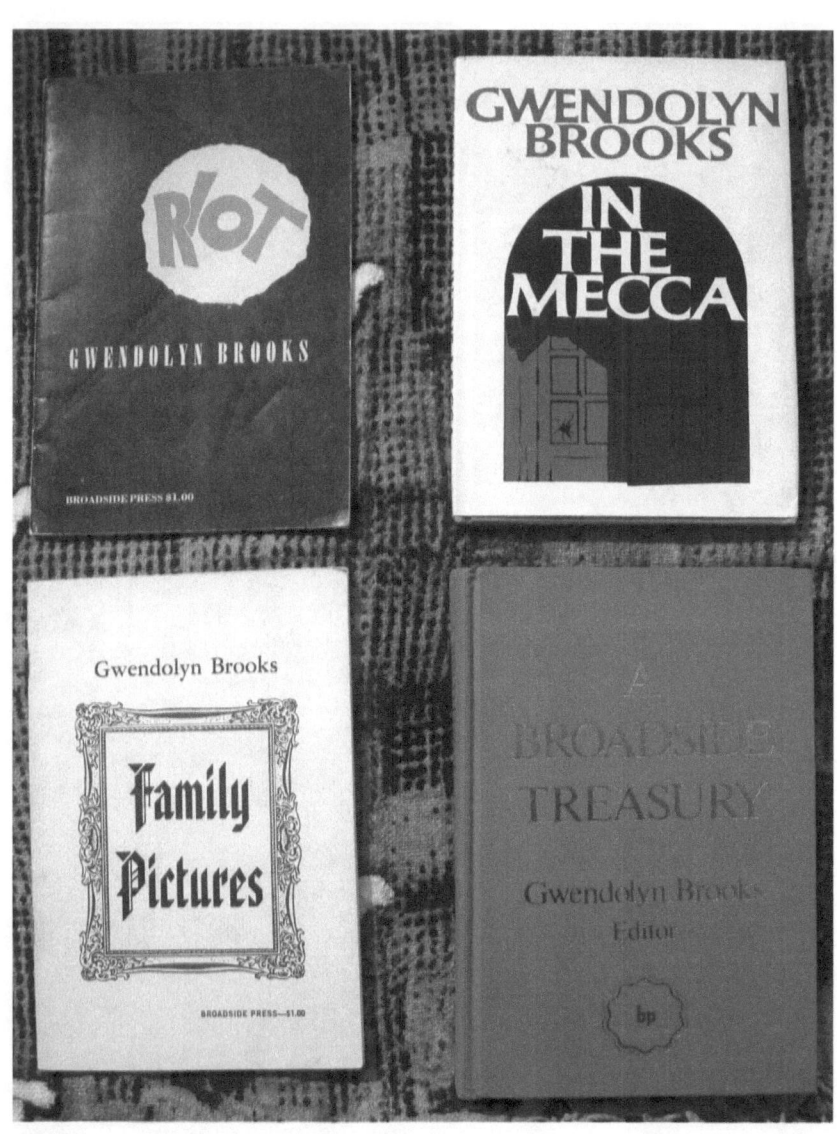

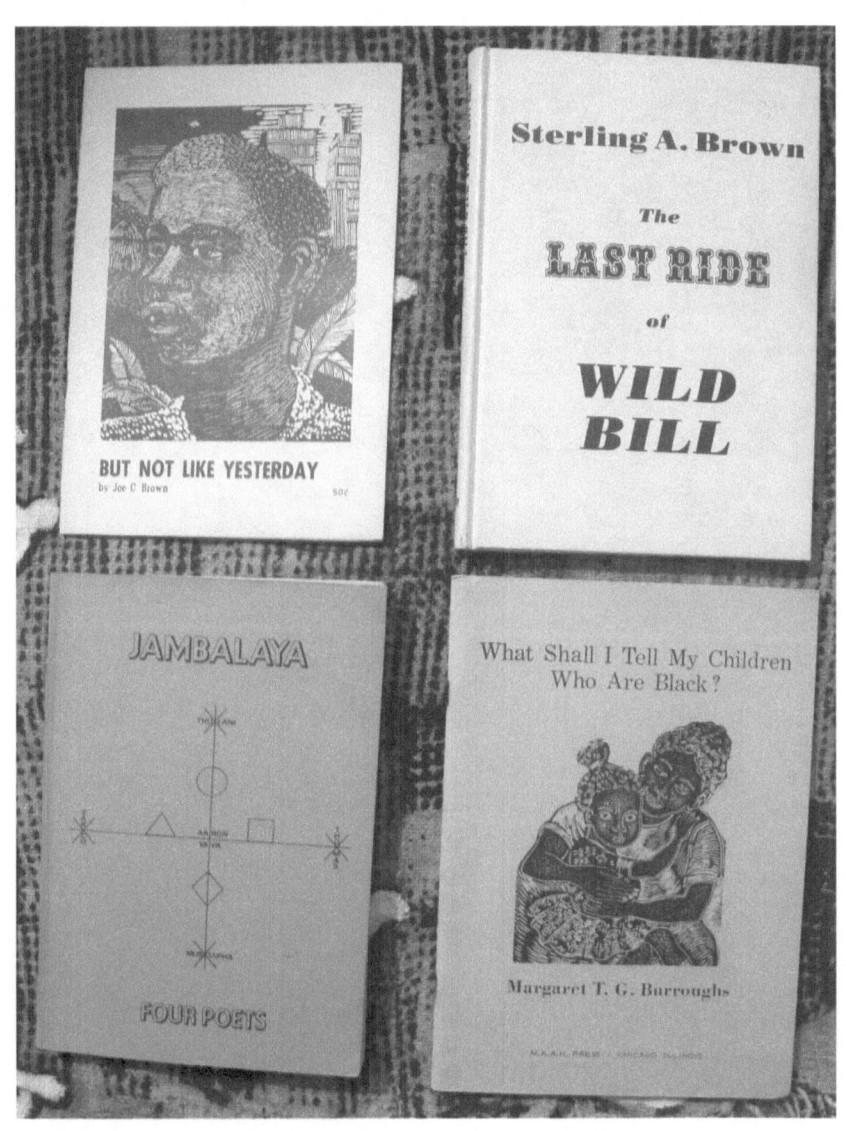

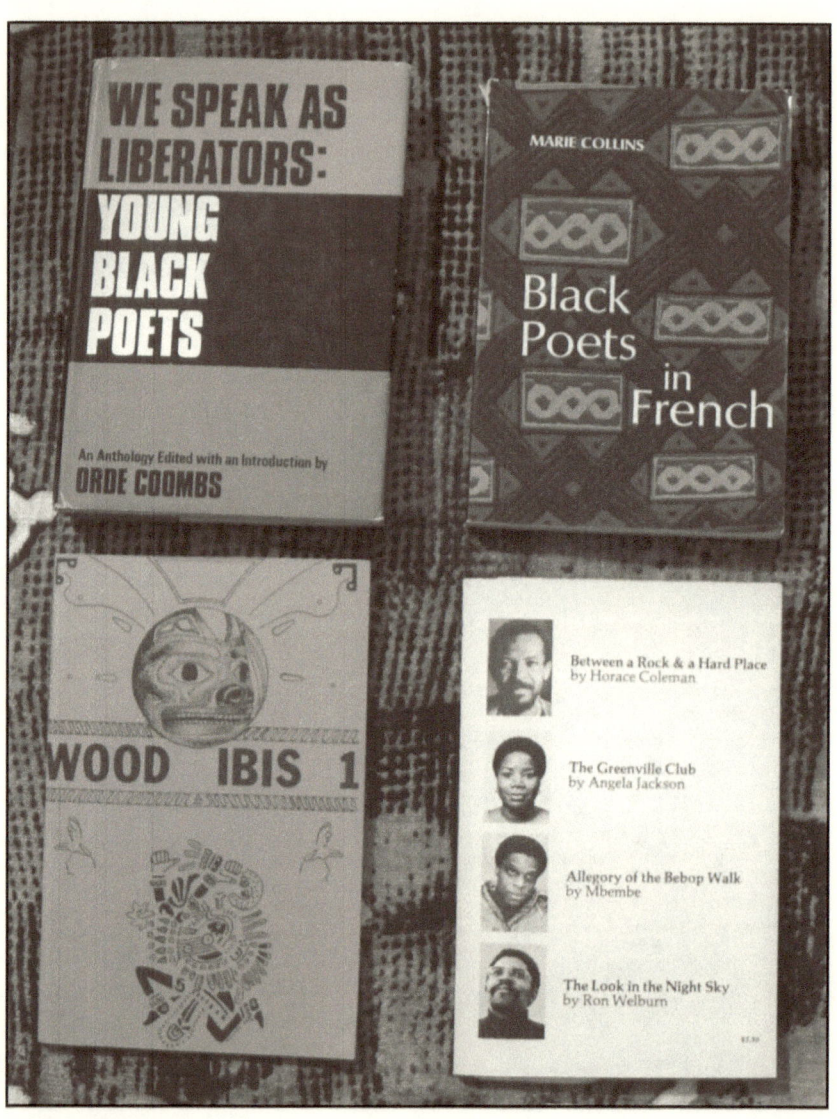

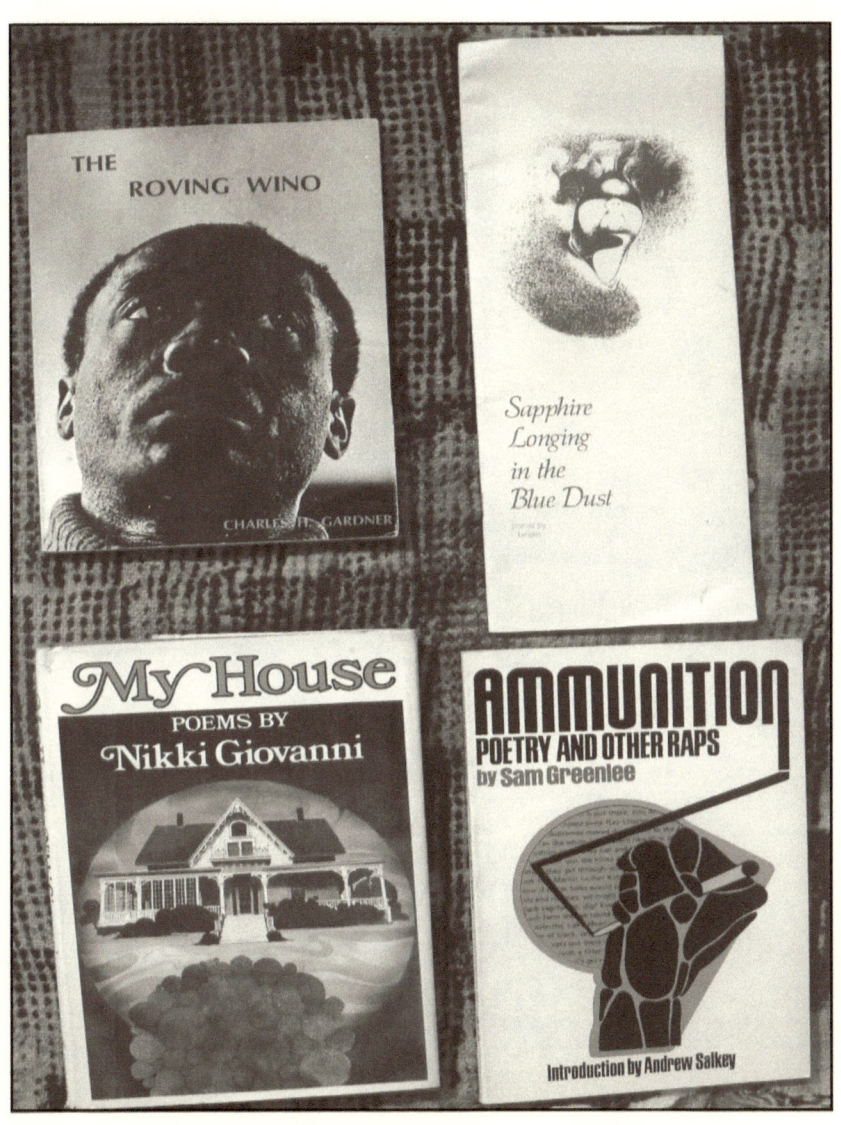

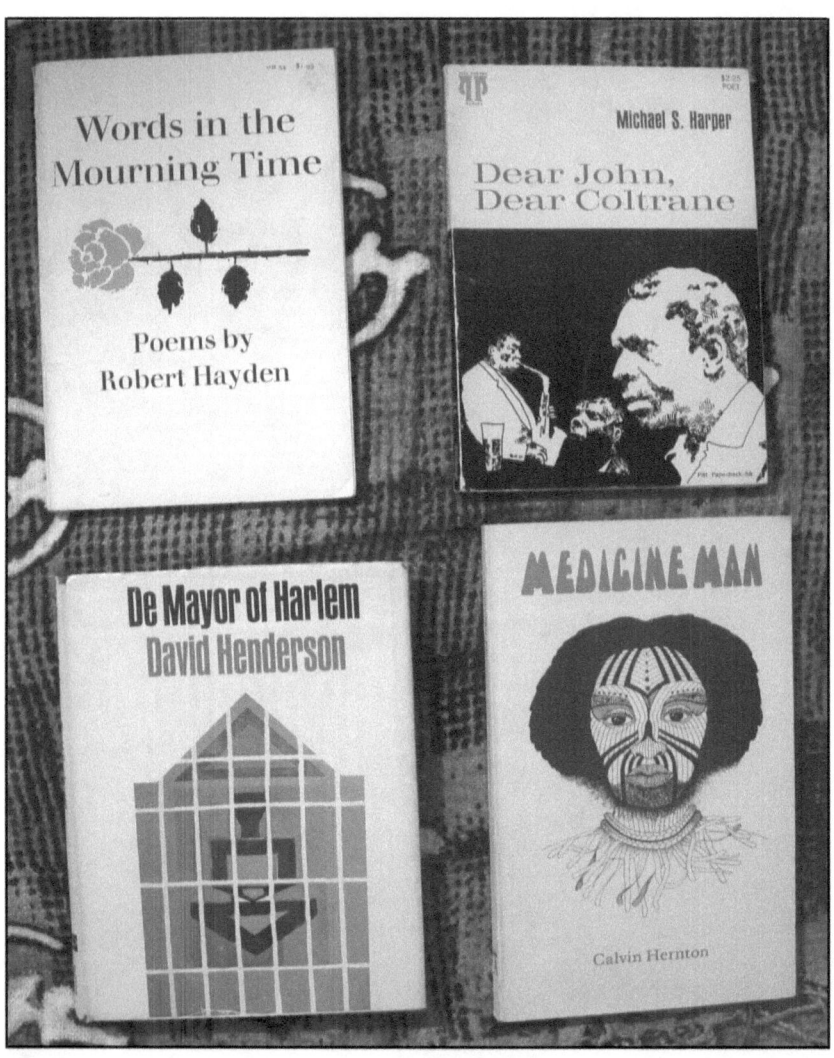

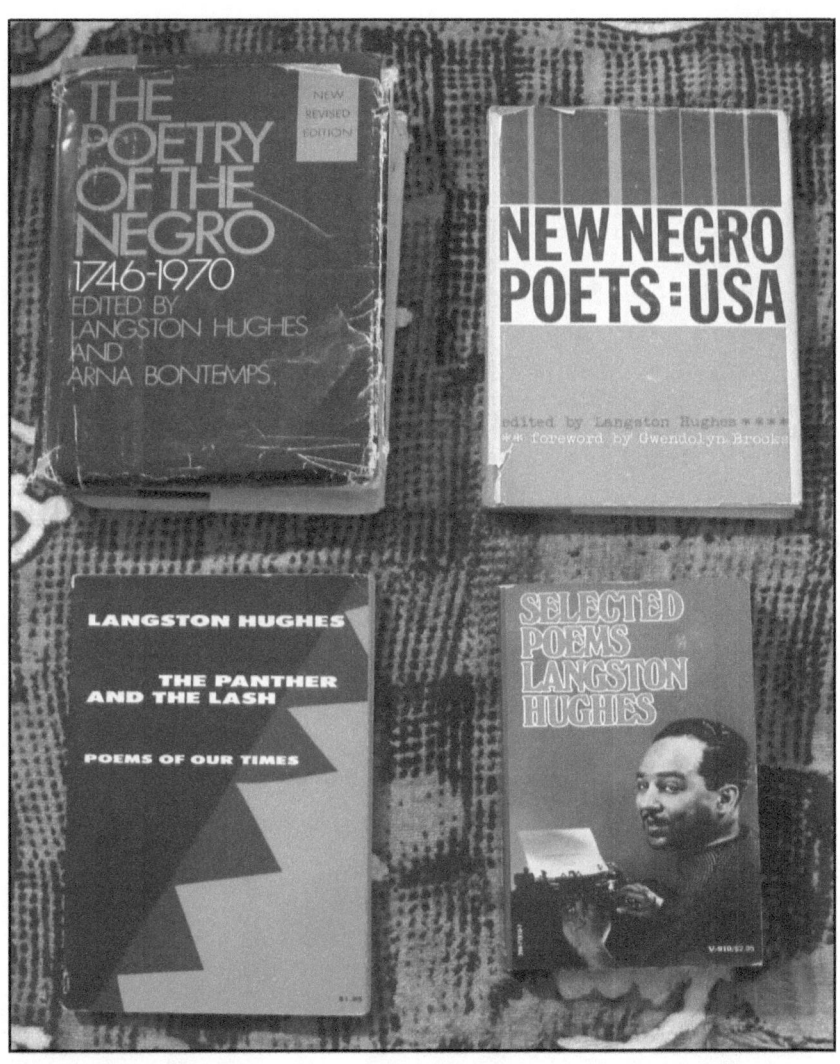

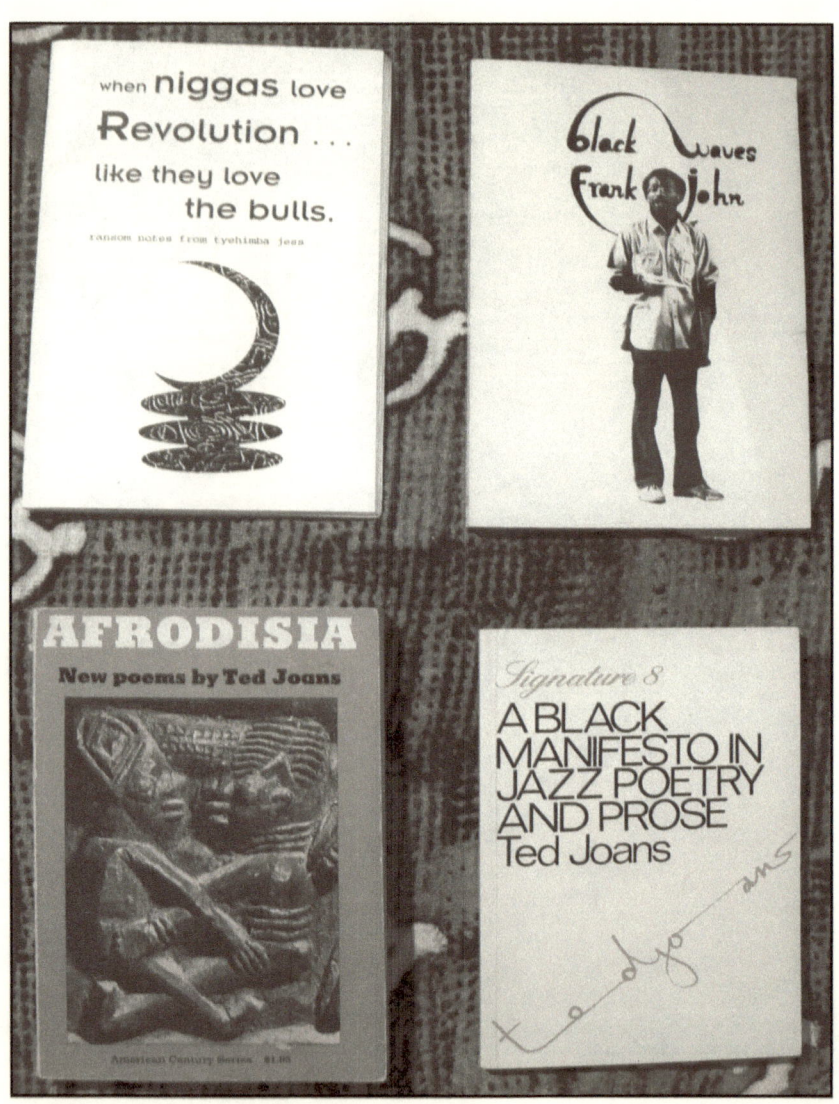

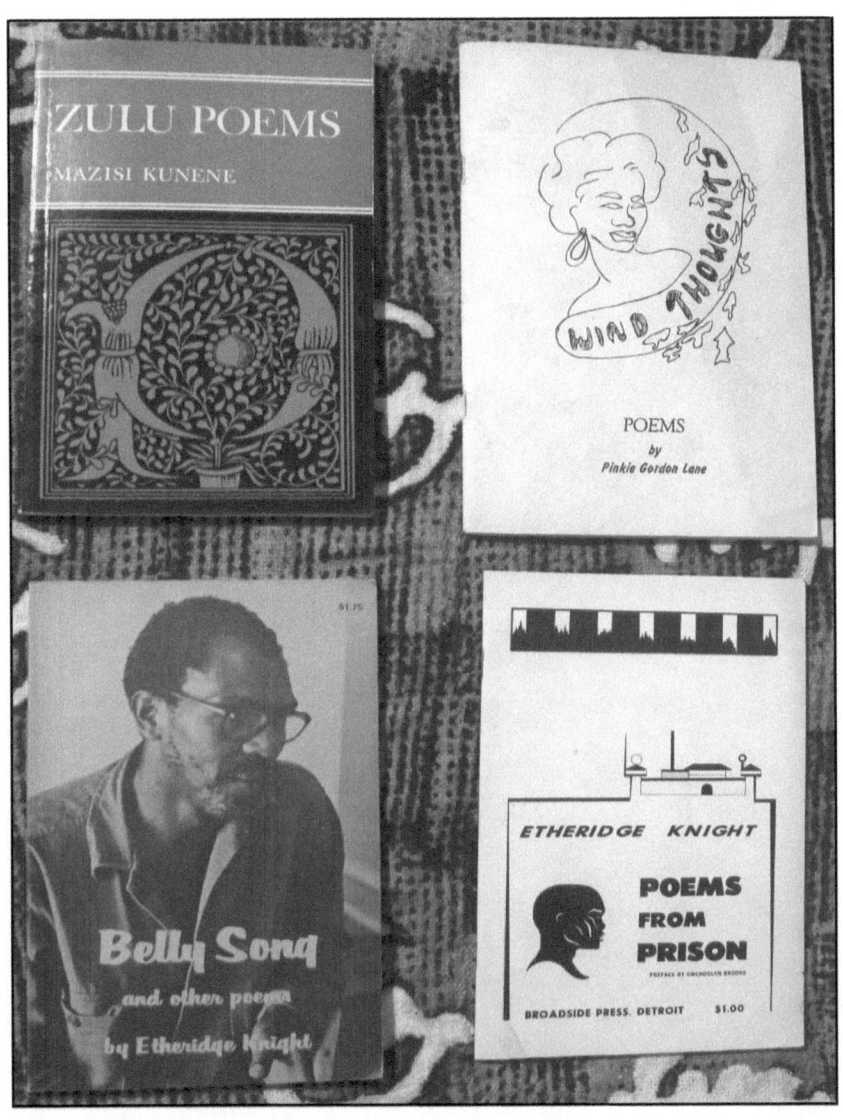

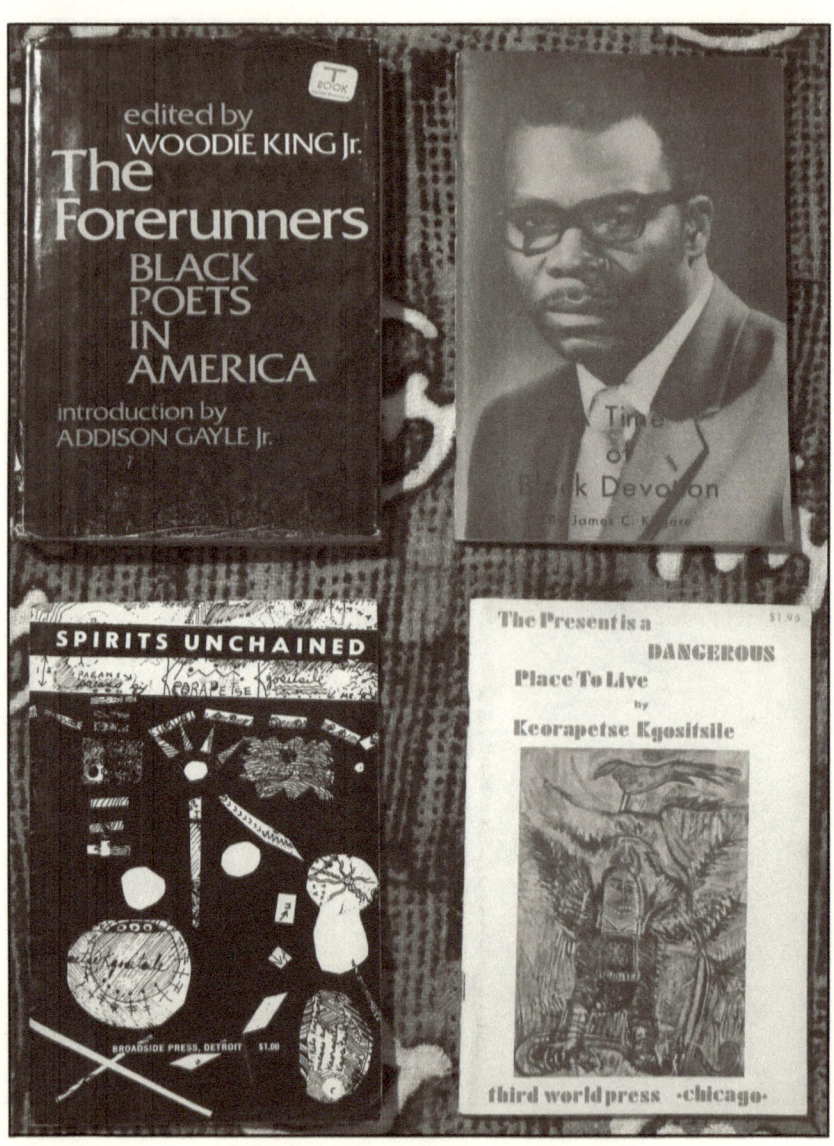

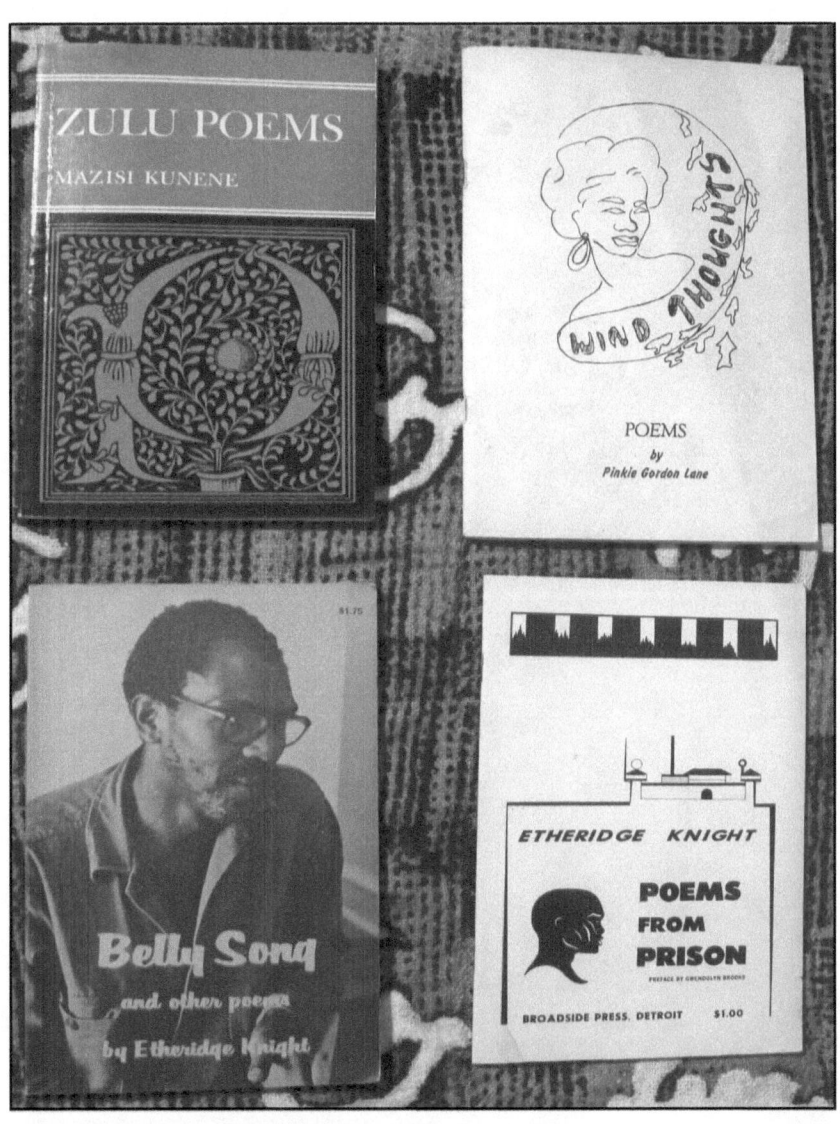

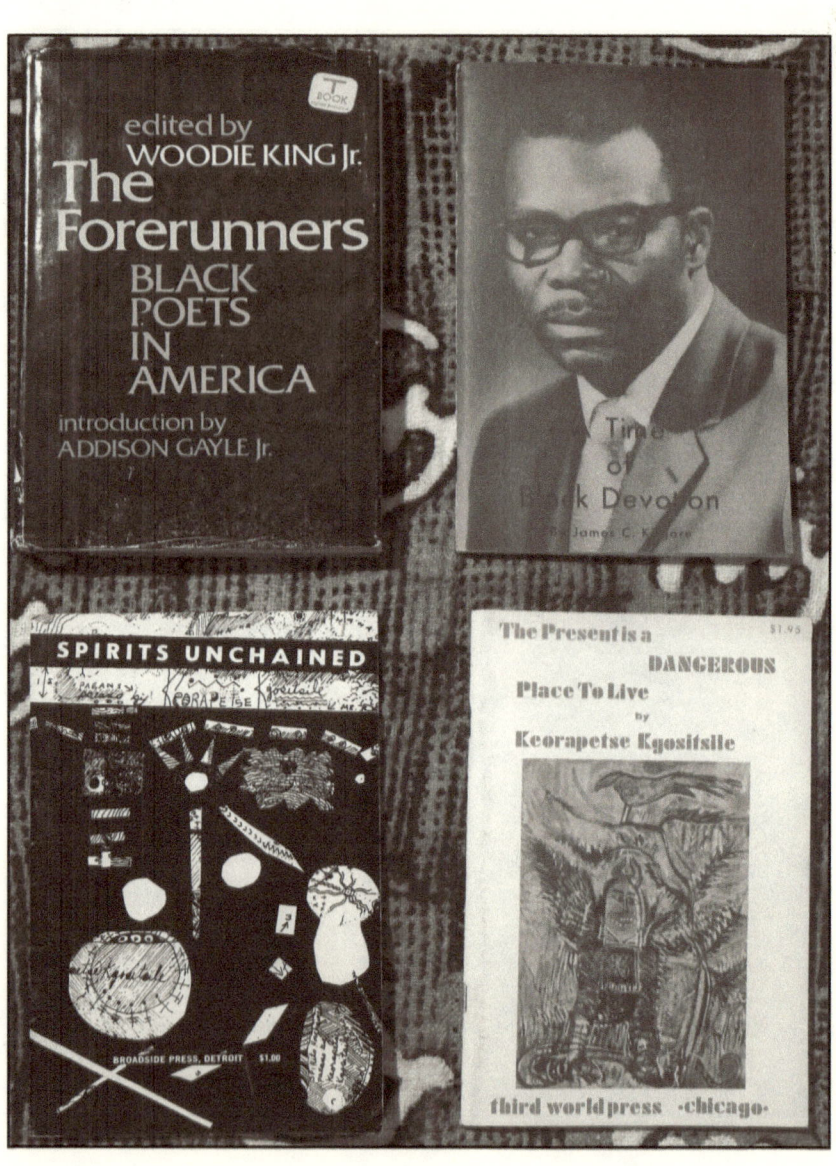

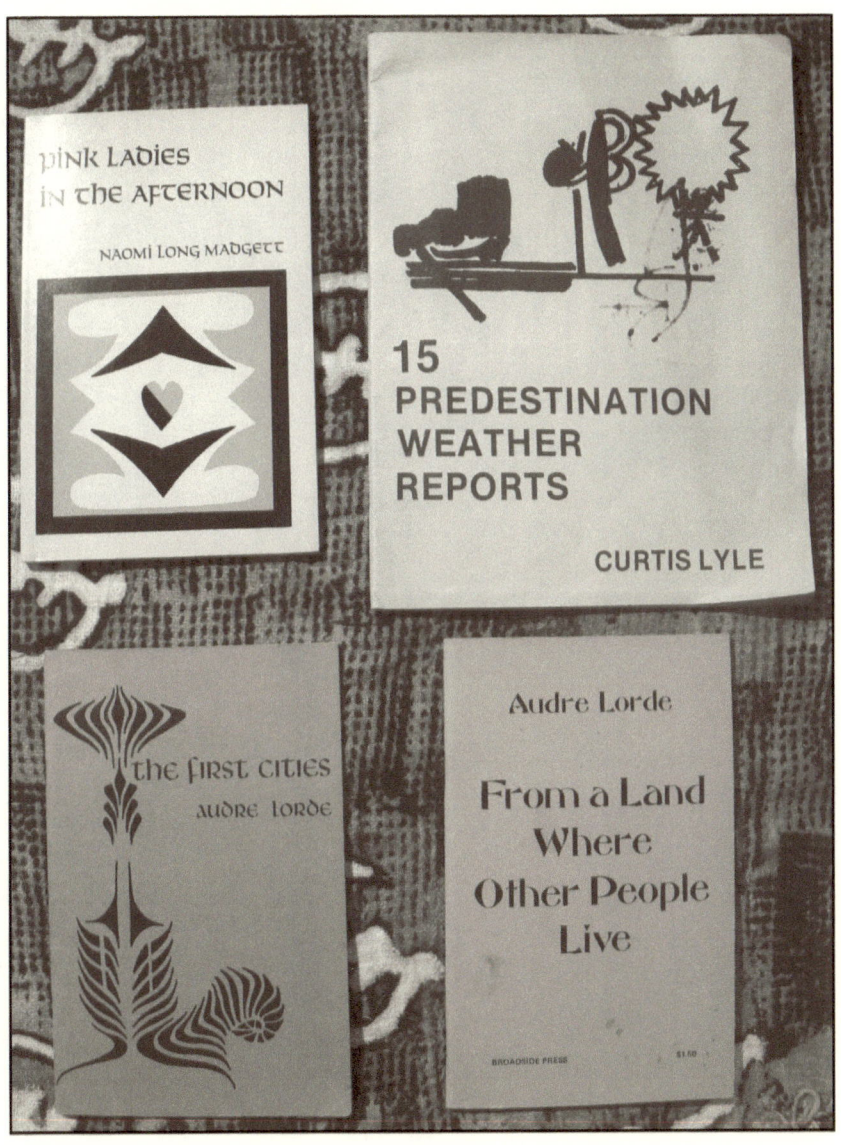

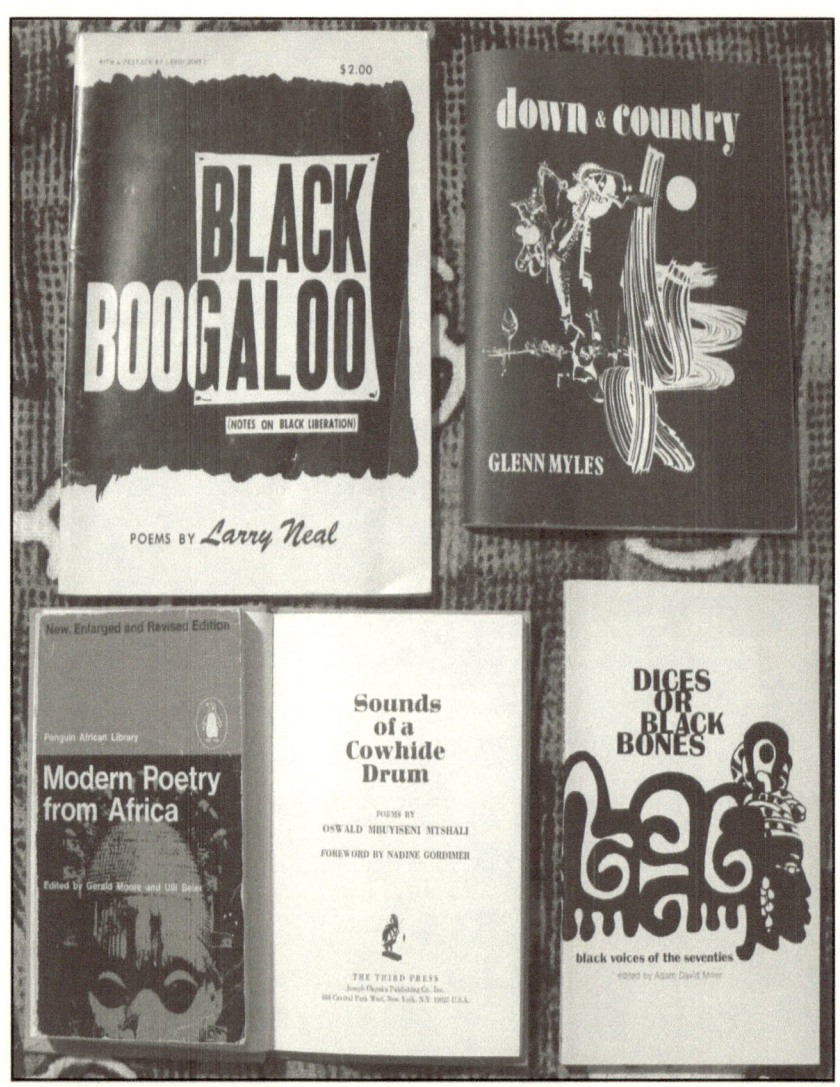

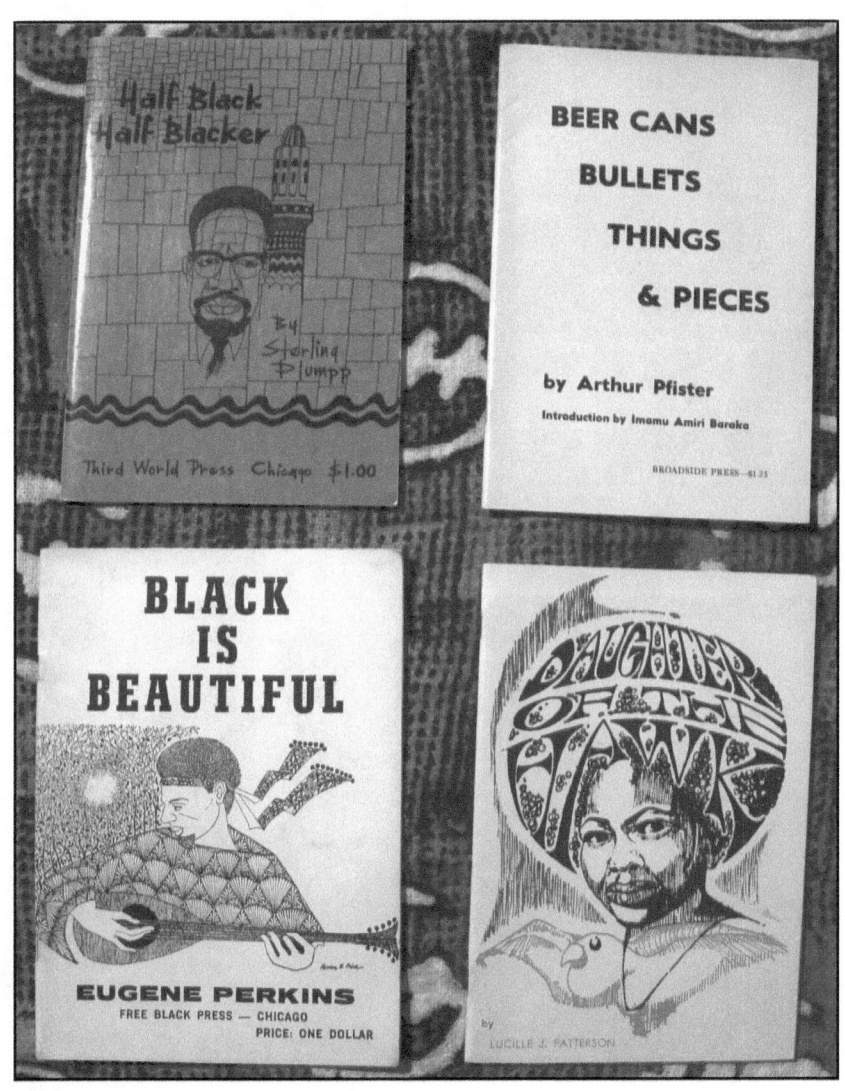

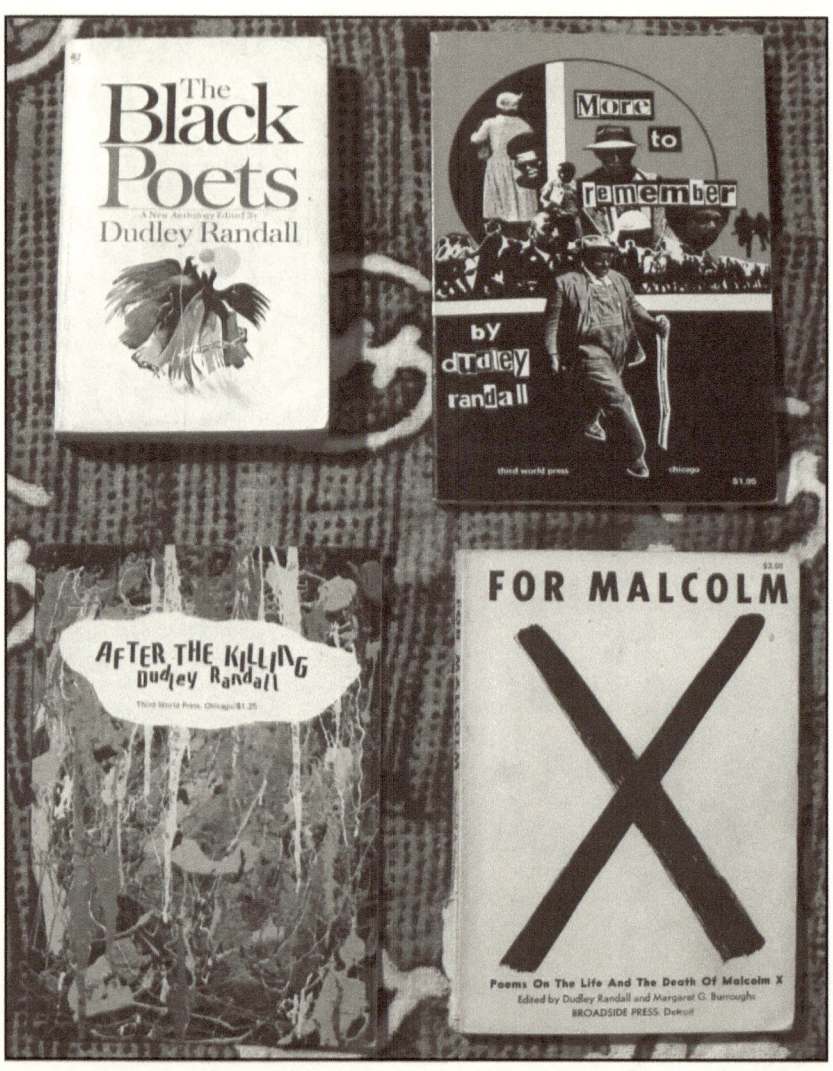

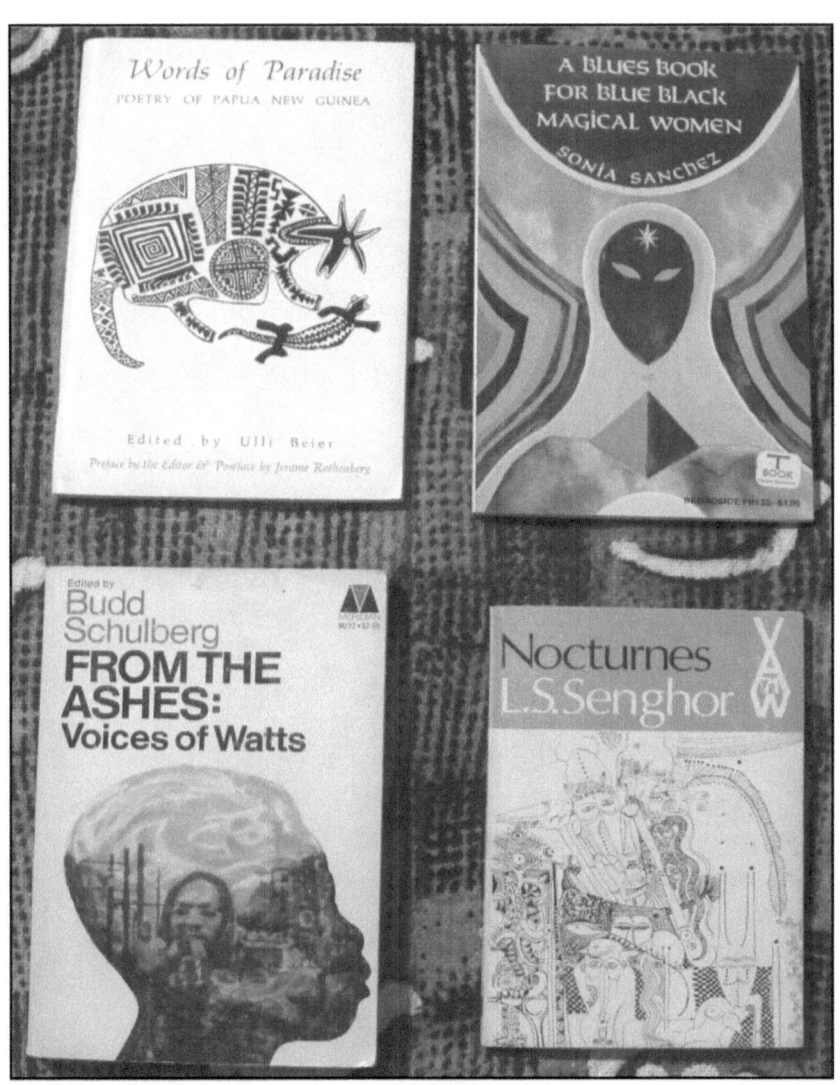

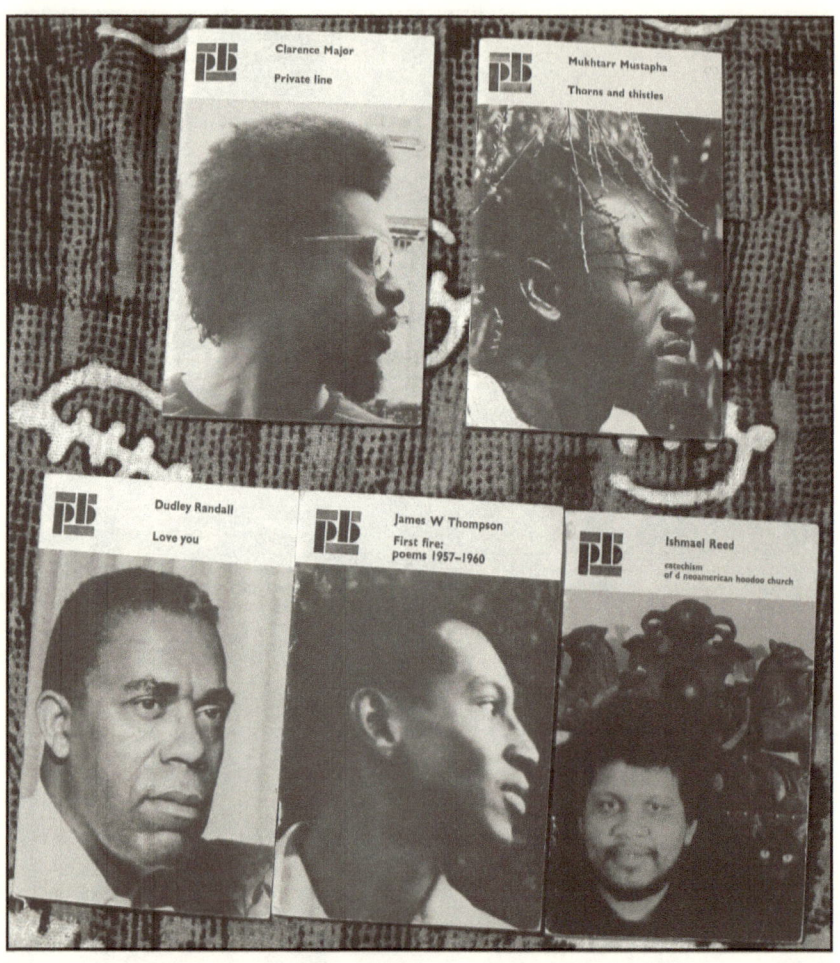

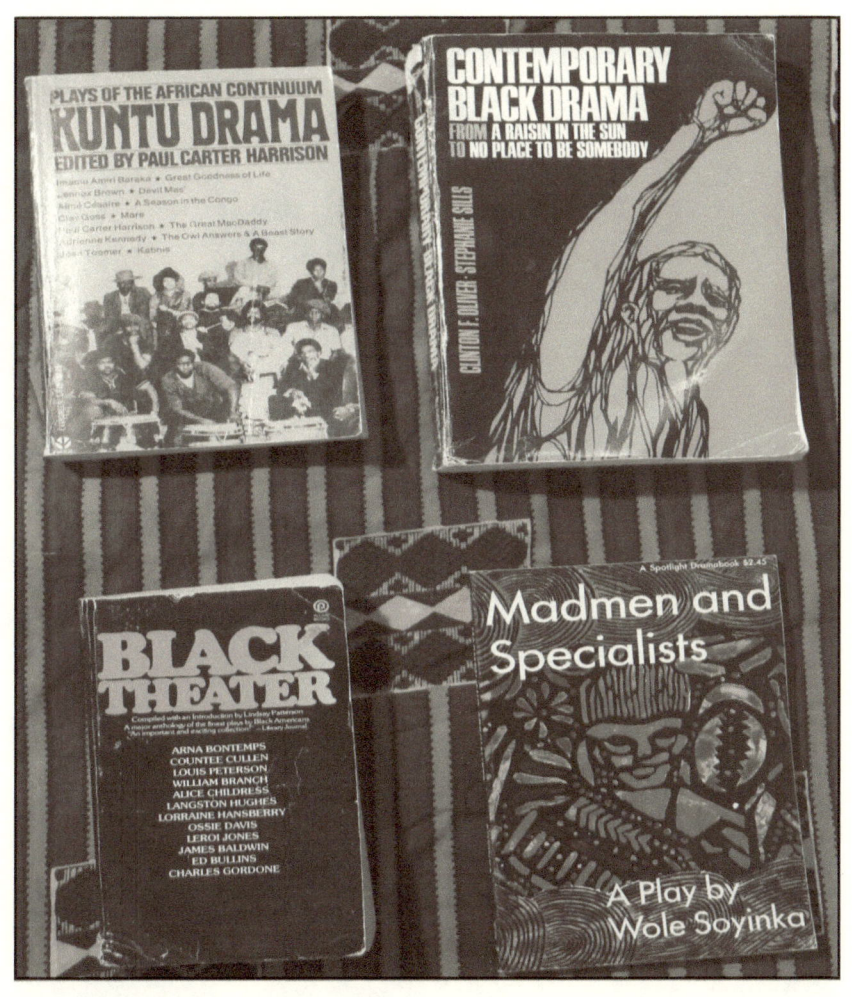

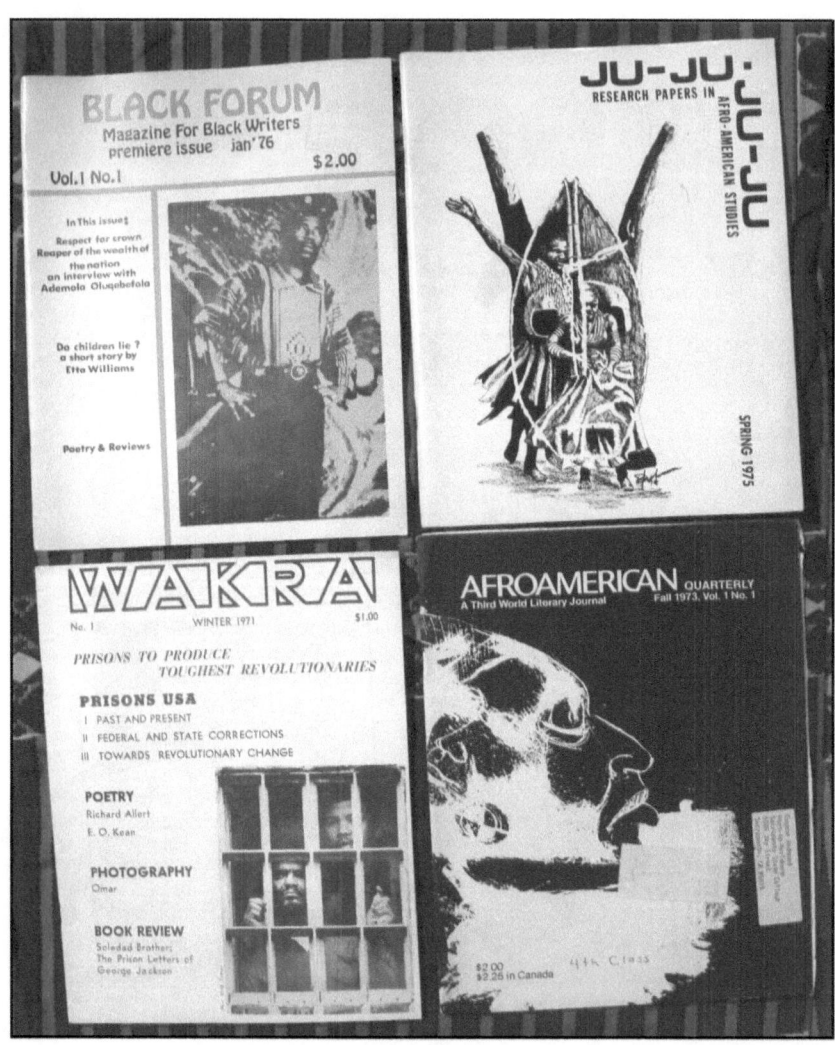

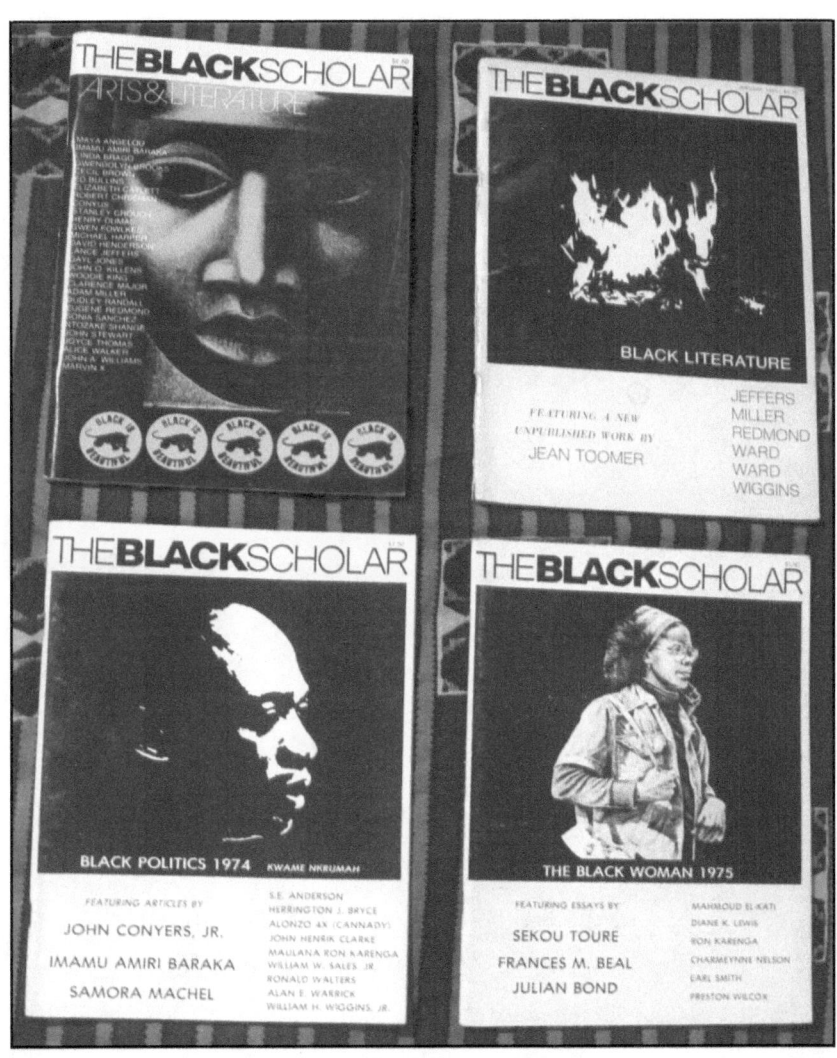

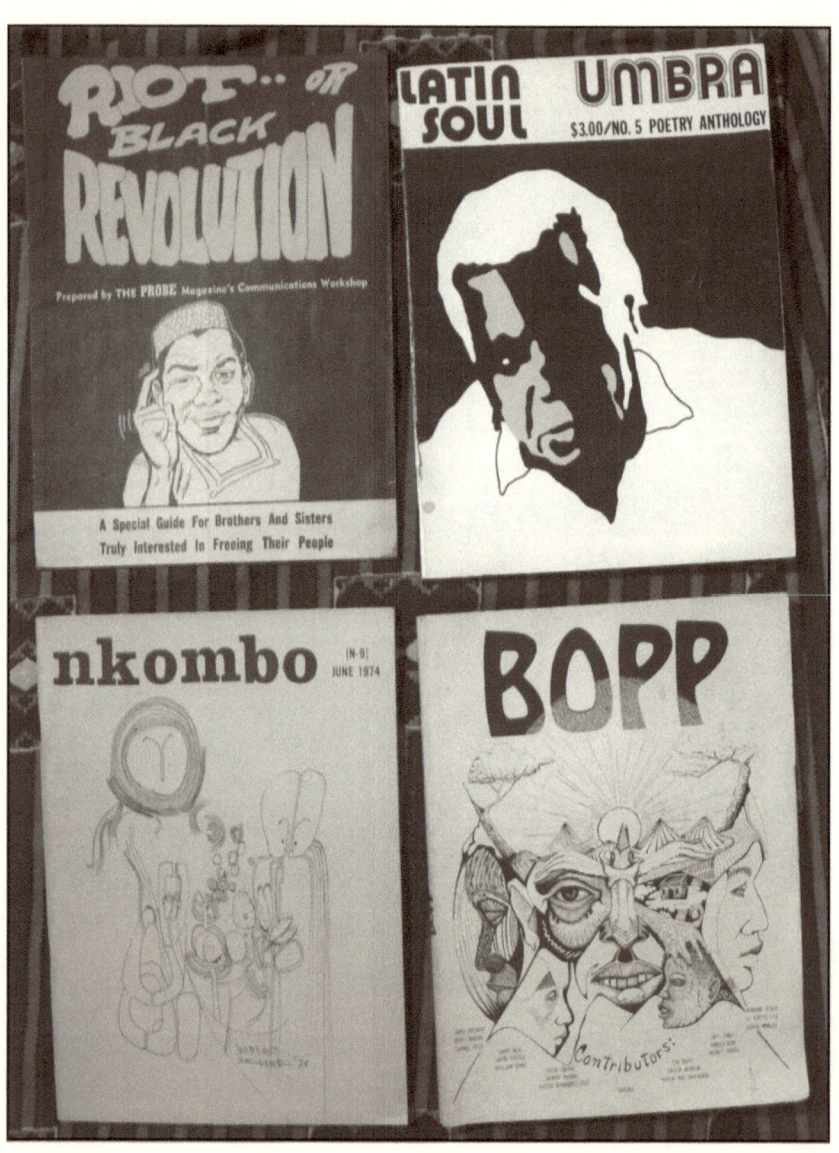

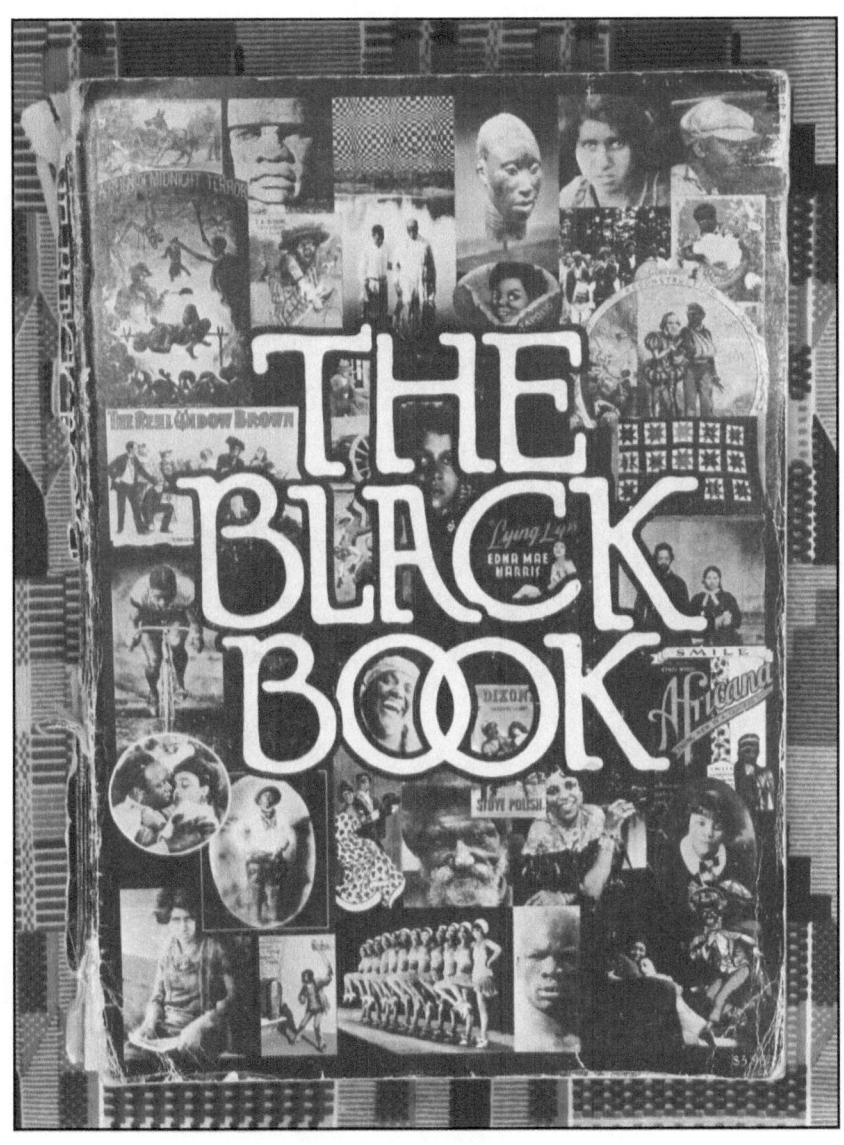

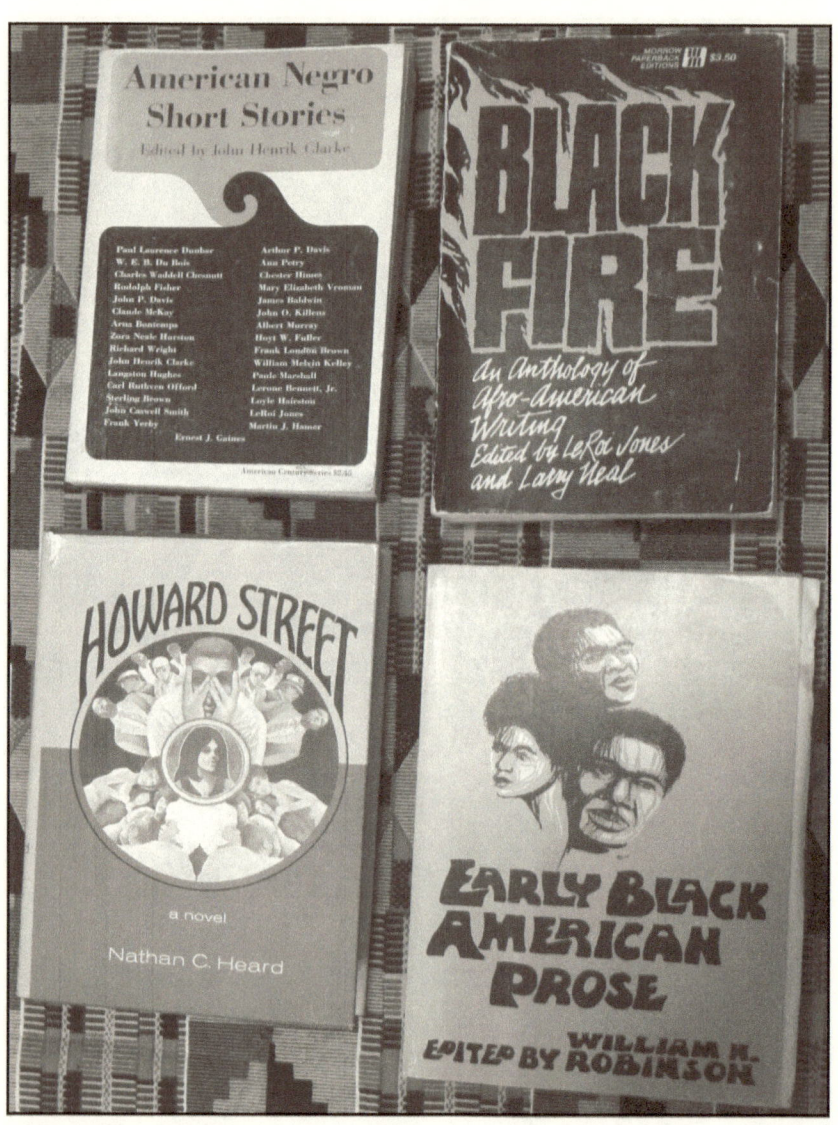

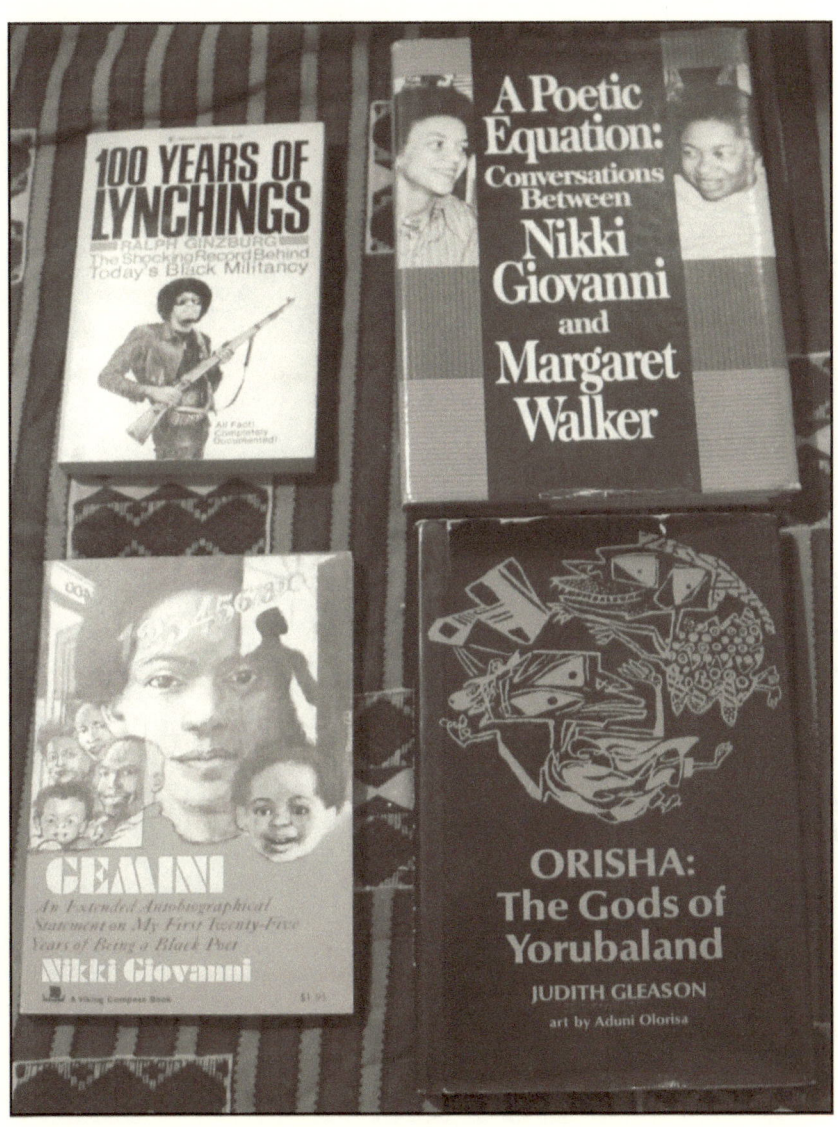

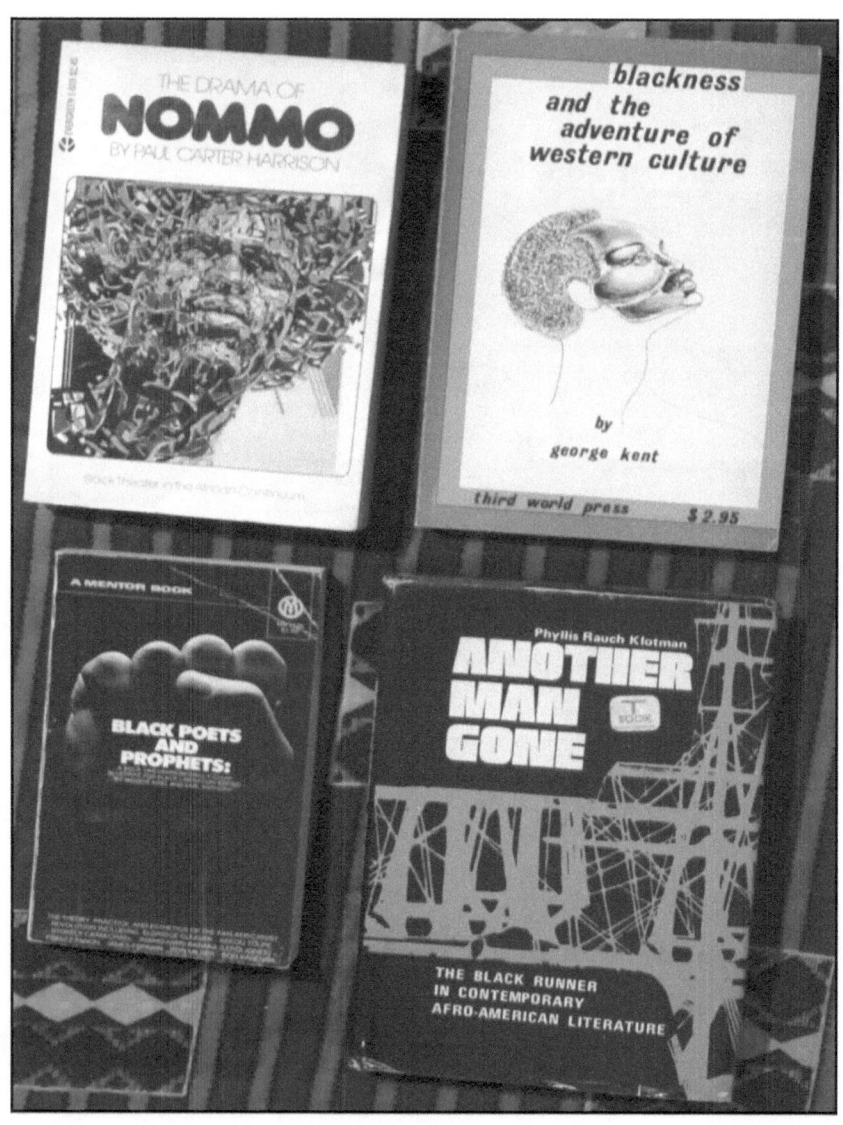

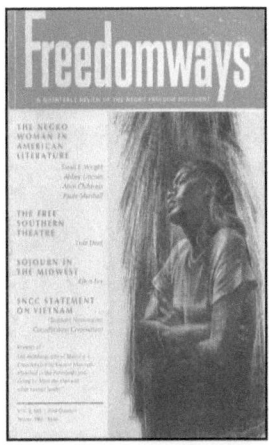
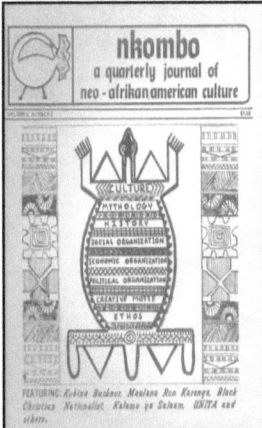
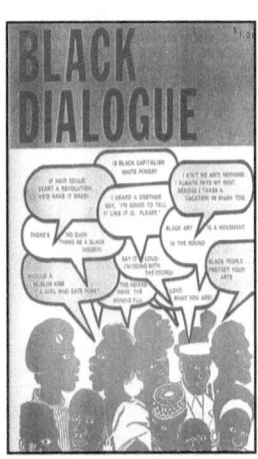

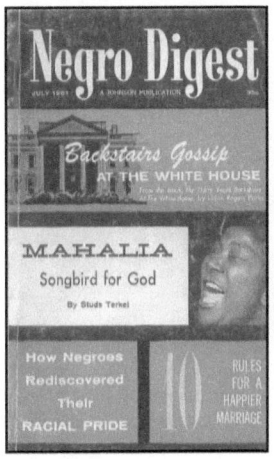
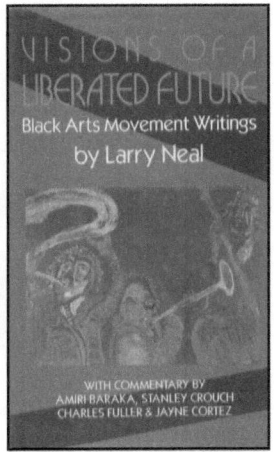
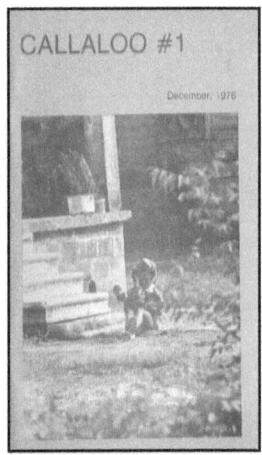

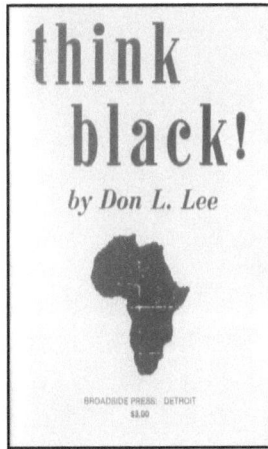
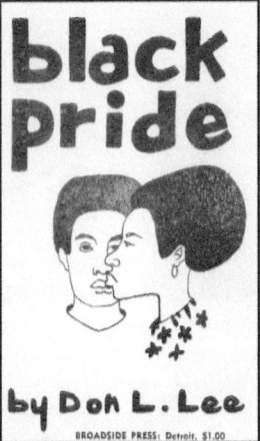
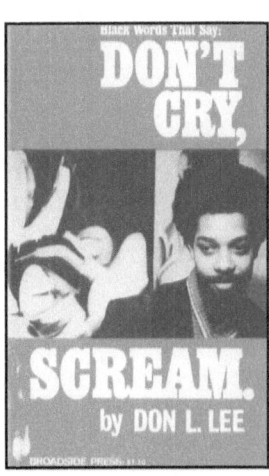

THE WAVES OF BLACK AESTHETICS
THE DEEP RIVER OF THE BLACK ARTS MOVEMENT
A Dialogue between Kalamu ya Salaam
and Margo Natalie Crawford
(Conducted August 2014)

Afro-Blue: James Baldwin in his short story "Sonny's Blues" (1957) depicts the blues as "deep water." When I hear your name, Deep River, it makes me think about the deep rivers of the black aesthetic experience.

Langston Hughes says "I've Known Rivers" and Baldwin says: "He wanted Sonny to leave the shoreline and strike out for the deep water. He was Sonny's witness that deep water and drowning were not the same thing—he had been there, and he knew. And he wanted Sonny to know. He was waiting for Sonny to do the things on the keys which would let Creole know that Sonny was in the water."

But let me explain my name. I call myself "Afro-Blue" as a way of escaping other prisms like "Afro-pessimism" and, also, "Afro-centrism." When I read *The Magic of Juju*, I felt the "deep water" of the Black Arts Movement. In the midst of some of the current art of drowning, I sometimes feel nostalgic for this movement that predates me. I think the children of the Black Power movement feel the presence of its absence. Do you feel nostalgic about the Black Arts Movement? Why did you write The Magic of Juju?

Deep River: Why not write about the Black Arts Movement? Everybody has an autobiography—I mean that literally. Everybody has a story to tell: how I came to be who I am. I happened to have been born during interesting times.

Under the influence of Langston Hughes, I decided early on to pursue writing. That was nearly fifty years ago. So that is one reason: self reflection, i.e. thinking about how I became who I am, why and what were the ramifications of the choices I made.

Another reason is—and this is in no particular order—I did not see any books on our work, on the Black Arts Movement. Tons of Harlem Renaissance work, bunches of books on the Black Panthers, but where were the books on the Black Arts Movement, a movement that was more far reaching that the Harlem Renaissance, which by the way I think is both misnamed and misunderstood (I'll come back to that in a minute). Moreover, I'm sure the absence of books on the Black Arts Movement is not an accident but rather part of a systemic effort at erasing our history.

Writing *The Magic of Juju* is itself an act of defiance. I know—check that, I should say "I believe" because I don't have hard evidence in hand—I believe that the academy has actively discouraged detailed investigations of the Black Arts Movement primarily because of the politics. Although most critics will not say so outright, the reality is that the Black Arts Movement is generally characterized as racist because, to use a shorthand, we were perceived as "hating whites."

Now, who is in charge of the academy? For sure it's not politically active Blacks, nor is it—Gates and a handful of others notwithstanding—academically oriented Blacks. Sure, a few individuals with considerable influence, and some might even argue with more than a little power exist, but considering the literally thousands of higher-ed institutions, the overwhelming majority of gate keepers are not only racially white, they have a white consciousness, which, in order to remain white, necessarily means excluding blacks and other people of color.

To put it bluntly, you cannot remain "white" and be intimate with "non-whites," which is why race mixing, i.e. miscegenation, has a pejorative connotation. If one is truly democratic, then one is open to the world. We who are called African American have been open. True, our openness has not been always by choice, but we have learned to live with a spectrum of color, rather than some dark essential. Elijah Muhammad was obviously of mixed racial heritage—if you catch my meaning.

Black consciousness is not a reflection of biological essentialism. (I know this seems a bit off the path from explaining why I wrote *The Magic of Juju*, but this is an essential aspect of the real answer.) For me, Black consciousness is a political concept, not a biological concept. I define Blackness as color, culture, and consciousness. Moreover, color is the least important element and consciousness the most important element.

Color is raw biology. For African Americans that rawness means, to use that loaded term, "miscegenation." Indeed, for us in the diaspora, and particularly for those of us in the good old U.S. of A., there is no purity in blackness. We are the original melting pot. We are America at its biological best in that, whether by choice or by circumstance, we embrace all elements.

Culture is collective behavior, views, and values. Certainly an individual can manifest a culture, but the culture itself is developed at a collective level.

Consciousness is identity both personal and social.

Consciousness is the crux of blackness precisely because biology is not a choice; you don't choose your parents, your ancestors. Culture is collective and thus never simply the result of individual action. We are born into cultures and as we humans come to consciousness we have the opportunity to shape the cultures into which we were born or to assimilate into a different culture. Consciousness is dynamic, ever changing. Of course we can go Jungian and talk about the collective consciousness of a specific group of people in a particular time and space. In any case, whether consciously, subconsciously, or unconsciously, we humans make choices.

With whom and with what do we identify? That is the ultimate determinant of our behavior at the level of choice. Of course we don't control all elements of our lives—but concerning the myriad of matters over which we do have a choice, consciousness, or the lack thereof, becomes the key to determining our behavior and to a large extent determining our destiny.

The big, two-part question is: "With whom do we identify and how do we actualize our identity?" That was a key element of the Black Arts Movement. We identified with working class Black people, which effectively often, but not necessarily, put us at odds with many academics who are petite bourgeoisie to the max.

I'm defining class in terms of relationship to the means of production and accumulation of wealth. Those who sell their labor to earn a living are working class. Those who manage the labor of others or who offer professional services are the petite bourgeoisie. The bourgeoisie are those who earn their living and accumulate wealth based on earning profits, collecting rent and/or interest accrued from their property, both intellectual and material.

That's a simplistic thumbnail, but it's important to understand this distinction because most of the people who write books are petite bourgeoisie in their orientation whether they are actually petite bourgeoisie in their consciousness. For example, just because you are a licensed professional, a Ph.D. or an M.D. or J.D., your degree doesn't necessarily tell us with whom you identify and in whose interest you work.

In general, however, the petite bourgeoisie identifies with the bourgeoisie rather than the working class. One can immediately see the conflict that the Black Arts Movement had with academics. There is a similar dynamic happening with hip hop, except because of the commercial success of hip hop within the capitalist society, there is an acceptance of hip hop in academic circles far greater than the academic acceptance of the Black Arts Movement. In America, money will change you and change how you are viewed and are accepted by mainstream society.

Part of *The Magic of Juju*, the concept, is the reality that juju transforms. Blackness is not static, unchanging. Baraka called it the "changing same." The key, though, is that we change both ourselves and our environment. Any study of Black culture necessarily has to be a study of change within a given society, a given space and time, whether we are looking locally, regionally, nationally or internationally. We set the parameters of our study—and even those parameters will change over time—then we proceed to study what happens/happened and why. We might even venture a guess about what will happen next.

I'm taking the time to sketch out some of these definitions because otherwise we cannot have a real dialogue if we don't share a common understanding. It's not about agreement but rather about epistemology, how it is we know whatever it is we think we know. The first step in knowing is having a common language. In Black culture the common tongue is first music and then oratory and kinetics, and only at a tertiary level, literacy. That is a big difference between Black culture and what is commonly called White culture. White culture in the U.S.A. validates literacy, business, and technology.

You want a glimpse into a Black person's consciousness? Check out the music they listen to—not the books they read or the movies they watch—and if they don't listen to music, there better be some major extenuating circumstances, otherwise you're not dealing with a conscious Black person. Notice, I said "music" as a general category rather than a specific genre of music.

I've written extensively about music. During my days as a music critic I won two ASCAP Deems Taylor awards for excellence in writing about music. The reason I mention that is to make clear that I choose not to identify with the mainstream even though I have the ability to compete and excel in the mainstream. Black Arts Movement artists chose not to identify with the mainstream even though we were capable of doing so. Blackness, consciousness is just that: a conscious choice rather than a biological default.

Moreover, our blackness includes whiteness, redness, brownness, yellowness and any other human "ness" there is. All of that is part of who we are. The expansiveness of Blackness is a major threat to those who want to be White. Our very being threatens White existence. We are tar babies. Touch us and get stuck.

Take the issue of hair—remember, I'm still talking about why I wrote *The Magic of Juju*. Why is hair care a multi-million dollar industry among Black people? Because hair is more than hair. The aesthetic is a conditioning (and I mean all the possible plays on the word "conditioning," from consciousness and socialization, to physical alteration and fetishization). We know what Lupita's hair looks like. And we know what the hair Beyoncé wears looks like. That spectrum is our reality.

Lupita represents—and I'm sure her reality may change over time as I'm certain there will be massive pressure on her—Lupita represents a return of the Black aesthetic in terms of women's hair. Yeah, she was born in Mexico to Kenyan parents and spent much of her childhood in Kenya, but she had higher education right here in the U.S.A., the most damaging place in the world for blacks who strive to be both black and beautiful. How many sisters in the arts world who aspire to win academy awards wear short naturals?

A big fro is a political statement. Dreadlocks are a style. But a short natural—that's African. Black African. And that's what the Black Arts Movement was about: reclaiming the aesthetic definition of black beauty. But not in a binary black only, or black is just one way. No, Black is a spectrum, a spectrum which includes basic black, natural black.

So, another reason I wrote the book was because we

needed to define ourselves and defend ourselves, our beautiful Black selves. And look, to be clear, this is not an issue for women only to change themselves. I said before and will repeat it: a majority, not all, but certainly a majority of Black women who wear weaves, wigs, and chemically treated hair do so because of the attitude of Black men towards Black women and how men want women to wear their hair. I should also add this: consider the negative attitude of many males toward Black women who do not in one way or another emulate a white aesthetic.

I know conscious black men and conscious black women are going to disagree about this, but I am not talking about a minority among the mass of our people, I'm talking about the dominant outlook in this new millennium, an outlook that validates and values a white hair aesthetic, which is precisely the aesthetic the Black Arts Movement explicitly fought against.

Within the Black Arts Movement, all our limitations and negativities notwithstanding, we championed natural Black hair and liberated ourselves from the tyranny of a white hair aesthetic. I recognize we all have the right to wear our hair howsoever we choose, including the right to choose to emulate, imitate, and identify with whites, but when we do emulate others we inherently reject ourselves and have to go to unnatural lengths to achieve our desired goal of looking like something we're not. Hair. Black hair. Natural Black hair was a major reason I wrote *The Magic of Juju*.

Afro-Blue: Too many black men were claiming literal ownership of black women's hair (and bodies) during the BAM. In Carolivia Herron's novel Thereafter Johnnie, as Eva tells Johnnie the story of her rape, she begins with images of her memories of the black consciousness reading room, and the D.C. black space before she moves to the discussion of her memories of being raped. As she remembers the "black consciousness reading room" she recalls that "there was always at least one coal black political activist who cursed me, cursed my high yellow skin." The white man who rapes Eva also curses her "high yellow" skin. During the rape, he exclaims, "You're a crazed high-yellow nigger." Herron connects the violence that shapes ways of seeing the "high yellow" whether tied to the Black Nationalism gaze or the

white gaze.

Eva pauses, in the middle of her discussion of the "blacker than thou" sentiment of the Black Consciousness Reading Room, to explain to Johnnie that she imagined herself as the fortuneteller who knew that the black messiah "will be a girl, and she won't be in Harlem, and she won't raise [the true black nation], and the nation will not be true black." In this extended passage, Eva critiques the desire for racial purity in Black Nationalism and exposes the common violence of the white anti-black, anti-yellow gaze and anti-yellow black nationalists. Eva sets up a trajectory from memories of the Black Consciousness Reading Room to the lesbian commune to the rape that occurs outside of the Old Carnegie Library. There is a movement from the black "reading room" to the "reading room" that may signify "whiteness," the Old Carnegie Library.

As Eva tells Johnnie about her movement through these racialized spaces, she thinks deeply about the ways in which her body has been placed within ideological maps that have become as concrete as actual sidewalks and the hard, cold stone of the Old Carnegie Library where she is raped. Eva muses, "I am defined between perpendicular and horizontal, I am a soft lady lying on a mat, I am sinking how I sink. Often space congeals around me; I accept the air and push it back again." Eva attempts to locate herself, but the image of "space congealing around [her]" conveys the presence of absence, the negative space that shapes Eva after the rape. Locating the dislocated seems to be Eva's intention as she "accepts the air," the space that has hardened around her. The "soft lady's" attempt to push this hard air is a poignant image of the attempt to push against the mold, the template, the "perpendiculars and horizontals" that define this "naked prophet, yellow-skinned and sleeping, plump and lovely, newly raped and fallen."

The love of private (black) body space is complicated. The 1960s love affair with blackness leads to a "thrill is gone" sentiment when lovers still feel the love but do not want or need to express that love in the same way. When the lovers take it for granted, blackness can, on the body level, be what Richard Iton calls "the black fantastic." It may seem odd that Julia Field's poem "Art," with the lines

"Whenever I goes to black art shows, I sees The ugliest black women in the whole world" would be published in the most central BAM magazine, Black World. Both this poem and Fields' poem "I Loves a Wig" are published in a 1975 issue of Black World, the same year that Mahogany was first released. In these poems, Fields imagines the point of view of a woman who is "black folk" and fully skeptical about the natural black beauty ethos of both the art of the BAM and the everyday life encounters between black "smart people" and the folk. Fields begins "I Loves a Wig" with the question "Precious Lord, what am I to do with smart people, That want me to get rid of my wig." The most intriguing part of this poem is the reclamation of intelligence as that which enables someone to know that the visual is the zone of play, not truth. Fields writes, "Wigs is for intelligent, sophisticated people—not Fools that think that things is what they is or what they seems." Fields' emphasis on the common black person's reaction to the "sophisticated" person's investment in natural black beauty dramatizes the popular, everyday life complexity of black aesthetics. The speaker in the poem enjoys wearing a wig because it is labor-free and because "all wigs have good hair." This notion of good hair is, of course, the madness that the BAM rages against, but the speaker in the poem is also critiquing the very notion of good hair as she implies that just as "all wigs have good hair," all people have "good" hair. In this poem, the black fantastic emerges when the trauma of black self-hatred is denaturalized in such a fantastical manner. During the BAM, it was so easy to think that a black woman insisting on her self-love while wearing a wig is delusional, but Fields, in this poem, makes readers step into this world of seeming delusion and begin to understand the "love" and pleasure that the speaker feels when she puts on that which Haki Madhubuti, in "On Seeing Diana Go Maddddddddd" (1970), describes as "other people's hair."

Field's poem "Art" is published, in Black World, on the pages immediately before "I Loves a Wig." In "Art," Fields depicts the gendered dimension of some investments in natural black beauty and the gendered dimension of some erasures of the black fantastic. After the opening line "I am glad that no revolutionary artist has ever made any/ Painting of me," the speaker in the poem proceeds to state, "The person who can make the ugliest picture of a black/ Woman is a black man." Fields imagines a black woman who looks at BAM paintings and sculpture and sees "blunt, basic, and ugly." This woman craves more adorned images; she wants to see more glamour. The idealization of the unadorned black woman, during the BAM, was, often, the attempt by black men to purge themselves of the dominant culture images of white feminine beauty; black women were imagined as the pure, "basic" beauty that did not need flowing hair or any intentionally seductive flair. But this stripping of black women to the "natural black beauty" ideal, as Fields shows in her poem "Art," shuts down the play and performance that can shape the pleasure of performances of femininity. Some BAM women writers such as Julia Fields refused to accept this cancelling out of the play of black femininity.

Deep River: I agree with you and with Julia Fields: male attempts at control, and even ownership, of female bodies is wrong on both a physical and a theoretical level. We in BAM had two problems. First, we had a major blind spot in not recognizing the depth and significance of sexism within ourselves and within the society as a whole. Some of us even thought that sexism was a white disease that could be eradicated just by getting rid of white control of our lives. A rather widespread although unarticulated assumption was that we as blacks could be in this white supremacist society and not be as deeply affected by the ills of this society as our oppressors and exploiters were.

My analysis is that the deeper problem was not the manifestation of sexism but rather the acceptance of race as a defining factor. Even as we fought against racism in terms of fighting against obvious racial restrictions, we made a major mistake in assuming that aspects of our personalities, of our very being, were essentially defined by race. Our blackness does not necessarily define us in any way; in reality through our behavior, we as humans who happen to be black define our blackness, which means effectively our blackness is mutable, dynamic not static.

Indeed, the very concept of blackness is a white concept. I know this is a shocking statement coming from someone grounded in the Black Arts Movement, nonetheless the reality is that prior to the European and Arabic slave trades, we did not define ourselves based on skin color, or on this Eurocentric social construct popularly known as race.

Moreover, the European and Arabic slave trades had a major difference: religion. Even though Christianity and Islam share similar roots the major difference is that Islam is not overtly racial. Islam prohibits visual depictions of God. Among Muslims, God literally has no color. In Christianity, Jesus is generally depicted as a white man. Even the liberation theology of the twentieth century in Latin America or of the post-fifties movements in the United States, even those movements had to deal with the "what color is God" question.

One answer was that God was all colors. Another answer was that God was black. In both cases, God is racial. Conceiving of God in racial terms is the problem, especially within eras where there is white domination. To be clear, I am arguing that an essentialist philosophy is a fundamental problem, howsoever that essentialism manifests itself.

While making race central to our social definitions is a dead end, the conundrum is that the social constrictions of white supremacy do not allow non-racial social organization among those whom it oppresses and exploits. In other words we are forced to be black, or alternatively and worse yet, we are encouraged to assimilate, as much as possible, into Eurocentric, ipso facto "white" aesthetics and social philosophies.

This discussion gets deep. For example, consider mathematics, which is usually taught as devoid of racism, i.e. numbers have no color. What is hidden in that view is European appropriation of non-European developments. The number system we used is Arabic, but more than simply a case of borrowing the zero from Arabic sources, which, by the way, the Arabs got from the Hindus. Modern math is impossible without using the Arabic numbering system, but we are not taught this because that undercuts the notion of white racial superiority.

I make it plain with my students when I challenge them to do division with Roman numerals. We don't even have to bring up algebra, you can't easily do basic arithmetic with Roman numerals. If we look at this example in isolation from numerous other examples, such as the racial depiction of God or the notion that blood, rather than DNA, carries basic human traits, and that blood is racial, once we accept those notions we have problems when we attempt to revolt against white supremacy. Our major problem is that even as we revolt, we are philosophically replicating that which we are revolting against.

Given the virulence of white supremacy, and the social ubiquity of its dominance, especially in the twentieth century on planet Earth, we were in a difficult position. In other words, we had to go through it to get out of it, we had to band together to fight it, but we limited ourselves when we used race to define ourselves and our fight. For me, Amilcar Cabral was key to philosophically and socially offering an understanding and methodology for resisting white supremacy without falling into the trap of advocating black supremacy on the one hand and/ or a specious color-blindness on the other hand.

It is impossible not to see race in a racially defined world. What was and remains possible is to move beyond racial essentialism. Or to put it in scientific terms, let's use DNA and not blood to define ourselves. When we use DNA we end accepting social truths about our selves, such as mixed heritage, that racial dominant categorization thoroughly resists.

I realize that the particulars of this discussion may seem like a major deviation from our consideration of BAM, but some of us were grappling with these issues. Although such issues were not the major focus of our work, we nevertheless did make some attempts in this regard. Maulana Karenga termed it "expansion without erasure or eradication." The corollary was the Amiri Baraka saying, "If we don't change change, change is going to change us."

Without knowing what the future would look like, we knew that some sort of transformation was inevitable. Change is fundamental. Indeed, existence itself is a process of change.

Of course, there is a difference between quantitative and qualitative change on both the physical and the social level. I do not believe in racial essentialism of any sort. White people are not devils in essence. I recognize that the history of our encounters demonstrates conclusively that many whites have acted at monstrous levels of behavior towards us non-whites, as well as towards other whites, but at the same time there have been whites who fought against white supremacy, against colonialism, capitalism, imperialism and other negative "isms." We are usually not taught about those examples, and certainly such examples were not dominant nor the majority in our history in the United States, but they existed nonetheless.

Just as I do not believe in racial essentialism, I also do not believe in gender essentialism. Without a doubt we live in a patriarchal society within which manhood is defined in sexist ways. That reality does not mean that men cannot change, that men have no choice about how they relate to women. Just as whites are not intrinsically racial devils, neither are men intrinsically gender devils, even though the behavior of most whites and the behavior of most men can easily lead one to conclude that racism/sexism are intrinsic characteristics.

So, essentialism is the first major problem. However, there is a second problem, one that is both easier to understand while much harder to deal with, and that is the problem of analytical decontextualization.

There is an old joke: Two young fish were swimming side by side when they encountered an older fish headed in the direction that the two younger fish were coming from. The older fish greeted them and asked, "How's the water back there?" The younger fish had no factual answer so they just said, "Okay." After the older fish swam on one of the younger fish turned to the companion fish and asked, "What's water?"

Many of us have no real understanding of the society we live in, of the era we live in, of how we are shaped and respond to the physical and social realities of our particular time and place. In short, we have no understanding of our water. Indeed, many of us are not even aware we are in water.

This absence of deep analysis, this absence of water awareness and knowledge, leads us to make a static analysis that elevates specifics and parts to the level of the general and whole. This problem is especially acute when we characterize social realities as though they were static, unchanging. What may be true at a given moment, can morph into the exact opposite at a later moment. I believe in dialectics. Everything must change. Existence is itself a measurement of change; that which does not change does not actually exist.

Again, this is rather rarified air, but I believe that a deep dialectical analysis is necessary if we are to avoid the trap of essentialism. So, yes, BAM was sexist initially but by the early seventies we also find fierce debates and major change happening. Not only is it important that we not "throw out the baby with the bath water," it is equally if not more important that we recognize there is a constant need for baths on a regular basis. We must always remember that we can always do more, that indeed, we have to do more. We have to change the water with each bath. We need clean water to both nourish and bath ourselves. For the entirety of our lives, we will need to drink and bathe, to execute and critique.

On the one hand I wanted to map out a general overview of BAM, but there was another issue. I also wrote the book because I knew for sure there were going to be Whites writing about the movement and getting their work published. I'm not sure how many conscious Black folk were going to write about the movement and be able to get published. There are two aspects there: the actual writing and the quality thereof, is one aspect, and getting published is the other.

I completed the manuscript over a decade ago. Getting it published is a whole other issue. While I wasn't certain when I wrote it how it would be published, I was certain that if I didn't write it, it would never be published. So one step at a time. First, write it. Then, get it published.

I knew I could write this book, not only because I was a participant who had writing skills, but also because I had access and an ideology, in addition to writing skills. I had access to key people who would share information and ideas with me—some of those people are no longer with us. I had an ideology that impelled me to do this important work, an ideology that was not one of racial essentialism, but rather one of openness and inclusion even as it has a particular orientation—my blackness does not shun contact with any other human being.

Finally, I wrote the book because the battle for self-determination, self-defense, and self-respect is far from over. Indeed we are still trudging our way up the rough side of the mountain.

As for feeling nostalgic, I have no time for backwards thinking, which is what nostalgia is, i.e. backwards thinking. To long for the past is natural, especially once we reach adulthood and assume adult responsibilities. In the face of the daily burdens of life, it is no surprise that we become nostalgic. Moreover, when we get old, we long to be young again.

This emphasis on nostalgia for the past but avoidance of the actual study of our history is especially the case in modern U.S.A., with its obsession with youthfulness and aversion to analyzing history even as it romanticizes the past. Indeed, in order to successfully romanticize the past, it is necessary to avoid analyzing our history. Uncritically celebrating bygone periods requires that we avoid dealing with contradictions and complications in favor of proclaiming slogans and simplicities. Social amnesia and ignorance is a deadly combination that is pushed by capitalism as a means to sell us products that we would otherwise have no reason to buy, and to keep us compliant with systemic rules and regulations.

Juju was not just a struggle to create something new. At its core my book, our ideology, our whole movement, was also an attempt, a very serious attempt, to discover, uncover and embrace the old, the hidden, the forgotten, i.e. our history. When Trane blew Afro-Blue he did so after having studied Sidney Bechet, hence pulling out the soprano saxophone. Coltrane was not the first to play the soprano saxophone but he was the man who made the soprano popular in modern jazz. In order for Trane to get to "My Favorite Things," it was necessary to study the past. Indeed, in jazz in particular, everybody who creates something that is both new and influential has necessarily had to master something that came before the new. To create something new, you've got to intimately know something old.

The American character is obsessed with newness, with starting over, with the latest this and that, with the newest model car or phone, with the latest book or recording, with speed and instant gratification. Check this paradox; a black aesthetic in the U.S.A. by definition requires us to embrace the past even though most of the time we do so unconsciously. Take hip hop: that art form could not exist as it is without drawing on the past. In that sense, Blackness in the U.S.A. is the art of remixing, i.e. making something new out of something old. We make new music by remixing old music, a combination of collage over a groove.

Here is where it gets tricky. Modern America trends on newness. Black America expresses itself as a remix. Why? Whites are trying to escape the Old World. Blacks are trying to recreate the Old World. They left Europe and came to America. We were stolen from Africa and brought to America. They chose to leave Europe, we had no choice about leaving Africa. Our relationship to our roots is fundamentally different. Even though there is a fundamental difference with far reaching ramifications for each of us, the fact remains that the price of the American ticket for both of us was the same: severance from our traditional home root.

We did not want to leave, they either did not want to stay or were not able to stay. I've read beaucoup history books, but I've never read that fundamental distinction placed in the foreground when it comes to interpreting so-called American history. To simply call ourselves a nation of immigrants completely obfuscates the binary difference between how Whites got here and how the majority of Blacks got here.

Yes, the majority population in this society is of immigrant origin, but there were critical differences in the immigration process and what that means for our individual and collective psyches. Plus, they could always go back. For us to return was not so simple.

Consider Liberia and how fucked up that colonization was. DuBois wrote about Liberia, the African country that was dominated by ex-slaves repatriated from America. It was not a pretty picture. Most of us know nothing about Liberia. Wilson can go to England. Emile can go to France. Jose can go to Spain. So forth and so on. Where in the hell do Otis and Odessa go? We sure don't need another Liberia.

I'm a Pan-Africanist politically, but I'm also a Black American culturally. The Black Arts Movement never got the chance to fully address that conundrum of where to go and what to do. And before somebody completely misunderstands what I'm pointing out, let me just say: dual citizenship. It doesn't have to be an either/or binary, it can be a both/and dialectic.

For me personally my intimate dealings with Africa began with the Sixth Pan-African Congress in Tanzania in 1974 and that initial phase ended with Festac in Nigeria in 1977. I was a delegate to Six-Pac. Although I was a board member of the American delegation, I did not attend Festac because I could not stay the required three weeks.

Most of the people who write about or have an interest in the Black Arts Movement are not aware of the extent of the contacts between our movement and the continent. The seventies were also the high point of direct support for the African liberation movements on the continent.

If you don't know anything about Six-Pac or Festac, if you are ignorant of the Frelimo, MPLA and ANC/PAC connections, if you don't know about those and a number of other exchanges and intersections, then you cannot fully understand that Africa was not an abstraction for us. Politically and culturally, Africa was a factual, concrete reality and not just a romantic dream.

When we talk about the past, I believe we need to study the recent past as much as we need to study the historic past, indeed studying the sixties and the seventies is more important than studying sixteenth and seventeenth century African history.

I do a lot of writing about the past, about history both from a personal standpoint in terms of my own life, and from a human standpoint. Back in the eighties, I wrote and published a major autobiographical statement. I am currently finishing off a second major autobiographical piece that concentrates on my transition from adolescence to adulthood. My rejection of nostalgia is not a rejection of history nor a refusal to literally dig my roots—"dig" as in investigate as well as "dig" as in appreciate or desire/like.

Additionally, a short-sighted or limited emphasis on our immigrant roots too often causes us to overlook or down-play the significance of how this society treated the indigenous population that was here before the immigrants arrived.

I know this is a long answer to your simple and straight forward, two part question: nostalgia and why I wrote Juju. So, let's pause a moment and dialogue. I'm sure you have some questions, and if not questions, some cogent observations.

Afro-Blue: Was the movement dangerous? Was it a life or death struggle?

Deep River: Ask Henry Dumas. Within a society controlled by, or should I say dominated by, white supremacy, any and all independently thinking and independently acting negroes are ipso facto dangerous. The "negro" is the creation of white supremacy, or as brother Baraka poetically termed it: How Africans became negroes. A shorthand history might be Fulani (or any number of other specific groupings) > Africans >niggers > negroes> New Negroes > blacks > African-Americans > African-Americans + niggers (also niggas) + mixed + post-black blacks. In that equation, the symbol ">" represents transformation of the previous into the following through conscious and/or popular nomination (i.e. naming). The process of naming is the nommo process.

Afro-Blue: How did the movement's Black Nationalism relate to Marxism?

Deep River: It was a fight, a sharp conflict that was more than just a question of what came first, race or class. The real battle was for the hearts and minds of the same audience, black people. Although we were only 13 percent or so of the national population, we were by far the single most important labor force in the initial development of economic wealth in the U.S.A. Beyond being the source of wealth, we were also, as an identifiable group, the ones who had the greatest anti-establishment capacity precisely because we were not so easily bought off as white workers had been, nor were we easily shunted aside as Asian railroad workers and today's Chicano migrant agricultural workers have been. Also worth noting in this regard is that the "native Americans" were never a major source of labor and thus were subject to outright genocide. White America out and out eliminated red America.

The problem for Marxism was how to incorporate self-identified blacks into an ideology that had zero understanding of what Marxists critiqued as racial identity politics. My example of highlighting this conundrum is that although they were both communists, Russia and China did not get along. Why not, since both were Marxists shouldn't they have been together? Well the Chinese had no intention of giving up their "Chinese" identity or of sublimating their Chinese identity solely to a class identity. Yes they wanted a working class revolution, but they also wanted a Chinese identity.

BAM adherents identified with the Chinese. Our New Orleans formation in partnership with the U.S.-China Peoples Friendship association organized a 1977 trip to China and spent a little over two weeks traveling throughout China, engaging in discussions and exchanges. We put out leaflets and organized programs when we returned with pictures of our delegation taken in China and headlines such as "Black Nationalists in Red China."

I had no similar desire to go to Russia. We viewed China as part of the Third World. Rightly or wrongly, we viewed Russia as white. If you look at BAM publications from the sixties and seventies the evidence is immediately apparent: we celebrated the struggles of red, black, brown, and yellow peoples worldwide and even included Middle Eastern people, particularly the Palestinian peoples, because we saw them as fellow victims of Western imperialism.

The Third World in general was where the militant struggles were happening. A more nuanced analysis might discuss the global north/south divide, as well as the east/west, and communism/capitalism battles, to which we would sometimes add the Christian/Islam religious battles. It is important to add that none of the other Third-World-based religions were as vigorous (some would say virulent) in their missionary zeal and seemingly obsessive urge to convert, usually through physical domination and appropriation; or, as they put it in their holy book, "Thou shall have no other gods before me." This was interpreted as no human being should have any religion other than Christianity.

While it is not inaccurate to focus on the Marxist/nationalist conflict as a defining factor for analyzing BAM, there are other elements: Third World/First World (and we even went in for arguing that we were the original and authentic First World rather than Europe+U.S.A.—this particular train of thought was best exemplified by the transition of Negro Digest > Black World > First World literary magazine under Hoyt Fuller's editorship). Other areas of contention included Christian/Muslim, and after the seventies, the gender battles, the struggles around overcoming and defeating sexism and patriarchy.

Moreover, beyond the battles themselves on both an ideological and an actual day-to-day social struggle basis, there was the fact that within the United States, black people were critical to all of these struggles as both the object/audience of these struggles and, more importantly, as the agents/activists carrying these struggles forward. In labor matters, A. Philip Randolph arguably was one of the most successful labor leaders of the twentieth century, followed by Cesar Chavez; in terms of gender politics there are so many major black women who stand out as activists, such as Angela Davis and Kathleen Cleaver, but also specifically as feminist writers (Audre Lorde, Alice Walker, Ntozake Shange, Michelle Wallace). We as a people not only had the cause, the reason to wage these struggles, we also had the will and the capacity to directly engage the system, and in so doing to inspire others "to get up and get involved," to use the language of the time.

Another factor is the Caribbean, Central America, and South America axis and our connections to that axis. Examples of foci of struggle in those regions that we directly related to and which in return directly influenced us were Haiti, Jamaica, and Grenada in the Caribbean; Nicaragua in Central America, and Brazil and Chile in South America. Those were not the only struggles but they were the leading places with which we in BAM were familiar and to which we related. These struggles deeply influenced our outlook and literary output.

Afro-Blue: We are only now beginning to understand the regional flows of the movement. What distinguished the Southern Black Arts Movement from other parts of the movement?

Deep River: The major distinction is that we had a long history of self directed social development in all spheres of activity and thus easily conceptualized doing for self without relying in any way on the dominant system for support, especially in terms of audience and basic economic survival. Our existence was not based solely on white benevolence and/or patronage. Of course there was and remains a major relationship between philanthropy and the arts, particularly Ford and Rockefeller, the two major foundations in funding arts programs by black people.

However, my point is that throughout the south we had the lived examples of black people organizing apart from the dominant society and without the support of the dominant society. We, as artists with varying degrees of consciousness, assumed the same philosophical outlook and practical stance in our day-to-day operations.

I will note that Louisiana was a little different because whereas most other areas in the south had their own distinctive mono-culture, Louisiana had three distinct cultures situated within what might be termed "New Orleans culture." In addition to Black and Creole culture, we had Cajun culture, and general Southern Anglo culture. Even in that case, the most distinguishing factor is the same "do for self" thrust that is a hallmark of black Southern existence. With the exception of the up-south city of Chicago, most of the northern urban areas did not have as strong a black "do for self" social basis. In the North, there was more of a push for social equality and social acceptance across the board. These two different outlooks are exemplified in the differences between black functions in Chicago compared and contrasted to black functions in Detroit, both of which were important locales of BAM activities.

In the Chicago/Detroit tale of two cities, we see certain elements played out to logical conclusions. For example, there is no surprise in the fact that although the black Muslims got their start in Detroit (1930), in the sixties their base and greatest achievements were in Chicago. Then there are the two major BAM era publishing companies: Broadside in Detroit and Third World Press in Chicago. A case study of the dynamic of these two cities both individually and in comparison to each other deserves to be done if we are to fully understand some of the major issues of BAM in particular and modern black life in northern urban areas in general. In a similar, although not quite as fully differentiated manner, one could do a study of black life and social expressions on the west coast with the comparison of Los Angeles to the Bay Area (with the interesting twist of the internal Oakland/San Francisco dynamic).

Time and time again we see the eternal African in the Americas question raised and grappled with: Do we integrate or separate (which is fundamentally different from segregate)?

Each objective has its own particular strengths and weaknesses. The integrationists have to struggle to avoid total assimilation leading to self-erasure. The separatists have to struggle to avoid isolation leading to social irrelevance and eventual obsolescence.

Afro-Blue, I think the question you raised about Marxism/ nationalism is too complex a question to be easily or quickly answered, but at the same time the question does cut to the fundamental question that we face in America. If I might play on a Shakespearean theme—even though I am not and have never been a fan of Shakespeare, I think he articulated an appropriate question when he said, "To be or not to be, that is the question." As a good dialectician will note, it is a false formulation to pose the question as an either/or dualism, when in fact it is really a both/and dialectic, precisely because in terms of consciousness and ideology, some formerly enslaved Africans will choose to remain African- or Black-oriented while others will choose to become Americans. The BAM choice was to be "African."

Actually, the true BAM choice was to be "black." The distinction between "Black" and "African" is that "Black" validated one's being as authentic without having to have a direct tie to a particular African geo-political, or even cultural, entity.

Indeed, my expanded view of Africaness itself asserts that Africa is a people identity more than a geographical identity, and that whatever Africa's descendants are doing as a self-defined people is as much African as is anything being done on the continent of Africa itself. I know that's a controversial statement, but nevertheless that's my belief.

Afro-Blue: I am the daughter of the Black Arts Movement, and like Ntozake Shange, I could say, "Even though they didn't know they were going to have a girl!" But I claim the Deep River of the movement. Why did people sometimes forget, during the movement, that the water was deep enough for Black Power feminism?

Deep River: Because most of us men, if not, to one degree or another, "all of us men," were patriarchal and thus saw feminism as our enemy. Let me cut to the core of my analysis, an analysis that is undergoing constant evolution, but never loses sight of the fundamental principle of self-determination and the support of everyone and anyone to advocate and effectuate their own self-determination, especially on a gender basis. I believe that nationalism as internationally practiced in the nineteenth, twentieth,and twenty-first centuries is problematic and requires patriarchy to exist. Moreover, the Christian belief that "God gave man dominion over the earth" is the religious and philosophical justification for patriarchy.

Here I will use a short hand and employ a metaphor: land is looked at as feminine. The insistence on private property as a bedrock principle of social organization, especially when that private property includes "real estate" is the basis for justifying male domination of women including the desire for women to be submissive to men.

At the risk of being totally misunderstood, I assert my belief that nationalism is not only a major problem, but that an advocacy of nationalism is a sine qua non of sexism and its various manifestations. The waving of national flags is one thing, however the phallic image of the flag pole stuck into the ground with some material waving in the wind as a signification of ownership is a recreation of the male desire to sexually control and dominate the female in the missionary sexual position. The idea/ideal of saluting a flag is an ideological genuflecting to patriarchal power.

On the contrary to the implication of your question, I don't think that "the water was deep enough." I think that black power feminism hit on the fundamental contradiction of nationalism and thus the two could not co-exist; we could not have nationalism and feminism in the same movement. One of the two dynamics had to be in the lead. By 1980 when we published Our Women Keep Our Skies From Falling, I had consciously chosen to uphold feminism and stopped referring to myself as a Pan-African nationalist and instead just said Pan-Africanist.

On the continent itself, I belief a major problem is that there are no African defined nations but rather European defined nations trying to force themselves to be these various nations with each one struggling with the issue of how to identify the self when you have one particular grouping (commonly called tribe) in a position of leadership, if not outright dominance over other groupings.

We have bought into the Eurocentric formulation of male domination of land, i.e. nationalism, so thoroughly that we think of the problem as "How to make the nation work," when really the question ought to be "Do we really need the Euro-defined nation?" Maybe we need to re-look at Booker T. Washington's often derided formulation, dust it off, up-date it and consider it as a political statement of supporting diversity: i.e. in matters purely social, be as separate as the fingers, in matters of mutual defense and development work as a fist.

I believe our diversity must include women as agents of their own existence and we should destroy the dynamic of women as objects of male desire and control, i.e. patriarchy, and by extension, nationalism.

There was a reason, even though we were not always conscious of why it was so, that black feminism and Black Nationalism could not co-exist. Indeed, let's take it one logical step further. Within the post civil rights era in the United States, black feminism is black power in action.

The basic principle of black power is not power based on our race, but rather the power of agency: the rights and prerogatives of self-determination regardless of whomsoever we humans may be and howsoever we choose to define ourselves. Within the black community, women are the most exploited. When black women organize themselves, speak for themselves, define and defend themselves that is the ultimate expression of black agency. In that regard, those who are last put themselves first and decide for themselves how they want to live their lives regardless of what others might think, either from within or from outside the community.

Implicit in the advocacy of feminism is not only open support for women's rights to self-determination, but also open support for what is now called LGBT (lesbian, gay, bi-sexual, and transgender) rights of self determination. Patriarchy has no broad human rights position precisely because patriarchy denies agency to women to determine their lives. Any philosophy that denies the rights of the other is flat wrong.

Moreover, to be progressive means that you stand up not only for your own agency, but that you respect and champion the agency of others. Agency begins with self, and ends with self. Control yourself and respect other selves, howsoever the other defines their self, howsoever we define who is the other. Respect all others, respect all "selves."

With that in mind, within our communities you cannot get any blacker than black women defining themselves: exercising the agency to determine how they will live their lives. That is the most thoroughgoing revolution that can happen in our community. And of course the fundamental or bedrock principle remains: the doers are, or should be, the decision makers.

Afro-Blue: During the movement, which women made you begin to first hear the sounds of Black Power feminism?

Deep River: On a personal level, in the sense of women I knew and talked with over the years: Michelle Wallace and Toni Cade Bambara. And though I did not have an extensive personal relationship with her and have not read all of her works, nevertheless, I have to include Audre Lorde as a major influence. On an ideological level based on what I read and/or what I saw in their work and example: Ntozake Shange, Abbey Lincoln, Nina Simone, Alice Walker, and Gayle Jones (particularly her beautiful and important Brazilian-based book, Song for Anninho).

On the level of important feminine influences that did not specifically call themselves feminist in the seventies: Mari Evans and Sonia Sanchez, both of whom I was close to personally. Finally, as symbols of courage and resistance, Fanny Lou Hamer and Assata Shakur. I didn't know Mrs. Hamer personally, but I did meet and hang out with Assata in Havana, Cuba in 1984. Assata's autobiography is critically important. Of course, this category of influences most definitely includes Angela Davis, although for me not as ideologically important as the others I just mentioned.

Afro-Blue: On the deepest (or most shallow registers), what are the untold stories of how people responded to the movement's

insistence on black people being with each other and breaking out of intimate relations with white people?

Deep River: Being in the deep South, I would not use the term "breaking out of intimate relations with white people" because that was not a prevalent mode where I was located. At the same time I don't want to give the impression that it was unusual or unheard of. In New Orleans we have a long, deep and wide history of inter-racial relations. That's part of who we are. To put it in provocative terms, for us blackness includes whiteness as an element of our blackness. We had members of BLKARTSOUTH who were naturally blond-haired and had blue, light grey, or green eyes, but their parents were black and they consciously identified themselves as black and identified with all other working class blacks.

I didn't have any close friends or even close co-workers who were in interracial relationships that broke up because of the black power movement.

Afro-Blue: Why couldn't many of the men in the movement see that their particular ways of enacting liberation struggles were sometimes denying black women their right to liberate themselves, without male control of their self-determination as black women?

Deep River: It wasn't just men who were blind. For a number of reasons (including, but not limited to, the effort to resurrect black manhood), the centrality of gender limitations on women as a major problem to be solved was not initially apparent to most people both male and female. Indeed, the presumption was that when segregation and racism were destroyed, women would be free also. We did not fully understand that yes, once we achieved civil rights women would also be free in the sense that black women as well as black men would have the right to vote, but our political freedom in that sense did not address women's need for rights as a gender, which was and is distinct from, and in many important ways larger than, women's needs for rights as part of a racial identity.

In the eighties, especially by its detractors, feminism was

conceptualized as an attack on manhood, and feminism was, as a result, defensively rejected by many men and some women because feminism was perceived as anti-males rather than what feminism actually is: i.e. anti-patriarchy. Conceptually we generally focused on two hurdles. First, we believed we had to support black manhood, encourage black males to stand up and take leadership roles as men. Second, although those of us who believed in self-identified agency for black women were certainly a numerical minority, some of us also believed we had to do the necessary ideological work of identifying the differences between manhood and patriarchy. In our society manhood and patriarchy are often bound at the groin and viewed as inseparable, but they are actually far from the same, far from inseparable. Because of the confusion that results when we don't distinguish manhood from patriarchy, it was then and remains now difficult for us men to address sexism, and its constrictions and oppression of women.

Afro-Blue: Aren't some of the critics of the BAM the direct beneficiaries of it?

Deep River: Without a doubt. We were aware that our struggles created better conditions for everyone and not just for those who agreed with us. In fact, we can go a step further and point out that it was our identity politics and struggles for self-determination, self-defense and self-respect that either directly inspired or at the very least created social openings for the next big wave of social struggle: feminism following the civil rights/black power struggles of the seventies in concert with the anti-war movement. The difference is that with the end of the Vietnam War in 1975, the anti-war movement quickly receded, but the sixties black power movement continued to flower and thrive throughout the decade of the seventies.

I argue that within the Black community the major beneficiaries were those blacks who were working within formerly all white or predominantly white social organizations, which now had black caucuses, as well as new openings and promotions for people of color. The mainstream decided to be more inclusive in the face of the revolutionary thrusts to overthrow the status quo. Which brings us back to the major question inclusion and assimilation versus continued exclusion and separation.

Regardless of how one felt or what one thought, the overwhelming reality was that we in mass were here and were not going to go anywhere else. By the eighties, it was clear to many of us that our people in general, and the vast majority of our leadership, had chosen accommodation with the status quo through efforts at inclusion and assimilation. In a classic case of unintended consequences, the struggle for black power facilitated and often served as a catalyst for assimilation. In that sense, our black critics were often the chief beneficiaries of the power struggle.

Afro-Blue: How did travel to Africa and other places shape the movement?

Deep River: While the majority of our people obviously did not physically travel to Africa, there was widespread support for the liberation struggles of the sixties, seventies, and eighties that were raging across the African continent and throughout the third world. Africa was not just a location of nostalgia and romantic yearnings, Africa was a focus of armed struggle, a laboratory for liberation efforts at social reconstruction, and the focus of efforts to create new societies, new men and women.

At one point we argued that our struggle was not about going "back to Africa," rather we were about going "forward with Africa."

Afro-Blue: Yes, the process of black consciousness-raising was transnational and the word "Black" was a unifying concept that enabled people to see the global nature of white supremacy. During the 1970s, U.S. mobilizations of the word greatly inspired a similar hailing process in the South African Black Consciousness movement. During the 1975-1976 trial, Steve Biko, the founder of Black Consciousness in South Africa, is asked to explain why black South Africans refer to themselves as "Black" as opposed to "brown." As the trial puts "blackness" itself on trial, Biko and

Judge Boshoff have the following exchange:

> Judge Boshoff: But now why do you refer to you people as blacks? Why not brown people? I mean you people are more brown than black.
> Biko: In the same way as I think white people are more pink and yellow and pale than white.
> Judge Boshoff: Quite…but now why do you not use the word brown then?
> Biko: No, I think really, historically, we have been defined as black people, and when we reject the term non-white and take upon ourselves the right to call ourselves what we think we are, we have got available in front of us a whole number of alternatives.

Biko claims the power of the word "Black" when it is reclaimed as a strategy of decolonizing the mind.

But, moving to other questions…. On the deepest registers, did the movement teach people to rethink the relation between struggle and aesthetics?

Deep River: I would not phrase it in the active and conscious terms of the movement teaching people to "rethink." I think the lessons we drew were often the results of trial and error, and the results of learning from each other, especially from the mistakes and setbacks. Indeed, we had very few long term successes.

Personally, my biggest lesson came in 1974 when I and a small group of activists had the opportunity to have a private session with President Julius Nyerere of Tanzania. I had a huge amount of respect for Mwalimu (Swahili for teacher), as president Nyerere was popularly called. I remember asking a question about state relations and support for the then ongoing liberation battles throughout southern Africa. President Nyerere answered my question with the observation that "all governments are conservative." When I tried to assert that surely the Tanzania example of front line support for the liberation movements and their efforts at Ujamaa, or African socialism were…. He cut me off and repeated with appropriate emphasis: "All Governments are conservative." They will all do whatever it takes to maintain power.

Nyerere was also clear in his acknowledgement and analysis of the depth of contradictions Tanzania and other countries were struggling to overcome, particularly what to do with large groups of literate, but relatively unskilled, young people. I questioned why there were four or five people involved in the process when one went into the bank to exchange money. Nyerere bottom-lined the answer by pointing out that if they didn't employ these people, these same people would become an opposition that would overwhelm the movement as a whole and the government in particular.

In later reflection I identified not only with that moment and understood that there was no simple solution to the complex problem of not simply how to get free, but rather how to construct a working model of a liberated society, I also soberly considered that the problem of neocolonialism would be our make or break moment.

Afro-Blue, when you earlier asked about beneficiaries of the struggle who not only were not active participants, but indeed who were often critics and opponents of the struggle, you were approaching the problem without necessarily identifying the syndrome. I suggest to you that what you describe is simply one of the major manifestations of the neocolonial problem. One interesting twist is that many of the people who directly benefited think they got those positions/benefits because they earned them or deserved them, rather than because of the struggle of others to create the opportunities for those who were capable to achieve positions.

To be clear, I do not argue that people did not and do not deserve positions within the system, nor do I argue that they are incapable of doing their jobs. That is not the case. Rather I argue that the question is not "Do we get to be overseers and even slave owners?" No, the real question is "Can we build a diverse and equitable society?" Those who favor inclusion try to do so within the system. Those who favor self-determination try to do so outside of the system. So far, neither of us has been very successful when it comes to the benefit of the masses of working class black people, although it is true that black petite bourgeoisie, primarily college educated, black professionals and a handful of athletes and entertainers have had some measure of individual political and economic success as exemplified by people such as President Obama, Supreme Court Justice Clarence Thomas, media mogul Oprah Winfield, and sports figures such as Tiger Woods, the Williams sisters, and LeBron James.

We could choose to go further into this discussion of neocolonialism and examine the entertainment sphere, or we could ask the question apart from paradigm shifts in how the various industries operate including craft and aesthetic concerns. Most important of all, we could ask what I consider to be the number one question: What benefit for the masses of black people have resulted from these particular successes?

Afro-Blue: Yes, Greg Thomas asks a similar question: How does "post-black" distance itself from "most black"? The creation of distance from "recognizable" black aesthetics by some twenty-first century black artists makes blackness the exterior that enables access to the highbrow interior. And when we think through the generational gaps at the core of critiques of artists such as Kara Walker, we might recognize that many of the artists' own repudiation of the Black Arts movement is the problem. Some of the younger artists themselves do not recognize the "black aesthetics unbound" ethos of the Black Arts Movement.

Deep River: Blacks not advocating blackness is not a problem; that's a choice, indeed a right. Be whatever you want to be. Ultimately, that's what we were fighting for. We were not fighting for black power in the exclusive sense, or even in the oppositional sense of black against white, rather we were fighting for our rights of self-determination, self-defense, and self-respect; rights, which some of us came to believe should not only be accorded to us, but should be available to all. The Magic of Juju was precisely the foregrounding of the struggle for agency, i.e. self-definition, self-defense, and self-respect regardless of race or gender.

Mao said, "Away with all pests." Backward thinking is the biggest pest. To paraphrase Nkrumah, "Forward ever, backward never," i.e. even if we want to, we cannot return to our past. If we are wise we grow up, mature, and take responsibility for dealing with our present and preparing for our future. A major part of fulfilling that responsibility is studying and learning from our past, our successes and our failures, what worked and why, what didn't work and why, and using those lessons to assist us in moving on.

The Magic of Juju is not about returning to the sixties and seventies. *The Magic of Juju* is my contribution to the contemporary generation who must and, I believe, who will make their own decisions in dealing with their own realities and in attempting to make real their own visions. In that regard, The Magic of Juju is an attempt to provide information and evidence for this current generation to make sense of their history, present and future.

Haki Madhubuti published *From Plan to Planet* in 1973 as a joint publication from Detroit's Broadside Press and Chicago's Institute of Positive Education, which is the education cohort of the social formation that is also responsible for Third World Press. The subtitle of that book was: *Life Studies: The Need for Afrikan Minds and Institutions*. That need is even stronger today. We need minds and institutions to address our current conditions.

It is no accident that *The Magic of Juju* is published by Third World Press rather than by a university press or a mainstream press. It is not enough to think about things, we must do things. The doers are not only the decision makers, the doers are the only ones who truly develop.

I was in China in 1977 when Deng Chao Ping was rehabilitated. His line was "It doesn't matter what color the cat is as long as it catches the mouse." Our reply was that if the black cat does not catch a mouse it will be dependent on the white cat for survival. It always matters whether we can do for self.

At a concert, the great blues musician Lightin' Hopkins began by tuning up his guitar and immediately afterward said a phrase that sums up my foundation philosophy. A stage hand had previously brought out Hopkins' guitar and had tuned it up before Lightin' came on. When Hopkins ambled onstage about five minutes later, the master sat down, picked up his guitar and proceeded to tune up again. When he was satisfied with the sound, he said—and I will never forget this, will always try to live this—"A guitar ain't tuned, unless you done tuned it yourself."

We have to tune our guitars. Each singer must not only sing

their song, we must tune our own guitars, whomsoever "we" might be. The real Magic of Juju is the transformatory power of self-determination at all levels and in all aspects: social, philosophical, spiritual. In all aspects, each of us as human beings in self-identified social formations should do for self. That's the lesson, the power, and The Magic of Juju.

Margo Natalie Crawford is Associate Professor of African American literature, global black studies, and radical black feminism in the Department of English at Cornell University. She is the author of *Black Post-Blackness: The Black Arts Movement and 21st Century Aesthetics* (forthcoming, University of Illinois Press) and Dilution *Anxiety and the Black Phallus* (2008, Ohio State University Press). She is the coeditor of *New Thoughts on the Black Arts Movement* (2006, Rutgers University Press). Her essays appear in a wide range of books and journals, including *The Psychic Hold of Slavery, The Trouble With Post-Blackness, Want to Start a Revolution?, The Cambridge Companion to American Poetry Post-1945, SOULS, Black Renaissance Noire, Black Camera, Publishing Blackness*, and the exhibition catalog for the 2013 AfriCOBRA exhibit at the DuSable Museum.

INDEX

Ahmed, A. Muhammad (Max Stanford) – 16-17
Baker, Houston – 161-162, 163
Baraka, Amiri (see also LeRoi Jones) – 5, 26, 31-32, 90, 96-97, 161, 189
Bell, Bernard W. – 58, 58-59
Black Books Bulletin – 83
Black Dialogue – 67-68, 68-69, 69-70
The Black Scholar – 78
Black Theatre – 120-121
Blumenthal, Bob – 135-136, 136
Bourne, St. Clair – 142-143, 143, 144
Briscoe, Joe – 3
Brown, James – 125, 126, 146
Burroughs, Margaret – 21
Byrd, Donald – 151-152, 154
Carmichael, Stokely – 15-16, 130
Cayou, Nontsizi – 155
Chrisman, Robert – 78
Coleman, Wanda – 121
Combahee River Collective Statement – 180, 181
Dent, Tom – xiv, 115-116, 167
Dixon, Brenda – 153-154
Drama Review (1968 Black Theatre Issue) - 34
Emery, Lynne Fauley – 148, 150
Evidence Records – 126-127
Fowler, Dr. Carolyn – 53, 53-54, 76-77
Fuller, Hoyt – 28, 46-47, 79, 80-81
Gaither, Edmund Barry - 156-157
Gayle, Addison – 98, 168-169, 175-176, 189-190
Gerald, Carolyn – see Dr. Carolyn Fowler
Goncalves, Dingane Joe – 20, 70, 74, 75-76
Green, Kim – 106
Harper, Michael - 129
Henderson, Stephen – 60-61, 174, 174-175
Himes, Chester – 89
Jackmon, Marvin (Marvin X) – 72
Jarrell, Wadsworth – 157-159
Johnson, Abby A. – 39
Jones, LeRoi (see also Amiri Baraka) – 2, 71
Jordan, Norman – 183
Karenga, Maulana – 49-50, 188
King Jr., Woodie – 176-177
LaBrie, Aubrey – 67

Lee, Don L.(see also Haki Madhubuti) – 128, 130
Lincoln, Abbey – 186
Long, Richard A. – 81-82, 147
Madhubuti, Haki (see also Don L. Lee) – 51-52, 85-86
Major, Clarence – 72
Marsh, Dave – 124-125
Masilela, Ntongela – 140-141
Moore, William – 145
Neal, Larry – 21-22, 22-24, 50, 56, 117-118, 118, 131, 191
Newton, Michael – 33,
O'Neal, John – 114-115
Porter, Tom – 191
Primus, Marc – 110-111, 112
Randall, Dudley – 21, 62-63
Redmond, Eugene – 61-62,
Reed, Ishmael – 88, 90-91, 95, 188
Rhines, Jesse Algeron – 137-138, 138-139
Richards, Sandra - 151
Roach, Max – 133
Rodgers, Rod – 149
Rowell, Charles – 167-168, 170, 171, 171-172
Sanders, Leslie Catherine – 118-119
Scott-Heron, Gil – 105
Shange, Ntozake – 179-180
Sheridan, Art – 67-68
Smith, David Lionel – 164-165, 165-166
Soulbook – 66
Taylor, Clyde – 141-142
Toure, Askia Muhammad – 8, 128, 186-187
Turner, Darwin – 84-85
Weinstein, Norman C. – 132, 133
X, Malcolm (El Hajj Malik el Shabazz) – 20, 29
Zolla, Jawole Willa Jo – 152, 152-153

Books and Recordings by Kalamu ya Salaam

Poetry

The Blues Merchant

Hofu Ni Kwenu

Pamoja Tutashinda

Ibura

Iron Flowers

Revolutionary Love

A Nation of Poets

Essays

Our Women Keep Our Skies From Falling

What Is Life?

Children's Literature

Herufi, An Alphabet Reader

Who Will Speak For Us? (with Tayari kwa Salaam)

Anthologies

Word Up: Black Poetry of the 80s From The Deep South

Fertile Ground – Memories & Visions (with Kysha N. Brown)

360 Degrees – A Revolution Of Black Poets (with Kwame Alexander)

From A Bend In The River – 100 New Orleans Poets

Students at the Center (SAC) Publications

SAC (sacnola.com) is an independent writing program in the public schools of New Orleans

Men We Love, Men We Hate (edited with Jim Randels)

Who Am I? (edited with Jim Randels)

The Long Ride (edited with Jim Randels)

Next Steps (edited with Jim Randels)

Ways Of Laughing (editor)

Recordings

My Story, My Song

A Nation of Poets (Amiri Baraka, Askia Muhammad Toure, Haki Madhubuti, Kalamu ya Salaam, Mari Evans, Pearl Cleage, Sonia Sanchez, and Wanda Coleman)

Film Features

When Love Hurts

Baby Love

www.ingramcontent.com/pod-product-compliance
Lightning Source LLC
Chambersburg PA
CBHW020313290526
45785CB00007B/2782